LIBRARY LIT. 18- The Best of 1987

edited by

BILL KATZ

The Scarecrow Press, Inc.
Metuchen, N.J., & London
1988

British Library Cataloguing-in-Publication data available

ISBN 0-8108-2163-X
Library of Congress Catalog Card No. 78-154842

CONTENTS

PUBLISHER'S NOTE

The new editor of The Best of Library Lit. is Dr. Jane Anne Hanni-gan, Professor Emerita, School of Library Service, Columbia University. Dr. Hannigan has published widely in the professional literature in monographs and journal articles. She has been a Series Editor for the Association of American School Librarians and Neal-Schuman Publishers and has served on the Editorial Boards for School Media Quarterly, The International Journal of Instructional Media, and Phaedrus: An Annual of Research in Children's Literature. In 1984 she received the Beta Phi Mu Award from the American Library Association for Distinguished Service to Education for Librarianship.

All nominations for articles for consideration for inclusion in future issues of The Best of Library Lit. should be sent to Dr. Jane Anne Hannigan, c/o Scarecrow Press, Inc., 52 Liberty Street, P.O. Box 4167, Metuchen, NJ 08840.

HERE'S LOOKING AT YOU, KATZ!

I don't like being the bearer of bad tidings, but, even with the bad news, it is at the same time a pleasure. I have been asked to pay tribute to a man who has been a friend for a long, long time, and one who has had a giant and lasting impact upon the literature of librarianship.

This volume, Library Lit. 18--The Best of 1987, will be the last under the editorship of Bill Katz. From the beginning, with "The Best of 1970" published in 1971, Bill Katz has been the glue that has held this project together and the force that has given it its character and shaped its taste and range. The new editor will inherit not just a firm foundation but a monument--and a very large pair of shoes to fill. The good news is that, although those familiar two four-letter words will no longer appear on the title-page, Bill Katz will continue as a member of the jury that annually makes the final selection of articles to appear in Library Lit.

Back in the sixties somewhere I wrote an extremely critical article on the library press. Its essential premise was that uncontrolled proliferation of library periodicals had led to publication of more and more dross, just to fill the space available (a sort of early Parkinson's Law). The relatively few flowers in our literature were all but invisible among the surrounding mounds of garbage. In retrospect, it may be that in that howl of protest was the germ of the idea that was to emerge as the Library Lit. series.

When I took over the editorial reins at Scarecrow, all I had to do was find the right person to translate the idea into reality. It had to be someone well acquainted with the literature, a person who read voraciously and over a wide range, someone with inspiration, energy and an understanding of what distinguishes good writing from puff and ponderousness, a person with a proven record of editorial ability. Who else but Bill Katz? I never had a second choice.

For most of the first decade of Library Lit. Bill and I were the only two permanent jury members. Others we chose together; they were all people with editorial experience and/or unquestioned writing ability. All of those jurors made valuable contributions, but it was Bill Katz who really defined the scope and style of Library Lit. Some articles were suggested by librarians in the field, some by individual jurors, but most of the 200 or so pieces Bill brought to the jury each year (from which the final 30 would be selected) had been mined from far and wide by Katz himself. He it was who placed a determined emphasis on the <u>literature</u> in library lit., he who ranged well beyond the usual national, state and regional library periodicals to others, international and foreign. And he, too, who looked well beyond <u>library</u> periodicals for writing of relevance and interest to librarians and students of librarianship. Looking back over just a couple of the annuals as I wrote this tribute, I discovered contributions from <u>Science</u>, <u>The Indexer</u>, <u>The New Yorker</u>, <u>Papers of the Bibliographical Society</u>, <u>Dissent</u> and <u>Quaerendo</u>. How many librarians would ever have seen the excellent article on printing as a factor in world history, reprinted from the last-named of these journals, but for Bill Katz and <u>Library Lit.</u>?

In the Foreword to <u>Life Goes On</u>, Lawrence Clark Powell's most recent excursion in autobiography, I asked: "How does one explain the education for a profession that leaves its graduates ignorant of its <u>own</u> giants, those who have shaped or given character or inspiration to that profession?" The question was provoked by an encounter with two librarians who asked me, "Who's Larry Powell?"

Bill Katz has not been much involved in the politics of librarianship or the turbulence of ALA and other library conventions. In fact he has shunned public exposure like the plague, concentrating instead on his teaching, his writing, his editing--all areas in which he has made an unparalleled mark upon his profession. Given his superb reference book, <u>Magazines for Libraries</u>, his standard textbook and several volumes of readings on reference work, his editorship for years of <u>The Reference Librarian</u>, his decades-long service as editor of LJ's "Magazines" column, plus eighteen years of <u>Library Lit.</u>--and much else--he may be one of the few giants of our profession whose name and contributions are known to <u>all</u> library school students of the past quarter-century.

As we bid farewell to Bill as founding--and thus far, only-- editor of <u>Library Lit.</u>, it remains only to ask whether this now hardy annual has been a success, whether it has achieved what we all hoped. Reviewing a recent volume in the series, that perceptive evaluator of the written word in our profession, Norman Stevens, said: "This most recent selection ... demonstrates that library literature is alive and, on the whole, well.... We should, at long last, put to rest the myth that library literature is a disgrace to the profession."

If Norman Stevens is correct in his assessment (and when is he ever wrong?), some of the credit for this dramatic change since my near-obituary for the library press in the early sixties must surely go to Bill Katz and his long stewardship of <u>Library Lit</u>. For that, and much more, one hopes that the profession is grateful to this man who has brought so much of worth to our attention. Certainly his publishers at Scarecrow, past and present, feel a deep sense of gratitude for his efforts and achievements. You will be missed, Bill. Now what can we think up for you to do next?

Eric Moon
President
Scarecrow Press, 1969-78

INTRODUCTION

In a world of uncertainties, one of the few sure things these days seems to be another edition of this collection which honors the work of writers concerned with librarians and libraries. This is the 18th year of the commonplace book, and far and wide through the land it takes its place on the shelf with other volumes, other voices in the series.

It seems evident that the approaches to literature in the field improve. Each year, despite the sometimes exquisite protests of reviewers, the group of articles demonstrates the various layers of interest of those who are involved with libraries. Yes, libraries. Not information centers, not media slam palaces, nor public policy pits-- just marvelous libraries.

Of the myriads of articles examined from just as many periodicals, the scale seems to be tipping back in favor of books and readers. Note, for example, that we have a new category in this prize-winning group called "Publishing, Books, and Reading." This does not mean the link between readers and books was ever in real danger, only that for a time new technologies and the mystic quality of machines lost contact with the reasons libraries have been about since Ur, and before. They have a history of serving readers, not managers, not computers, and certainly not educated illiterates. The demoniac power of time is settling it all in favor of librarians involved with shaping and reshaping ideas, or helping people in their quest for such formulations.

As more garbage is pumped into the system, as more disinformation floods the world, the role of the librarian becomes increasingly important. It is the necessity to separate out the recognized good from the not-so-always-recognized bad which justifies our existence. It explains, too, on a smaller scale what the jury is about when it meets each year to put this book together.

Given a choice among a hundred or more articles, the members are asked to select around thirty of the "best". It's not all that easy, nor are the results ever totally satisfactory, but over the years there has developed a program of evaluation which seems to work well enough.

The editor first sifts through the majority of periodicals involved with library literature. An effort is made to isolate those articles which are involved with the ongoing interests of librarians. The selected articles and those suggested along the way by other jury members as well as followers of this series are then presented to the jury for evaluation. The members meet together and fight it out over a period of one late afternoon.

The members consider the importance of the message, the course of the argument and the style of presentation in selecting or rejecting an article. The methodology for gathering and sifting data, the truth of the internal and external observations, as well as the sincerity of the voice, is important.

In the all too human game of writing for libraries and librarians much is made of the sheer power of repetition. One can, for example, never say too much about online searching, user studies or the puzzlement of information patterns. Much of this is evangelical rather than original. It has its place, but not in this collection, which prods the judges to pay attention to originality, imagination and significance of intelligence.

It is wonderful to find year in and year out such thought-provoking articles. The disagreeable aspect of it all is in narrowing the field to around 30. If you, the reader, wish to help, send the Editor articles which you believe should be in next year's volume. (Yes, Virginia, there will be another year, and another and another....) The only limitation is that the piece have something to do with libraries and librarians and be published between October and October, i.e., in this collection the approximate dates of publication are from October 1, 1986, to October 1, 1987.

The 1987 Jury

John Berry, editor-in-chief of Library Journal; Mary K. Chelton, former co-editor of VOYA; Arthur Curley, editor of Collection Building; Norman Horrocks, Vice President, Editorial, Scarecrow Press; Pat Schuman, President, Neal-Schuman Publishers; and the undersigned.

Thank you, Nancy

None of this would have been possible without the intelligent enthusiasm of Nancy Slater, my graduate assistant.

--Bill Katz

Part I

LIBRARIES AND LIBRARIANS

PIONEERS IN PUBLIC LIBRARY
SERVICE TO YOUNG ADULTS*

Joan Atkinson

A look backward may produce nostalgia if the past appears to offer
a simpler, more manageable existence than the present. Or the past
may be viewed rather academically, worthy of exploration just because it is there. Neither of these approaches would do justice to
the four leaders whose biographies are presented here. The heritage
they left is, in Henry Steele Commager's phrase, a "usable past,"
because their spirit of pioneering is absolutely essential to the present
and future of public library service to young adults.

The people I have chosen have many traits in common, but
each is an individual with a personality all her own and a unique
place in the development of young adult services. The composite
picture may suggest the qualities youth services needs today in its
advocates, and a look at individual strengths may help each of us
to identify the ways our specific talents fit into the larger picture.
The leaders are Mabel Williams and Margaret Scoggin of the New
York Public Library; Jean Roos of the Cleveland Public Library;
and Margaret Edwards of Baltimore's Enoch Pratt Free Library.

Mabel Williams (1887-1985)

Mabel Williams, who initiated and administered library service
for young adults at the New York Public Library (NYPL) between
1916 and 1951, was the administrator par excellence that most of us
would like either to have or to be. She worked hard herself, believed
in the importance of what she was doing, adapted the program of
service to the social context, and appreciated and encouraged the
special qualities of each staff member. Her managerial style was
informal, personal, and flexible.

Williams was a New Englander, educated at Simmons College,
Boston, where she took the library course and received her B.S.

*Reprinted by permission of the author and publisher from Top of
the News 43:1 (Fall 1986) 27-44; copyright © 1986 by the American
Library Association.

degree in 1909. She became a high school librarian and was speaking
at a Massachusetts Library Association meeting in 1916 when Anne
Carroll Moore, then head of Children's Services at NYPL, heard her
and was impressed. Williams became Moore's assistant later that
year and in 1919 was appointed supervisor of Work with Schools,
a position in which she instituted the first systematic service offered
for young adults by a public library.[1]

   The thrust of Williams' work between 1916 and 1930 was schools.
By 1919 New York City had thirty-nine licensed librarians in the city's
twenty-seven high schools.[2] The junior highs were not, however,
as well provided, and NYPL's class visit program targeted eighth
grade, aiming to acquaint students with the adult section of their
public library branches before they scattered to high schools. Up
until 1926 Williams was the only staff member assigned full time for
secondary school class visitations and in 1921 alone 2,445 class visits
were scheduled. Williams conducted many of these and trained branch
personnel to help as well. Her energetic work resulted in the hiring
of Amelia Munson in 1926 to take responsibility for continuation schools,
the forerunners of vocational and industrial schools. She also pushed
to have a trained school and reference assistant assigned to each
branch.

   Williams believed in the importance of young adults in society
and empathized with their vulnerability. Her 1945-46 annual report
asserted: "Adolescents are the victims of the times. When there
is a depression, we try to keep them young. When there is a war,
we push them into adult responsibility."[3] She advocated understanding on the part of the library of young adults' special needs,
calling this the "heart of the matter."[4]

   To Mabel Williams, the capstone of public library service was
its attention to the individual. Her visionary suggestion for meeting
young people who did not voluntarily enter the library was a "fleet
of book wagons going to schools, business centers and factories, at
convenient hours, with enough librarians to give all the personal
help needed." The individual contact was absolutely essential in
her view: "It is impossible to accept a compromise that will bring
books to many centers without these interpreting, friendly librarians."[5] For the reluctant reader, realistic reading guidance was
quite as important as for the avid reader: "If we don't [help bridge
the gap from juvenile to adult reading], we must surrender this
special group of young people to the moving pictures, the newsstand
and their limited environment because they must go searching for
answers to their questions in the surroundings available and intelligible to them."[6]

   The growth and change in young adult work in the branches
between 1930 and 1951 are a testimony to Williams' patience and persistence. Attitudes toward young adults changed gradually, as older
branch librarians who "killed youth's exuberance at the door," were

replaced by staff who knew Williams and respected her objectives.[7] Branch activities also changed. With the onset of the depression and the unemployment of masses of youth, Williams promoted clubs (a recognized part of children's work) for teenagers and also established lounges and browsing rooms. Clubs usually featured reading but also focused on current events, drama, or hobbies. Their activities were tremendously varied including reviewing books for young people; writing and performing plays; producing a newspaper; puppetmaking; equipping a darkroom and exhibiting photography; meeting with authors, poets, and other prestigious guests; and sponsoring trips to museums, theaters, and other sites.[8] Williams also established browsing rooms and lounges or "living rooms" in some branches depending on the neighborhood's need for a place for teenage social interaction and the branch's physical set-up.

Two other innovative contributions of Williams' administration were of major importance: establishment of the Nathan Straus Branch and publication of Books for the Teen Age. The Nathan Straus Branch, which existed in its own building from 1941 to 1953, served as a laboratory library for work with young adults under the direction of Margaret Scoggin. Books for the Teen Age, an annual listing of books of interest to young adults, actually began as "Books for Young People" and was published in Branch Library Books News beginning in 1929. Williams' introduction to the first list makes clear the distinction she saw between school and public library service:

> This list is primarily for use in the adult sections of the
> Library, to suggest books to boys and girls when they are
> first transferred from the Children's Rooms. It is not ex-
> pected to replace any of the lists now used by the schools.
> High School lists are naturally affected by the curriculum and
> the desire to give pupils an opportunity of knowing all
> forms of literature before leaving school. Furthermore,
> their use is dependent not only on inclination but also on
> compulsion, because of the various checking-up methods used
> in the schools. This list, on the other hand, includes only
> those books which boys and girls are known to have enjoyed
> either through their own discovery or the suggestion of a
> friend, a teacher, a librarian, or through the impetus re-
> ceived from book talks or reading clubs.[9]

Lillian Morrison, NYPL's coordinator of Young Adult Services from 1968 to 1982 points out: "It is hard to realize in these days of free reading, what school was like in 1929. Often one textbook was used. Classics were heavily emphasized for outside reading, and recreational reading related to personal interest was pretty much ignored. So a list of this kind filled a great need."[10] The celebration of the list's unveiling is still a gala event at NYPL, occurring usually in February and bringing together librarians, teachers, publishers, and authors. After her retirement Mabel Williams continued to attend these gatherings, including the fiftieth anniversary celebration in 1980 when she was ninety-three.

Williams' administration was characterized by its personal quality, flexibility, and informality. She interviewed job applicants and looked for enthusiasm, a "human touch," and a book background. Then preferences were also important to her: some liked booktalking, others preferred reference work. She appreciated both. She said, "What I loved about the whole thing was the placing of librarians where they'd be happy doing what they could do well."[11] Training was informal. The trainee might go with Williams on a class visit, observe her, and ask questions. Later the recruit would deliver a sample booktalk before Williams. No special structure was required; whatever worked best for the individual was acepted. Class visits varied and might comprise a number of elements: library instruction; booktalks; introduction to the resources, layout, and rules of the adult department; programs involving games, contests, listening time with the Victrola, or formal or informal discussions; browsing time and individual reading guidance. Monthly meetings encouraged the librarians to develop their own philosophy of service as they were drawn into discussions of specific issues or problems or books. Lillian Morrison observed,

> Miss Williams had the ability to discover possibilities in the people who worked there and let them flower. She seemed so interested in what she was learning from you and made you feel excited about the work. She was one of the most humble people, but you respected her for her knowledge, for her feeling for people, her quiet effectiveness and appreciation of quality and vision in others when she saw it.[12]

In 1942 the name of the office was changed to the Office of Work with Schools and Young People, the addition of "and Young People" emphasizing services for all youth, not simply those in schools. In 1946 NYPL established the Reference Department, which took responsibility for reference work in the branches but left ill-defined who was to provide it for young adults. From 1946 to 1951 Williams' task was determining which services could be offered by her staff, which was down to twenty-five after a high of sixty-nine in 1939. One approach was hiring field workers, not assigned to any one branch, who made class visits during school hours and did floor work in several branches in the afternoons. Another approach was as-signing a school and reference librarian to cover two branches. Thus, at the time of her retirement, Mabel Williams had witnessed both tremendous expansion during the thirties and a disheartening cutback of service to young adults after World War II.

Mabel Williams attracted to the department a highly committed staff; her influence can still be felt today. As early as 1926, with the hiring of Amelia Munson, she began to build. A few years later Margaret Scoggin joined School Work, and when she progressed to the point where she was about to take another job that would offer more challenge, Williams managed to get the building that became the Nathan Straus Branch for Scoggin to design and run as a youth

library.[13] By the time of Williams' retirement she had prepared
Scoggin in every aspect of the work, so the transition from her
administration to Scoggin's seemed effortless. A dozen other talented
and competent youth specialists were readying themselves for the
years ahead, including future coordinators Lillian Morrison and Ruth
Rausen.

The quiet effectiveness of Williams' work was finally recognized
officially by the American Library Association in 1980 when she was
the recipient of the Grolier award, given for outstanding library work
with young people. The Grolier Citation reads, in part, "She envisioned programs and activities that recognized children and young
adults as citizens of the community regardless of age, grade, intelligence quotient, race, or creed. Her philosophy was ahead of its
time, and remains timeless in its application to meet the needs of
youth throughout the country."[14]

Mabel Williams lived for ninety-eight years! Ruth Rausen,
present coordinator of Young Adult Services, remarked that Williams
was spry, alert, and interested in the activity of the office until her
death on November 17, 1985.[15] The qualities that made her a much-
honored administrator were memorialized in NYPL's press release on
the occasion of her death, which contains the following tribute written
by Lillian Morrison:

> A wise woman, with a great sense of humor and a deep under-
> standing of the young, she was a wonderful flexible adminis-
> trator whose philosophy, though unobtrusive, was a great
> influence and whose forte was discovering the special talents
> of her librarians, giving them free rein, to the great benefit
> of the young people of New York City. Her contributions
> continue through the work of all of us who are still serving
> teenagers in the public library, not only in New York but
> in other library systems around the country.[16]

Margaret Scoggin (1905-1968)

Margaret Scoggin shared many qualities with her mentor, Mabel
Williams. She shared her administrative skills, her empathy with
young adults, her conviction of the library's importance in their
lives, and her vitality and warmth. During the twenty-five years
the two worked together at NYPL, Williams steered Scoggin toward
opportunities for experimentation and growth that she knew the
younger woman thrived upon.[17] At Williams' retirement in 1951,
Scoggin succeeded her as superintendent of Work with Schools and
Young People.

From the Midwest, Scoggin was born in Caruthersville, Missouri, April 14, 1905. She described her forebears as people who
followed pioneering trails through North Carolina, Virginia, Mississippi,

Georgia, and Tennessee. The men were lawyers, ministers, and
doctors distributing books, Bibles, and medicines from their saddle-
bags.[18] Her childhood recollection of a library was of that of her
older brother, a professor of Greek, Latin, and Sanskrit at the
University of Missouri in Columbia. Scoggin graduated as valedictorian
from Columbia High School in 1922 and attended Radcliffe College,
where she majored in English and classical studies. In 1926 she
graduated magna cum laude and was elected to Phi Beta Kappa.
During her senior year she lived at Denison House, a university
settlement house in Boston, and taught English to foreign students,
an activity that may have spurred her interest in youth work.[19]

    Scoggin applied for summer work in 1926 with New York Public
Library because she wished to live in New York City. For the next
two years she moved from position to position in several branches, coming to know and admire Mabel Williams. After spending a year (1929)
attending the School of Librarianship at the University of London, she
was appointed in 1930 librarian in charge of school and reference work
at NYPL's George Bruce Branch. Scoggin adopted Williams' philosophy
of providing young people with books that interested them and of
helping them discover their interests via library clubs, programs, and
involvement in book selection and reviewing. From 1935 to 1940 she
supervised work with vocational and industrial high schools, and in
1940 when a building on East 32nd Street was made available through
the estate of Nathan Straus, she became the designer of both facility
and services of the first public library dedicated exclusively for the
use of people under twenty-one years old.

    "How she loved it!" Williams recalled Scoggin's response to
the challenge of complete freedom. Scoggin oversaw all phases of
the work from gutting the old building to selecting furniture for
the new. She insisted that a welcoming atmosphere be created by
the use of good lighting and bright colors, an innovation at the time.
Her vision for the new library was that it serve the needs of both
young people and professionals. It should be a laboratory where
young people found a model collection of books old and new reflecting
the diversity of their interests, hobbies, problems, and hopes.
Planned to be a center for their experimentation, it was to include
a printing press with lists and broadsides, a Victrola and record
collection, a radio and a movie projector--these to "yield valuable
information as well as fruitful entertainment." For persons working
with youth she intended the Nathan Straus Branch to be a laboratory
for research on reading interests, for observation and for acquaintance with the newest materials. "Perhaps its philosophy," said
Scoggin, "may be best expressed as a profund hope. May young
people find here a symbol of stability in a confused world ... proof
and promise that certain human values do endure and cannot per-
ish."[20] The journal kept by the Nathan Straus staff and available
today in NYPL's Office for Young Adult Services is testimony to
its success. Literally thousands of visitors from around the world
journeyed to observe and request services during the years 1941

to 1953, when the collection and services were moved to their present location at the Donnell Library Center on 53rd Street.

Scoggin took to heart Williams' belief that the library must become a social institution, interpreting, selecting and writing, if need be, books to meet the needs of young people.[21] In all she compiled six anthologies of stories to interest teenagers, the first Chucklebait (1945) dedicated to Mabel Williams, "who first interested me in reading for fun." Others followed: Love of Danger (1947), More Chucklebait (1949), The Edge of Danger (1951), Battle Stations (1953), and Escapes and Rescues (1960). She was coediting a science fiction anthology at the time of her death.

One of the most successful programs of the Nathan Straus Library was its teenage book reviewers' group, who were to read widely and "express their honest opinions." A monthly bulletin, "Circulatin' the News," presented their views to publishers and librarians. Excerpts, included with the annual "Books for Young People" list beginning in 1946, show the critical sophistication developed by these readers, who used the terms shaky, forced, imitative, original, and musical to describe style or language. The 1948 excerpts show that young people as far away as Maryland and Minneapolis also participated. The reviewing program expanded to radio in 1946 with Scoggin moderating a weekly "Young Book Reviewers" broadcast that was taped and aired on other stations around the country. It is now called "Teen Age Book Talk" and has won several awards.

Energetic in seeking out cooperative ventures, Scoggin engaged in a variety of professional activities. As early as 1928, she addressed the American Library Association on the topic of service to young people. She was secretary of ALA's Young People's Reading Round Table in 1936 and in 1940, chair. In 1942 she became an ALA councilor and in 1950 chaired ALA's International Relations Committee. When the New York Library Association established a Children's and Young Adult Services Division (1951), Margaret Scoggin became its first chair. She also influenced the profession by teaching at St. John's University for many years in the 1940s and 1950s and at Simmons College in Boston, where she traveled once a week during 1952 to institute a young adult course. Her professional writings are numerous, beginning in the early 1930s and continuing until shortly before her death.

Scoggin enjoyed travel, feeling it promoted brotherhood and understanding. In addition to her year in London in 1929, she led a group of cyclists through the Scandinavian countries on a youth hostel trip during the summer of 1938. When the American Library Association and the Rockefeller Foundation cooperated after World War II to organize an international youth library in Munich, Germany, Scoggin was the natural choice as adviser. Once she was on site, however, she found herself working long hours to help the librarians

weed and classify 8,000 books from twenty-four countries and to
organize programs that would attract young people. After much effort
the library opened in 1949. While in Europe, Scoggin also toured
other libraries for UNESCO and on her return campaigned for books
to be included in CARE packages.

Back home, Scoggin became assistant to Williams, who was approaching retirement and obviously intended Scoggin to be her suc-
cessor. At this time administrative changes were coming in NYPL.
Because the city administration wished to reduce costs it began to
apply scientific management techniques. Ralph Beals, NYPL director,
considered combining the children's and young people's offices as a
cost-cutting measure. It was the strength of the leadership of
Williams and Scoggin, who emphasized the close relation of young
people's and adult work, that influenced NYPL to maintain a separate
young people's department, [22] which in 1956 was named Office of
Work with Young Adults, as it remains today. Scoggin became coordinator of the office, a position she held until shortly before her
death.

Scoggin's outstanding accomplishments were recognized by
several awards. In 1952 she received the Constance Lindsay Skinner
Award of the Women's National Book Association. In 1956 she received
the Lane Bryant Award and the Marshall Field Award. For her accomplishments in encouraging young adult reading, she received the
Grolier award in 1960.

Margaret Scoggin died on July 11, 1968, at the age of sixty-
three. She had worked for forty-one years for the New York Public
Library. Lillian Morrison, who followed her as coordinator of NYPL's
Office for Young Adult Services, remarked: "She had great rapport
with the young. Her brainpower and productivity were staggering,
to say nothing of her generosity to those who worked under her."[23]
Emma Cohn described her as appearing like an avenging angel when
a branch assistant had a problem and called for help.[24] Others
remembered her modest demeanor, contagious enthusiasm, and constant
search for challenge. "The tailored stern appearance of the tall,
slim, brown-eyed, gray-haired librarian belied the boundless energy,
intellectual brilliance, remarkable wit and inner warmth that shone
through when she was with 'her' young people." Several days before
her death the American Library Association presented her with a
tribute which read in part:

> Her ideas of library service for young adults have brought
> her authority and eminence in the field. Her simplicity and
> integrity of character have won her respect of young people
> throughout the world. Her wisdom and understanding,
> and above all her sense of humor, have been guiding lights
> for her colleagues and associates. We honor Margaret Scog-
> gin as one of our truly dedicated public servants.[25]

Jean Carolyn Roos (1891-1982)

Jean Roos was Mabel Williams' counterpart in the Cleveland
Public Library (CPL), where she worked in youth services for
thirty-seven years. From 1925 to 1940 Roos was head of the Robert
Louis Stevenson Room for young people and from 1940 until her retirement in 1959 she was supervisor of the Youth Department.

Born in Buffalo, New York, March 9, 1891, Roos attended the
University of Buffalo and Cleveland College. She received her cer-
tificate from Western Reserve University's School of Library Science
in 1928. She combined an awareness of social conditions and a focus
on cooperation with youth-serving agencies outside the library in
order to meet the needs of young adults both in and out of school.

Organization of the Stevenson Room in 1925 was Cleveland's
innovation in public library service to young adults. CPL director
Linda Eastman observed in her 1925 annual report that the "inter-
mediate" still being served in the children's room who wanted "by
fair means or foul, to get into the adult room" was an urgent library
problem.[26] The Stevenson Room was to provide special service
for the fourteen- to twenty-one-year-old, by having a trained staff
and a collection of adult books selected with the interests of young
readers in mind. Jean Roos, who had been assistant to Annie Spenser
Cutter, head of the School Department, was selected as head. Roos
established liaisons to promote Stevenson Room activities to young
people who gravitated to the popular library and to distribute introductory cards to young people who approached the information desk.
Adult departments also called the Stevenson Room for help in the high
school reference area, and by 1934 Roos was pleased with the inter-
divisional cooperation that had evolved.

In 1938 Charles Rush was appointed CPL's director, an important move for youth services because Rush was one of the earliest
advocates of public library commitment to strong programs for young
adults. He made persuasive speeches to this effect at conferences
of the American Library Association in 1925 and 1927.[27] A reorganization by Rush created two new supervision offices, the Adult
Education Department and the Office for Service to Youth, the latter
renamed the Youth Department in 1943.

As supervisor of the new department Roos was directly responsible to the director of the library and gained increased authority
for hiring and training staff for branches and providing in-service
training for other librarians. The role of the youth librarians in
the branches posed a problem, however, because they reported directly to the branch heads, who could approve or reject programming
and could schedule their activities in a way that maximized routine
branch duties and minimized work in the youth specialty. Roos conducted monthly meetings of the young people's librarians to discuss
book selection and other issues. Although she also scheduled one

afternoon a week to visit branches, work with the branches was not
her strong point. The monthly meetings were later described by
some of the young people's librarians as deadly and static. Roos
was perceived as presiding over a big corporation meeting where
there was no policy discussion or even any discussion of any kind.
Her strong personality dominated, and to differ with her demanded
an equally strong personality. The result was that very little programming over the years was reported from the branches.[28]

Instead, activities were centered at the Main Library where
Roos had the freedom and authority to initiate and carry out policy.
Roos directed a major effort toward out-of-school youth, who numbered
64.8 percent of sixteen- and seventeen-year-olds in 1920; 40.9 percent in 1930; and 19.5 percent in 1940. In the late 1920s the library
sent a form called a new job card to young people under seventeen
who had been issued work permits; the new job card informed them
of the services of the branch nearest them and invited them to use
library materials. When in the early 1930s the clerical work became
overwhelming, Roos tried contacting young people through fifty
major employers of minors with introductory library cards. Another
approach she tried was to have high school librarians distribute introductory cards to graduates and others leaving school. Results
of these efforts were hard to measure and only the latter showed
real returns.[29]

In the late 1930s and 1940s Roos shifted the effort to serve
out-of-school youth away from direct contact, which Mabel Williams
saw as crucial, and toward reaching them through other social agencies. In 1938 a deposit collection was placed in the offices of the
National Youth Administration (NYA) and invitations to the Stevenson
Room were given to young people who applied for NYA aid. NYA
vocational guidance counselors also recommended the library's pamphlet
files and other vocational materials. In the early 1940s Roos was
active on at least twenty youth-advocacy committees in Cleveland.
Her role was to bring needed materials to the attention of other youth
workers and invite groups to visit the library. The high point of
this activity was 1949 when 514 groups visited the library and Roos
contacted 912 groups outside the library.[30]

Toward the end of World War II, Roos initiated a popular program that continued for seventeen years (1945-62). Cosponsored by
four community groups, it was called "Roads to World Understanding."
Roos wrote, "The emphasis of each program is understanding the way
people live, think and act--not political ideologies."[31] Each program
featured a country of interest. Formats varied, including panel
discussions, guest speakers, films, slides, music of the country,
demonstrations, and dances. An exhibit lined the corridor to the
library auditorium and used materials from the Cleveland Art Museum;
library books, maps, and magazines; and pen-pal letters of members
of the Cleveland Press World Friends' Club (80,000 members) who
corresponded with young people throughout the world. Part of the

success of the program, which drew from 250 to 600 participants during its first year, was its timeliness. The young adults had fathers, brothers, and uncles who had fought abroad. Also, two-thirds of Cleveland's population were first- or second-generation Americans. Another factor in the program's success was that an active youth advisory committee of about twenty-five young adults assisted the sponsors. Another CPL program that had a long and productive existence was the Poetry Group (1927-42). The group was devoted to writing original poetry and met to hear each other's work and offer encouragement. Prominent guests were sometimes invited, including Langston Hughes in 1935. Two publications resulted from this group, "Preludes to Poetry" (1928) and "More Preludes to Poetry" (1942). Like Mabel Williams, Jean Roos directed the compilation of a number of bibliographies and book lists to provide indirect reading guidance. The best-known is Patterns in Reading (1954, 1961), an annotated subject grouping of 1,600 titles around 75 "patterns." The progression within each pattern was from easy to more complex books.

In 1943 Cleveland Public Library experimented, as New York Public had done with the Nathan Straus Branch in 1941, in converting the Alta Branch library into a facility mainly for the use of young people and placing it under the jurisdiction of the Youth Department. The branch head, Mary Meyer, made it a place teenagers wanted to visit by using bright colors and starting clubs and programming. The neighborhood, basically one of nonreaders, had a fairly homogeneous population, mostly Italian, and stability. Throughout the experiment the Branch Department objected to what it perceived as the focus on social work rather than library work; Roos and Meyer argued that the situation in the neighborhood made that approach necessary. In 1955 Alta was returned to the Branch Department's authority and although it continued theoretically to be an experiment in work with young people, its programming was indistinguishable from that of other branches. A similar attempt in 1956 at the Hough Branch to serve young people's needs by special programming brought about frustration and disappointment, and the experiment was scrapped after four years. CPL had tried, but staff, resources, and commitment to specialized service were insufficient to surmount the overwhelming social problems involved in these experiments.[32]

Class visitations and booktalking for secondary schools were not major activities in Cleveland as they were in New York because of the difference in the public library's relation to schools. Cleveland had a unique arrangement in which school library service was under the supervision of the public library from 1895 to 1968. In her early years in the Stevenson Room, Roos handled selection for the schools. School librarians worked in the public library during summers, Christmas holidays, and afternoons. Details of the arrangement shifted through the years, but Roos felt the school librarians had the broad background needed to booktalk and give reading guidance. Public librarians needed to go to schools only for special occasions.

Roos articulated her philosophy in professional literature and speeches. Her 1940 speech and article, "Laying the Foundation," maintained that adult service rested on four cornerstones: children's work, school library work, young adult work, and service to parents, teachers, social workers, and leaders of youth groups of all kinds. She saw the inattention to young adult work producing a library building that looked "somewhat like the Leaning Tower of Pisa."[33] The current structure failed to produce a natural movement from children's to adult reading and use. Just five years before her retirement Roos wrote "Young People and Public Libraries,"[34] a brief history of the development of young adult services. It emphasized reading guidance and the special public relations role of the young adult librarian with other community agencies serving youth.

In addition to her interest in youth-serving agencies, Roos also participated actively in the American Library Association. She helped organize the Young People's Reading Round Table, was an ALA councilor, and served as president in 1947-48 of the newly formed Division of Libraries for Children and Young People. Like Margaret Scoggin, she taught for many years, in her case on the faculty of the School of Library Science of Western Reserve University. After her retirement from the Cleveland Public Library, Roos was acting librarian for Martin County Public Library. She later moved to Florida and died there March 21, 1982, at the age of ninety-one.

Jean Roos fought battles within the library to establish young adult services as a vital library function. She emphasized direct and indirect reading guidance. Using youth advisory committees, she planned programs and activities that were pertinent to young adults. She was highly visible in the community and worked persistently with other youth workers to guarantee access to ideas for both in-school and out-of-school youth.

Margaret Edwards (1902-1988) [See Editor's Note on page 21]

Margaret Alexander Edwards was the architect of young adult work, called "Y work," at Baltimore's Enoch Pratt Free Library, where she worked for thirty years, from 1932 to 1962. Her zealous commitment to her principles and her persuasive communication skills deserve emulation.

Born October 23, 1902, in Childress, Texas, Margaret Edwards came to library work via schoolteaching. She received her B.A. degree from Trinity University in Waxahachie, Texas, in 1922; her M.A. from Columbia University in 1928; and her B.S. in library science also from Columbia in 1937. During her childhood, the family's physical remoteness on their West Texas farm meant that library service and a varied supply of books were not accessible. The family cherished its collection of Dickens, Scott, and other masterpieces and read the King James version of the Bible aloud regularly. Edwards memorized nine psalms for her ninth birthday. Before interviewing with Joseph Wheeler for the training program at Enoch Pratt in 1932, she taught English in small Texas towns for five years and Latin in Towson, Maryland, until a disagreement with a supervisor resulted in her being fired. From the beginning, youth work interested Edwards, and when the new central building opened in 1933 with a separate alcove in the popular library set aside for teenage use, she was assigned to work there three hours a day. As the work developed, the position became full-time in 1937. Edwards visited NYPL to observe its program and to talk to Mabel Williams. She returned "bursting with ideas" and began to establish branch collections and to recruit assistants in each of the branches, a task completed by 1940.[35]

As coordinator Edwards was in the same administrative bind that Roos experienced in Cleveland: the Y librarians had dual accountability: to branch heads and to the coordinator. The outcome differed, however. Edwards' vigor and forceful personality plus strong administrative support for the youth specialty resulted in her prescribing the training program she believed in and receiving cooperation from the branches in carrying out her plans.

Edwards had the ability to select and bring out the best in good people. Her training program was formally structured and rigorous, in keeping with the importance of the objectives to be achieved: promotion of world citizenship through reading and understanding the implications of United States citizenship. An integral part of her philosophy was that the aims could best be realized through books that touched the reader emotionally. Since growth in literary appreciation was not the objective, Y librarians had to be retrained in their analysis of books to emphasize what personal understanding might derive from reading. First, of course, the librarians must be well read.

Edwards demanded excellence. She began with individual training. The new assistant checked titles already read from NYPL's Books for the Teen Age list and discussed with Edwards the objectives of reading. She then chose 300 more titles for the assistant to read and discuss with her. These discussions, which included ten books each, emphasized book selection principles, techniques for presentation of the book on the floor of the library, procedures for developing readers, and effective speaking. Some assistants described these sessions as grueling, others as demanding and thought-provoking. Despite the hard work Anna Anthony Curry felt they were effective because the skills were immediately transferrable to the actual work situation. Being successful in floor work built confidence. Monthly meetings, also a part of the training, were for inspiration and ideas, not book reviewing. A controversial title might be debated; librarians might listen to a booktalk before and after coaching; techniques for helping shelf-sitters get moving might be the topic. Librarians saw these sessions as exciting, stimulating, or provocative but never as

dull. Sometimes the director even appeared to debate or listen to
debate on a title or issue. The third aspect of training was in booktalking, and Edwards' requirements were precise, including type
of incident selected for telling, voice modulation, and memorization
of the talk. Beginning in 1956 all booktalks were typed in triplicate
with two copies kept in the office and available for use by other Y
librarians. Some librarians liked the tight structure; others found
it inhibiting. Edwards contended that the rigor was necessary to
produce the desired result: work carried out so smoothly it appeared
effortless.[36]

Edwards had wanted to work closely with schools from the beginning, believing that through schools the broadest cross section
of young people was reached, but it was not until 1943 that arrangements were worked out for conducting a systematic class visitation
program. The visits followed a prescribed routine: librarians distributed booklists of about 260 titles divided into categories, students
were asked to call out numbers of books they would like to hear
briefly summarized, a long (nine-minute) booktalk would be followed
by more short ones and finally by another long talk. Some Y librarians were critical of the "mechanical structure of the visit" and
would have preferred informal rapping or at least flexibility. Edwards was firm, however, and uniformity prevailed.[37] Effectiveness of the program was not scientifically measured, but most of
those involved agreed that class visits successfully met Edwards'
objective of humanizing books, the library, and the librarian.

In one respect Edwards' philosophy of work with schools was
dramatically different from that of NYPL or CPL. She resisted the
reference function. As her branch Y librarians responded more and
more in the late 1950s to the pressure of providing school-assignment
help and some instruction in use of reference tools, especially the
card catalog, her response was: "I hate it. I think that the catalog
is the librarian's tool ... you take all these hordes of people and
teach them to use the catalog, and they don't want to learn and do
not learn." After Sputnik, the emphasis on upgrading education,
particularly in the sciences, brought more and more pressure for
youth reference service, and finally in 1961 Edwards capitulated.
Reference work was recognized officially as the province of librarians
who "received general instruction in reference work through in-
service training meetings."[38]

Edwards described herself once as rough and ready, and one
of her service programs certainly bore this out. In a 1934 speech
Mabel Williams had envisioned a fleet of book wagons taking the
library to people who would not come to it. Margaret Edwards actually
practiced that innovative outreach in the summers of 1942, 1943,
and 1944. With a horse and a wagon marked "The Pratt Library's
Book Wagon. Borrow Books Here," she traveled the streets of Baltimore, distributing books in neighborhoods of low library use. The
first summer she issued library cards to 456 new borrowers and

estimated that in four hours she circulated as many books as the
branch generally did in an eight-hour day.[39] The next two summers were equally successful and, Edwards felt, did the librarians
as much good as the residents. Demands of the project was high,
however, requiring eighteen-hour days of hard work on Edwards'
part. After her marriage in 1945 she could not continue at that
pace, and the experiment was dropped.

Edwards took the book wagon to both black and white neighborhoods of racially segregated Baltimore. In his bequest establishing
the library, Enoch Pratt had asserted that it "shall be open for all,
rich and poor, without distinction of race or color...". The reality
left much to be desired. Augusta Baker, a Baltimore native and
later coordinator of Children's Services at NYPL, remembers blacks
as being restricted to the "black" branch, regardless of where they
lived. Nor was the library amenable to hiring blacks, as Baker found
when she applied for a job there in 1933, although by 1946 there
were two black professionals on the staff.

Margaret Edwards was determined to include blacks in her
programming. She noted that at one time Pratt did not send vacation
reading lists to black schools and insisted, with Wheeler's backing,
that this omission be rectified. When in 1945 she planned a Book
Week masquerade party at the main library, black students were
invited and came. White librarians did class visits at black schools
before the Supreme Court desegregation decision of 1954, and Edwards worked with the superintendent of black schools to organize
a series of film programs, which she reported in 1943 had gained
new readers for the library and provided stimulating entertainment
in the community. Film programming was not an ongoing activity,
however, as Edwards' priorities were class visits to schools and booktalking. She said of these:

> We have always in our school visits assumed that everyone
> was liberal and unprejudiced. In all the schools we gave
> booktalks on <u>Black Like Me</u> and other books of social signifi-
> cance, as if all the audiences were concerned for all Ameri-
> cans. The fact that teenagers are not, as a rule, prejudiced,
> helped.[40]

Perhaps Edwards' greatest contribution was her ability to release talent in people that they did not know they had. Anna Anthony
Curry,Enoch Pratt's current director, was the first black librarian
in Y work. Interviewed in 1970, she described Edwards as her
mentor:

> My relationship with Mrs. Edwards was a very special kind
> of relationship that transcended superior and fledgling. It
> was a one-to-one relationship probing my intellect. For the
> first time I thought about things and had an opportunity to
> express ideas that never had come to the surface. I began

to be very proud of myself. I wanted passionately to do
whatever she wanted me to do. It suddenly became important
to be a good librarian ... and as a black librarian, it seemed
doubly important because I realized as I grew up what limited
experiences I had with black librarians and I felt there are
a great many young people who would profit from an experience
and exposure with me. I've never felt, frankly, that anything I had done since I left Y has been quite as important
as what I did as a Y librarian.[41]

At the 1986 ALA program, "On the Shoulders of Giants," Lillian
Bradshaw, honored as one of the profession's giants, mentioned
Margaret Edwards as a motivating force in her life. At Edwards'
retirement, she left other leaders ready to continue the work at
Enoch Pratt: Sara Siebert, who followed her as coordinator, Linda
Lapides, and others. She was a leader who made leaders.

Both before and after her retirement in 1962 Edwards contributed to the profession by her teaching, lecturing, and writing. She
was a visiting professor in library schools at McGill University,
Rutgers University, Catholic University, the University of Texas,
and the University of Montana. Her major, lasting contribution is
the book The Fair Garden and the Swarm of Beasts (1969, 1974),
which describes her philosophy and practice of young adult librarianship with inimitable wit and persuasiveness. She lectured and held
workshops throughout the United States. In April 1976 she was
keynote speaker for a conference at the University of Alabama. When
I met her plane, I was immediately struck by her independence,
vigor, and determination. Her first words to me were: "You'll
have to carry my suitcase, as I've had an accident on my farm with
my wheelbarrow and have three broken ribs. I've had to sleep sitting
up for the last two nights." Edwards continues at eighty-four to
live on her farm in Joppa, Maryland. Linda Lapides summarized
Edwards' personal traits: her greatest quality is the ability to inspire
others to carry on the work. She believed that the ideas found in
books are civilizing, and she cared about books because she cared
about people and wanted them to develop imagination and understanding that comes from reading books. She was brilliant, fast on her
feet, able to laugh at herself and convinced that a sense of humor
was important for everyone, certainly for teenagers. Life never
seemed grim with her. She challenged her staff. We worked in-
credibly hard. We were proud to be part of the Edwards' team.

Conclusion

These pioneers were more alike than different. They all worked
for thirty years or more in one library system, focusing their abun-
dant energies primarily on their profession. They were college-
educated at a time when the range of careers for educated women was
quite restricted and the practice of combining career and marriage

was unusual, to say the least. Only one of them married, in midlife, and had no children.

Besides energy, they had in common a willingness to adventure, experiment, perhaps fail, and then pursue their aims in other ways. Whether it was Margaret Edwards with the horse and wagon enticing readers or Jean Roos aligning the library with other social agencies to contact out-of-school youth, there was a reluctance to accept the library's role as that of serving only young adults who walked through its doors. The missionary zeal, the belief that what they were doing was vitally important was always with them. They accepted the necessity of working within their social environment, whether it was segregated Baltimore, cosmopolitan New York, or predominantly ethnic Cleveland, and of adapting programming and services to social conditions and needs. They were effective communicators both with their administrations, their teenage patrons, and the library profession. They left a tremendous body of pertinent professional literature, and the professional organizations they founded and supported still flourish. Perhaps best of all they had a zest for living and found life quite satisfying. Certainly they had longevity--two lived into their nineties, one is now in her eighties.

The pioneers had the wit to see what needed to be done and the tenacity to seek out people who could be inspired to share their vision. They knew that in order to make a real difference, service to young adults had to be ongoing and institutionalized. We are still fighting the same fight--to get young adult work recognized and established. To win we need the flexibility, quiet affectiveness, warmth, and empathy with people of Mabel Williams; the intellectual depth, vitality, dedication and search for challenge of Margaret Scoggin; the social awareness, commitment to cooperation, persistence, and spirit of youth-advocacy of Jean Roos; and the forthrightness, optimism about human potential, persuasiveness, and capacity to inspire of Margaret Edwards. These pioneers are our "usable past," our inspiration for getting the job done.

References and Notes

1. The American Library Association, The ALA Yearbook, (Chicago: American Library Assn., 1981), p. 79.
2. Miriam Braverman, Youth, Society and the Public Library (Chicago: American Library Assn., 1979), p. 23. Braverman's work is the major history of the early development of young adult services in New York Public Library, Cleveland Public Library, and Enoch Pratt Free Library. This article relies heavily on it, especially for establishing the context in which these leaders worked.
3. Ibid., p. 108.
4. For a complete treatment of Williams' philosophy, see Mabel Williams, "'Seventeen' and the Public Library," Library Journal 59:821-23 (Nov. 1934).

5. Ibid., p. 822.
6. Ibid., p. 823.
7. Mabel Williams, "Young People in the Public Library," American Library Association Bulletin 33:158-62.
8. Braverman, p. 38-42.
9. Lillian Morrison, "Fifty Years of 'Books for the Teen Age,'" School Library Journal 26:44-50 (Dec. 1979).
10. Ibid., p. 48.
11. Braverman, p. 61.
12. Ibid., p. 63.
13. Ibid., p. 52.
14. The ALA Yearbook, 1981, p. 79.
15. Interview with Ruth Rausen, July 7, 1986.
16. News release, New York Public Library, November 1985.
17. Braverman, p. 52.
18. Current Biography Yearbook (1952), S.V. "Scoggin, Margaret Clara."
19. Mary K. Chelton, "Scoggin, Margaret Clara," in ALA World Encyclopedia of Library and Information Services (1980).
20. Margeret C. Scoggin, "The Nathan Straus Branch for Children and Young People," Branch Library Book News 18:96-97 (June 1941).
21. Williams, p. 823.
22. Braverman, p. 65.
23. Morrison, p. 44.
24. Interview with Emma Cohn, July 7, 1986.
25. Beverly Lowy, "Scoggin, Margaret Clara," in Dictionary of American Library Biography (1978). For Scoggin's presentation of her philosophy of service see "First Catch Your Hare," American Library Association Bulletin 53:55-60 (Jan. 1959).
26. Braverman, p. 117.
27. For complete information see Charles E. Rush, "Reaching Boys and Girls Out of School," American Library Association Bulletin 19:142-45 (July 1925), and "The Interdependence of Adult and Juvenile Departments," American Library Association Bulletin 21:298-301 (Oct. 1927).
28. Braverman, p. 123-26.
29. Ibid., p. 150.
30. Ibid., p. 140.
31. For a full discussion of the program, see Jean C. Roos, "A Youth Department Points the Way," Library Journal 72:279-82 (Feb. 15, 1947).
32. Braverman, p. 158-67.
33. Jean C. Roos, "Laying the Foundation," American Library Association Bulletin 34:448-54, 490 (Sept. 1940).
34. Jean C. Roos, "Young People and Public Libraries," Library Trends 3:129-40 (Oct. 1954).
35. Braverman, p. 181.
36. Margaret A. Edwards, "Many a Thousand Brick," Library Journal 81:1282-85 (May 15, 1956).
37. Braverman, p. 200.

38. Ibid., p. 224.
39. Margaret Edwards, The Fair Garden and the Swarm of Beasts
    (New York: Hawthorn, 1974), p. 55.
40. Braverman, p. 234.
41. Braverman, p. 1971.

Editor's Note

Margaret Alexander Edwards died on April 19, 1988, after a
stroke. The American Library Association, meeting in July, honored
her with a memorial resolution. It acknowledged her contribution to
Enoch Pratt Free Library and to young people in Baltimore, her
"legacy of excellence to libraries around the world" and her influence
on the profession through her intellectual vitality and commitment,
her writings, and her training of capable successors.

Perhaps her most significant memorial she wrote herself in her
will, which bequeathed her estate of over half a million dollars to
further the philosophy she believed and practiced. She wrote:

> It is my observation that in the lives of most people, mean-
> ingful experience is rare and that without it, it is difficult
> to understand one's self or to establish good relations with
> others. Since I believe the book supplements experience and
> since I have faith in young people and am concerned that
> they read--not only for their personal enjoyment and enrich-
> ment but so that they may equip themselves to remake society
> --I bequeath the bulk of my estate to further the personal
> reading of young adults ... I should like what worldly goods
> I leave behind to be used to experiment with ways of
> effectively promoting the reading of young adults and of in-
> spiring young adult librarians to realize the importance of
> reading and to perfect themselves as readers' advisors."

Her Trustees are three of her former "Y" librarians: Anna Curry,
Ray Fry, and Sara Siebert.

CONVERSATION, A NEW PARADIGM
FOR LIBRARIANSHIP?*

Joan M. Bechtel

That these are challenging, often difficult, times for academic libraries is no news to anyone in the library world. Concern for
professionalism, with its attention to accountability and responsibility,
abounds. Unprecedented growth in technology provides vast new
opportunities for communication, and the availability of information
far outstrips most people's capacity to digest it all. In the face of
this information explosion, it is ironic that academic librarians are
casting about for an appropriate myth or model for library service.
Witness the ACRL Third National Conference (April 4-7, 1984), called
to address the issue of the present and future direction of academic
libraries. While several of the participants in that conference called
for a new paradigm for librarianship or suggested possibilities in the
search for one, a compelling new image for trenchant library service
was not found. While critics charge that academic libraries are not
sufficiently integrated into the central concerns of the college or university and that librarians have their own, independent agendas,
librarians responsible for present services as well as plans for the
future are uneasy. Perhaps it is an overstatement to say that academic librarians are drifting in a vast sea of information and technological advances, searching for an appropriate course of action.
Nevertheless, we appear to have lost the stabilizing rudder of confidence in who we are and what we are to do. As a more powerful
alternative to the images of librarianship already available or proposed,
I suggest that we begin to think of libraries as centers for conversation and of ourselves as mediators of and participants in the conversations of the world.

OLD IMAGES

Libraries in the past have been labeled "The heart of the college
or university," "the center of our intellectual life,"[1] or a "warehouse

*Reprinted by permission of the author and publisher from College
and Research Libraries 47:3 (May 1986) 219-224; copyright ©1986 by
the American Library Association.

for storing books." If the "heart of the college" cliché is correct, heaven help the educational world; the library functioning as the heart of the college works about as well as the Jarvik 7. Fortunately, however, for the colleges and universities of the land, the library never was the "heart of the college," and today the claim is little more than sentimental garbage trotted out by presidents and deans when they are required to say something flattering about libraries; neither the speaker nor the hearers believe it. As a paradigm for library service it provides no clues to the services needed in the university, nor does it help to clarify the role of librarians in the educational process.

The characterization of libraries as the "center of our intellectual life" is not much better because that center is often elsewhere, in a group of scholars working on a problem, in a laboratory where the professor and students are testing a hypothesis, in a group of friends who meet regularly for study and discussion, in a classroom, or even in a student's room or a faculty member's office as he or she reads, thinks, and writes.[2]

In the university or college, libraries are more often viewed, one suspects, as warehouses for the storage of books and other materials, rather than hearts or centers of intellectual activity. And as storehouses, dusty places that one occasionally visits to recover some bit or piece that is useful, they require little more than custodial care. As such, they are not often regarded as a top priority in academic institutions, much less as central to the life of the mind and the educational process. While few librarians would accept the warehouse image, many view their libraries as their particular province. In the warehouse imagery, there clearly is no guide for dynamic library service.

THE BUSINESS MODEL

In order to reconceptualize librarianship for an uncertain future and in the hope of finding a new image, Kaye Gapen suggested using Mary Parker Follet's "Law of the Situation" question: "What business are we really in?"[3] Her response was that libraries have been in the package (book) delivery business. In the future, she says, libraries will be in the information delivery business, a change that will radically alter what librarians do. While the notion of information delivery rather than package delivery serves to enlarge the possible content of that which is delivered and points to the use of modern technologies, it does not indicate a more active role for librarians either in seeking to serve new clientele or in serving present users better, nor does it force librarians into the center of the critical-thinking processes of the university.

Both the question, "What business?" and the answer, "Information delivery," smack of mail-order houses, consumerism, profit, efficiency, and the popular culture. They make librarians delivery

boys or Purolator truck drivers or Federal Express administrators.
They transform library users into consumers and books and information into commodities to be used and discarded. All become part of
the consumer, disposable society. The result is that the institution
that ought to resist the dehumanizing, competitive, degrading aspects
of modern culture has ended up adopting the corporate world as its
guru. Criticism of the profit-and-loss orientation, of efficiency as a
primary value, and of an ends-directed stance is muted or cut off.

Given the business orientation of our culture, it is not surprising that libraries are tempted to look at the corporate model in the
search for an energizing, rejuvenating image. Appropriating a new
image of librarianship from the world of commerce, however, will
only serve, as Parson says, to "fix the limits of the possible."[4]
Conceiving of the business of libraries as information delivery will do
nothing to redirect librarians' "strict identification with the library
as an agency or institution to an identification with the client or
library user"[5] because the focus of the business world is on its
own survival, not on the enhancement of the quality of life. Furthermore, the business model encourages continuing the old pattern of
making the delivery in response to a patron request. The burden for
initiating the request, knowing what to ask for, and evaluating the
information provided all rests with the patron or, at best, depends
upon the library's effectiveness in marketing the products and services
it chooses. What remains as highest priority is improving the efficiency of the delivery system rather than seeking to understand and
meet the needs of the library user.

MISSION AND GOALS

Having no controlling paradigm for guidance and seeking to
improve library service, librarians in the last ten years or so have
placed greater and greater emphasis upon the need to articulate a
clear statement of mission and goals. These often relate to regularly
updated, long-range plans. Surely these are needed; no library can
function responsibly without them. The problem, however, is in
identifying the library with its mission and goals rather than looking
for its intrinsic being or value.

The difficulty with goals is that they are rigid, resistant to
change, often self-limiting, and that they focus on the achievements
of the person or group articulating the goals--a focus that is isolating
and, therefore, grossly inappropriate for defining a service organization. Originating in the self-perceptions of a group, goals tend to
promote a competitive stance. The group may see itself as standing
against competing groups or institutions, sometimes even those it
seeks to serve. A statement of goals has no built-in mechanism for
periodic review, criticism, or evolution. When it is adjusted to meet
new situations or to take advantage of new technologies, the new set
merely takes the place of the old. Worse yet, constantly changing

statements of mission or goals lead to a sense of instability, insecurity, and loss of identity. Further, when a library is identified and characterized solely by its goals, it is end-oriented and end-justified. The ends or purposes it serves and how well or how poorly they are met define the institution.

The notion of mission has a problem as well. While a sense of mission is not isolating, as goals are, mission does have an inherently self-referential character that emphasizes the person or group with the mission rather than those it wishes to serve. A larger, transcending vision is needed, one that seeks to identify the intrinsic value of libraries in relation to society and one that will continually inform and correct the mission and goals of a library. The conversation model discussed below may supply the dynamic, organic paradigm needed to bring academic libraries into a more intimate relationship with the central concerns of the educational world.

THE CONVERSATION
OF A LIBRARY

Libraries, if they are true to their original and intrinsic being, seek primarily to collect people and ideas rather than books and to facilitate conversation among people rather than merely to organize, store, and deliver information. To be sure, libraries have traditionally collected the documents of human imagination and action. In doing so they have preserved the ideas and events of history and have become the centers for ongoing conversations in which people speak their opinions, criticize others', and enlarge or restrict the scope of the discussion. Scholars state their thesis in writing, add information to the topic, argue with each other, and even change the direction of the conversation. The primary task, then, of the academic library is to introduce students to the world of scholarly dialogue that spans both space and time and to provide students with the knowledge and skills they need to tap into conversations on an infinite variety of topics and to participate in the critical inquiry and debate on those issues.

In its earliest meanings conversation meant "living or having one's being in a place or among persons, living together, intercourse, society, intimacy, or engagement with things in the way of ... study" as well as the "resulting condition of acquaintance or intimacy with a matter."[6] It had to do with people living with people and sharing intimately their experiences and ideas, their very lives. Conversation was and is an essential activity of human beings and one that informs, critically evaluates, and provides energy and renewal for their life together.

Conversation can be of utmost seriousness as philosophers debate truth, beauty, and justice, world leaders hold a summit meeting, labor and industry meet at the bargaining table, or students prepare for a class session on plate tectonics. Conversation can be purely playful, recreation in the best sense of the word, as friends gather around the fire after a skiing expedition, as the library softball team plans to take on the student intramural champs, or colleagues engage in punning or exchange new jokes. Intercourse, the most intimate expression of communication, wholeness, and integration, reflects the quality and character of conversation, the most general and inclusive activity of human connectedness.

The preservation of crucial conversations, the first task of libraries, served not only to preserve the record, but more importantly to ensure the continuation of significant conversations already in progress. The intrinsic value of libraries, therefore, is not so much lodged in the collection of information as it is in their relational value. Insofar as libraries make intercourse possible among people and even enter into that intercourse themselves, they are true to their original value. Insofar as they serve to bring people into relationship with each other, they are true to their principal purpose. Conversation, essential to the quality of life of Homo sapiens, provides the occasion and mode for intimate, significant, and ongoing engagement of human beings with each other in society. Libraries bear the critical burden of preserving, facilitating, and participating in those conversations.

Paradigmatic of the original and inherent purpose of libraries, conversation appropriated as the controlling image for librarianship can significantly inform the articulation of mission and goals, collection development policies, services, and the role and character of librarians as well as the organizational structures and procedures of libraries. Adopting the conversational mode may, in fact, provide enduring and powerful direction for all aspects of library service and, in emphasizing participation and process over ends, would provide the internal and ongoing mechanism for evolution and change.

Mission and Goals

Adopting the promotion of and participation in conversation as the primary task of libraries suggests that librarians searching for suitable missions and goals in the educational setting return to the old notion of vocation or calling. By thinking about calling, one places the focus outside the library and suggests the need to respond to voices other than the library's own. The library and librarians responding to the call of the educational enterprise immediately find themselves in a dynamic, relational stance, not in a passive, isolated one. Discovering the proper vocation of the library then becomes an ongoing process of conversation with those involved in teaching and learning, in which resolution of differences and refreshment of purposes can occur.

Collection Development and Services

Focusing on the enlargement of conversation in the educational environment demands that librarians ask questions about the needs of faculty and students. Which recorded conversations are needed to support the curriculum of this particular institution? What are the impediments to participation in scholarly discussion? What do students need to assist them in becoming active participants in intellectual dialogue? What library services will encourage faculty and student interaction on significant issues? What are the needs of faculty in pursuing their teaching and research? The answers to such questions concerning collection development and services will necessarily come out of continuing conversation with faculty and students, both individually and in the governance structure of the college. Surely the whole range of possibilities--reference service, database searching, term paper consultations, bibliographic instruction, and, one hopes, new possibilities for services not yet envisioned--will be explored in order to bring about the widest participation in the intellectual inquiry.

Bibliographic Instruction

In the development of citation indexing the conversational paradigm has already influenced entrée to scholarly works. Built on the notion that scholars talk to each other in their writings, citation indexes provide users with access to the contributions of all the participants in a particular discussion through the list of footnotes found in a book or article and through the list of articles and books that subsequently cite the central work.

Pushing the paradigm further, it can significantly inform bibliographic instruction by suggesting that students be invited to discover and participate in discussions that span the globe and the centuries. Using the library, students in the 1980s can enter a dialogue with Plato, Machiavelli, and Ghandi on the relationship of the individual to the state. They can participate in conversations on world hunger, euthanasia, and drug abuse. Books, journal articles, and other library materials, understood in their original and proper relationship to each other, represent the opinions and arguments in the ongoing conversations on these issues. The aim of bibliographic instruction becomes one of enabling students to be active and critical in the encounter with other minds. The usual student attempt to assemble a collection of "good quotes" and a lengthy list of references will not do. Furthermore, librarians providing instruction cannot be content with teaching library organization and use of library tools.

The questions for a student become Which conversation do I want to enter? Where and how do I find that conversation? Who are the participants in the discussion thus far? Are there disagreements that I need to know about? How do I assess the value and quality

of the various contributions to the conversation and can I make a
significant comment on the issue or problem? Instruction, therefore,
will include analysis of the problem to discover which conversation a
student seeks, instruction on where and how to locate what has been
said on the topic, and evaluation of the various contributions to the
conversation. Clearly, this includes discovering the qualifications
of the participants in the discussion and their particular points of
view and assessing their value for the student's particular interest
or concern. Bibliographic instruction will encourage and assist students to think critically about the search process, teaching them to
use the process itself to refine and narrow a topic and to use the
results in the development of their own position on the issue. The
proper task of bibliographic instruction becomes teaching critical thinking and enabling participation in intellectual inquiry. The focus is
on the process of scholarly dialogue, not on the organization of the
library or the production of term papers. The result is that the
librarians find themselves intimately engaged with students and faculty
as they explore what it means to think critically.

Character and Role of Librarians

Appropriate library response to the call of the university to
pursue critical thinking requires librarians who are educators--library
educators, to be sure, whose special and primary task is to facilitate
scholarly conversation in the educational environment. Such a role
requires librarians who are or can become library and educational
generalists, whose critical facilities can be continually honed and
sharpened in the dialogue with faculty and students, who are themselves active in the life of the mind and, above all, who relish analysis and examination of significant issues.

A second master's degree in a subject area taught at the college or university is useful for librarians in demonstrating their ability
to participate in significant scholarly conversation. More importantly,
however, effective bibliographic instruction can best be provided by
one who is active in and excited about his or her own research and
writing.

Required also will be primary commitment to the educational
process, not to the library as an independent entity. Working with
faculty as fully professional partners in the pursuit of learning
clearly requires professional commitment that is not restricted to
forty hours a week, eleven months a year. Neither striving to become faculty members nor content with being custodians of the library,
librarians must primarily be concerned with continually seeking and
providing library services that will enhance the educational process,
that will enlarge participation in intellectual dialogue.

Organizational Considerations

If librarians are primarily to be promoters of conversation, they must themselves be able to participate fully in the conversations of the library and the university. While it does not dictate any particular form of library organization, providing the context for free and open conversation among the library staff necessarily includes a leveling of hierarchical structures and a loosening of rigid hierarchical control. This is as important for the growth of the collection and success of the library in meeting the needs of its users as it is for the growth of individual librarians. Creativity, one suspects, most often comes in the interchange between people and not in individual heads thinking in isolation; individual, intellectual, and, therefore, professional growth occurs most significantly in the agora of free and open debate.

In addition to loosening the bonds of traditional library structures, the barriers of narrow specialization within librarianship need to be broken down. The separation of technical services and reference activities may have been effective and efficient in the past. However, the antipathy, jealousy and competition such division fostered between individuals and departments within the library can no longer be tolerated. The explosion of information that is forcing more careful choice of materials for a particular collection and the radically improved organizing and accessing of materials afforded by computers both underscore the fact that the traditional separation of cataloging and reference is artificial. Librarians intimately involved with faculty and students and with each other in planning and executing library services must be active in and knowledgeable about all aspects of library service.

CONCLUSION

The conversational mode, intrinsic to the nature of libraries, may provide the paradigm, context, and impetus needed for reconceptualizing academic librarianship. Committed to bringing together, in conversation and dialogue, voices from the past with those of the present, African voices with Spanish and English, young voices with old, men with women, and librarians with faculty, students, and administrators, the academic library will not only provide access to conversations, but will also continually participate in discussion with those it seeks to serve. The extent of the librarians' task, much like the structure of conversation, is open-ended. There is always a great deal more to do; there is much more to say and many more voices to be heard.

References and Notes

1. Archibald MacLeish, "The Premise of Meaning," The American

Scholar 41:359 (Summer 1972), quoted by Charles Martell, "Myths, Schooling, and the Practice of Librarianship," College and Research Libraries 45:376 (Sept. 1984).

2. I question Martell's assertion that "Intellectual life centers first in one's own being " (ibid., p. 377). The life of the mind is nourished and encouraged, first by parents and family. Subsequently it is fed and grows in the encounter with more and more of the world. Intellectual life, it seems to me, cannot occur in isolation; it thrives in interaction with others.

3. Kaye Gapen, "Myths and Realities: University Libraries," College and Research Libraries 45:356 (Sept. 1984).

4. Willie L. Parson, "User Perspective on a New Paradigm for Librarianship," College and Research Libraries 45:370 (Sept. 1984).

5. Ibid., p. 372.

6. The Oxford English Dictionary (Oxford: Clarendon Pr., 1970), V.II-C, p. 940.

WHAT IS THE USE OF ARCHIVES?
A CHALLENGE FOR THE PROFESSION*

Bruce W. Dearstyne

What is the significance and impact of research in archives? What difference does research in archives make--in terms of individual enlightenment, solution of practical problems, benefits to the public good, scholarly advances, growing human self-understanding, or additions to the sum total of human knowledge? In short, what is the use of archives?

Most archivists would find it difficult to answer such questions, either for their own repository or for all archival programs. Archivists have given relatively little attention to the issue of who uses their materials and what difference that use makes. The profession has concentrated on developing and refining a body of theory and techniques on appraisal, arrangement and description, physical preservation, and reference services to researchers. Yet the ultimate goal of archival work is to identify and preserve information that is put to use by people for some deliberate purpose. The value of the records archivists so carefully collect and preserve depends on the importance of their information, and that, in turn, depends on who uses the records and for what purposes. Furthermore, the research use of the material is one important basis of convincing appeals for program resources and support--an important consideration, since many of the nation's archival programs are underdeveloped and underfunded.

For many reasons, the question of research use of archives is important but until recently the issue has received little attention and

*Reprinted by permission of the author and publisher from The American Archivist 50:1 (Winter 1987) 76-87; copyright © 1987 by The Society of American Archivists. This article is a revised version of a paper read at the annual meeting of the Society of American Archivists, September 1984, Washington, D.C. The article reflects the author's own views and not necessarily those of the New York State Archives, the National Association of Government Archives and Record Administrators, or the Society of American Archivists Task Force on Archives and Society.

analysis. Archivists need to analyze the use of holdings in order
to more clearly define their professional mission, to help persuade
resource allocators that archival work is significant, and to gain the
general public's attention and support for the importance of the archival function in society. This article advances a framework for
analyzing and suggestions for dealing with this neglected issue.

Now is an appropriate time for facing this important question.
The past few years have been a period of growth and change in the
archival world, of questioning traditional approaches, and of searching
for new directions. Indeed, the recent past may someday be known
as the Age of Archival Analysis because of the many important studies
that have been carried out. For instance, forty-three of the states
have completed assessment and reporting projects which, taken together, constitute the most searching analysis of historical records
programming ever undertaken. The Society of American Archivists'
Task Force on Goals and Priorities has issued the profession's first
comprehensive statement on long-term objectives. The Task Force
on Archives and Society has been probing the public's "image" of
archival work and searching for ways to improve public understanding
and support. These studies have raised quesitons about the nature
and purposes of archival work and have led to new insights and plans
for the future.[1]

This healthy spirit of archival self-evaluation is evident in the
writings on archivists' relations with researchers. Mary Jo Pugh,
Elsie Freeman, and William Joyce, for instance, have demonstrated
major defects in the ways archivists serve researchers. They suggest
that archivists do not really know their clientele and that they have
an inaccurate notion of the information researchers need and how they
seek it.[2] Roy C. Turnbaugh has suggested that archivists produce
finding aids that are either ignored or are difficult to use and that
archivists cling to outdated concepts inappropriate for modern researchers' approaches and needs.[3] William J. Maher and Paul Conway have proposed systematic ways to improve tracking and measuring
of research use of archival holdings.[4] The general conclusion of
these studies is that more systematic user studies are needed, as are
improved services to researchers.

Archivists need to do more, however, than just study users and
refine the reference services traditionally rendered. They must
address fundamental questions, heretofore largely ignored, about the
relationship between archivists and researchers and about the nature
and significance of research use of archival materials. There are at
least six areas where analysis and new approaches are needed: (1)
tracking and studying research use, (2) interpreting and reporting
on the significance of that use, (3) promoting increased use, (4)
emphasizing use as a means of garnering program support, (5) reaching out to the researcher community as a partner in dealing with
difficult archival problems, and (6) expanding the concept of

reference service to a broader notion of researcher service or public service. These ideas are developed in detail below.

First, <u>archivists must develop more effective, realistic means of tracking and analyzing use.</u> As a profession, we have been too complacent and disinterested in systematically keeping track of research use of holdings. Even the best archival literature reflects this indifference. The standard text in the manuscripts field casually suggests that "...probably the curator will keep a record" of use, primarily to guide future acquisitions decisions, monitor frequency of use, detect theft--and to assemble figures for the annual report.[5] The SAA basic manual on reference advises recording researchers' identities, research topics, and the records they use, but it gives little guidance on how to interpret and report this information.[6]

The state assessment reports reveal the shocking fact that many repositories do not even keep counts of researchers. In Virginia, for instance, 42 percent of repositories surveyed reported they did not know the number of researchers served annually. In Kentucky, the figure was 50 percent. In North Dakota, it was an incredible 69 percent.[7] Furthermore, most repositories that keep a count do not interpret the numbers or attempt to draw conclusions about or report on their significance. The State Archives of New Jersey, for instance, counts researchers but does not keep track of "types of researchers or purposes of record use."[8]

Merely counting and recording the numbers of researchers and categorizing them under a few headings conceived by the archivist tells little about the significance and impact of research use. Archivists must move beyond this superficial "numbers" approach. "Many archives have a few numbers to show that their holdings are used," observes William J. Maher. But without analysis, "most archivists' understanding of the use of their holdings is sketchy at best." This hampers them in making program modifications intended to increase and facilitate use, and it deprives them of "an important tool to justify programs and secure greater resources." Maher has proposed helpful methodologies for regular analysis of daily use and for specialized studies of specific aspects of reference services.[9] His work should serve as the basis for further analysis and development in this area.

Paul Conway has gone even further in a pioneering article certain to provoke much-needed discussion and debate in the profession. He advocates "a comprehensive, profession-wide program of user studies" and has proposed a framework for "the basic elements of information that should be recorded, analyzed, and shared among archivists to assess programs and services." In Conway's proposed scheme, archivists would measure and assess three elements of reference services: (1) quality--how well archivists understand and meet the information needs of their users; (2) integrity--how well archivists balance their obligations to preserve materials against their obligations to make them available; and (3) value--the effects of use on

individuals, groups, and society as a whole. Conway also provides
a form to serve as the basis for gathering information needed to pursue the analyses he advocates.[10] While Conway's detailed scheme
may prove too complex for some repositories to implement, his work
has nonetheless clearly called attention to the need for repositories
to focus on the interchange between archivist and researcher and to
seek deeper insight into researchers' use of archives.

More discussion and development is needed. The profession
needs more and better tools for monitoring research use. The forms,
procedures, and approaches should gather information needed to
thoroughly understand researchers' purposes and the significance
of the information derived from the archival material. Of course,
the gathering of such information would require cooperation on the
part of researchers. These key questions would need answering:

- What was the exact subject and purpose of the research?

- How did the researcher find out about the repository and the
  materials? What are the implications for the repository's
  finding aids and public relations efforts?

- What records were used?

- What was the researcher's information need? What were the
  questions that he or she needed to answer?

- Did the researcher find the information sought, anticipated,
  or needed?

- How rich and extensive was the information gleaned from
  the records? How significant was the information for the
  researcher's purposes?

- Did the information cast new light on or lead to a new interpretation of the subject being researched?

- Did study of the material suggest or open important new
  lines of inquiry for the researcher?

- Did study of the material uncover or suggest other sources
  for the researcher to pursue?

Second, archivists need to find better means of measuring and
interpreting the significance of research use. Few archival institutions
have carried out systematic user studies. The profession has never
produced a national report on "Research in Archives: Significance and
Impact." Such studies are needed to clarify for ourselves and to
enable us to explain to others the importance of research in archives.

If significance is equated with numbers, then the majority of use probably is genealogical. Certainly genealogical research is important in a nation made up of immigrants' descendants with considerable interest in personal and family "roots." Research by academic historians is also important, though the degree of reliance that historians place on archival sources needs further study.[11] But archivists' traditional concerns with genealogists and historians may cause them to miss an important point about use: numbers do not necessarily equal significance. Not all users should be counted equally because some uses, measured in terms of the archival program's mission and in terms of the utility of the information derived, may be more significant than others. The key to understanding the difficult issue of significance of use is to derive and apply reasonable, consistent standards of measurement. Archivists need to develop at least two types of standards.

One standard is the significance of the research use in terms of the archival program's own mission and priorities. Every program should include in its mission statement, planning documents, or in some other written form a statement of why it exists, what records it aims to collect, what it aims to document, and what types of research it is most interested in encouraging and supporting. A state archival program, for instance, may decide that its primary client is state government. A repository that collects medical records may decide that its primary mission is to support medical research. A community historical society may decide that its primary interest is to support research in local history. The intention is not to deprive anyone of access to the records or to slight any researcher's work but, instead, to indicate preferences and priorites. Without such a settled indication, the repository has little choice but to regard all research interests and topics as equal. With such an indication, there is an established benchmark against which to measure significance of use.

The second standard of measurement is more complicated; it focuses on the significance of the topic, ramifications of the research, and dissemination of the results. Here the objective is to look beyond "use" in the elementary sense--directly seeking and deriving information from archival material. Instead, the focus turns to ultimate users and beneficiaries--"people who may never visit an archives but utilize archival information indirectly."[12] Among the key questions in applying this standard might be the following: Did the research provide significant new information about an important subject? Are there legal ramifications to the research findings? Will the welfare of an individual or group be affected? Will important institutional or public undertakings be affected or significantly redirected? How will the conclusions and results of the research be disseminated? Who can be expected to study and use the results, and for what purposes? And what changes can be expected as a result of the use of this information?

A number of recent studies have pointed the way toward further development of this second type of standard. The Connecticut and

New York historical records assessment reports, for instance, demonstrate that there are many uses of historical records that are not
always apparent to the general public or even to archivists. These
reports provide examples of practical uses of historical records with
far-reaching implications. Businesses, governments, and other institutions need archival records for retrospective policy analysis and to
provide continuity in administration. Government records document
the responsibilities of government and the rights of its citizens.
They are often essential in legal matters--to document agreements,
substantiate claims, and prove contentions.

Engineers use old plans, maps, sketches, reports, and specifications for information on the location, age, and physical characteristics of the infrastructure. Historical preservationists use photographs, blueprints, and drawings to determine the original appearance
of buildings, reveal structural elements, and guide authentic restoration. Environmental researchers use historical records to study land
use patterns, water use, and other environmental issues. Medical
researchers use patient files and other records to understand genetic
and familial diseases and to trace the impact of epidemics. Seismolo-
gists use descriptions of earthquakes in diaries to determine the location and magnitude of previous quakes. Educators use historical
records to supplement textbook and lecture presentations, giving local
history courses an immediacy and letting students study key source
materials. The New York report concludes emphatically that "historical records are important to the well-being of New York and to the
welfare of its citizens ... historical records have a variety of immediate, practical uses with everyday implications for all of us." The
Connecticut report agrees: "clearly, historical records play a larger
role in our lives than most people suspect."[13]

A brochure issued by the SAA's Task Force on Archives and
Society plays up the same theme. It suggests that archival material
can be used to protect citizens' rights, increase business profits,
preserve historic buildings, provide administrative continuity, and
educate and entertain, as well as to sustain genealogical and historical
research. "In one way or another, directly or indirectly, you [the
public] use, benefit from and have a definite stake in the preservation
of archives," it concludes.[14]

How should archivists improve their abilities to track and
measure use? One simple device is the exit interview, which allows
the archivist to ask about the researcher's use of the records and
about the extent and importance of the information derived. Archivists need not and should not forget about researchers after they go
out of the repository's door. One way of keeping in touch and finding out the results of the research is to send out questionnnaires to
researchers some weeks or months after their visit. The questionnaires can identify how the information from the archives contributed
to the overall research effort and determine the publication or other
dissemination of the results. Analysis of citations to archival resources

in professional literature is another way of gauging the significance and extent of research use. Archivists can help organize sessions at professional meetings to encourage researchers to discuss their use of archival material. Archivists should also consider publishing explanations of particularly important or innovative uses of the material in their repositories.

As a third new approach, <u>archivists must confront the problem of underutilization of archival resources.</u> Archivists have traditionally measured use in terms of how many times a collection or document is used or how many researchers call, write, or visit during a given period of time. This focus on numbers rather than significance has obscured the need for a more realistic measure of the adequacy of use. That measure might be as follows: To what extent have the records been used by people who had an information need that was (or could have been) satisfied by research in the records? No matter how archivists measure adequacy of use, however, there are several reasons why archival resources are underutilized.

First, a large percentage of the nation's archival resources are so poorly maintained, incompletely processed, and inadequately described that they are virtually inaccessible. Archivists are not to blame; the underlying reason for this state of affairs is lack of sufficient resources and people. In California, according to its state assessment report, most repositories are "understaffed, underbudgeted, and without a clear direction of what to collect or how to provide for the physical care of their holdings." In Kentucky, the financial resources of the vast majority of historical records repositories are inadequate by any standards." In North Carolina, repositories have "responsibilities that exceed their resources." And in New York, "most historical records repositories lack the facilities, resources, and staff expertise to carry out core functions in a minimally acceptable way."[15]

This lack of resources is at least partially due to archivists' difficulties in gaining public attention and support. There is a vicious cycle here, however, for such support would be easier to obtain if records use could be increased and more effectively tracked and publicized. In any case, lack of resources means that many collections are sitting in a sort of archival abeyance--unprocessed and unusable.

Furthermore, as the assessment reports reveal, a shockingly large percentage of repositories have inadequate finding aids or none at all. Many do not report accessions or holdings to the <u>National Union Catalog of Manuscripts Collections</u>, scholarly journals, or anywhere else researchers would encounter the information. As the California assessment report observed, "the public is unlikely to use materials well if they do not know the materials exist."[16]

A second major reason for low incidence of use is that archivists are too often satisfied to serve only the limited reference traffic that happens to come their way. Archival reference has been too narrowly conceptualized as a passive, reactive service that is not activated until a letter arrives, the phone rings, or a researcher comes through the door. Archivists have not realized that promoting maximum appropriate use of their holdings should be a centerpiece of the archival mission. They have not concentrated on encouraging and expanding use of materials by those people and groups whose information needs could be satisfied by research in archival holdings. "Archives have some of the best kept secrets in the country," notes the director of a manuscripts collection. "We as archivists may know some of these secrets, but we have not made an effort to share them with those for whom the secrets can be important. We cannot blame the public for not utilizing our resources and not appreciating our value.... We have not made our story known."[17]

The state assessment reports bear out this view. In Pennsylvania, for instance, "materials [in archival repositories] are not being used to any great extent" largely because researchers simply do not know the material exists."18] A summary of the state government sections of the reports concludes that "the posture of state archives toward researchers is generally passive. Despite archivists' claim that their records are essential to the continuity and effective administration of government, little evidence supports that claim. [There is] little evidence that state archivists have clearly defined the products of their work or have convincingly demonstrated the value of these products to their states."[19] A summary of the sections on historical records repositories notes that "lack of public understanding and regard leads to underfunding of historical records repositories and underutilization of their holdings. The process has a circular effect in that low use perpetuates low funding which prevents repositories from upgrading the management of their collections which might in turn increase their use."[20]

As the SAA's Planning for the Archival Profession concludes, "at present, the many possible uses of archives are not widely recognized and archival records are underused ... the archival community must reduce existing barriers and undertake positive steps to promote the use of archives."[21] A massive campaign is needed--one that includes educational and promotional efforts that reach out to researchers, more widespread dissemination of descriptive information on archival records, and aggressive appeals to researchers whose work would be enriched by using archival materials.

There is a third obstacle to greater utilization of archives: with few exceptions, college and university students are not taught to use archival materials for research. There is no adequate publication explaining research in archives; the closest substitute is Philip Brooks' Research in Archives, a short, outdated work that is not well known in scholarly circles.[22] There are few college research methodology courses that cover archival materials. Archivists need to reach out to and cooperate with historians and other professionals whose research interests and needs should naturally lead them into archival repositories. More writing is needed about the content, research importance, and usefulness of archival material. Archivists should work with professionals to develop courses that lead students "to expand their awareness of what documentation is available, how it grew out of and affected the historical 'event' under study, and to help them make more creative use of available documents."[23] Repositories should sponsor workshops and seminars to show researchers how to use archival sources and to introduce them to materials in specific subject fields.

A fourth new line of attack follows logically from the three discussed above. Archivists need to focus attention on and publicize significant use of their material in order to improve support for archival programs. The challenge is to convince the public of the value and impact of research use of archival materials. David Gracy has argued that the public perceives archivists as "permanently humped, moleish, aged creatures who shuffle musty documents in dust-filled attics for a purpose uncertain."[24] One way to correct at least the "purpose uncertain" part of that misconception is to make known the significance and importance of archival work.

The place to begin is at home. A recent SAA study revealed that the people who control and allocate resources for archival programs tend to view archivists as scholarly, dedicated professionals who are not assertive or deserving of increased program support. "...the purposes, uses, and contributions of the archives have to be made more vivid--more explicit, more concrete, and repeated in various ways [through] communication of a steady flow of examples to heighten awareness and appreciation of what is being gotten for the money," says the report. "Archivists need to translate their importance into more power. That requires more self-assertion, more concerted action, and being less sympathetic to our understanding of the resource allocators' budget problems."[25]

Making the case to resource allocators is a good start, but archivists also need to direct the public's attention to the use of archival material. As one state assessment report pointed out, "it is easy to ignore [historical records]. They do not crowd the streets, nor do they complain, write letters, lobby, or vote ... they are known only to a few."[26] But how do archivists get the message across to the public? Archivists provided the following suggestions and insights to the Task Force on Archives and Society:

> A university archivist: "...the view of the public toward us will never significantly change unless we alter our practice of catering almost exclusively to the scholarly community. Outreach (particularly to non-traditional users) needs to be recognized as important a function of an archival program as reference or processing. We've got to do more than just be custodians. Practical uses for records need to be identified

and developed. Once that is accomplished, and the public
is using our records, we won't need to change our image;
we will have done it already."

The associate director of a university manuscripts collection:
"Although some sections of society will probably never appreciate the importance of preserving our documentary heritage, they may well respond to the practical uses of archives.
Compiling examples of archival uses which increase efficiency,
reduce costs or generally make life easier, would greatly enhance our image."

A Canadian provincial archivist: "It is a good plan to indicate
the overall services to the citizens at large which a properly
run archives can provide. Once one gets away from the
academic world, the reality of services rendered to local
(non-professional) historians, practicing architects and engineers, linguists, genealogists, economists, political scientists,
statisticians, administrators, etc., can be demonstrated effectively."

A municipal preservation planner: "...public entities never
know when or where litigation might arise. They never know
what records they might need for what ... social purpose
... the use of pedantic explanations is not relevant to those
who have to balance budgets, social needs, and costs....
We have to prove to the politician that we have a well thought
out product, and sell it using techniques familiar to the
business."

And finally, the director of a religious archives: "The profession desperately needs more discussion of how to make
manuscript repositories valuable to the nonscholar, the non-
genealogist. Most archival finding aids are so hard for non-
specialists to use. The whole mind set of archivists has to
be changed to make them more open to the needs of the
general public.... It does seem that archives are tough to
kill. But that is not necessarily a good thing. Maybe they
are tough to kill because the staff will meekly accept inadequate resources to do an overwhelming job."[27]

What these perceptive archivists are saying, in effect, is that
archivists need to revise the way they think about themselves, their
services, and the use of their materials by researchers. Archivists
need a marketing strategy and orientation--to increase significant
research use of their holdings and to make known the message of
the significance of that use.[28]

A fifth approach that archivists need to develop is to draw on
the assistance of users in selected areas of archival work. Archivists
usually think of users only as a clientele to be served. In fact,

researchers and researcher groups can be approached to assist archivists in critical areas of their work. One such area is appraisal. Too often, archivists appraise records in an intellectual vacuum and do not consult with the intended beneficiaries of appraisal work and decisions. In many cases, it would be helpful to seek the advice of researchers in the field before making a final decision on whether to keep or discard records. In another article in this issue, Larry Hackman advocates going further and working toward the establishment of documentation strategies to ensure adequate documentation of issues, activities, functions, and subjects. Such strategies would be developed and implemented by ongoing mechanisms that would involve documentation creators and users, as well as archivists. Under this approach, users would become archivists' partners in carefully deciding what documentation should be retained and what could be discarded. [29]

A second area in which archivists and users should hold intensive discussions is the development of automated systems and data bases. As the computer increases archivists' ability to store and manipulate descriptive information on holdings, they need to ask key questions: Where and how do users encounter this information? How do they access it? What topical, subject, and geographical approaches do users pursue when accessing historical records? Do systems that make sense to archivists also make sense to users? If archivists do not consult with users, they may construct expensive and complex automated systems that frustrate the very people they should be designed to serve.

A third area in which users can and should work closely with archivists is advocacy for archival programs. Users should be leaders in campaigning for strong, adequately supported archival programs. Archivists need to cultivate researcher groups, to encourage them to play this role when appropriate, and to provide them with needed information on budgetary and program development needs.

Finally, archivists need to consider merging reference, outreach, and public programs into a new, aggressive, proactive public service concept that is integrated into the total archival program. Reference has been too narrowly conceptualized as a passive, reactive function isolated from the rest of the archival program. In many repositories, no one has total responsibility for coordinating all efforts relating to promotion and use of records. Archivists need to begin merging reference, outreach, and public programming efforts into a systematic management approach that stimulates program development and leads to increased research use. The limited work of the reference archivist would gradually be superseded by a new type of archival endeavor. "Public service" or "researcher service" archivists would have several key responsibilities, and their work would be carefully related to the rest of the archival program. The range of responsibilities might include the following:

- Answering reference inquiries and assisting researchers who visit the repository.

- Predetermining at least part of the reference traffic by continually reaching out to research groups that could benefit from using the records and openly advocating research use.

- Promptly reporting new accessions to journals and other sources that potential users are likely to see.

- Writing articles for non-archival professional journals and newsletters on the nature, content, and research potential of holdings, particularly underutilized holdings.

- Proposing sessions at professional meetings on archival resources and making presentations on the research potential of holdings.

- Holding conferences and workshops and producing publications and other materials on how to do research in archival material.

- Carefully tracking the use of records and monitoring and measuring the impact and significance of the research.

- Continuously reporting--through the media, exhibits, audiovisual shows, program reports, lectures, and elsewhere-- on the significance and impact of research use of archives.

- Carefully monitoring and analyzing research use and utilizing the resulting information for planning and management decisions on appraisal of new records, reappraisal and deaccessioning of unused records, arrangement and description priorities, conservation needs, and microfilming and publication plans.

What is the use of archives? To adequately address this question, archivists need to reassess some long-held assumptions and develop some new approaches to their work. This article certainly raises more questions and issues than it settles; it is intended to initiate discussion of an important challenge to which the archival profession should turn its attention. If we do so, we may find answers to the question "What is the use of archives?" that will benefit our programs, our profession, our users, and our society.

References

1.   Larry J. Hackman, "A Perspective on American Archives," Public Historian 8 (Summer 1986): 10-28, provides an excellent summary of recent developments.

2. Mary Jo Pugh, "The Illusion of Omniscience: Subject Access and The Reference Archivist," American Archivist 45 (Winter 1982): 33-44; Elsie Freeman, "In the Eye of the Beholder: Archives Administration from the User's Point of View," American Archivist 47 (Spring 1984): 111-23; William L. Joyce, "Archivists and Research Use," American Archivist 47 (Spring 1984): 124-33.

3. Roy C. Turnbaugh, "Living With a Guide," American Archivist 46 (Fall 1983): 451; Turnbaugh, "Archival Mission and User Studies," Midwestern Archivist 11, no. 1 (1986): 27-33.

4. William J. Maher, "The Use of User Studies," Midwestern Archivist 11, no. 1 (1986): 15-26; Paul Conway, "Facts and Frameworks: An Approach to Studying the Users of Archives," American Archivist 49 (Fall 1986): 393-407; Conway, "Research in Presidential Libraries: A User Survey," Midwestern Archivist 11, no. 1 (1986): 35-56. See also Jacqueline Goggin, "The Indirect Approach: A Study of Scholarly Use of Black and Women's Organizational Records in the Library of Congress Manuscript Division," Midwestern Archivist 11, no. 1 (1986): 57-67.

5. Kenneth Duckett, Modern Manuscripts (Nashville: American Association for State and Local History, 1975), 239-40.

6. Sue E. Holbert, Archives and Manuscripts: Reference and Access (Chicago: Society of American Archivists, 1977), 23.

7. Virginia State Historical Records Advisory Board, Public and Private Records Repositories in Virginia: A Needs Assessment Report (Richmond: 1983), 110; Kentucky Historical Records Advisory Board, Historical Records Needs Assessment Final Report (Frankfort, 1983): 31; North Dakota State Historical Records Advisory Board, North Dakota's Forgotten Heritage: Public and Private Records as Historical Documents (Bismark: 1983), 34. Other state reports bear out this pattern. The figures are slightly misleading, however, because the smaller repositories are primarily the most lax about maintaining such statistics.

8. New Jersey State Historical Records Advisory Board, New Jersey Records Assessment and Reporting Project (Trenton: 1983), 8.

9. Maher, "Use of User Studies," 15.

10. Conway, "Facts and Frameworks," 394 and passim.

11. See Fredric Miller, "Use, Appraisal, and Research: A Case Study of Social History," American Archivist 49 (Fall 1986): 371-92 for thoughful analysis in the area of social history.

12. Conway, "Facts and Frameworks," 396.

13. Connecticut Historical Records Advisory Board, Final Report of Historical Records Assessment Project, 1982-1983 (n.p.: 1983), 1-5; New York State Historical Records Advisory Board, Toward a Usable Past: Historical Records in the Empire State (Albany: 1984), 19-24. Oddly enough, few of the state assessment projects sought users' views of archival affairs or included in their reports any discussion of the significance of use of archival material.

14. "Who is the 'I' in Archives," brochure, (Chicago: Society of American Archivists, 1985).

15. California State Historical Records Advisory Board, Final Report
     of the California State Archives Assessment Project (Sacramento:
     1983), 22; Kentucky Historical Records Advisory Board, Historical
     Records Needs Assessment, 29; North Carolina State Historical
     Records Advisory Board, North Carolina Historical Records As-
     sessment Report (Raleigh: 1983), 40; New York State Historical
     Records Advisory Board, Toward a Usable Past, 53.
16. California State Historical Records Advisory Board, Final Report,
     7.
17. Gordon O. Hendrickson to Frank Mackaman, 13 January 1984,
     Records of SAA Task Force on Archives and Society.
18. Leon J. Stout, Historical Records in Pennsylvania (Harrisburg:
     1983), 13.
19. Edwin C. Bridges, "State Government Records Programs," in
     Documenting America: Assessing the Condition of Historical
     Records in the States, ed. Lisa Weber (Albany: National As-
     sociation of State Archives and Records Administrators, 1984),
     8.
20. William L. Joyce, "Historical Records Repositories," in Document-
     ing America, 39.
21. Planning for the Archival Profession: A Report of the SAA Task
     Force on Goals and Priorities (Chicago: Society of American
     Archivists, 1986), 22.
22. Philip C. Brooks, Research in Archives (Chicago: University
     of Chicago, 1969).
23. Clark Elliot, ed., Understanding Progress as Process: Docu-
     mentation of the History of Science and Technology in the United
     States (n.p.: 1983), 52-53.
24. David B. Gracy, "Archives and Society: The First Archival
     Revolution," American Archivist 47 (Winter 1984): 8.
25. Social Research, Inc., The Image of Archivists: Resource Al-
     locators' Perception (Chicago: Society of American Archivists,
     1984), 4.
26. Preserving Arizona's Historical Records: The Final Report of
     the Arizona Historical Records Needs and Assessment Project
     (Phoenix: 1983), i.
27. Elizabeth C. Stewart to Frank Mackaman, 4 January 1984; Anne
     R. Kenney to Mackaman, 14 December 1983; A. D. Ridge to Mack-
     aman, 23 December 1983; Caroline Gallacci to Mackaman, 15
     December 1983; and Robert L. Shuster to Mackaman, 10 January
     1984; Records of the SAA Task Force on Archives and Society.
28. For a perceptive elaboration of this theme, see Elsie Freeman,
     "Buying Quarter Inch Holes: Public Support Through Results,"
     Midwestern Archivist 10, no. 2 (1985): 89-97.
29. See Larry J. Hackman and Joan Warnow-Blewett, "The Documen-
     tation Strategy Process: A model and a Case Study," American
     Archivist 50 (Winter 1987): 12-47.

THE MYTH OF THE
REFERENCE INTERVIEW*

Robert Hauptman

> It is an obvious truism to every librarian who works at an
> information or reference desk that inquirers seldom ask at
> first for what they want.
>
> Robert S. Taylor

> There are times, in fact some claim more times than librarians
> are willing to admit, when a person asks a question--just a
> question, no more, no less.
>
> Bill Katz

> Most of the library users who put questions to the librarian
> know exactly what they need and ask for it clearly.
>
> Denis Grogan

The amount of research done on the reference or information interview is staggering.[1]   Innumerable commentators, from different
fields, have mused, felt, discovered, theorized, opined, and suggested that library users are shy, confused, deceptive, or inarticulate, and they are therefore basically incapable of indicating their
real needs. Beleaguered reference librarians are further distracted
from their appointed tasks by authors who have insisted that although
information is certainly important, creative impetus or experience is
as well. Here patrons not only cannot formulate their needs, they
also really do not know what they want. And so the librarian is
called upon to appreciate "a personal gestalt" in an open-ended,
creative session, analogous, apparently, to a stint with one's analyst.
[2] All of this is compounded by those who note that the nonverbal
aspects of communication are as important as the articulated query.
Furthermore, the reference librarian too must be careful with facial
expressions, head and hand gestures, and even make sympathetic
clucking noises when appropriate! [3] Nevertheless, it is virtually
impossible to accept the assertion that sixty-five percent of the

*Reprinted by permission of the author and publisher from Reference
Librarian 16 (Winter, 1987) 47-52; copyright © 1987 by The Haworth
Press, Inc. All rights reserved.

"social meaning" of a conversation is relayed nonverbally.[4] This
means that the patrons' paralinguistic and kinesic responses are twice
as important as their articulated queries. Furthermore, as Lewis
Thomas points out,

> There may even be odorants that fire off receptors in our
> olfactory epithelia without our being conscious of smell,
> including signals exchanged involuntarily between human
> beings. Wiener has proposed, on intuitive grounds, that
> defects and misinterpretations in such a communication system
> may be an unexplored territory for psychiatry. [And library
> science, presumably.][5]

Readers may object that Thomas is stretching things almost beyond
endurance, but all of the material on defective patrons, creativity,
paralinguistics, and kinesics is equally exaggerative. There can be
little doubt that patrons' queries must sometimes be clarified through
concise questioning. This, however, is a far cry from a full-fledged,
complex reference interview. It is, additionally, difficult to understand
Geraldine B. King's insistence on discovering patrons' motivations and
objectives. (Why they are interested in a topic. What use they will
make of the information.) In fact, King's probing about Dick Turpin
and highwaymen, in her example of correct interviewing technique,
only squelches the patron's creativity. [6] As Fred Batt perceptively
observes, "Sometimes the reference interview impedes the flow of
information."[7]

The Myth Revealed

Because the reference interview comes up frequently in the
literature, is highly touted, and appears to be both practically and
theoretically justified, it comes as a disconcerting intellectual shock
to discover that it is, at least partially, a myth. During the course
of answering tens of thousands of queries at two academic research
libraries, I was struck by the infrequent necessity of posing a complex series of questions in order to ascertain the patrons' real needs.
To confirm this general impression, I kept careful track of 1,074
questions asked during a 101 hour period (5/9/83-7/27/83). The results were revelatory. Some questions, to be sure, required brief
discussion, but only six queries demanded extensive interviewing.[8]
Patrons who asked for library locations were satisfied with the directions. Those who needed a biographical source for Martin Luther King
manifested delight in the tendered material.

There are, of course, patrons who request The Encyclopedia
Americana in order to do a survey of Oklahoma state statutes, but
clients only infrequently cite inappropriate sources or really do not
know what they want. The misleading implication of the literature is
that a long-winded, convoluted reference interview, complete with
nonverbal observations, is a mandatory part of virtually every exchange. My experience indicates that this is simply untrue.

Because the evaluation of the reference interview is so overwhelmingly positive, it occurred to me that I might be doing an inadequate job. Perhaps all of those patrons who asked for the MLA
International Bibliography really wanted the Humanities Index or
Grzimek's Animal Life Encyclopedia; those who needed film reviews of
Annie Hall, really were looking for quotations of Robert Hall stock;
and those who needed straight-forward facts--like how many 1978
foreign automobiles were sold to punk rockers--naturally had ulterior
motives, which only a carefully orchestrated interview could elicit.
One possible solution to this dilemma was to bother patrons with in-
quisitive probes: "Are you really looking for a history of Colombia?
Perhaps you would find a list of cocaine dealers more useful? Why
are you interested in buttermilk?" But such a superfluous procedure
would only alienate patrons.

Instead of teasing people, I decided to observe a diversified
group of reference librarians at work. I, therefore, visited eight
libraries in order to learn just how one should utilize the reference
interview effectively.[9] I learned very little. During the eight
hours of observation librarians conducted no interviews. The closest
anyone came was an exchange concerning a demand for a "list of books
on fashion" by which the librarian immediately discovered the patron
meant a computer-produced bibliography. Similarly, a "catalogue"
was transmogrified into an index through one simple question. This
type of inarticulate confusion occurred only three or four times out
of a total of 229 questions.

It should also be noted that librarians may pose many counter-
questions simply because they are inept, inefficient, incapable of answering, or unable to locate material. For example, one librarian did
not know what GNP meant, and even after finding out led the patron
to the wrong tool. One suggested the card catalog for articles on
music! She was unfamiliar with The Music Index. Another, upon
being told that Journalism Quarterly could not be located in the serials microform listing, asked what periodical index the patron had
used. The relevancy of this query escapes me; the listing was apparently simply faulty. Sometimes the patron knows more than the
librarian: an extremely inarticulate person asked me for an almanac.
I wondered why, and he indicated that he was looking for the marriage
laws of each state. I mentioned that the almanac was an inappropriate
tool, but that he was welcome to try. He returned, and I asked if
I could help him further. He said no and walked away. I looked in
the almanac and there they were!

Roads to Error

After begrudgingly conceding that brief questioning or even a
full-fledged interview is, at times, useful, it is necessary to emphasize
that too much misleading, abstract, and theoretical material on the
subject is published. It is time for those involved in reference work

to concentrate on substantive multidisciplinary knowledge. Then they could provide responses, preferably correct ones, to carefully articulated queries. There is an increasing consensus (with which I agree) that reference librarians are doing an inadequate job. Ten years ago, David E. House described an experiment in which twenty librarians were asked for information on the artist David Shepherd. When one considers the general nature of the sources, the sixty percent rate of failure to provide any information at all is extremely disheartening.[10]

More recently, Marcia J. Myers and Jassim M. Jirjees have put together a collaborative volume consisting of material excerpted from their dissertations. The researchers posed a total of forty-nine telephone queries in each of forty-five academic libraries. About fifty percent of the responses were acceptable. This is certainly a dismal showing.[11] Examples could be multiplied easily, but there is really no need to do this; the results are invariably the same: reference librarians fail to provide adequate answers in about half the cases. Perhaps they are too busy interviewing patrons.

Very few investigations of the reference interview conclude that it is often unnecessary or even counterproductive. Thus, we should be grateful to two authors who disagree with the accepted point of view. In Mary Jo Lynch's experiment, interviews occurred in less than one half of all possible instances. Furthermore, the interviews resulted in important changes in only thirteen percent of the cases.[12] Samuel Rothstein, in his extensive historical overview, sums up the situation nicely:

> I suggest that we may have gone too far in the direction of self-consciousness and elaboration. Too much of our research confirms the obvious, and some of the training programs, with their emphasis on surface mannerisms, seem more suitable for telephone operators and encyclopedia sales people than for members of a learned profession.
>
> Above all, I charge that we keep complicating where we should be simplifying.[13]

References

1. See, for example, two lengthy and only partially overlapping bibliographical surveys: Wayne W. Crouch, "The Information Interview: A Comprehensive Bibliography and an Analysis of the Literature," ERIC Document, ED 180 501 (1979) and O. Gene Norman, "The Reference Interview; An Annotated Bibliography," Reference Services Review, 7 (1) (Jan/Mar 1979), 71-77. Bill Katz, allocates part of a chapter in the second volume of his Introduction to Reference Work (New York: McGraw Hill, 1982) to the interview: Denis Grogan devotes an entire thirty-five

page chapter to it (<u>Practical Reference Work</u> [London: Clive Bingley, 1979]); and Gerald Jahoda, et al. think that it merits two chapters in their <u>Librarian and Reference Queries; A Systematic Approach</u> (New York: Academic Press, 1980).

2. Don McFadyen, "The Psychology of Inquiry: Reference Service and the Concept of Information/Experience," <u>Journal of Librarianship</u>, 7 (1) (January 1975), 2-11 passim.

3. Virginia Boucher, "Nonverbal Communication and the Library Reference Interview," <u>RQ</u>, 16 (1) (Fall 1976), 27-32, passim.

4. Joanna López Muñoz, "The Significance of Nonverbal Communication in the Reference Interview," <u>RQ</u>, 16 (3) (Spring 1977), 220.

5. Lewis Thomas, "Vibes," in his <u>The Lives of a Cell: Notes of a Biology Watcher</u> (New York: Viking, 1974), p. 40. (Those who are impressed by this sort of thing might also consider chronemics, haptics, proxemics, etc.)

6. Geraldine B. King. "The Reference Interview," <u>RQ</u>, 12 (2) (Winter 1972), 158-159.

7. Fred Batt, oral communication. Consider, for example, the following overheard interchange: Patron: "Where are the encyclopedias?" Reference librarian: "There are, of course, a great many encyclopedias, arranged by call number on the shelves. The general encyclopedias are on the table over there." Patron: "I'm looking for the <u>Encyclopaedia Britannica</u>." Reference librarian (Pointing to the table): "It's over there."

8. A patron requested a specific reference title; he really was seeking bibliographical information on a journal. The book, however, was an appropriate source for this. Another patron asked for an almanac, which was inappropriate, since he was searching for a map of Annapolis. A third needed phone books and phonefiche; both of these did help him locate radio stations, but ultimately he had to turn to other sources. A fourth desired an index to French magazines; he was looking for duck hunting journals. Next, there was a broad question on Ian Fleming's novels and the derived films. It turned out that the patron wished to know something quite specific about six of these films, but I had automatically answered his question. Finally, a general query concerning the oil industry hid the true question, which dealt with the business of oil wells.

9. The eight major academic libraries are at North Texas State University: one hour of observation, 51 questions posed, no interviews; Texas Woman's University: one and a half hours, 22 questions, no interviews; University of Oklahoma: one half hour, 24 questions, no interviews; Central State University (Oklahoma): one hour, 20 questions, no interviews; Washburn University: one hour, 18 questions, no interviews; University of Kansas: one hour, 22 questions, no interviews; Iowa State University: one hour, 32 questions, no interviews; University of Minnesota: one hour, 40 questions, no interviews. These statistics do not include telephone queries nor four exchanges that I was unable to hear.

10. David E. House, "Reference Efficiency or Reference Deficiency,"

Library Association Record, 76 (11) (November 1974), 222-223.
11. Marcia J. Myers, Jassim M. Jirjees, The Accuracy of Telephone Reference/Information Services in Academic Libraries: Two Studies (Metuchen, NJ: Scarecrow, 1983).
12. Mary Jo Lynch, "Reference Interviews in Public Libraries," The Library Quarterly 48 (2) (April 1978), 133-134, 137.
13. Samuel Rothstein, "Across the Desk: 100 Years of Reference Encounters," Canadian Library Journal, 34 (5) (October 1977), 397.

ATTACKING THE MYTHS
OF SMALL LIBRARIES*

Thomas J. Hennen, Jr.

In 1948, the ALA Committee on Post-war Planning published A National Plan for Library Service. In that epochal volume, Carleton B. Joeckel and Amy Winslow reflected Franklin D. Roosevelt's statement that one third of the nation was ill-housed, ill-fed, and ill-clothed. They reported that one quarter of the nation, mostly rural, had no public library services. Another quarter of the nation, they said, lived near small libraries with woefully inadequate services.

To extend and improve libraries, Joeckel and Winslow prescribed an ambitious program of federal, state, and local funding based on "wider units of service," centralized technical and administrative functions, resource sharing, reorganization, and consolidation.

Forty years ago, most of the 7,500 public libraries serviced populations of less than 25,000. Today, of the 8,600 libraries, 78 percent serve populations of less than 25,000. Most new libraries are suburban. In 1986, only some 5 percent of the nation has no legal access to a library. But what portion of the nation is still ill-served?

An honest and objective observer of most small libraries in America today must sadly say that despite some progress, Lowell Martin's words in A National Plan still ring true: "The first hard truth that confronts an observer of American public libraries is that they have stopped far short of their potential. The second is that at isolated places, and in partial fashion, they have performed an educational function that is unique and significant."

The concept of wider units of service arose because in many areas even counties were, and still are, an inadequate tax and population base for modern library services; thus library systems incorporating a number of counties and a minimum population and tax base

*Reprinted by permission of the author and publisher from American Libraries 17:11 (December 1986) 830–834; copyright © 1986 by the American Library Association.

were established. Was the system idea, based on a belief that "bigger is better," born of undue American optimism after World War II? If so, how does the idea now compare to the post-Vietnam reappraisal that "small is beautiful?" Some of the prevailing myths and the harsh realities of library service by small public libraries bear examination in the light of such questions.

MYTH #1: SMALL IS BEAUTIFUL
BECAUSE IT'S MORE PERSONAL

Myth number one is that small public library service is more friendly and personal. In truth, quality of service depends on the leadership of the director and the commitment of the staff. One can get as cold and impersonal a response from people in a small library as in the largest. Often one has to be part of the inner circle of regulars to get friendly service, regardless of library size.

If small size alone meant personal service, road show carnivals would be friendlier than Disney World. Try them both and see for yourself. Commitment to personal service is what counts, not size.

MYTH #2: SMALL LIBRARIES COLLECT
ONLY BESTSELLERS

All small Soviet libraries may have nearly the same collections, just as most chain bookstores in America do, but not so our small public libraries. Our collections are probably more diverse than large library collections. Book selection is shared by many staff in larger libraries, and individual idiosyncracies, biases, and preferences are subordinated. In a small library, the director is often the sole selector. This is both the beauty and the bane of small libraries. A bibliographic archaeologist could easily trace the tenures of chief librarians in most small libraries by examining the bibliographic layers of purchasing represented in annual acquisitions lists: a failed poet here, a skydiver or sociologist there.

Small library collections can become so skewed as to be totally irrelevant. More often, they adequately reflect most of the needs of the community as seen through the slightly rose-colored glasses of the chief librarians.

Librarians need to devise methods of balancing collections to the true needs of all local citizens without developing the cold standardization of chain bookstores or small Soviet public libraries. The very difficulty of the task may cause us to shy away from truly effective, coordinated collection development, yet the diverse needs of the actual and potential clientele of small libraries demand that it be undertaken.

MYTH #3:   SMALL LIBRARIES SERVE
TOWNSPEOPLE AND FARMERS

Another common myth is that small libraries serve mostly farmers and small-town residents. Since World War II, however, most of the one thousand or so new small libraries have been autonomous suburban libraries. The result is a patchwork of small units duplicating many of the technical and administrative functions that the National Plan envisioned would be better accomplished in wider units of service. Notable exceptions, like Hennepin County in Minnesota and Baltimore County in Maryland, prove the viability of the plan's proposals.

In rural areas, there are fewer farmers every year and town populations remain stable; yet, rural populations overall continue to grow. The myth of farm/small-town service ignores an important post-World War II development, the emergence of YRPIES (Young Rural Professionals), who are close cousins to trendy YUPPIES. The YRPIES are busily gentrifying rural America wherever it comes within a 75-mile radius of urban sprawl.

Before the extension of interstate highways, very few nonfarmers lived in rural areas. Now people can commute long distances to jobs in urban centers and affluent city workers are moving farther and farther out. The trend is accelerated as high-tech industries move to industrial parks along interstate bypasses.

YRPIES are young, educated, and affluent. They use schools, libraries, and other tax-supported services at a higher rate than their farm neighbors. Many of their homes are assessed at a value far above those of city or farm dwellers, yet the new residents are usually taxed at their neighbors' far lower mill rates because of outmoded property tax structures. YRPIES, on their property tax islands amid corn and wheat fields, cannot be taxed at the higher rate their library use dictates without disproportionately taxing overburdened farmers. This affects community services planning, especially library planning. Libraries are singularly susceptible to shifts in property tax distributions. The irony is that they provide people-related services primarily on a property tax base.

Small rural libraries have historically served the needs of small-town residents fairly well. Farm families have fared less well. YRPIES and other, less affluent rural non-farm residents fare better than farmers, but live farther away from the libraries and consequently use them less. Small libraries rarely design service programs specifically for them. Bookmobiles, books by mail, or other extension services usually simply extend traditional small-town services and materials. To gain the credibility needed to firmly establish an adequate tax and population base for library services over widely dispersed and divergent areas, far more attention must be paid to the true library needs of the surrounding constituencies.

MYTH #4:   SMALL LIBRARIES "RAPE"
RESOURCES OF LARGE LIBRARIES

The "resource rape" of large libraries is the latest in a line of
myths perpetuated by misguided observers.   Do small and rural libraries borrow more than they lend? Undoubtedly. National data,
by library size, easily support such a conclusion.[1]   Does such net
borrowing amount to resource rape of larger libraries? No; the
wrong resources are being considered.

Nearly all discussions on interlibrary loan focus on materials
loaned (net lending) rather than on staff commitment to the process.
The "net lending" load so frequently cited is nearly irrelevant. If
all the interloans in a year were concentrated on a given day, they
would amount to less than one-tenth percent of total lending stock.
This is true in every population category from the largest library to
the smallest. No one could seriously argue that such minor amounts
significantly affect access to any library's primary clientele.

The biggest resource of any library, small or large, is its
staff, where 60 percent or more of any funding is concentrated. The
staff spends the same amount of time to handle any interlibrary loan
request, whether the item is being lent or borrowed. Staff time committed to interlibrary loan is the relevant factor, not net lending.
Participation in interlibrary loan networks is often state mandated.
Where it is not required by law, it is overwhelmingly encouraged by
the library community in the name of resource sharing and cooperation.

Nationally, there is a direct and absolutely consistent correlation
between the size of a public library and the staff burden that interlibrary loan presents: The smaller the library, the larger the staff
workload per interlibrary loan handled. In many states larger libraries are compensated for interlibrary loan. Moreover, recent data
demonstrate that many small libraries are actually net lenders besides
handling more activity per staff member,[2] owing to advances in
bibliographic tools based on computer technology and telecommunications networks.

If "resource rape" has occurred, the smallest libraries have been
the victims. They are required to participate in interloan, made to
feel shame at their net borrowing demands, and yet must deal with
the greatest volume per employee. As is so often the case, the victim
has been blamed.

MYTH #5:   LOCAL AUTONOMY
ENSURES BETTER SERVICE

Many, if not most, librarians and library trustees firmly believe
in the myth that the community values the local autonomy of its library. Bigger is not better because it is bureaucratic and distant

from community control, they say. The truth is that local autonomy is more important to the local city councils, trustees, and directors of small libraries than to the public. The public wants a well stocked, maintained, and staffed library, not autonomy for its own sake. Autonomy can easily lead to service programs totally irrelevant to community needs. The library map of America is littered with many autonomous local agencies with wholly inadequate buildings, untrained staff, and useless collections. Citizens have been tragically robbed of an invaluable educational resource. When such agencies are allowed to be dignified with the name of "public library," all adequate and excellent libraries everywhere are demeaned.

Library leaders, often pushed by directors jealous of their prerogatives, have allowed the system ideal of "wider units of service" to be too closely tied to interlibrary loan. Then it is "discovered" that interlibrary loan amounts to less than 1 percent of circulation and that it is (can anyone be truly surprised?) labor intensive and expensive.[3] Then, in the style of the most reactionary city council member at a library budget hearing, such critics ignore any and all user benefits and focus on costs alone. The straw man of interlibrary loan is thus ceremoniously hanged and the grand design of systems thereby falsely declared a failure. Autonomous municipal libraries are discovered to be the best of all possible worlds. Direct state and federal funding for collection development is then demanded as preferable to the dollars "wasted" on interlibrary loan and the systems erroneously tied solely to it.

As interlibrary loan detractors focus on costs, they lose sight of total value to library users. Public libraries nationwide borrow over five million items annually on interlibrary loan. Without it, libraries would have to deny the request or buy the item. At a conservative $15 per item, buying would require adding $75 million to the $250 million book budgets of American libraries. A one-third increase in book budgets is unlikely in these stringent economic times.

Perhaps, having lost sight of our objectives, we have redoubled our efforts. Library system development was not designed to provide interlibrary loan. That is just the carrot with which to draw reluctant libraries into a cooperative framework. The true purpose was, and still is, to extend library services. Direct state and federal funding to autonomous municipal libraries will not ensure extension of services to areas lacking population density or tax-base, any more than system development focused too heavily on interlibrary loan has or ever will. Complete local autonomy can mean the autonomy to provide inadequate service or none at all to vast numbers of our citizens. We cannot and should not allow this.

THE JOB AHEAD

For too long we have let the self-serving, shortsighted objections of autonomous municipal libraries stand in the way of adequate service to all library users. Why not eat those Lake Woebegon Powdermilk Biscuits, the ones that give shy people the strength to do what needs to be done, and work to extend and improve service in geographic areas and "wider units of service" with an adequate population and tax base? We must stop concentrating on limp appeals to networking or resource sharing. Now is the time to consolidate tax levies, refine administrative services, and improve services to all citizens, not just those in urban or suburban municipalities.

Forty years ago Lowell Martin observed that small public libraries were stalled "far short of their potential." They still are. They will remain so until we recognize that the important issues are not small as opposed to large units, or local autonomy as opposed to tax equity, or even resource sharing as opposed to resource hoarding. The paramount issue is to ensure that no portion of this nation is without easy access to quality public library service.

References

1. National Center for Educational Statistics, U.S. Department of Education. Statistics of Public Libraries, 1981-82. Public Library Association, American Library Association, 1985. p. 110.
2. Abbott, Peter and Kavanaugh, Rosemary. "Electronic Resource Sharing Changes Interloan Patterns." Library Journal (October 1, 1986) p. 56-58.
3. Ballard, Tom. "Knowin' All Them Things That Ain't So: Managing Today's Public Library," in Occasional Papers of the University of Illinois Graduate School of Library and Information Science. Number 168. March 1985.

MEASURES OF EXCELLENCE:
THE SEARCH FOR THE GOLD STANDARD*

Virginia H. Holtz

Many of the preceding Janet Doe lecturers have been able to share
with you reminiscences of personal encounters with Janet Doe. I
only met her once, when I was very new to MLA, at an annual meeting
banquet. I've wondered since why that single encounter many years
ago left such an indelible impression. Janet Doe was among the first
of those who have set for me a "gold standard" for what MLA and
MLA members should be, through the example of her enthusiasm for
the fellowship and ideas of colleagues, young and old, a joy in the
task to be done, and pleasure in accomplishment, no matter whose.
Among her enduring gifts to this associaiton, renewed at each annual
meeting, is this open, generous, ad joyful sharing of each other's
company, insights, and accomplishments.

Selecting the topic for the Janet Doe lecture is an experience
in and of itself. In my case, it took on overtones of an exorcism.
It was not so much that I chose a topic, but that I fulfilled a need
to resolve a number of recurring questions, questions that arose repeatedly and independently in various contexts.

Why, in this decade, is our profession so urgently preoccupied
with the production of professional standards, guidelines, statistical
analyses of library data, and other evaluation measures? Not only
health sciences librarians, but those in all branches of our profession
are seriously and simultaneously concerned with these issues.

Why are some of the values we hold so enduring, and will they
continue to persist in the face of changes confronting our profession?

Why do we repeatedly find ourselves in the position of having to

*Reprinted by permission of the author and publisher from the Bulletin
of the Medical Library Association 74:4 (October 1986) 305-314;
copyright © by the Medical Library Association. Janet Doe Lecture on
the History or Philosophy of Medical Librarianship presented May
21, 1986, at the Eighty-sixth Annual Meeting of the Medical Library
Association, Minneapolis, Minnesota.

pause in our work to redefine old familiar terms like information or
knowledge, or to develop working definitions for subsets of these
once serviceable terms?

Is there a common thread that ties all of these issues together?
I believe there is, and that is why I want to talk to you about some
of the values we as health sciences librarians hold and preserve and
the goals we derive from them as a gold standard for our profession,
about the tools we use to measure our achievements of those goals
and some of the controversies that surround them, and about paradigms and changes that result in paradigms lost, found, and in transition. In the process, knowingly and unknowingly, I will doubtless
do some violence to concepts borrowed from other fields by bending
them too far. But I beg your indulgence. Especially in times of
change, disciplines that are to survive and be successful must expand their sights and consider fields surrounding or even quite remote from their own for useful pieces of theory with which to expand
or change their own frame of reference in useful ways.

The roots of this discussion are bound up in our history, which
is a fairly long one, filled with examples of developing values and
judgments about quality and excellence. However, the purposeful
development of formal tools to measure excellence in the field of librarianship in general has taken place largely in the last century and,
in the field of health sciences librarianship, in the last twenty-five
to thirty years.

During this time, librarians have shown an enduring concern for
those instruments of measurement that include standards, guidelines,
collections of data and statistics, planning processes or outlines, and
other such tools. The persistence of this concern implies that these
instruments fill a basic need in our profession and that their absence
in any readily perceived form generates unrest. There is little doubt,
given the effort expended on the production, revision, and discussion
of these tools, that they play a fundamental role in the current practice of librarianship.

One of the most basic needs of individuals and, indeed, of institutions (as groups of individuals with a common purpose) is to be
able to identify their place in their universe, personal and professional
As a group, the tools addressed here help to establish the base from
which librarians act, to describe what they do, to identify their
peers for various purposes, and to measure their "goodness" on a
variety of scales. They help librarians and libraries generally to
establish their overall individual identities.

Beyond this function, these instruments also are used, and sometimes misused, to serve a wide variety of less abstract purposes:
for example, to establish starting points such as baselines or minimal
values, or to determine targets such as benchmarks, norms, or best
practices. In other cases they are used to facilitate communications

between a functional unit, the library, and the bodies with which it interacts, such as user groups, peer groups, or more commonly, re-source controllers outside of the library, such as deans, chancellors, hospital administrators, managers, or boards of directors. Whatever these purposes, these tools provide a kind of gold standard against which libraries are measured.

In the last century, and especially in the last twenty-five years, such measures have attracted the attention not only of a growing number of librarians, but of administrators outside of the library field and others as well. This phenomenon appears to be related to a num-ber of forces, including the tremendous growth in recorded information; the increasing professional distance over the past century between those who develop and maintain the library and those who use its resources; a growing number of devices and systems, in addition to print on paper, for carrying recorded information; an overall increased complexity in the process of information storage and retrieval; the growth of other professions for which information handling is a major concern; and, in some sense, the maturing of our own profession.

It is clear that some forms of evaluation for health sciences li-braries were in operation earlier than this century, but formalization of the applied measures and values is recent. Indeed, the early literature of libraries and librarianship is full of implied values, many of which are preserved for better or worse in their formal successors.

Communities and Paradigms

Before considering some of the various individual mechanisms for evaluation in more detail, it would be useful to consider how discipline-oriented communities organize their knowledge, values, beliefs, and community experience for further study and practice. A useful model to consider is the one presented by Thomas Kuhn in The Structure of Scientific Revolutions [1].

This slim volume deals with the concept of paradigms and how they function in science. It draws its examples from the history of science and describes a process of paradigm development that has close parallels in librarianship.

In order to be clear about Kuhn's view of paradigms, it is im-portant to understand his concept of a scientific community. Such a community consists of the practitioners of a scientific specialty. The members "have undergone similar education and professional ini-tiations; in the process, they have absorbed the same technical liter-ature and drawn many of the same lessons from it. Usually the boun-daries of that standard literature mark the limits for a scientific sub-ject matter, and each community ordinarily has a subject matter of its own" [2]. Major communities also share membership in professional societies. Certainly this description fits the scholars and practitioners in our field.

Communities of this sort are the producers and validators of
scientific knowledge about their disciplines and share a common paradigm, or disciplinary matrix. This matrix is made up of such things
as a set of commonly shared beliefs in Symbolic generalizations that
are basic to the current practice of the discipline and allow easy communication; belief in particular models; widely shared values for
judging such things as scientific theories, the social goals of the
community, and the accuracy of predictions; and shared examples
that illustrate the community's commonly held beliefs and are often
referred to in the teaching and scientific literature of the discipline.

Around these features of this shared professional matrix have
aggregated over time less tangible elements such as shared general
knowledge and intuition about the discipline. This rich and complex
structure, taken as a whole, gives the community a common frame of
reference for seeing and interpreting the world around it.

I am assuming that we as librarians constitute such a community
and, as health sciences librarians, a specialized subgroup of the more
general community of librarians. I am also assuming that we share a
common paradigm, but that even within our special community there
are overlapping subspecialties, including librarians who serve specific
environments exemplified by teaching hospitals, community hospitals,
or academic settings, or those who pursue subspecialties (media or
automation, for example). We certainly share in common our library-
oriented education, a body of literature, our professional organizations,
our concern with appropriate education for ourselves and our successors, easy communication within our profession, and many values,
models, and examples that we use to understand, describe, and teach
librarianship. These and other subtle influences make up the fabric
of our paradigm. Kuhn also holds that for a scientific community a
mature paradigm helps to define areas in which research is needed--
puzzles which need to be solved.

This model of how science works appears to be a useful one within
which to examine what has been going on within librarianship, especially as it relates to our evaluation mechanisms. The components
Kuhn identifies as being part of a scientific paradigm are important
to evaluation.

With their common view of the world, librarians by definition also
hold in common various interlocking beliefs, standards, and values.
Some of these are also shared not only by the communities of scholars
and practitioners we serve, but by the general public as well. Some
are so deeply embedded in our history and practice that even as we
discuss and intellectualize change, we honor these beliefs in practice.
This behavior is consistent with Kuhn's observation that until an acceptable alternative is found, old paradigmatic behavior will persist.
We need an organizing structure even if it is defective. More than
three centuries ago Francis Bacon said, "Truth emerges more readily
from error than confusion" [3].

Some Common Values

Three examples of widely held tenets of librarianship are the belief in the power of print on paper as a carrier of information, the value of the volume as a measure of what libraries do and are, and the importance of comprehensiveness in collections of information. It is interesting to note that each of these examples not only persists in many aspects of what we do today, but each has its roots in the very first concepts of what a library was and did.

It seems to be stating the obvious to say that the book, especially the book published through the use of movable type, was the first important carrier of information, aside from the mind of man. The printed word and the book that contained it were such successful technologies for recording, preserving, and transmitting information that no rival techniques for these purposes were needed; none appeared for centuries. The need and the technology were such a perfect fit that it became common practice to describe collections of mankind's recorded knowledge in terms of the physical carrier of the information, the book or volume, rather than in terms of the content itself. The natural human tendency to collect information and, in large subgroups of humanity, to try to collect all information relevant to a specific purpose, is so basic to civilization as to be a survival technique. This tendency is particularly pronounced in scholarly communities.

These values and beliefs are so deeply embedded in our history, practice, and value systems and have persisted so long without being questioned or challenged by alternatives that we are only beginning to examine and understand the attributes that made them successful and durable.

As long as there were no successful alternatives to print on paper, there was nothing to compare it to; its many powerful characteristics remained for all intents and purposes invisible. The book has been declared to be as basic and versatile a development as the wheel.

In recent years, however, the repeated challenges to print by alternative technologies have begun to peel away the layers of mysticism and reveal by comparison those characteristics of print on paper that make it an enduring technology and earn it a place in our value system. Initially, it inspired enthusiasm for its ability to provide an extended group memory, a stable and unchanging record of important facts, discoveries, and events. More recently, however, these purposes have also been served by other technologies.

Little by little, over time, print's competitors have revealed some of its basic characteristics. It is directly accessible by the reader who has it in hand. It is very versatile, accommodating with reasonable facility the storage and use of a wide variety of information, including collections of data, facts, interpretations of facts, extended philosophical treatises, poetry and other creative literature, news reports, political treatises, and many other types of content. Individual volumes are very portable, and personal copies accommodate marginal notes, underlining, and other forms of personal enhancement. Among the most important characteristics of print on paper is its stability, not only as a physical format (we feel almost betrayed by the deterioration of things printed on high-acid papers), but as an intellectual record. Users rely on finding the same information in the same words and the same order each time they return to a volume. Over time, the book and journal, the most persistent forms of printed material, have been engineered for human use. The end result is an artifact that comes in a relatively limited range of sizes, weights, paper colors, and print formats found to be most suitable for human use. It is no wonder that print and the book persist.

The second value, the use of the volume as a standard measure of library quality, is closely related to the value we give to print on paper as a powerful information carrier. As the printed sheet is the carrier for information, the volume is the carrier for the printed sheet. The association between information and the book or volume is so strong that one has come to represent the other. The volume has become a kind of common denominator that we use when we try to describe in a uniform way the intellectual content and, therefore, the value of a library. We try to find volume equivalents for present formats that don't logically come in volumes so that we can have a standard unit by which to measure the library's contents. We also measure the use of library collections in terms of the number of volumes borrowed, used, or reshelved. The volume is the closest thing we have to a measure for units of information.

The fact that we still place great value on the size of a library or the number of volumes held, in spite of some substantial challenges to that approach in the recent past of librarianship, demonstrates how strongly we, as a community, hold a belief in comprehensiveness. We, as librarians, want to collect everything relevant to our enterprise and, failing that, because of limitations in our facilities or resources or support or mission, we try to be comprehensive within a limited discipline or time frame. But, at the same time, we want to be assured that another library or agency is collecting the rest and will preserve it and make it available to us and to our users. Librarians are not alone in holding this value. The users of libraries not only value comprehensiveness, but often assume it, as the form of their questions frequently indicates. A new paradigm for librarianship would have to accommodate, replace, or otherwise deal with values as deeply rooted as these.

Although paradigms provide the stability we as communities need in order to accomplish our study and practice, they also must be able to change, sometimes dramatically, if they are not to deny progress. It seems clear that the discipline of librarianship has shared a common paradigm for a substantial period of time and that it is now undergoing a paradigm shift--a process also described in some detail by Kuhn.

Paradigms Lost and in Transition

Paradigms that operate according to Kuhn's description have within them the seeds of their own change. One of the most basic functions of a paradigm is to provide a framework for further study and elucidation of the discipline. In the natural course of events it is likely that members of the community will discover anomalies-- differences between expected outcomes and reality. A growing awareness of anomalies is one of the first symptoms of a paradigm shift, followed by the "gradual and simultaneous emergence of observational and conceptual recognition and the consequent change of paradigm"[4]. This process can be a long one, and it often encounters resistance. Indeed, the emergence of important new theories and discoveries and technological changes that replace previously standard beliefs, procedures, or technologies intrinsic to the old paradigm precipitate a growing professional crisis.

This crisis period is characterized by a time of pronounced professional insecurity generated by the failure of existing rules to predict appropriate outcomes. The matrix becomes increasingly complex and cumbersome in an effort to explore and encompass anomalies. Theories become increasingly vague and less useful, and there is a proliferation of versions of basic theory. The research in the discipline, instead of proceeding in an orderly and understandable way, guided by the shared conceptual framework, begins to become unfocused and directed by the views of competing schools rather than by one unified discipline. This crisis is described by Kuhn as not only normal, but necessary to progress. History repeatedly demonstrates that the solutions to many such crisis-precipitating problems were at least partially anticipated during a period when there was no crisis. However, in the absence of a crisis, there is no incentive to abandon a functioning, if disabled, paradigm or to attempt to look at the world in a new way and to readjust the basic tenets of the discipline.

Another basic requirement for paradigm change is the existence of an alternate paradigm. Because the presence of such a conceptual structure is basic to the function of a science, a community does not reject one paradigm until another is available to take its place. However, crisis has the effect of loosening the rules of the existing paradigm in ways that allow alternate views of the professional world to proliferate. The emergence of a new paradigm is seldom, if ever, uncontroversial. Changing paradigms does not simply involve the fine tuning of the old worldview but a basic "reconstruction of the field from new fundamentals, a reconstruction that changes some of the field's most elementary, theoretical generalizations as well as many of its methods and applications" [5] and the reorientation of the community to these changes.

Another characteristic of paradigm shift observed by Kuhn is that, almost always, those who invent a new paradigm are either very

young or very new to the field whose paradigm they change. These
people, less committed to the traditional rules of the existing paradigm, are particularly likely to see that the old rules don't work and
to conceive a new set.

A new paradigm can have the effect of subdividing an old community, redirecting an existing one, or providing a unifying theory
linking together a group of lower-level theories. Early signs seem to
indicate that we are moving in the direction of developing, in conjunction with others, a unifying theory for information handling.

One other sort of change a paradigm can undergo--one critical
to Kuhn's description--is a transition to maturity. Only after achieving maturity does a paradigm allow for normal puzzle-solving activity.
It then provides a framework for research that facilitates the identification of problems or puzzles needing attention and accommodates
successful solutions into its overall structure. Research then achieves
again a more orderly and directed progress.

The concepts of stable and shifting paradigms, of communities
of interest which, over time, subdivide, change, or unite with other
communities to form new or different disciplines or subdisciplines or
remain stable, are all useful concepts within which to examine evaluation mechanisms. The combined values, rules, models, and experiences we share make it possible for us to create standards and planning and evaluation frameworks and to interpret statistics in ways
that are meaningful for the entire community.

Evaluation Measures

At this point, it would probably be most useful to consider some
of the mechanisms we have used to create the gold standard by which
we evaluate our work and our libraries.

The oldest system of measurement is the numerical measure. From
the earliest histories of libraries came descriptions in terms of the
size of the collections. In our own branch of librarianship, we see
the persistence of this sort of account. It seems reasonable to pre-
sume the authors of these reports were trying to tell us about library
characteristics they viewed as important, and so the characteristics
they describe may be seen as their preliminary criteria for evaluation.

In the field of medicine, information was a scarce commodity for
a very long period of time. Books and then journals were not at
first held in significant numbers by medical practitioners, so the
pooling of information resources was a highly useful thing to do. The
size of the composite collection was then, and for a long time there-
after, the most important measure of the library's usefulness. Medical
education was often sketchy, and the information-hungry practitioner
was ideally omnivorous in his reading habits. Information resources

were scarce and information changed only slowly. The reader had
little trouble finding his way among the meager resources, and relatively little was required in the way of organization. It is little wonder
then that early descriptions of medical libraries, like those of libraries
in general, deal almost exclusively with the number of volumes in the
collection.

In the Bulletin of the Medical Library Association, as late as 1902
there appear several notes or brief articles about established or emerging libraries, and they are described in similar terms. The library
of the Surgeon General's Office is represented as a magnificent collection with 142,490 books and 238,772 pamphlets. The library of the
Medical Society of Kings, Brooklyn, in December of 1901 was described
as having 600 current periodicals regularly on file, 35,000 volumes,
and more than 20,000 pamphlets. With duplicates, there were nearly
50,000 volumes in the library. Other libraries are similarly described.

Conversely, even at this early date the size of the information
base was beginning to be a problem for library and reader alike. The
Boston Medical Library, at about the turn of the century, reduced
its collection by 1,082 books in a "new departure" in library administration by discarding all but the first or last editions of handbooks
and general treatises while preserving classics, works embodying
original research, and special monographs. This made room for the
display of 504 current periodicals, "that all important class of literature" [6]. By 1932, an editorial in the Indiana State Medical Journal
complained, "[I]t is interesting to know that if one should begin to
read everything medical that was written last year, and should spend
eight hours a day, six days a week and fifty weeks a year, it would
take him in the neighborhood of one hundred years to do it. At that
time our well-read man would actually be ninety-nine years behind the
times" [7].

As the literature of medicine became too large for any one person
to read and absorb, it became all the more important for libraries
to collect and preserve books and journals so they could be made
available when they were needed. While the comprehensiveness of the
collection continued to be a widely held value in some libraries and
the number of volumes remained the prime measure of a library's
quality, the concept of the limited practical collection emerged as
early as 1912. "There are two types of medical libraries. The first
is the great city library where the authors and teachers consult the
history as well as the progress of medicine, and the second is the
small, practical working library for the busy practitioner" [8].

Other criteria for quality also began to emerge at the turn of the
century. Use statistics, including circulation and reading room at-
tendance, were reported and the importance of convenience, immediacy
of access, and browsing were mentioned. Because of the growing
size of the collections and the need to organize them and provide
access to them, the presence of an assistant or librarian was also

found desirable by 1914. Informal reports of this nature illustrate
the growing set of criteria that began to characterize the successful
library.

The birth of formal library statistics occurred in the United States
with the first publication of library statistics in the 1850s and 1870s;
however, the first regularly recurring health sciences library statistics began with the collection of academic health sciences library data
in 1975. This work was first compiled by Donald Hendrix, then librarian at the University of Texas Health Science Center at Dallas,
and is continued as the Annual Statistics of Medical School Libraries
in the United States and Canada by the Houston Academy of Medicine
Texas Medical Center and the Association of Academic Health Science
Library Directors. Another series of reports of statistical data collection and analysis of health-related libraries done by Rees and Crawford in 1969, 1973, and 1979 included all types of libraries [9].

These works were preceded by several other significant statistical
studies, especially those of Darling in 1956, the Medical Library Association in 1959, Bloomquist in 1962, Keenan in 1964, Geisler and Yast
in 1964, and the Medical Library Association in 1966 [10, 11]. Bloomquist, for example, gave summary data for eighty-four medical school
libraries on volumes held, volumes added, periodical subscriptions,
various expenditures, and number of staff. The composite data were
not only reported but were compared with some numerical "standards"
established on the basis of expert knowledge and opinion. Recommendations were made about improvements in academic medical libraries
in terms of minimum numbers of volumes (100,000) and subscriptions
(1,200-1,500) [12].

The two national associations of health sciences librarians, the
Medical Library Association and the Association of Academic Health
Sciences Library Directors, continue to be concerned with the collection and analysis of data as an important part of their work in
assisting their members to monitor and evaluate libraries and library
service. An examination of recent reports demonstrates that data
collection and statistical analysis of that data is growing more complex
and comprehensive, and that the size of collections as measured in
volumes and the size of staff and expenditures continue to be considered significant measures for study and analysis. In addition,
output measures are given in terms of volumes (or issues) circulated,
borrowed, or loaned on interlibrary loan. Some of the most problematic and controversial data and data collection issues revolve around
attempts to measure the collection and use of materials that are not
perceived as being countable as volumes and the evaluation of information services that are difficult to define in terms of discrete, easily
and consistently measurable units.

In the library community at large and in the research community
in particular, the recent emphasis is away from measures of what a
library collects or spends and toward a concern with output or performance measures. Examples are Zweizig and Rodger's 1962 publication

Output Measures for Public Libraries [13] and Kantor's 1984 work
Objective Performance Measures for Academic and Research Libraries
[14], both of which provide workbook approaches to arriving at suggested measures of library effectiveness based on data collected for
the purpose. The public library work uses some of the old standbys,
such as volumes circulated and numbers of users, in more complex
combination, as well as different categories of data collected on a
sampling basis. The Kantor work is a minitext in statistics, but offers three examples of methods intended to capture information about
the quality of library service.

Taken as a whole, library statistics have provided useful raw
data on which to base some initial minimal numerical standards and
impressions about libraries. They have allowed institutions to identify
their place among peer organizations and have provided a kind of
shorthand description of a library's characteristics and accomplishments for communication in and out of the library.

In the health sciences arena, however, the application of even
simple data gathering and analysis of a national multi-institution basis
is very uneven. It is most highly developed for academic institutions
and least well developed for small community hospitals. However,
strong interest in the development and improvement of data collection
and analysis is prevalent in all the subspecialties of our discipline,
and our national associations are actively exploring the potential of
this tool.

Given the increasing variability of the institutions served by health
sciences libraries, interinstitutional comparisons of even complex statistics are not always productive. Neither do all of the factors we
may wish to evaluate lend themselves to numerical measures. In these
cases, a more abstract tool, such as a set of authoritative performance
standards, may best serve the purpose.

Aside from technical standards, which are usually unambiguous,
authoritative, and uniformly applied by those who adopt them, performance standards come in a variety of forms, many of which are
generalized abstractions of a desired goal.

Implied standards have been used to evaluate general and health-
related libraries for as long as there has been one library to measure
against another. Formalized and documented standards are a much
more recent phenomenon. The two major objections to standards are
opposite sides of the same coin. They are seen as being either so
specific that they are rapidly outdated or not widely applicable, or
so general that achievement is not really measured. Efforts to resolve
this basic conflict have been relatively unsuccessful. Except in times
when the majority of libraries of a certain type are considerably sub-
standard and specific targets based on the practice of more successful
libraries can be used to set beneficially high targets, numeric and
other highly specific standards tend to do more harm than good.

After a time, they have the effect of preserving the status quo rather than advancing the state of the libraries they are intended to help. As the number and discrete types of libraries increase, standards become more difficult to write. Eventually, most types of libraries have adopted guidelines or planning outlines that provide common frameworks for individual libraries to use in setting their own specific performance objectives in the context of their specific institutions, mission, practice, and priorities. One of the most farsighted and far-ranging versions prepared for health sciences libraries was the set of guidelines produced by the Joint Committee of the Association of American Medical Colleges and the Medical Library Association, Guidelines for Medical School Libraries [15]. A set of current guidelines produced by a joint task force of the Association of Academic Health Science Library Directors and the Medical Library Associaiton will soon be published [16].

The development of standards for libraries in the United States has spanned the period from about 1917, when ALA first took up the question, to the present day, when standards, guidelines, planning outlines, and other such tools are again receiving considerable attention. This professional unrest, search for stabilizing standards, and broad interest in collecting and analyzing data can all be seen as classic signs of an impending paradigm shift.

Paradigms Found

It is paradoxical that as we seek to understand and explain our professional world by simplifying it, we make it more complex by adding to its conceptual framework. When the framework finally becomes too complex through our increased efforts to deal with anomalies or exceptions to our expectations, we need and therefore seek new unifying principles to simplify our world again. This, in essence, is a paradigm change.

If some of our old abstractions (values) have to change, what will our new values look like? If Kuhn is correct, at least some of these new values could be and probably are already a part of our present system. They, along with existing and emerging technologies, methods theories, and the like, will fall into place and, when they do, the shift to the new way of thinking about all of these things and their place in our professional universe will be complete.

A classic example of such a shift in thinking was inadvertently described in a recent issue of Library Journal. A writer in the "News" section describes an assortment of views of the future, including the one elaborated in the Matheson-Cooper Report, Academic Information in the Academic Health Science Center [17]. He describes the first reactions to this report of some individuals he labels Matheson's "followers." They "characteristically spoke of not understanding her message until after many rereadings of her paper, and then having

it all come clear in a flash of light" [18]. Though the reviewer is
uneasy with this kind of sudden conversion in thinking, it is in fact
typical of individuals undergoing a partial or complete paradigm shift.

What will our new worldview be? In Kuhn's view, we will know
it when we see it. We will almost instantly feel at home in it and it
will open up vistas of inquiry and study that are logical and interesting to us. This last idea, incidentally, also has a corollary in the
concept of "frameworks" for management information systems, where
research is described as filling a niche in a framework.

Assume, for a time, that the new central focus is recorded information in its many permutations, as many of the current theoreti-
cians suggest. Aside from the fact that this suggestion seems: a)
nothing new, b) simply a description of what we have always done,
or c) inconceivable, consider the following. A new paradigm is not
necessarily based on new and unfamiliar elements; it may be simply
a new way of seeing existing components along with new ones.

Think about the following scenario. The information user, rather
than the library, and information per se, rather than the instruments
which carry it, have become the central concerns of our discipline.
This shift in thinking has been brought about because our old frame
of reference is becoming too complex to be useful as it tries to provide
appropriate ways of evaluating and explaining relationships between
the many emerging information formats, subspecialties, methodologies,
and values emerging in librarianship. The rapidly developing information handling potential of computers, electronic storage, and communication devices precipitates a paradigm crisis by providing many
powerful alternate mechanisms for recording, manipulating, storing,
retrieving, and communicating information.

From this new viewpoint some old central values remain intact,
while others take a new place in the structure where their new role
is clearer. Still others have ceased to be functional and disappear.
Take, for example, the concepts cited earlier: the importance of
print, the volume as measure of the quality of a library, and comprehensiveness.

As long as print was the sole or dominant form of information
representation, there was only a superficial need to examine the qualities that made it so powerful a conveyor. Over time, most of the
challengers to print, though each was highly touted at its inception,
have failed to supersede print on paper, but have made visible some
of the enduring and important qualities of print. The wide application
of electronic formats, the first <u>successful</u> competitor to print, highlights other important characteristics of print as well as those of the
competing formats, and the appropriate uses of each continue to evolve.

What emerges over time is not only a clearer picture of the relative
characteristics of print as opposed to electronic and other formats

but, more basic and important, a more complete understanding of the various types of information that need handling. Initially, these are labeled data, information, and knowledge.

The first of these categories, data, is characterized as files of relatively brief, discrete, value-neutral bits of fact or data-like elements that often require further manipulation to be useful. Though each data element is relatively small, the files in which they are organized are of variable sizes. Often, the part the user ultimately wants is small relative to the size of the whole file. This class of information, formerly represented in fact books, indexes and abstracts, data collections, and the like, moves quickly and without controversy to electronic formats.

Information, the second overall category, is made up of components that are larger than data-like elements and more complex. They are based on value judgments and insights about data and other information and knowledge. They range from preliminary findings or conclusions to relatively well-synthesized summaries. This sort of information formerly appeared in journals, articles, brief reports, case studies, and letters. This information may be unstable over time. Some forms of this type, especially those requiring rapid communication, move to online electronic journals quickly, while others continue to be more economically distributed in print or on compact "specialty disks" composed of the latest issues of several related publications.

The third category, called knowledge, is usually more comprehensive and complex than information; it is based on value judgments and on acceptance over time as best interpretation or best practice. Knowledge is the most stable of the three information elements and the most difficult to change. Knowledge continues to be represented largely in the print format as review articles, textbooks, and annual reviews, since this form is least likely to need dynamic manipulation and requires a measure of stability. Important exceptions to this general observation include expert systems, annual reviews that are online (like other current awareness materials), and experiments with electronic textbooks in rapidly changing fields. This category is the slowest overall to adapt to electronic formats fully, although notable exceptions provide grist for the research mill. An interesting compromise is the dynamic electronic expert system, of which a stable "snapshot" is taken at intervals for research and archival use.

The same process of categorization is taking place in defining types of information use, information users, and other components of the information process.

It is widely understood that this typology of information is primitive and that further study will continue to reveal its full structure and the relationships among the parts. Incongruities in the application of these categories help to identify areas where study is needed.

In this scenario, the volume as a measure of the intellectual content as well as size of the library's information resources has been, in large part, replaced by the concept of units of information. These new measures have developed from a better understanding of the characteristics of information and how it can be measured. As these measures are relatively new and do not yet fully encompass all information services offered, they are still a topic of much research and are still hotly debated at professional meetings. It is significant that these debates sometimes stimulate proposals to return to volumes or volume equivalents as the uniform measure. Although much information is available in forms other than print, the langugage of print persists in other formats, and some electronic publications appear in "volumes" and "editions."

Comprehensiveness is as strongly held a value as ever and again appears in some sense to be achievable. The subtle shift from comprehensivensss of ownership to comprehensiveness of access was gradual. It was conceptually almost complete even before the paradigm shift.

As a practice, comprehensiveness of access was threatened and almost defeated by the complexity of communication networks that became so diverse in technology and standards and so convoluted in structure as to be unmanageable. This precipitated a crisis and resulted in serious attention to international standardization of hardware and protocols.

The focus of this new information-based science is the investigation of the basic attributes of information and information carriers, uses and users, and their needs. The practical application of this science involves finding best matches among users, carriers, and information based on known characteristics. Unexplained misfits are identified and provide further grist for the research mill, which then seeks further clarification of attributes. There is a close integration of the research and practice environments, especially in the areas of theory testing and anomaly identification.

Scholars and practitioners from a number of previously discrete disciplines are drawn into this common enterprise, where over time a common technical language is developed to describe common phenomena. These had been variously described and studied from varying points of view under the old discrete disciplines.

From the developing framework that underpins this refocused discipline emerges a comprehensive set of beliefs, values, and standards by which the profession operates and evaluates itself. Units of information, the new quantitative measure, has subcategories that accommodate units of education and consultation provided by the library.

Quality of service via the new user-centered network is considered in terms of ease of access, comprehensiveness of service and resources accessible, quality and versatility of information management programs, speed of service, and effectiveness of the educational program for users in the area of personal information management.

Administrative effectiveness is evaluated in terms of cost per unit of information accessed or other service used, the effectiveness of planning and evaluation of resources and services, and the integration of information services with the overall goals of the host institution or community.

If this scenario and its new gold standard seem out of focus, or wrong-headed or otherwise unacceptable, it is only one of the many we could explore. Feel free to create your own. It's fun to write the future! On the other hand, it may seem so obvious as to be hardly worth stating. It is important to remember that when our paradigm shifts, it will not leave us strangers in a strange land but rather professionally home at last.

We may not even notice that it has happened.

References

1. Kuhn, T. S. The structure of scientific revolutions, 2d ed., enlarged. Chicago: University of Chicago Press, 1970.
2. Ibid., p. 177.
3. Bacon, F. Cited in: Kuhn, T. S. The structure of scientific revolutions, p. 18.
4. Kuhn, T. S. The structure of scientific revolutions, p. 62.
5. Ibid., p. 85.
6. Library items. Bull Med Libr Assoc 1902 Jan-Apr; 1 (1-2): 32-5.
7. "Keeping up with the literature (editorial)." J Indiana State Med Assoc 1932 Feb; 25 (2): 88-9.
8. Black, C. E. "The small medical library." Bull Med Libr Assoc 1912 Oct; 2 (2): 13-8.
9. Crawford, S. "Health science libraries in the United States: I. overview of the post-World War II years." Bull Med Libr Assoc 1983 Jan; 71 (1): 16-20.
10. Keenan, E. L. "Medical library statistics." Bull Med Libr Assoc 1965 Apr; 53 (2): 196-203.
11. Committee on Surveys and Statistics of the Medical Library Association. Library statistics of schools in the health sciences: part I. Bull Med Libr Assoc 1966 July; 54 (3): 206-29.
12. Bloomquist H. "The status and needs of medical school libraries in the United States." J Med Educ 1963 Mar; 28 (3): 145-63.
13. Zweizig D, Rodger, E. J. Output measures for public libraries. Chicago: American Library Association, 1982.
14. Kantor, P. Objective performance measures for academic research libraries. Washington, D.C.: Association of Research Libraries, 1984.

15. "Guidelines for medical school libraries." J Med Educ 1965 Jan; 40 (1, pt. 1).

16. Association of Academic Health Sciences Library Directors/Medical Library Association Joint Task Force to Develop Guidelines for Academic Health Sciences Libraries. Challenge to action: planning and evaluation guidelines for academic health science librarians. (In press.)

17. Matheson, N. W., Cooper, J. A. D. "Academic information in the academic health sciences center: roles for the library in information management." J Med Educ 1982 Oct; 57 (10, pt. 2): 1-93.

18. "News." Libr J 1986 Mar 1; 111 (5): 24.

IMPROVING THE USE OF PRISON LAW LIBRARIES: A MODEST PROPOSAL*

Christopher E. Smith

I. INTRODUCTION

Prison law libraries play a central role in the protection of constitutional rights for prisoners. The U.S. Supreme Court declared in Bounds v. Smith [1] that, in order to fulfill the right of meaningful access to the courts, prisoners must be provided with either law libraries or assistance from persons trained in the law.[2] These resources are required to assist incarcerated offenders in the preparation of petitions and lawsuits to be filed in court. Legal actions by or on behalf of prisoners have served as the basis for judicial recognition and protection of the entire range of constitutional rights possessed by inmates in correctional institutions.[3] Because prison authorities constitutionally are required to provide only law libraries or legal assistance,[4] a number of commentators have argued that legal assistance is more valuable to prisoners than law libraries are.[5] Some correctional institutions, however, have opted to provide only libraries. Thus, many incarcerated criminal offenders must rely solely upon prison law libraries for effectuation of their right of meaningful access to the courts and for judicial enforcement of their other constitutional rights.

The American Association of Law Libraries has demonstrated its justifiable concerns about the adequacy of prison law libraries through its Committee on Law Library Service to Prisoners,[6] checklist of recommended collections for prison libraries, and list of available services.[7] Other organizations have published manuals for prisoner litigation.[8] However, law librarians and prisoners' advocates should not bear the primary responsibility for monitoring the quality of prison law libraries. The entire legal community should be concerned about improving prison libraries, which are so important for protecting prisoners' constitutional rights.

*Reprinted by permission of the author from Law Library Journal 79:2 (Spring 1987) 227-239; copyright © 1987 by Christopher E. Smith.

This article proposes one means of improving use of prison law libraries. Based upon experiences in one prison,[9] this article describes how, through the cooperation of law libraries, law schools, and correctional institutions, the entire legal system can benefit from using law students as legal research instructors in prison law libraries. In the student-run Prisoner Counseling Project at the University of Washington School of Law, volunteer upperclass students taught legal research and writing inside a maximum-security state correctional institution under the sponsorship of the prison's Black Prisoners Caucus. The Washington program provides a model for discussing the potential benefits of using law students to improve prisoners' use of the resources in prison law libraries.

A focus on prison law libraries does not constitute an endorsement of libraries as the most efficacious means for fulfilling the right of meaningful access to the courts under Bounds v. Smith. As one commentator has noted, an emphasis on improving prison law libraries by supplying instruction manuals and recommended collections lists suffers from a serious defect: "In effect, each represents the idea that prison inmates are capable of doing legal research and each ignores the reality that prisoners, as a group, are illiterate and have only the slightest chance of effectively using legal resource materials."[10] The provision of legal assistance to prisoners would be more effective and is essential for truly protecting the constitutional rights of all prisoners. However, because federal court decisions interpreting Bounds have indicated that the provision of legal assistance for prisoners is not constitutionally required,[11] many prisoners are forced to rely upon prison law libraries for their only access to legal resources. While this article recognizes that law libraries alone cannot protect the constitutional rights of most prisoners, the proposed teaching program is an attempt to make the best of a difficult situation. The harsh reality of prisoner dependence upon inadequate law libraries dictates that every effort be made to encourage the effective use of prison law libraries.

II. PRISONER DEPENDENCE UPON LAW LIBRARIES

A. Judicial Development

The development of prisoners' right to a law library as a component of meaningful access to the courts has been well described elsewhere.[12] In essence, the United States Supreme Court, in the seminal case of Bounds v. Smith, held that "the fundamental constitutional right of access to the courts requires prison authorities to assist inmates in the preparation and filing of meaningful legal papers by providing prisoners with adequate law libraries or adequate assistance from persons trained in the law."[13] The Bounds decision left it to correctional officials to develop adequate plans involving libraries, legal services, or both to provide the necessary legal resources for prisoners.

Subsequently, lower federal courts attempted to order prison
officials to provide legal services in addition to libraries, but in recent
decisions, the courts of appeals have stepped in to preserve and limit
the holding of <u>Bounds</u>. The courts of appeals have insisted that
<u>Bounds</u> requires either libraries or legal assistance, but not both.
For example, in <u>Cepulonis v. Fair</u>, the First Circuit vacated a district
court order requiring prison officials to obtain the services of upper-
class law students to assist prisoners.[14] The Eleventh Circuit in
<u>Hooks v. Wainwright</u> similarly interpreted <u>Bounds</u> to prevent a district
court from ordering the state of Florida to provide legal assistance
to prisoners in addition to law libraries,[15] as did the Ninth Circuit
in <u>Lindquist v. Idaho State Board of Corrections</u>.[16] As a result
of these decisions, it is clear that many correctional institutions, if
they so choose, can provide only law libraries for their inmates.

B. Growth in Prison Populations and litigation

The inadequacy of prisoners' being dependent on law libraries
for legal information is exacerbated by the growth in prison populations. In 1984, 445,381 criminal offenders were incarcerated in correctional institutions,[17] nearly a 48 percent increase over prison
populations in 1979.[18] This increase in prison populations is primarily due to stiffer sentencing policies in recent years,[19] and the
increase probably will continue into the twenty-first century.[20]
As a result, prison law libraries must be available to serve the needs
of an ever-growing number of people who, at some point, may need
to consider initiating a legal action in order to vindicate their constitutional rights.

Litigation by prisoners also has increased significantly in the
past two decades. In 1970, 15,997 prisoner petitions were filed in
United States district courts;[21] by 1985, that figure had climbed
to 33,468.[22] The most significant increases have occurred in civil
rights suits against correctional officials by state prisoners[23] using
42 U.S.C. 1983.[24] These actions increased from 2,030 in 1970[25]
to 18,491 in 1985,[26] when they constituted nearly 7 percent of all
civil filings in United States district courts.[27] Most of these cases
are brought by pro se litigants.[28] The typical prisoner initiating
a court action lacks formal training in the law, has little education,
and is indigent.[29] Not surprisingly, most prisoners' actions are
dismissed without a hearing in the early stages of the judicial process.[30]

The increasing volume of litigation by prisoners has led to
criticisms that the federal courts are overburdened by such cases.[31]
As Supreme Court Justice Harry Blackmun has noted, "Prisoners,
especially those who proceed <u>pro se</u>, are popular candidates for the
group likely to present consistently frivolous claims."[32] There are
indications that federal courts have become less active in upholding
prisoners' rights by intervening into correctional institutions.[33]

Whether or not most prisoners' petitions should be considered by the federal courts, many inmates must file all types of grievances in the form of legal actions because correctional institutions often lack effective grievance procedures and other alternative dispute resolution mechanisms.[34]   Thus, prison law libraries are essential for enabling prisoners to assert all types of complaints and legal claims.

In spite of the large number of prisoners' cases that are terminated, the Supreme Court specifically has recognized the potential for prisoners to raise important legal issues by using prison law libraries.   The Court's opinion in Bounds stated that "this Court's experience indicates that pro se petitioners are capable of using lawbooks to file cases raising claims that are serious and legitimate even if ultimately unsuccessful."[35]   This statement emphasizes the Court's expectation that law libraries will enable prisoners to prepare effective legal claims.   The heavy reliance upon prison law libraries by the federal courts and by prisoners underscores the need for the legal community to make these library resources as effective as possible in order to uphold constitutional protections within correctional institutions.

C.   The State of Prison Law Libraries

It is relatively easy for someone with legal training, upon entering a prison law library, to discover deficiencies that hamper effective usage of legal materials by prisoners.[36]   It is much more difficult to define or systematically measure effectiveness in prison law libraries.[37]   Two nationwide surveys help illustrate the deficiencies in prison law libraries that law student teaching programs could help ameliorate.

A study in 1973 found grave deficiencies in prison library collections, including the fact that 54 percent of state and 20 percent of federal prisons did not even have legal dictionaries in their libraries.[38]   Such deficiencies place the inmate in an extremely difficult position when seeking access to and understanding of relevant legal concepts.   If prisoners themselves cannot find necessary legal information, their only option is to ask someone for assistance. However, because nearly 89 percent of prison law libraries were staffed by persons without training in library science or law,[39] personnel resources obviously were not geared toward maximizing the effectiveness of law libraries for prisoners.   The 1973 survey indicated a need for persons trained in law to provide assistance in the use of prison law libraries.

In 1981, a national study revealed that 42 of 103 prisons provided no legal assistance for prisoners in preparing habeas corpus petitions and civil rights complaints.[40]   Twenty-one other prisons provided only inmate clerks to give legal assistance to prisoners.[41] Thus, prisoners in many institutions must rely on law library materials to gain access to the courts.[42] In addition, a majority of prisons had no one with formal legal training to answer prisoners' questions about research and use of the library. Only twenty-two of the prisons had librarians with training in library science; forty-six had no law librarian at all.[43]

Because few correctional institutions have trained personnel for instructing prisoners on how to undertake legal research, law students can fill this void by teaching classes on proper use of legal materials.

III. THE TEACHING PROGRAM

A. The Basic Concept

Upper-class law students in all law schools have received instruction and experience in legal research and writing through required first-year courses. Although law students may lack confidence in their legal research skills, they possess extensive systematized knowledge about legal research materials when compared to prisoners.

In the program at the University of Washington, it was evident that the prisoners needed basic information about how to undertake legal research. Those prisoners experienced at using the law library regularly conducted legal research by thumbing through volumes of Federal Supplement and Federal Reporter 2d looking for cases involving prisons. Law student instructors made a significant contribution to the prisoners' education simply by explaining the use of digests and creating exercises that required inmates to look for various cases and legal concepts within the digests. In addition, even the few experienced "jailhouse lawyers"[44] who had successfully litigated cases were not familiar with the use of Shepard's Citations. Again, simple explanations and exercises served immediately to improve the quality of the prisoners' research.

The classes conducted by law students had the additional benefit of providing instruction for the law librarian, a part-time employee with a bachelor's degree in education, who had been attempting unsuccessfully to learn the basics of legal research through "trial and error" self-education. Thus, the prison law librarian was able to use the information from the classes to better assist the prisoners in effectively using the library's resources.

These examples illustrate how simple the prison library teaching programs can be. The prisoners' need for information about legal research can be so basic that law students can make a contribution just by explaining how to use case reporters, digests, and other legal materials.

The extent and complexity of teaching programs can depend upon the interest and commitment of law students, law schools, law librarians, prisoners, and correctional officials. The success of any program is obviously dependent upon cooperation among all of these different groups. If interest and commitment are sufficiently high, then there are possibilities for more advanced legal research courses. For example, in the Washington program, a member of the law school's moot court team taught a class in legal writing for prisoners who made the commitment to attend class every week and complete written assignments. The advanced class assisted prisoners in identifying legal issues, refining the presentation of arguments, and improving overall writing skills.

The library research classes were held in a less formal atmosphere. Classes met weekly and were open to all interested prisoners. Some prisoners attended regularly, but the lectures and exercises were kept simple enough to include those prisoners who attended only occasionally.

The "law students as teachers" concept can be used to create programs to fit various needs within correctional institutions. The teaching concept can be expanded to include prisoners in other educational activities related to law. For example, the Washington program included a mock civil trial inside the prison using prisoners as jurors and law students as attorneys. This exercise was a project for the law students' trial advocacy class and served as the culmination of the year's education programs. The trial served as a useful vehicle for generating mutually enlightening discussion between law students and prisoners concerning courts and law.

B. Relevant Factors for Program Development

In order to develop a teaching program, there must be sufficient interest among the law students who will participate. The necessary commitment could come either through formal sponsorship as part of the law school's credited programs or, as at the University of Washington, through the voluntary efforts of an extracurricular student organization.

Due to the inherent limitations of traditional classroom instruction, law schools have developed innovative clinical programs to enable students to master the practicing attorney's essential knowledge and skills.[45] These clinical programs typically place students in an advocate's role for actual legal cases under the supervision of faculty attorneys. A few law school clinical programs involve the representation of prisoners.[46] Law schools, with the cooperation of correctional institutions, could create similar learning experiences outside the classroom by awarding academic credit or otherwise officially sanctioning teaching programs at prison law libraries. While such programs would require faculty supervision, training sessions for the student-

instructors, and research papers concerning the teaching experience
within the correctional setting, the involvement of law school resources
would create the potential for offering prisoners a variety of legal
research and writing classes. Classes could be designed to fit the
diverse levels of knowledge and skills evident within any prison population.

Because legal assistance, rather than the use of law libraries,
is essential for securing meaningful access to the courts, one might
consider that law students' efforts would be better spent in providing
legal services for prisoners rather than in teaching legal research.
However, such legal assistance programs, unlike teaching programs,
require sponsorship and supervision from law schools or practicing
attorneys. Teaching programs can be implemented by law student
volunteers in cooperation with correctional institutions.

The Washington program officially had a faculty advisor and was
sanctioned as a student organization by the law school. However,
in effect, the program was entirely student-initiated and student-run.
The information learned in first-year classes, with some preparation
for the conditions within the prison environment,[47] was enough for
students to be able to convey simple, valuable information about legal
research. Although training for law student-instructors concerning
both legal research and teaching techniques would be desirable, the
need for legal assistance within prisons can be so glaring that valuable classes can be taught without extensive training.

Because there is flexibility in creating teaching programs, other
interested individuals, such as law librarians, could begin a program.
Law librarians initially could recruit law student volunteers and make
arrangements with correctional officials. Law librarians also would
serve an important role as advisory resources for law student-instructors when prisoners raise questions about legal research issues that
require the students to seek professional assistance. In addition,
student-instructors may need advice on how to present legal research
concepts and information. Law librarians, whether affiliated with
law schools or not, can be important for initiating, supervising, or
advising legal research teaching programs.

The cooperation of correctional officials is essential for any
program. Some prison officials may be reluctant to permit any teaching programs within their institutions for fear that law library classes
will only serve to generate additional legal actions against them.
However, with the requirements of Bounds, the increasing professionalization of correctional administrators,[48] and the prevalence of
education programs for prisoners,[49] many administrators would
welcome teaching programs as beneficial to the institution and prisoners.

The interest, cooperation, and participation of prisoners is also
necessary. In the Washington program, the Black Prisoners Caucus
served as the sponsor of the teaching program. By agreement between

the Caucus and the law students, the teaching program, unlike other prisoner organization-sponsored activities, was completely open and had participation by a broad cross-section of the prison population. The Caucus disseminated information about the program throughout the prison and helped to plan activities such as the mock civil trial and the legal writing class. Acceptance and cooperation from the prisoners enables the program to tailor classes to meet the legal research needs and interests within the prison.

C. Potential Problems

The sponsorship of teaching programs can create problems. If the program is initiated by the correctional institution without participation by prisoners, then the law students may lack legitimacy and, in the eyes of the prisoners, may be associated with the prison administration. To promote participation and acceptance by the prison population, attempts should be made to include prisoners in the planning and sponsorship of a teaching program.

In any prison program, law students must become aware of the social structure and interactions within the prison environment in order to avoid manipulation and cooptation by the prisoners.[50] Law students must take particular care to maintain their proper role as instructors because prisoners may seek to gain legal advice and advocacy assistance from them. The potential seriousness of this problem dictates that every program hold preliminary orientation sessions to discuss the prison environment with someone experienced in dealing with prisoners.

Any education program for prisoners faces certain fundamental and insurmountable difficulties. Two noteworthy problems are the deficient educational backgrounds of most prisoners and the lack of needed materials.[51] The high illiteracy rate and lack of basic academic skills will prevent many inmates from benefitting from a teaching program.[52] Thus, law student-instructors must seek to make lectures and exercises as open and flexible as possible. The prisoners who participated in the Washington program ranged from functional illiterates to college graduates. It was extremely difficult to keep the attention of all prisoners in a long lecture, so instructors learned to be innovative in creating legal research exercises aimed at differing levels of ability.

These problems are shared by all education programs within correctional institutions. Yet, there are dozens of education programs operating successfully at prisons throughout the country.[53] Directories of groups and institutions offering such programs [54] can provide informational resources for people interested in establishing prison library teaching programs. Such organizations as the Correctional Education Association may offer expertise or even participation in designing law programs that can avoid certain problems and pitfalls.

IV. BENEFICIAL EFFECTS

Teaching programs in prison law libraries potentially can benefit all participants as well as the court system and the legal profession. Teaching programs clearly are not a panacea for the problems related to protecting prisoners' constitutional rights, however. The extent to which prisoners benefit depends upon the effectiveness of the individual program. The key point is not that one should expect to solve major problems within the legal system, but that teaching programs provide those involved an opportunity to experience concrete positive effects while working toward the protection of prisoners' rights.

Working in prisons can enhance law students' legal education. Students are placed in close and regular contact with a segment of society intimately affected by the legal system. Students in the Washington program gained practical knowledge and useful insights concerning litigation from discussions with experienced jailhouse lawyers who participated in classes.[55]

In addition to first-hand knowledge about and awareness of the criminal justice system, students can solidify and refine their own understanding of legal research. Studies have shown that many attorneys lack confidence and competence in conducting legal research. [56] Students who teach legal research are forced to prepare presentations, develop legal research exercises, and seek advice from law librarians, and thus can strengthen their grasp of research techniques.

Many law libraries provide legal reference assistance to prisoners,[57] and inmates' requests are often highly problematic because prisoners lack knowledge about the law. According to one law librarian:

> We have received inmate requests that contained so little information that we could not provide reference assistance without first soliciting more information from the patron. Other requests have presented us with such a complex snarl of facts and issues that we had difficulty knowing where to begin. Some requests have been veiled pleas for legal advice.[58]

Involvement in a prison teaching program permits law librarians to contribute to both prisoners' and law students' understanding of legal research. This, in turn, can benefit law librarians because these groups are able to improve the quality and specificity of their requests for research assistance.

Prisoners, of course, will benefit by better understanding legal research, which will enhance their right of meaningful access to the courts and better protect their other constitutional rights if they need to file actions in court. Although the idea of rehabilitating prisoners is fraught with controversy,[59] some have argued that active participation in legal matters enables prisoners to avoid destructive feelings of bitterness and hopelessness.[60] In any case, contact with an educational program may have additional personal benefits for individual prisoners.

Providing legal assistance to prisoners tends to reduce litigation because counselors trained in law can discourage frivolous or non-meritorious legal actions.[61] Although pro se litigants do not have the expertise of an attorney, improved legal research and education can help prisoners determine whether they have valid legal claims before they try to file suits that will be dismissed instantly. Prisoners with legal assistance also will be more effective in presenting legitimate legal issues. This will allow the federal courts to pay more attention to the clearly stated, valid legal claims from prisoners.

Lawyers have a professional responsibility to assist in making legal counsel available to individuals in need of assistance.[62] This responsibility traditionally has been fulfilled through pro bono work, in which the profession encourages every attorney to participate.[63] In this era of declining public funding for legal aid programs, the American Bar Association has advocated that all members of the profession participate in pro bono programs. According to the president of the ABA, "Our profession will not have met its obligation fully until every lawyer is participating in some way in these (pro bono program) efforts."[64] This professional ethic for public service potentially can be imbued in future lawyers through their participation as law students in programs for indigent citizens. A prison library teaching program is one type of experience that will expose law students to public service activities. Thus, law students can be initiated and acclimated into this important value of their intended profession, and the legal profession as a whole benefits.

Lawyers also heavily influence legislative branches of government,[65] which enact sentencing laws and make policy decisions concerning the criminal justice system. Exposing future lawyers to correctional institutions may help develop more informed policies regarding prisoners' rights. A number of programs have been designed to expose lawyers and legislators to the criminal justice system in order to foster public policies based upon direct knowledge and experience. [66] The goals of these programs can be accomplished through prison teaching programs involving law students who will become future leaders.

V. CONCLUSION

For many prisoners, the right of meaningful access to the courts enunciated by the Supreme Court in Bounds is dependent solely upon effective use of prison law libraries. The deficiencies of these libraries create an opportunity for members of the legal community to initiate efforts to increase the adequacy of legal resources available to prisoners. By developing programs that use law students as teachers in prison libraries, various components of the legal system can benefit while working to ensure constitutional protections for prisoners. Although the benefits will be limited in extent, the importance of the goals involved should outweigh any uncertainty about predicted results. It is not often that mutually beneficial relationships can be identified in the service of protecting constitutional rights and enhancing the integrity of the judicial system. Thus, prison library teaching programs present an excellent opportunity for innovative efforts aimed at influencing society in a positive way.

References

1. Bounds v. Smith, 430 U.S. 817 (1977).
2. Id. at 828.
3. See J. Jacobs, New Perspectives On Prisons and Imprisonment 33-60 (1983) (on the impacts of the prisoners' rights movement).
4. See, e.g., Hooks v. Wainwright, 775 F.2d 1433, 1434 (11th Cir. 1985).
5. See, e.g., Flores, "Bounds and Reality: Lawbooks Alone Do Not a Lawyer Make," 77 Law Libr. J. 275, 287 (1984-85); Turner, When Prisoners Sue: A Study of Prisoner Section 1983 Suits in the Federal Courts," 92 Harv. L. Rev. 610, 655-56 (1979).
6. Now the Subcommittee on Institutional Services of the Contemporary Social Problems Special Interest Section.
7. Reeves, "The Evolving Law of Prison Law Libraries," 3 New Eng. J. On Prison L. 131, 149, 160 (1976); Poe, "A Spark of Hope for Prisoners," 66 Law Libr. J. 59 (1973); Werner, "The Present Legal Status and Conditions of Prison Law Libraries," 66 Law Libr. J. 259, 267 (1973).
8. See Flores, supra note 5, at 285-86.
9. As a student at the University of Washington School of Law, I was a legal research instructor inside a maximum-security state prison. The examples used in this article are drawn from my experiences as a law student teaching in a prison law library.
10. Flores, supra note 5, at 286.
11. See, e.g., Lindquist v. Idaho State Board of Corrections, 776 F. 2d 851, 854-55 (9th Cir. 1985).
12. See Ryan, "Access to the Courts: Prisoners' Right to a Law Library," 26 How. L. J. 91 (1983).
13. 430 U.S. at 828.
14. Cepulonis v. Fair, 732 F.2d 1, 6 (1st Cir. 1984).
15. 775 F.2d at 1434-35.
16. Lindquist, 776 F. 2d at 854-55.
17. "Probation and Parole, 1984." Bureau of Justice. SD Statistics Bulletin, Feb. 1986 at 1, Table 1.
18. Id.
19. G. Cole, The American System of Criminal Justice 513-14 (4th ed. 1986).
20. See Rich & Barnett, "Model-Based U.S. Prison Population Projections," 45 Pub. Admin. Rev. 780, 780-81 (1985).

21. Bureau of Justice Statistics, U.S. Dep't of Justice, <u>Sourcebook Of Criminal Justice Statistics--1984</u> at 582-83, table 5.17 (1985).

22. <u>1985 Ann. Rep. Director Admin. Off. U.S. Cts.</u> 149, table 24 (bound with <u>Reports of the Proceedings Of the Judicial Conference Of the United States Held in Washington, D.C. March 6 and 7, 1985 and September 17 and 18, 1985)</u> [hereinafter <u>Ann. Rep.</u>].

23. The Supreme Court, through the decision in <u>Cooper v. Pate</u>, enabled prisoners to file civil rights suits against state officials. 378 U.S. 546 (1964).

24. Every person who, under color of any statute, ordinance, regulation, custom, or usage, of any State or Territory or the District of Columbia, subjects, or causes to be subjected, any citizen of the United States or other person within the jurisdiction thereof to the deprivation of any rights, privileges, or immunities secured by the Constitution and laws, shall be liable to the party injured in an action at law, suit in equity, or other proper proceeding for redress. 42 U.S.C. 1983 (1982).

25. <u>Bureau of Justice Statistics</u>, <u>supra</u> note 21, at table 5.17.

26. <u>Ann. Rep.</u>, <u>supra</u> note 22, at 149, table 24.

27. The 18,491 civil rights suits by state prisoners constituted 6.75 percent of the 273,670 total filings in 1985. <u>See id.</u> at 137, table 18 & 149, table 24.

28. In a study of prisoners' civil rights suits, the two districts with the lowest percentage of pro se actions by prisoners--the District of Massachusetts and the District of Vermont--had 85 and 78.4 percent pro se actions respectively. <u>See</u> Turner, <u>supra</u> note 5, at 617.

29. <u>See</u> Zeigler & Hermann, "The Invisible Litigant: An Inside View of Pro Se Actions in the Federal Courts," 47 <u>N.Y.U.L. Rev.</u> 159, 159 (1972).

30. Turner, <u>supra</u> note 5, at 617-18.

31. See Blackmun, "Section 1983 and Federal Protection of Individual Rights--Will the Statute Remain Alive or Fade Away?," 60 <u>N.Y.U.L. Rev.</u> 1, 2, 21 (1985).

32. <u>Id.</u> at 21.

33. See Robbins, "The Cry of <u>Wolfish</u> in the Federal Courts: The Future of Federal Judicial Intervention in Prison Administration", 71 <u>J. Crim. L. & Criminology</u> 211, 225 (1980); Note, "Eighth Amendment--A Significant Limit on Federal Court Activism in Ameliorating State Prison Conditions," 72 <u>J. Crim. L. & Criminology</u> 1345, 1373 (1981).

34. See Nat'l Inst. Corrections, U.S. Dep't of Justice, <u>Alternative Dispute Resolution Mechanisms for Prisoner Grievances</u> 5-10 (1984) (submitted by Silbert, Feeley, and Associates).

35. 430 U.S. at 826-27.

36. For example, law student-instructors in the Washington program discovered that the part-time librarian had placed all volumes of <u>Shepard's Citations</u> in a storage box because no one knew how to use them.

37. Flores, <u>supra</u> note 5, at 279.

38. Werner, <u>supra</u> note 7, at 266, table 11.

39. Id. at 266.

40. Ducey, Survey of Prisoner Access to the Courts: Local Ex-
     perimentation a' Bounds," 9 New Eng. J. on Crim. & Civ. Con-
     finement 47, 105-18 (1983).

41. Id.

42. Interestingly, nine prisons in the study indicated that they
     provide neither a law library nor legal assistance to prisoners.
     Id.

43. Id.

44. "Jailhouse lawyers" are prisoner-litigators who possess some
     legal knowledge and skills, and who sometimes provide legal as-
     sistance to other inmates.

45. See Grossman, "Clinical Legal Education: History and Diag-
     nosis," 26 J. Legal Educ. 162 (1974).

46. See, e.g., Note, "A Federal Litigation Program: For Students,
     Inmates and the Legal Profession," 4 Nova L. J. 377, 395-400
     (1980) (describing a program at Nova University).

47. In the Washington program, prison officials included the law
     students in an orientation session for all volunteers working
     within the prison. An administrator discussed the potential
     problems in working with inmates.

48. See J. Jacobs, supra note 3, at 47, 54-55, 57.

49. See Thomas, "Role of the Community College in Continuing Ed-
     ucation for the Correctional Inmate," 45 Fed. Probation, Dec.
     1981, at 41.

50. See Sykes, "The Society of Captives: The Defects of Total
     Power," in G. Cole, Criminal Justice: Law and Politics 321-35
     (4th ed. 1984).

51. Brodt & Hewitt, "Teaching 'Cons' about Crime and Justice:
     Experience with Non-Traditional Students in a Non-Traditional
     Setting," 35 J. Correctional Educ. 15, 16 (1984).

52. T. Clear & G. Cole, American Corrections 327-28 (1986).

53. See, e.g., U.S. Dep't of Educ.; Education in Correctional
     Settings (1985) (directory and descriptions of education programs
     for prisoners).

54. Id.

55. Several jailhouse lawyers attended legal research and writing
     classes because they enjoyed discussing legal issues with law
     students. Their participation in the classes also encouraged
     them to provide information to other inmates.

56. See Flores, supra note 5, at 280.

57. Poe, supra note 7, at 61.

58. St. Sauver-Reinecke, "Assisting Prisoners: Reference Guide-
     lines at Kratter Law Library, University of San Diego," 75
     Law Libr. J. 529, 529 (1982).

59. T. Clear & G. Cole, supra note 52, at 89-92.

60. According to one commentator, "The ability to initiate a lawsuit
     and realize one's civil rights reduces vulnerability and power-
     lessness. The ability to participate actively in a project which
     helps develop competence, usefulness, and legitimate political
     power removes much of the bitterness and hostility which

incarceration has come to develop." G. Alpert, Legal Rights of Prisoners 47 (1978).

61. See Turner, supra note 5, at 636; Flores, supra note 5, at 287.
62. Model Code of Professional Responsibility Canon 2 (1980).
63. Id. EC 2-25.

   Historically, the need for legal services of those unable to pay reasonable fees has been met in part by lawyers who donated their services or accepted court appointments on behalf of such individuals. The basic responsibility for providing legal services for those unable to pay ultimately rests upon the individual lawyer, and personal involvement in the problems of the disadvantaged can be one of the most rewarding experiences in the life of a lawyer. Every lawyer, regardless of professional prominence or professional workload, should find time to participate in serving the disadvantaged. The rendition of free legal services...continues to be an obligation of each lawyer.   Id.

64. Falsgraf, "President's Page: Access to Justice in 1986," 72 A. B. A. J., Feb. 1986, at 8.
65. For example, 251 of the 535 members of the 99th Congress were lawyers. R. Davidson & W. Oleszek, Congress and Its Members 110 (2d ed. 1985).
66. See Fink, "Jailed for 30 Hours, Lawmakers Get Insight on Prison Life," Hartford Courant, Feb. 2, 1986, at B1.

IMAGES OF LIBRARIES
IN SCIENCE FICTION*

Agnes M. Griffen

The study of science fiction has been described as one method of
futures research. The genre of speculative fiction can be used as
a tool to develop scenarios of libraries in the future. Alvin Toffler
suggests that "...science fiction throws open the whole of civilization
and its premises to constructive criticism.... Science fiction tries
out new epistemologies, new notions of causality, nonlinear time,
language and communication, and, simply by encouraging a new time-
bias (a greater future-consciousness), it leads to a kind of antici-
patory adaptability by the culture."[1]

In a review of this "literature of the future," one can identify
a typology of libraries as envisioned under various scenarios of the
future. Borrowing loosely from futures research, the cultures can
be described and the assumptions on which they are built can be
examined. Through the stories and the characters the reader may
glimpse users of libraries as well as varying formats in which information is conveyed. Certain conclusions can be made about what these
images might tell us about the yet-to-be-imagined or already-being-
invented libraries of the year 2000 and beyond.

Willis Harman, in An Incomplete Guide to the Future,[2] says
the function of futures research is to make our assumptions explicit.
Our assumptions can be about:

• what is possible--all the alternatives, as in the thousands
of scenarios that form the plots of science fiction novels;

• what is probable--the most likely alternatives, given criteria
and constraints; and

*Reprinted by permission of the author and the publisher from Library
Journal 112:14 (September 1, 1987) 137-142; copyright © 1987 by
Reed Publishing, USA, Div. of Reed Holdings, Inc.
This is based on a paper presented at a preconference on long-
range planning, Michigan Library Association, Flint, October 7, 1986.

• what is desirable--the alternative choice or combination of alternatives that we prefer because it fits our own value system, or that of the community with which we are designing a future.

Libraries of the Future

There are four types of libraries that can be found through an examination of the images, characters, plots, and perspectives of science fiction writing: 1) the completely computerized or roboticized library; 2) the rehumanized library; 3) the post-cataclysmic, reinvented library; and 4) the post-computer, mental high-tech library.

For the first type, we will go to such "computer-ruled worlds' as those inhabited by Harry Harrison's high-tech criminal-turned-interplanetary police detective in The Stainless Steel Rat for President,[3] and we will look in on one of the voyages of Ijon Tichy, as portrayed in Stanlislaw Lem's satirical The Star Diaries.[4] Ursula LeGuin's Always Coming Home is an excellent example of the second type, the rehumanized library, in a scenario where computers have led to a "radical decentralization [of civilization], leading to a complementary relationship between city and country and the development of a lifestyle which is oriented fundamentally toward cultural enrichment."[5]

The last two types embody variations on dystopia and utopia. Two older classics will be examined to ascertain the features of the dystopian library, which must be reinvented after a world cataclysm has brought humankind back to the Stone Age: George R. Stewart's Earth Abides,[6] originally published in 1949, and A Canticle for Leibowitz[7] (1959) by Walter M. Miller Jr. Finally, we will find the utopian, post-computer, mental high-tech library in Robert Silverberg's 1981 masterpiece of technical imagination, Majipoor Chronicles. [8]

The Roboticized Library

This first scenario is based on what Herman Kahn calls the "Basic Long Term-Multifold Trend." It assumes "the worldwide spread of a more or less [empirical, sensate, humanistic, utilitarian culture], the institutionalization of scientific and technological innovation, the expectation of continuous economic growth ... [with] an increasing capability for mass destruction [and] increasing tempo of change."[9]

Although the human race may have had to become more versatile in their use of languages and awareness of interspecies cultural differences, the information seekers and library users found in books of this type are not basically any different from those in the 20th Century. Often they have many more opportunities in their wired environments to get information at will, either at the flick of a wrist or with a muttered command to the surrounding, ubiquitous, interactive artificial intelligence which molds itself to the user's needs and skills. Memory storage devices used include cubes, capsules, cassettes, microfiche, and disks.

Anthropomorphized robots are sometimes used as terminals for information retrieval or for such "expert systems" tasks as solving crimes, as in Isaac Asimov's The Robots of Dawn.[10] In the third adventure of New York detective Elijah Baley, he is on his way to the planet Aurora to solve a case of roboticide. He uses the "useless time crossing space" to research the history, political science, and geography of Aurora by viewing "book-films" available in the spaceship's library.

In some of these novels, paper books still exist, either for archival or nostalgic reasons, or for the sake of novelty. Though the computer may rule their imagined worlds, some sf writers, however, actually prefer the book format (perhaps they are bibliophiles because they write books).

That great Polish comic novelist Stanislaw Lem pictures his hero Ijon Tichy in his rocket ship on his way to planet Ardeluria, "doing some serious boning up" on books stored on "bookshelves sagging beneath the weight of the loftiest fruits of the human spirit." In his pursuit of knowledge, the hero has found a clever way "to avoid the mistake of reading books [he] might already have leafed through," tossing each of the six thousand tomes he reads "out the hatch of the rocket," intending to collect them on the return trip.

The User Is King

What conclusions can be drawn about libraries in the more immediate future from these tales of spacefarers whiling away their time in space cabins filled with book-films, universities-on-disks, or the old book itself in its familiar form? Librarians are noticeable in their absence. The end user is in control.

The presence of a wide variety of media presents the muddled choices one faces in that online "paperless society" promised by Wilf Lancaster, which at least at this stage seems to generate even more paper at our workstations than ever accumulated on our desks. Ed Mignon concludes "that the most immediate impact of the new technology is likely to be 'the continuing diversification of the information environment rather than any radical changes in the design of primary library services.'"[11]

We can see in these fictional images the reflections of today's most computerized, multimedia libraries, with the addition of media even newer than the software, CDs, and CD-ROM of which some libraries are now so proud. Perhaps information will be captured in cubes or capsules, or in other formats of which we have not yet dreamed. Certainly there will be many more points of access to the library. Users will call up the master database and library on terminals from home or while traveling, or may be online from habitats in nearer space, locating specific items that could still be borrowed from some source in book form or printed out in hardcopy on demand, which is the more likely form of book that will be read in the year 2000. But that will depend to a great extent on the costs as well as the economics both of publishing and libraries.

One can only hope that if the human race can afford space colonization, unlimited and free access to information in many formats will be provided for all users. Maybe the technologies will bring the cost of information down to affordable levels for all public libraries. It may be up to library leaders to ensure this long-term result.

The Rehumanized Library

In this scenario the unobtrusive computer does not control the world as much as it makes possible "a kind of order and peace under which human freedom and dignity can develop to its full potential" and in which people can concentrate on arts and crafts or whatever is important to them. In LeGuin's Always Coming Home, a rural, agrarian, decentralized, post-industrial society is carried to an almost utopian extreme, but it is hardly a utopia. People still make war and kill each other, although on a more manageable tribal level.

In one small valley (located somewhere north of what used to be San Francisco) is the town of Sinshan, home of Stone Telling, a young girl of the Kesh people. Her story is beautifully told, set against a background sketched in as an "almost ethereal technology of the City, on the one hand, which had no use for heavy machinery, even their spaceships and stations being mere nerve and gossamer, and on the other hand ... the very loose, light, soft network of the human cultures ... in their small scale, great number, and endless diversity."

In this "global village," high-tech/high-touch scenario, the significant institutions include the world-wide computer network with its local exchange and terminals, located in the village "heyimas" or multipurpose community centers where all communal activities take place. "Computer terminals, each linked to nearby ground or satellite cities and hence to the entire vast network [operated by the City of Mind], were located in human communities worldwide. Any settled group of 50 or more people qualified for an exchange, which was installed at the request of the human community by the City robots, and maintained by both robot and human inspection and repair."

The image of the City of Mind is reminiscent of the vision of the ultimate "wired nation." This network of intercommunicating centers was "occupied by independent, self-contained, self-regulating communities of cybernetic devices or beings ... [whose] existence consisted essentially in information." It is not clear what role humans play other than to provide input on current events, as when Stone Telling returns from her exile in another town, she reports in to Wakwaha Exchange on what she has learned in her travels. Since the City of Mind runs so well, one assumes no humans are involved in its governance!

"Most messages and notices coming into the Wakwaha Exchange were held in short-term memory for 24 hours and then self-effaced," but some reports were "printed out on paper for circulation and perhaps for preservation in the Archives." LeGuin's thesis seems to be that when all basic information is in the computer and freely available to all, you can afford a very different approach to what you keep and don't keep in a library or archives, and much greater value is placed on oral transmission and preservation.

Librarians Freed from Paperwork

Librarians are described as "the more or less professional tellers of tales in prose and verse," while the library/archives/museum is in the care of a keeper, a kind of library assistant "who looked after things and put them away and took them out, all the things of the heyimas for the dances and the singing and teaching and giving." And what an assortment of media is found here! "...the costumes for the Summer dancers, the stones, the paintings on paper, cloth, and wood, the ranges of feathers, the caps, the musical instruments ... the writings, the books, the sweet and bitter herbs, the dried flowers...." Is it any wonder that such a collection must be weeded relentlessly, especially without a public catalog in sight?

A knowledgeable public librarian. Annette Klause, who advises readers on science fiction, points out that in this "archeology of the future, the librarian [has become] an important caretaker of the written and oral tradition. This person also performs the material for an audience, is instrumental in passing the heritage on, and can also contribute to its evolution as part of folklore."[12]

LeGuin has discovered what librarians have felt instinctively may be the ultimate role of the computer in libraries, to make library service like this possible. It is possible that someday librarians will be freed by cybernets from the responsibility of collecting, organizing, managing, and disseminating that vast amount of routine, daily information which threatens to overwhelm us all. Free to play a much more active role in the life of the community, to be scholar, poet, or storyteller, to concentrate on communicating with people, to pay attention to our living cultural heritage.

What kind of libraries are foreshadowed in LeGuin's images?

In this future, a computerized "learning web" links people and resources much as in Ivan Illich's concept of the "deschooled society,"
[13] with bibliographic and encyclopedia databases all accessible from
home, workplace, or library information center.

There would be more smaller, more selectively stocked community and neighborhood libraries that would, of course, be online to the
larger library centers, and anything could be printed out on demand.
The media would be almost as varied as the collection in the heyimas,
and as for collection management, the logical extension of the Baltimore County approach--keep it moving or toss it out--would be most
appropriate. There would be books and storytimes and creative activities of all sorts, and the librarian's and keeper's roles might be
similar to those in that future culture of the Kesh.

These libraries would be designed to bring nature indoors, with
lots of wood and plants and maybe a pool or running water in the
entry-way. There might be a small historical museum, or a theater
in the round doubling as a meeting room, and every part of the building, except for maybe a quiet room for study, would be in constant
use by community groups. Perhaps this particular scenario is already
beginning to unfold in some libraries. The year 2000, after all, is
only 13 years away.

The Reinvented Library

Those who read science fiction for escape may not be particularly fond of the many dystopias which appear with great regularity.
In the typical plot, male and female neo-savages ravage the country-
side along with fierce and horrible mutants, and the hero/heroine is
the only hope of civilization, etc. Nevertheless, some of the greatest
classics in speculative fiction are dystopias.

Stewart's Earth Abides and Miller's A Canticle for Leibowitz
are set in western North America, some centuries after the Great
Cataclysm. Both books focus on how humans would cope with the
aftermath of a worldwide catastrophe, whether it comes in thermonu-
clear or biogenetic form. The basic premise, of course, is that such
a disaster is inevitable and cyclical, given mankind's suicidal nature
and self-defeating proclivities. A major theme is the fragility of
human culture and civilization, which always hangs by a thread and
invariably depends for its future on the actions of one individual.

Earth Abides still has many messages for librarians today.
Since the biogenetic disaster that wipes out over one-third of the
human race in this book happens in the near future (it was published
in 1949), one gets an eerie feeling reading it now, because with the
passage of time it has become a contemporary novel set in the present
time. Concluding around the year 2000, it covers about 50 years in
the life of protagonist Isherwood Williams, who thus could be our
contemporary or older brother.

Ish escapes the virus through a coincidental and immunizing snake bite. He discovers through a trip to his parental home, with a swing out to observe the people jumping off the Golden Gate Bridge, that the remaining survivors are in shock or already insane. He determines that if he is to survive, he must have a purpose in living. He writes down the qualification behind his decision on a piece of paper: "Have will to live. Want to see what will happen in world without man, and how. Geographer." He realizes that his scientific education as well as his solitary nature have prepared him for life as an observer. He also muses that as a reader, he "had still available an important means of relaxation and escape. At the same time, he was more than a mere reader in that he knew also the means of research through books, and thus possessed a powerful tool for reconstruction."

When Ish finds Em, another survivor and a woman with whom he feels he can make a future, in a poignant scene she moves in with him because he has more books. "It was less trouble to move to the books than to move the books to them." Books and libraries become Ish's great hope as over the years his family grows and his household expands to include a loosely knit tribe of some 14 to 20 remnants of the human race who straggle in to escape solitary existence and create a community. Together they "push back the darkness" by having children to repopulate the world, thus keeping the human race from extinction.

The Lone Reader

It is not so much the survival of the human race that becomes the driving force in Ish's life but the realization that he is the only reader left. With the death of literacy, books and libraries, the whole cultural record and "wisdom by which civilization had been built, and could be rebuilt," would disappear into the darkness forever. Ish teaches the children "to read and write, because reading he felt was the key to everything else and writing was its counterpart."

Realizing that within his little tribe a new society is growing up "with almost no stored-up tradition ... a society that [is] not going to develop its traditions greatly by reading," Ish places all his hopes on his son Joey, the first and only one of his generation to learn to read, as the leader who will bring the tribe into the future and keep the flame of culture alive.

When Joey dies, Ish dismisses school in a gesture acknowledging that he is giving up on literacy. He must accept the fact that civilization will have to reinvent itself in another thousand years when the population again reaches the numbers that will require that complexity of civilization in which literacy and learning, books and libraries can thrive. In the end, Ish dies, aware that while the libraries have survived the fires that later had swept the area, the books may never again be read.

In Earth Abides, all knowledge is in books; the technology at
issue here is the technique of reading, which we call literacy. Culture requires a sense of time and calendar, and knowing how to write
and to read. Without these, civilization reverts to a primitive, super-
stitious stage, to oral literature, myths, and fables. Yet Ish op-
timistically muses: "Perhaps there were too many people, too many
old ways of thinking, too many books ... why should not the philo-
sopher welcome the wiping-out of it all and a new start and men playing the game with fresh rules? There would be, perhaps, more gain
than loss."

The Importance of Preservation

In A Canticle for Leibowitz, only few books and papers, the
"Memorabilia," survive. Deeply pessimistic, this three-part requiem
of the human race regards a world six centuries "After the Flame
Deluge" in which civilization has been bombed back to a new Dark
Age. In "the Great Simplification" that followed, the scientists and
scholars were all killed by the mob "for having helped to make the
earth what it had become."

Literacy is nonexistent and only a few monks of the Order of
St. Leibowitz dedicate their lives to: "preserve human history for
the great-great-great grandchildren of the simpletons who wanted it
destroyed.... Its members were either 'bookleggers' or 'memorizers,'
according to the tasks assigned. The bookleggers smuggled books
to the southwest desert and buried them there in kegs. The memorizers committed to rote memory entire volumes of history, sacred
writings, literature, and science, in case some unfortunate book smug-
gler was caught, tortured, and forced to reveal the location of the
kegs" to the simpleton mobs who wished to destroy all knowledge so
that it might never again cause such devastation to the human race.

"From the vast store of human knowledge, only a few kegs of
original books and a pitiful collection of hand-copied texts, rewritten
from memory, had survived in the possession of the Order by the
time the madness had ended. Now, after six centuries of darkness,
the monks still preserved this Memorabilia, studied it, copied and re-
copied it, and patiently waited.... It mattered not at all to them that
the knowledge they saved was useless.... Still, such knowledge had
a symbolic structure that was peculiar to itself, and at least the
symbol-interplay could be observed. To observe the way a knowledge
system is knit together is to learn at least a minimum knowledge-of-
knowledge, until someday--someday, or some century--an Integrator
would come, and things would be fitted together again."

The scholar or reader may be seen as this "Integrator" who can
fit things together by diciphering the meaning in books. In an age
of information overload and the exponential proliferation of knowledge,
no single librarian or scholar can comprehend in its entirety the
contents of any great central research library today.

The image of the Abbey of St. Leibowitz may be perceived as
the symbol of the cultural record and "the storehouse of ancient
wisdom." In that Citadel of Learning, the monk librarians keep the
light of civilization alive by preserving and conserving what remains
of the cumulative record of the human race, even sending the Memorabilia to the stars with a small colony of survivors when final destruction of the Earth is assured.

It is important to most librarians and certainly to many library
users that somewhere in the state, the regional network, the country,
or the world, the books and other documents that are cultural treas-
ures are kept safe and preserved for posterity. One of the most
hotly debated and controversial functions of libraries still is the final
discarding of a title or the erasure of any record, whether it be
cultural treasure or trivia. Librarians question their own role in
this, asking whether even an archivist or a historian really can know
what is worth preserving.

The Memorabilia can serve as a humbling reminder that the role
of the librarian and archivist is first and foremost to preserve the
human record for those who will come after us. As with the faithful
monks and abbots of the Order, whether we do it in hope or in despair is ultimately irrelevant to the task of keeping the Memorabilia
intact. The flame of literacy must be kept alive no matter how we
feel about the future. The Citadel of Learning has always depended
on the fidelity of librarians and keepers to this mission.

But today one might ask if this mission will continue to be appropriate to a world of fleeting video images, multimedia ephemera,
and databases which change momentarily. The human record itself
is in constant flux and, what's more, is subject to considerable downtime. Who will be keeping that record in permanent form? Who will
make sure that nothing of value is erased, especially minority opinions,
unpopular statistics, and political heresies? In the service of intellectual freedom, will librarians become copyists like the monks of the
Order of St. Leibowitz, endlessly taking recordings or snapshots of
the information flow in order to document and monitor the human
record in its self-renewing software format?

It may be time to consider just how a record that is always in
motion can be preserved. No one, not even in the emerging field of
information management, has tackled that yet. Or should that task
be considered not doable, making more appropriate the attitude of the
people of Kesh toward the collection of media in the heyimas? Should
one assume that everything of importance to people will be kept and
not worry about that part of the record which may never be preserved, even in the computer?

The Post-computer Library

The fourth scenario may not be at all probable for at least

another 500 to 1000 years. Nevertheless, it is included here in the belief that there are many things we have not yet dreamed of, and in the hope that a glimpse of such technologies may stimulate librarians to think more creatively about future formats and media for information storage and transfer.

In Robert Silverberg's Majipoor Chronicles the scenario assumes the transmission of knowledge through a recording technology that enables the library user to experience directly the experiences of others, the ultimate audiovisual encounter, if you will. He projects a future in which the technological flowering and fusion of electronics will make the mystical experience of wholeness available to all. This world presupposes an evolution of transformation of human consciousness as anticipated in all the traditions of mysticism and direct knowing. (An excellent description of this may be found in Marilyn Ferguson's The Aquarian Conspiracy.[14])

In the second volume, Majipoor Chronicles, young records clerk Hissune diverts himself from his boring tasks by forging a pass to get into the Register of Souls, where millions of people have left memory-readings. Every citizen "is allowed every ten years, beginning at the age of 20, to contribute to these vaults," which contain 8000-9000 years of such recordings. Using a control console, the reader can select any period, location, or individual.

Hissune picks a time, a continent, a ruling era, and specifies "anyone." He feels a mind flowing into his and "lets the soul of the other take possession of him." After several such experiences, Hissune begins to realize "that these stolen minutes in the Register of Souls are providing him with [the courses toward] his true education, his doctoral degree in life." Four years later, he stands alone under the cold, brilliant stars.

> So many of them! And one is Old Earth, from which all the billions and billions of humankind had sprung so long ago. Hissune stands as if entranced. Through him pours an overwhelming sense of all the long history of the cosmos, rushing upon him like an irrestible river. The Register of Souls contains the records of enough lives to keep him busy for half of eternity, he thinks, and yet what is in it is just the merest fraction of everything that has existed on all those worlds of all those stars. He wants to seize and engulf it all and make it part of him as he had made those other lives part of him, and of course that cannot be done, and even the thought of it dizzies him.

How many readers have had similar feelings when faced with the library? No matter how comprehensive our collections, how extensive our networks, or how learned we may become as subject specialists or experts of one kind or another, an attitude of humility toward the task of the librarian and researcher is always appropriate.

We will never be able to capture all of it in our libraries, or to teach
it all in our schools and universities. The best to which we can
ever aspire to provide for our students and library users is some
useful assistance and an introduction to the sources in which they
can follow their own individual quests for knowledge, their own
explorations of the "geography of the soul."

The Possible, Probable, Desirable

To fully understand the insights gained by examining information-
finding and library-like activities in these stories, one must return
to the initial assumptions about what is possible, what is probable,
and what is desirable among the alternative futures for the year 2000.

In the first concept, the completely computerized library resembles in many respects the most advanced and automated libraries of
today, and seems as reasonable to assume as manned space travel
which is foreshadowed even now in the interplanetary voyages of
robotic devices already underway. This vision of "more of the same,
only better," and of great diversification of media may be the most
probable of all four possible types of libraries.

The question is not whether this type can prevail in the future.
Rather, is it desirable? Is it what we want? If it is, will librarians
and users be able to persuade those who control the purse strings
of the electorate that the benefits of such easily accessible information
systems are worth the investment of tax money that will also have
to stretch to pay for the costs of space exploration and defense, not
to mention a few other priorities such as reducing the deficit, fighting
malnutrition, and guaranteeing a decent life for all?

The rehumanized library will have great appeal to those operational optimists who believe that the computer will bring liberation
from information overload rather than contribute to the insanity or
paralysis that can come from having too many choices and too many
demands for immediate and unthinking responses. The probability
of this future depends on whether the human race can ultimately stop
the arms race, achieve a condition of international understanding,
and harness technology so that such a global village and such a culturally enhanced lifestyle can come to pass.

Unfortunately, it does not appear as probable as the third
scenario, which assumes an inevitable total or near-total destruction
of all civilization and culture sometime in the not-so-distant future.
The web of civilization becomes fragile and torn, the destiny of humanity is rung once again on the bells of change, and language, counting, writing, reading, all the tools of human culture including, of
course, the library are destroyed and will have to be reinvented.

What should the attitude of librarians be to this highly probable

future? Does one take action against the darkness by teaching someone to read? Or does one shrug it off and say it would be no great
loss, agreeing with Ish in his final days that maybe a fresh start
would do humanity good since intelligent beings should have the capacity to re-create whatever culture is needed, and given time and
numbers, the flame of literacy and learning will be rekindled again
when it is required.

While the mental high-tech library is possible, it is not very
probable, at least for a century or two. It is almost comforting that
human nature itself does not change substantially, even though
mental and spiritual powers may be greatly enhanced in an evolutionary
leap. In fact, in all four of these scenarios, the people in the stories
make mistakes and commit sins against each other and are as ornery
and cantankerous as every one of us is today.

But most comforting of all, Hissune can be seen as the symbol
of the eternal reader, the self-learner who gains an education by
"letting the soul of the other take possession of him," which is what
has always happened in a very elemental sense in libraries, ˙ etween
the reader and the book, the viewer and the film, and perhaps sometimes even between the computer user and the databank. This too
does not change. As LeGuin states:

> The trust or confidence that can be established between
> writer and reader is real, though entirely mental; on both
> sides it consists in the willingness to animate, to project
> one's own thinking and feeling into a harmony with a not-
> yet-existent reader or a not-present and perhaps long-dead
> writer.... when the power of the relationship [between artist
> and audience] is not abused, when the trust is mutual, as
> when a parent tells a bedtime story or a teacher shares the
> treasures of the intellect or a poet speaks both to and for
> the listeners, real community is achieved; the occasion is
> sacred.[15]

Decide on a Future

I suggest a useful exercise: sit down sometime in a quiet
place and define and examine your own assumptions about the future,
both in general prospects for humanity at large and what you think
about the future of books and libraries, users and librarians, and
the facilities and settings in which they can best develop. If your
reading tastes do not include science fiction, for inspiration you might
start by reviewing several sets of assumptions which have been
developed by library colleagues.

Marilyn Gell Mason makes nine forecasts about "The Future of
the Public Library," including such predictions as: "The public
library of the future will be judged not by the size of its collections,

but by its success in providing information quickly and accurately....
Public libraries will develop an information infrastructure to provide
access to a growing and changing flow of information...." And in
a most optimistic tone: "Public libraries will not only survive, they
will flourish."[16]

Or try Lowell Martin's eight "ingredients that will go into the
new mix" of library, such as: "The responsive library will be easier
to use than most agencies today...." And: "On the inside of the
building you will know which city and library you are in without
looking at the name at the entrance.... The agency will be genuinely
multimedia, with print and image and sound organized around interests
and motivations of users."[17]

What matters is not so much whether these statements are based
on correct assumptions, but what you think about them in relation to
your own assumptions, at both unconscious and articulate levels.
After reviewing all possible futures and then narrowing the choices
down to what is actually probable, you can then decide what future
library scenario most closely reflects your own values and assumptions.
The purpose of such an exercise, which would also be appropriate
for a long-range planning committee, is to help you reach an understanding of what you think is a desirable future for libraries so that
you can make the right decisions, which one can hope may lead to
that future you anticipate.

References

1. Toffler, Alvin in Science Fiction at Large. ed. by Peter Nicholls,
    Harper, 1976, p. 118.
2. Harman, Willis. An Incomplete Guide to the Future. San Fran-
    cisco Bk. Co., 1976, p. 10.
3. Harrison, Harry. The Stainless Steel Rat for President. Ban-
    tam, 1982.
4. Lem, Stanislaw. The Star Diaries. HBJ, 1976.
5. LeGuin, Ursula K. Always Coming Home. with audiocassette,
    Music and Poetry of the Kesh, Harper, 1985.
6. Stewart, George R. Earth Abides. Houghton, 1949.
7. Miller, Walter M., Jr. A Canticle for Leibowitz. Lippincott,
    1959.
8. Silverberg, Robert. Majipoor Chronicles. Arbor House, 1981.
9. Kahn, Herman & Anthony J. Wiener. The Year 2000: a Frame-
    work for Speculation on the Next Thirty-Three Years. Mac-
    millan, 1976, p. 5, 7.
10. Asimov, Isaac. The Robots of Dawn. Ballantine, 1984.
11. Quoted by Edward M. Walters, in "The Future of the Book:
    a Historian's Perspective," Information Technology and Libraries,
    Mar. 1982, p. 21.
12. Klause, Annette, in memorandum to author, July 7, 1986.

13. Illich, Ivan. De-Schooling Society. Harper, 1970, 1972.
14. Ferguson, Marilyn, "Spiritual Adventure: Connection to the Source," in The Aquarian Conspiracy: Personal and Social Transformation in the 1980's. Tarcher, 1980, p. 361-386.
15. LeGuin, p. 503
16. Mason, Marilyn Gell, "The Future of the Public Library," LJ, Sept. 1, 1985, p. 136-139.
17. Martin, Lowell, "Should the Public Library Seek New Directions," address to Urban Libraries Council, Chicago, July 6, 1985, p. 11-12.

Part II

PUBLISHING, BOOKS AND READING

THE LITERARY-INDUSTRIAL COMPLEX*

Ted Solotaroff

As an editor who works in trade publishing, I lead a dual life. I come from the world of letters, a vague but real place that has given me my standards and shaped my skills, and that keeps a record of my performance. On the other hand, for the past 20 years I have been reporting, as we say there, to the world of publishing, a specific but increasingly unreal place where I earn my living and produce my goods, and where a different kind of record is kept.

Though these two worlds have probably never lived on easy terms with each other, they have shared a certain common ground of desire and function: the pen yearning for the press that disseminated and rewarded its words, the press yearning for the fine pens that enabled it to move upward in society from a business to a profession, to publishing as an institution of culture.

There matters stood some 20 years ago, when I came to work at New American Library. Hardcover publishing was still largely a genteel profession. The "houses" were, like the homes of the gentry, distinctive, stable, guided by tradition or at least by precedent, inner-directed in their values. They characteristically bore the names of their founders--Norton, Knopf, Scribner, Harper Brothers, Farrar Straus, Simon and Schuster, and so on--and had developed along the lines of a kind of idealized self-image of the founders: of their vision, taste, and interests, and those of the successors who were chosen to maintain the reputation. Hence the identity of the house was remarkably stable for an organization so vulnerable to the vicissitudes of the times and the market.

The main reason for this stability was that the identity of the house was framed, and its profitability stabilized, by its backlist: by the well-established titles that more or less sold themselves from year to year. This endowment, as it were, enabled a publisher to

*Reprinted by permission of the author and publisher from The New Republic 196:23 (June 8, 1987) 28-44; copyright © 1987 The New Republic. This essay appears in expanded form in A Few Good Voices in My Head. (Harper & Row, 1987).

refrain from the promiscuous pursuit of best-sellers. Moreover,
profits were expected to be modest and variable. In hardcover publishing, the ratio of the cover price to the acquisition and production
costs of a book was little better than 4-to-1; when the high overhead
of a labor-intensive product and a 40 percent discount to the seller
are added, one can see why a publisher who showed a net profit
of eight percent a year judged himself to be doing well. The publisher and perhaps the few other officers derived incomes sufficient
unto Fifth Avenue or Chappaqua; otherwise salaries were perhaps
a bit better than at a university or some other non-profit organization.

     Thus a publisher like Alfred Knopf, relying upon a franchise
author like Khalil Gibran and an occasional bonanza like Camus's
The Stranger (which he bought for $750), could develop a list of
authors of international standing, ranging from England to Japan,
from South America to Canada. Publishing for Knopf, a not untypical
son of the risen Jewish merchant class, was a means of joining commerce and culture in a cosmopolitan way, just as he cultivated a
refined lifestyle and an autocratic deportment. (He is supposed to
have said that he did not care to publish any author whom he would
not want to invite to dinner.) And one could point also to the
younger leading hardcover houses--Viking, Simon and Schuster, Random House, Farrar Straus--as similar examples of Jewish newcomers
using family money to establish houses that conformed to their desire to play an important cultural role in New York, much as their
counterparts were doing in Vienna, Berlin, and London.

     Even Simon and Schuster, which had something of the unin-
hibitedness of the Hollywood moguls about turning a buck, had its
own touch of class, as well as a shrewd awareness that quality paid,
which quickly made Pocket Books, its paperback subsidiary, pre-
eminent in the ragtag field of reprints that existed before the Second
World War. Viking and Random House, which began in the late
1920s, soon established themselves as leaders in literary and intellectual publishing by virtue of their aggressive pursuit of important
writers (Random House brought the famous court action that enabled
Ulysses to be published in America, and Viking published Joyce's
other books) and their innovative marketing, which produced the
Modern Library and the Viking Portables. Farrar Straus, which
began after the Second World War, was another bright star in the
publishing firmament; when I came to New York, in 1960, it had much
the same aura as Partisan Review (and there was none brighter).

     The older houses were typically more conservative in their
behavior, less eclectic and more parochial in their interests. As
a book and magazine publisher, Harper's served for many decades
as an arbiter of mainstream American culture, particularly in its
political and social concerns. By virtue of its magazine and its
editors, culminating in Maxwell Perkins, Scribner's had been a force
in American fiction ever since its great New York edition of Henry
James. W. W. Norton was more or less the publisher of record in

psychology and music; E. P. Dutton was known for its Americana
and nature books; Houghton Mifflin, like Little, Brown and the Atlantic Monthly Press, maintained the Yankee Brahmin strain in American
life and letters. Of course, these were all general publishers as
well, whose lists for a given season might not seem readily distin-
guishable from one another. But the perceived tradition and character
of each house was important in selecting editors and manuscripts,
in determining priorities and taking risks, in packaging and marketing
a book. A common attitude was that in a business as uncertain as
trade publishing it paid to know who you were and what you did
well.

A strong sense of identity and vocation was particularly apparent in two houses--New Directions and Grove Press. The scion
of a steel fortune and a poet himself, James Laughlin was the best
kind of patron, the kind who supports his authors by publishing
them; he devoted New Directions mainly to discovering and disseminating the canon of the modern tradition. Barney Rosset, a well-to-do
Irish-Jewish American with a bohemian streak, made Grove and its
magazine, Evergreen Review, into a forum for the international
avant-garde of the 1950s and '60s. As iconoclastic as his authors,
like Genet and Beckett, he went to court to appeal the Post Office's
banning of his unexpurgated edition of Lady Chatterley's Lover, and
subsequently defended his right to publish Tropic of Cancer and
Naked Lunch. According to Kenneth C. Davis, a publishing historian,
Rosset was "almost single-handedly responsible for the rewriting of
censorship laws in this country." Pursuing his various interests
in erotica, in profits, in modernism, in freedom of the press, in
showmanship, Rosset was withal a bookman. When Grove's marketing
manager asked Rosset why he was publishing a bilingual edition of
Neruda's poetry "when I can't sell poetry, let alone bilingual poetry,"
Rosset replied, "Because its important. We made a lot of money with
this and that and we've got to give a little of it back to the business
that made us the money."

Rosset belonged more to the paperback side of publishing
circa 1965 than to the hardcover one. That's where most of the cru-
saders and plungers were, much of the mission and the action, the
classiness and the gaminess. "The paperback revolution" was still
in full swing when I came to New American Library to start a literary-
intellectual paperback magazine. NAL was going through some
strange and, as it proved, prophetic times, but the vestigial spirit
of its two founders, Kurt Enoch and Victor Weybright, was still
there, though both had departed a few years before. The office
I was given had just been vacated by David Segal, who had launched
in the previous two years, as part of NAL's fledgling hardcover program, the novelists John Gardner, William H. Gass, and Cynthia
Ozick. In the next office was Arabel Porter, the tutelary spirit of
New World Writing, which had demonstrated a decade before that
editing a big little magazine for the mass market was not necessarily
an oxymoronic idea. Down the hall were the editors who worked on

Signet Classics and Mentor Books, which had brought much of the
best that had been thought and said into corner drugstores and
transportation terminals. And there was the kindred spirit of Sylvan
Barnet, who edited NAL's superb Shakespeare series.

NAL also made a big thing out of publishing Mickey Spillane
and Ian Fleming, among other "down market" authors who largely
supported the enterprise, but what surprised and instructed me was
that this practice mattered much less than I would have thought.
Coming, as I had, from Commentary and the New York intellectual
scene, where the distinctions between high-, middle-, and lowbrow
were rigorously and disdainfully preserved, I was struck at NAL by
the degree to which the right hand of commerce and the left hand
of culture knew, and even respected, what the other was doing.
E. L. Doctorow, who had preceded me by a few years, likes to recall that he was responsible for signing up Ayn Rand and Ian Fleming,
as well as for overseeing Signet Classics and NAL's science books.
There was a kind of synergy at NAL, the hustle and the aspiration
each pulling its oar.

This catholicity was also a part of the Enoch-Weybright legacy.
Enoch, a refugee, had been a pioneer of paperback publishing in
Europe. His Albatross Books, marketed for the English-reading
audience of the Continent, had put Joyce and Lawrence and Virginia
Woolf side by side with Ellery Queen and S. S. Van Dine. And this
vision of a broad market for inexpensive books that were the best
of their kind had lit up Weybright's mind. A farm boy from Maryland
who had made his way through journalism to the Office of War Information in London, Weybright was a man whose status drives were
matched only by his reading habits (he claimed to read 2,000 books
a year). They founded NAL to go after the mass as well as the
class market.

What drove NAL was Enoch and Weybright's combined energy
as very ambitious and cultivated men who demanded to be taken
seriously--not as "reprinters," the somewhat derogatory term that
the hardcover side used to mask its dependency on those who did
cheap editions of its books, but as culturally important and valuable
publishers, indeed as the new movers and shapers of the industry.
Dealing in the rough-and-tumble (and still somewhat shady) world
of the magazine distributors who handled most of their books no doubt
gave Enoch and Weybright a motive to polish their image. So, too,
did the congressional investigation in the mid-1950s of the allegedly
violent and licentious influence of paperbacks. But finally these
two publishers built their house upon a sense of vocation: they
would be cultural missionaries to the masses. "Good Reading for the
Millions" was the motto they stamped on the cover of each of their
books--Whitman's Democratic Vistas come true.

The conditions were right and ripe. There was the virtually
continuous expansion of the economy after the Second World War; the

dramatic spread of higher education due to the GI Bill; the federal subsidies that poured into the colleges and universities between Sputnik and the Great Society. These influences produced an educated middle class and a serious reading public that hardly existed before, as well as a huge campus market that was supplementing and increasingly replacing hardcover textbooks with paperbacks. Moreover, the nature of paperback distribution, in which the publisher set the quotas for the wholesalers, enabled a house like NAL to force its quality books into the market in the same "drop" with its Westerns, detective stories, and romances, and its reprints of last year's bestsellers. True, a lot of these books were returned unsold, but since mass-market books cost only a few cents a copy to produce (the ratio of cover price to production and distribution costs being more than double what it was in hardcover, and the royalty rates about half) one could afford to take risks.

Another advantage of paperback publishing at NAL was that its editorial group was small, versatile, quick on its feet, and trusted. Weybright, who in other ways put the "mega" back in megalomaniac, gave editors their heads. Doctorow tells a more or less typical story of jumping on the news of Adolph Eichmann's capture, calling up a knowledgeable journalist friend, and convincing him to write a quick book. A month after the event The Case Against Adolf Eichmann was in the racks, and went on to sell 500,000 copies. The success is less to the point than the venture itself. Good publishing at NAL was neither a crapshoot nor a market analysis: it was sensible risks in the pursuit of the interesting.

I came to NAL for precisely this pursuit, and when I began I had all the freedom and backing I could ask for. It would have been much the same if I had worked for Peter Mayer at Avon, or Oscar Dystel and Marc Jaffe at Bantam, as I did a few years later, or Ian Ballantine at his house. They were all astute rabbis of the paperback book, and fervent in its cause. Weybright himself summed up their careers:

> I had run the gauntlet and emerged with proof, widely acknowledged, that widespread cultivation of new and habitual readers of inexpensive books does not lead to vulgarization and the lowest common denominator of quality.... There was scarcely a notable author, contemporary or classical, who was not listed in the current volumes of paperback books in print.

II.

As it fell out, Weybright's words were a valedictory not only of his achievement but of NAL's, and eventually of the revolution he had helped to lead. He and Enoch were already diminishing legends when I arrived at NAL, because seven years earlier they had sold their company to the Los Angeles Times Mirror, a junior-size conglomerate. They had both fallen for the allure of the big time, an allure that was to work its will on other independent publishers, to much the same outcome. It was to prove typical, too, that the accord that had prevailed in a privately owned company was displaced by rivalry and jockeying in a subsidiary one, that the golden apple of corporate acquisition would produce discord. It was also typical that the man from the business side would prove to be the more effective conglomerateer. As head of the Times Mirror's book division, Enoch went from apparent strength to strength, acquiring World, whose highly successful Bible and dictionary provided a solid foundation on which to build; Harry Abrams, the leading art-book publisher; and a small English house, which was to be Enoch's beachhead in the U.K.

Meanwhile Weybright steadily lost ground. He had little or no influence in Enoch's acquisitions. He found his autonomy vanishing in his own sphere, and had to take on the responsibility for World's new titles when its editors resigned en masse. The brief but disastrous history that followed, which led, only a decade later, to the fall of NAL from the top place in paperback publishing to the depths of the second rank, and to the virtual demise of World and New English Library, is sketched in gall in the chapter "From Dream to Nightmare" in Weybright's memoir, The Making of a Publisher. Its account of misconception, mistrust, mismanagement, and mediocrity forms a paradigm of the fate of many of the trade publishing houses that in the next two decades climbed the magic beanstalk of increased operating capital, shares of stock, and reassuring promises, only to end up in the land of the hungry giants.

The theme that runs through Weybright's account is the subversion of publishing planning and practice by the corporate mentality. Toward the end, Weybright recounts a meeting with the executive of the management consulting firm that was now overseeing the book program: "'You are a purchasing--a procurement--executive,' Jack Vance said, 'and you must be responsive to marketing.'"

This, in a nutshell, became the story of much of trade publishing over the next 20 years. The main supporting characters are the conglomerates that bought publishing houses, the "procurement executives" who replaced the Weybrights (he resigned a month later, never to return to paperback publishing), the new bookstore chains, and the new breed of American book consumers. Together they have worked like a pincer movement to narrow the scope and prospects of literary and intellectual publishing in the book trade, to capture and exploit the new mass market of the age of consumerism and the culture of narcissism.

The typical publishing corporation or conglomerate subsidiary is only perfunctorily interested in providing "good reading for the millions." At the management level it works, thinks, and wills like

any other big business. Its paramount concern is not the integrity
of its product but the value of its shares, which is keyed to its
short-term profits, derived from the number and the profitability
of books it sells. The result has been to expand the volume of the
product (from 1965 to 1985 the number of published titles increased
by close to 25 percent in each decade) and to tailor the product
to the demand. This is more pronounced in paperback publishing,
where the invisible hand of the mass market is more coercive. But
it has increasingly affected hardcover publishing as well, both as
supplier to the reprinters and as a merchant looking for its piece
of the action at the chain bookstore in the shopping mall.

The action is in the books that service popular needs for information, instruction, entertainment, and fantasy, or, indeed, consumerism itself: the yearning to buy that has turned the shopping
mall into the church where so many families worship each weekend.
This explains the overwhelming shift in most publishing houses to
consumer-oriented titles: the proliferation of cookbooks and dieting
books; physical, mental, and spiritual self-help books; fad and cele-
brity books; and books on all stages of the life cycle from infant
care and child-rearing to retirement and estate planning. It also
explains the corollary development in fiction, the domination by the
masters of the categories--occult, romance, detective, spy, Western,
horror, and so on.

The mass market of the shopping mall has proved to be the
Great Leveler of the publishing business. The long-standing identities
that derived from the houses' traditional interests and purposes
have eroded, along with their backlists. With a few exceptions, the
major houses today are virtually indistinguishable. (Here, as elsewhere in this essay, I exclude Harper & Row, my present employer,
and Bessie Books, my publisher, from the discussion.) Like members
of a football team in the huddle, the publishing players are distinguished from one another mainly by their size and numbers (that is,
volume of sales). Authors, publishers, and editors move from one
house to another without missing a beat. Why shouldn't they? The
discourse they've left is the same they find: the subtle novel is
a "tough sell"; the one that isn't immediately topical is "marginal";
the crudely written, heavily plotted one is a "great read"; the slick
one, in which, typically, a gimmick meets a fad, is "popcorn." So,
too, with non-fiction, in which the well-informed book is elbowed
aside by the one that approaches its subject and its audience with
outflung arms, the main idea on its author's mind being money. By
attempting to standardize their product, the publishers have succeeded
in standardizing themselves.

How does the corporate mentality infiltrate a publishing house?
Let us begin with a not so hypothetical example. Telcom, a far-flung
media empire of newspapers, magazines, and TV and radio stations,
wants to own a New York publisher, for the prestige and the entre-
preneurial possibilities. It looks into Harbinger House, a distinguished

publisher of mostly quality books, which has been hit by high interest rates, soaring manufacturing and overhead costs, a flat book
market, and the IRS's recent policy of taxing inventory, which has
driven backlist publishing further to the wall and many important
books out of print. Harbinger has been losing some authors, and
failing to acquire others who belong on its list, because of the inflated advances offered by other houses for quality books "with commercial possibilities," which almost everyone occasionally wants to
publish so they can look themselves in the face while laughing all
the way to the bank. Moreover, Harbinger needs financing to capi-
talize on what it does well--particularly to expand its trade paperback line by acquiring undervalued titles from other publishers.

This looks good to the chief executive officer of Telcom.
Wanting to impress the Harbinger people with his urbanity and himself
with his high-mindedness, he assures them that the house's autonomy
will be fully respected. For a time not much changes, except Harbinger's cash flow. Then Telcom buys Premium Books, a mass-market
paperback house, to "mate" with Harbinger; they will now be able
to compete with similarly positioned companies for the super best-
sellers that seem to make all the difference. To coordinate his new
companies, to place them more symmetrically on Telcom's organizational
chart, and to "goose" their managements, the CEO sets up a new
division and places it under the supervision of Howard Green, a
Telcom executive who has no experience in publishing but was successful as the No. 2 man in Telcom's magazine division.

Green moves in with his team of financial and marketing analysts.
They quickly discover that book publishing is a very irrational and
uncertain business. For example, only 12 percent of Harbinger's
list is responsible for 78 percent of its profits. But the main problem
is what Harbinger doesn't publish. Breaking down its list and comparing its "major" titles (50,000 copies or more sold) with the Publishers Weekly hardcover and trade-paperback best-seller lists for
the previous year show that Harbinger was weak in occult fiction (one
title), suspense fiction (two), and romances (none). In non-fiction
it was even worse: inspirational books (none), humor (one), pets
(none), business and investment (none), and so on. In sum, the
analysis not only explains why Harbinger is still showing a negative
ROI (return on investment) after two years, but also confirms
Green's belief that its management may have an incurable case of
"egghead tunnel vision."

A similar analysis of Premium Books shows that it is cluttering
up its inventory with books like Doctor Zhivago, The Hedgehog and
the Fox, and The Last of the Just. It should eliminate all titles
that aren't moving at the rate of 1,000 copies a month, and should
not acquire any for which this rate of sale cannot be anticipated.
Premium, too, needs many more consumer-oriented titles--a line of
"clean romances" like Harlequin, biographies of celebrities, more
"blockbuster" novels (a million copies or more). Also, Telcom's ROI

would be substantially improved if Premium would acquire and co-publish more of its major acquisitions with Harbinger. At the next Telcom board meeting it is agreed that although a Robert Ludlum, a Carl Sagan, or a Stephen King comes high, that's where the investment should be. Acquiring King, as well as doing him in both editions plus a movie tie-in, is a license to print money, almost as exciting as picking off an undervalued corporation.

But a year passes and Harbinger's ROI has barely improved. The publisher explains to Green that most of the new high-priced authors he has acquired are still finishing their books, and that his expanded paperback line is running into heavy competition in the burgeoning field of trade paperbacks. Green needs more for the board meeting. He demands a major commercial acquisition before the meeting (for which Harbinger will badly overpay). All new acquisitions will henceforth be cleared with him; operating overhead for the next fiscal year will be cut by 15 percent; the quota of "major" titles will be doubled. After trying unsuccessfully to meet with Telcom's CEO, the publisher resigns. He is immediately replaced by an aggressive treasurer from another house with whom Telcom's "headhunter" agency has been negotiating. He brings his own editor in chief, from one of the big book clubs. And after a few months he convinces Green that Harbinger will be viable only if its entire operation is merged with Premium. Harbinger will maintain its editorial independence, though joint ventures will be more vigorously pursued.

Quickly a new Harbinger House begins to emerge. Poetry is cut back to a few authors who command substantial anthology fees. Literary criticism departs. History and biography become more popular and up-to-date. Fiction in particular comes under the new editor in chief's scrutiny. Does it have a page-turning plot, sympathetic characters, a punchy style, a topical subject, erotic steam? Is it, in short, a novel that he likes to read, and can sell to a reprinter for at least double its advance? Collections of stories are dubious unless the author has been consistently published in the New Yorker, and preferably in one or two of the women's magazines. Social and political criticism is similarly subjected to the standard of popular appeal: Is its author likely to be invited to the Phil Donahue show? So with psychology, biology, religion. "Don't tell me how good it is. Tell me who's going to buy it."

All of which has an effect on even the most independent, venturesome, quality-minded editor. He finds that his value to the house has been quantified: his salary and overhead are now expected to produce X times their total in the net sales of the books he acquires. The pressure affects the way he reads, judges, and even edits manuscripts. His attention and evaluation begin to shift from the characteristics that make a book unique to those that make it readily identifiable ("the new anti-yuppie novel"), from those that make it risky and interesting to those that make it promotable ("a

cross between Jay McInerny and Scott Fitzgerald"). If the former
characteristics significantly outweigh the latter, which is generally
the case with original or otherwise difficult work, he becomes less
and less willing or able to take the book on. In the new marketing
environment of Harbinger, he feels that his judgment is always on
the line, that to prevail with the moderately unusual manuscript he
must forget about doing the esoteric and the demanding one, even
though he knows in his heart, if he has a heart left, that the
author could be the next Italo Calvino or Susan Sontag or John
Berger.

Fortunately even bottom-line publishing doesn't lend itself
all that readily to the kind of controls that corporate minds like to
employ to tailor the book to the market. The reading tastes of the
serious book-buying public are still too idiosyncratic and unpredictable
for a computer to track. That is one reason why the beleaguered,
compromising editor at Harbinger House remains haunted by the
spirit of art and ideas. He knows that the literary or intellectual
work that strikes it rich can strike it very rich indeed, and for
years to come. First novels generally lose money, but how would
you like to have passed up The Bell Jar or The Catcher in the Rye
or Catch-22 or The Naked and the Dead or Invisible Man? A writer
whose first three or four novels didn't sell is hard to justify to the
sales force and the bookstore buyer, but how would you like to have
turned down The World According to Garp or The Golden Notebook
or The French Lieutenant's Woman? So the literary editor tries to
persuade his new publisher and editorial director to keep a margin
of imagination and seed money available for at least a few unlikely
submissions like The Lover and The Name of the Rose.

Still, the new pressures at Harbinger continue to push the
editor in the direction of the "major" titles. Since the authors of
such books are already being well published and cherished elsewhere,
he finds himself in the new role of raider and seducer for Harbinger.
Apart from its effect on his morale, such behavior tends to curtail
his independence and compromise his editorial role and skills. Besides more money, he doesn't have much to offer the best-selling
author except his flattery and Harbinger's prestige. But if he enters
on his knees, how is he to stand on his own two feet later and edit
this author? If he has reservations about his glibness, which he
wasn't about to mention during the courtship, how is he to establish
the ground to criticize it? He can't do much accommodating and
falsifying and groveling without losing respect for his own judgment,
which is what he mainly edits with. And so less serious editing will
be done at Harbinger.

Let us assume that the editor at the new Harbinger still has
some margin in which to persist, and some will to do so. He acquires,
say, a remarkable collection of coarse, enigmatic, but cumulatively
powerful stories about low life in Glasgow. He does everything right
for this exciting and important literary discovery, only to encounter

in the marketplace an even more onerous version of the books-as-product mentality. First, the bookstore chains, which now control 30 percent of the market and counting, and powerfully influence the rest of it. An article in Publishers Weekly a few years ago described the outlook at Waldenbooks, which now operates a thousand stores:

> All of its top executives strongly support the mass merchandising concepts (that is, of treating books like a product in the same way a manufacturer would merchandise a bar of soap). Hoffman [the president], who views romance titles with as much respect as literary works, experienced the selling power of mass merchandising techniques when he was an executive at Bell and Howell.

More recently, in the New York Times Magazine, Harry Hoffman amplified his view of the book market. One of his more telling points was that "time is a factor. People want something short that they can read in a night."

One can easily imagine the response that Harbinger's salesperson will receive when he presents our editor's unique book about some lost souls in Glasgow in their own idiom, a book for which the editor has fought to get an advance quota of 5,000 copies but no advertising budget. Even if the salesperson shares the editor's enthusiasm for the book, buyers at Waldenbooks and at B. Dalton, the other major "full-line" chain, will order no more than a few copies for 15 percent of their stores.

Let's assume that this "slow read" and "tough sell" receives critical acclaim. A rate of sale deemed acceptable for it has already been plugged into a central computer. If the book doesn't meet it in 90 days, it won't be in most of the stores when its reputation catches up with it. When the author's next book comes along, assuming the editor still has the credibility and heart to take it on, 30, or perhaps by then 35, percent of the market will be closed to it. An even more ominous phenomenon is the advent of the discount bookstore chains, which narrow the market even further by restricting their inventories to the quick and the dead: to best-selling types and remainders.

The trouble with both these chains is not that they exist: nobody in publishing is opposed to bringing more people into bookstores. It is that by expanding omnivorously they make it difficult for many independent booksellers to survive, particularly in communities where serious readers are not legion. It's not only that the full-line chains have taken to discounting some of the best-sellers to pull in customers, but also that because they buy books on a chainwide basis they get discounts six percent to eight percent higher from the publisher, even though it pays the same freight costs to send five copies of a book to B. Dalton in San Jose as it does to supply the independent there. More important, their

purchasing capacity enables them to receive many times more money
for co-op advertising and promotion from the publisher. They kill
off competition and distort the business by driving the larger independent stores to adopt their methods.

One of the ways the outpriced and outgunned independent
bookstore has fought back is by countering the impersonal, supermarket service of the chain store with increased attention to its
clientele, with programs of readings, discussions, and other events
that enable the store to serve as a center of the local literary community. This has worked well in places with high concentrations
of serious readers, like Minneapolis and Berkeley; but it's hard to
put across in Saratoga Springs or Tucson without some significant
help from the publishers. The endangered state of the local bookstore is particularly a problem for quality publishing, because the
store provides the advice, information, and service to readers that
gives the original collection of Glasgow stories a better chance. And
as independent bookstores vanish, like sentinels whose positions
have been overrun, and the chain merchandisers move in with their
store traffic control and target marketing plans, the reverberations
are registered back in New York, where amid talk of cutbacks here
and new lines there the transformation of publishing from partly a
profession to wholly a business broadens and accelerates.

In recent years the diversified conglomerates such as Telcom
have for the most part departed from the business of book publishing.
But their impact is still to be felt in the many houses that they badly
destabilized and the several that they killed (notably Fawcett, a major
paperback publisher) by their demands for unrealistic and quick
returns on the money they poured into them; by their arrogant or
ignorant meddling in publishing judgments and practices; and by
their firing, demoting, and undercutting of sound bookmen and book-
women as they brought in their conglomerateers or empowered those
within who rushed into their embrace. The conglomerateer has bred
an atmosphere of fear, cynicism, rapaciousness, and ignorance that
has been as destructive to serious publishing as any of the other
developments I've described. Its cost can be reckoned in the number
of sagacious and dedicated publishers, editors, and marketing executives who, like Victor Weybright, were driven out or demoralized
or corrupted.

The conglomerates' ravage of the publishing industry was compounded by the stagflation of the late 1970s and early 1980s. The
paperback houses fared particularly badly, and their cutbacks severely
reduced the subsidiary income many hardcover houses needed to make
ends meet. The books that were most adversely affected were the
so-called "mid-list" ones, which included most of the quality titles
by authors who did not have major sales, who were not "brand names."
But the older management, interested in preserving publishing as an
institution of culture, tended to be replaced and its natural heirs
superseded by a new managerial class that fell in smoothly with the

book-chain executives and buyers and store managers, for all of whom publishing was profits and losses and books were "product."

In this climate, during the late 1970s, of inflated advances, reprint sales, and a declining interest in most literary and intellectual titles, some important publishers and editors who had been committed to quality were, sadly, more or less overcome by the mass marketeer in themselves. And the intense competition for established or even potential "market leaders" that Thomas Whiteside described in The Blockbuster Phenomenon gave a new scope and impact to the wheeler-dealer literary agent and lawyer. They plugged the high voltage of Hollywood into the delicate circuitry of established author-publisher relationships, shorting out a good many of them and creating overloads of publishers' advances and authors' expectations from which both groups are still recovering.

In the latest round of mergers and acquisitions, the publishers who have adapted most successfully to supplying the demands of consumerism have been using their surplus capital to take over those that have not adapted as well, rationalizing and strengthening the tendencies I have been describing. Watch what happens to Doubleday now that it has been bought by the multinational firm of Bertlesman, which has presided over the transformation of Bantam from the brilliantly balanced purveyor of commerce and culture that I worked for in the 1970s to a mega-merchandiser of both hardcover and paperback products, most of whose huge monthly order form reads like a tour through a shopping mall bookstore (though Bantam's spirit may be reviving in its new imprint for publishing new writers).

III.

One can say, of course, that it's a free country; that the big publishers and booksellers are giving consumers the books they want; that there is no reason why books should be spared from the economic, social, and cultural forces that continue to massify all the other media; that relative to the products of the radio and television networks, the film industry, and the newspaper and magazine chains, there is still much quality of thought and art in book publishing. One can talk about the twilight of the print era, the culture of narcissism, the rock-bottom state of the zeitgeist during the past decade. One can say all this ... and also believe that there is more to be said.

I think that in viewing the big time as its proper place in society, much of the publishing business has sold itself a bill of goods. It has largely sold out its cultural purpose to its commercial one, thereby losing the vision and the energy and the realism that guided and empowered publishers like Knopf, Cerf, Klopfer, Harold Guinzberg, Cass Canfield, Kurt Wolff, Ballantine, Enoch, Weybright, and others. The truth is that the basic economics of the trade book have not changed since the days of aggressive cultural ambition and modest economic expectation. If anything, the spread between costs and receivables has contracted, because of the chain stores' higher discounts and promotion charges. It's true that publishers have been able to put out many more of the mass merchandise titles for which the chains have expanded the market, but they are also taking book returns that are three and four times what they used to be. Even by corporate standards profit margins remain slim and capricious.

Yet because they are corporations, the bigger houses have big-time overheads: six-figure salaries for the officers, substantial fees to the directors, skyscraper rents for office space and executive apartments in the city, limousine service, and the other perks of the boardroom. It's no wonder, then, that there has been the frantic pressure for blockbuster books by name-brand authors and by celebrities, the competition for which leads to bloated advances, bloated promotion costs and services, and bloated risk.

When a blockbuster or two fail, the effect on the rest of the list can be grievous indeed. Quality books are the most badly affected, for they lose the pittance of advertising money that their authors count on to develop a reputation that may sustain their careers. Moreover, the attitude toward acquisitions hardens against the gifted, serious, inexpensive submission, but grows starry-eyed about the big commercial property that can be published quickly. As the CEO and his number-crunchers exert themselves, publishing decisions become more reckless and shortsighted. During the past couple of years, the lords of the market share, the counselors of the quick fix, the believers in the divine rights of the ROI have been laying waste lists and careers in trade publishing in an even more relentless and benighted way.

What can be done, meanwhile, to keep the profession of publishing alive as an institution of culture? Obviously, the giant houses aren't going to take themselves off the Big Board or become small again. But it's not too much to ask that their CEOs and other top executives mull over some serious questions. Given the narrow profit margins of trade publishing, is it sound business to saddle it with the inflated salaries that corporate officers receive? They are four to five times those of senior editors and marketing people, who are willing to work in publishing for less money than they would earn in a more profitable business. (Not to mention the junior staff, who barely subsist on their salaries.) Why should officers not accept the same facts of economic life?

Does a publishing house really need the towering midtown location that pushes its overhead further through the roof? Are the new breed of executives in the right to flood the market with non-books that may or may not increase their market share, but surely drive out genuine books and degrade the business? Does sound publishing follow from the pressure to increase short-term profits and return on investment levels that belong to a more profitable and

stable business? The truth is that the opulent corporate style rein-
forces the expansionist corporate mentality, institutionalizing the
motive energy of greed and envy.

Envy and greed lead one to think big. Respect and care lead
one to think small. Thinking small pays attention, in Paul Goodman's
words, to "the object, the function, the program, the task, the
need," while thinking big pays "immense attention to the role, procedure, prestige, and profit." What would thinking small, or at
least smaller, be like? It would wonder if this cookbook is really
useful, or just another packageable and promotable piece of merchandise. It would ask whether you would give this book of pop psychology or spirituality to a troubled friend. Thinking smaller would
mean inquiring whether the house is acquiring and scheduling more
books than it can publish well--does it habitually disrupt its publishing program and undermine professional standards by rushing
out books in the fourth fiscal quarter to inflate its annual volume
and profit figures?

Thinking smaller also concerns the climate of the editorial
group. Does it foster independent judgment, cooperation, initiative,
painstakingness, and pride? Or power roles, committee decisions,
crass opportunism, pressure, rivalry, fear, and the depreciation of
editorial skills? Are editors encouraged to be the allies or the ex-
ploiters of their authors? Is the house promoting big books unduly
and small ones hardly at all? Are the salespeople able to sell its
list, as well as those of the other publishers they represent, effectively? Does 20 percent of its list (the figure publishers use to
justify doing the other 80 percent) really make a significant contribution to genuine culture and public enlightenment? Thinking smaller,
in short, puts one in touch with the values that probably led one
to come into publishing in the first place, with the values that were
found in the good publishing houses 20 years ago.

By the same token, if you are a CEO, or an officer, or an
editorial or marketing executive, and these values mean little or
nothing to you, why do you persist in such a low-margin and capricious business? Is it to bask in the prestige of publishing even
as you undermine the values and practice that created it? In asking
the corporate publishing executive to think smaller and more seriously
about purposes and methods, I am trying not to turn the clock back,
but to take account of the facts as they now stand. I am pleading
with him, or her, not only to moderate this heedless momentum in
the direction of mediocrity and unreality, but also to make better
use of the capital and other resources that are available.

After all, a big house can spend more to promote a worthy
book and author than a small one can. Why doesn't it do so as a
matter of course? It costs about $1,500 to put a young or little-
known author whose book has received compelling reviews on the
literary map by advertising it in a leading journal of opinion. The

same amount will buy full-page ads in four leading little magazines
that further position an author in the world of letters. When you
realize that this very modest budget is about three percent to five
percent of the budget for the big commercial book by the name-brand
writer, which will soon be shouting for attention all by itself in bookstore windows across America, you can see why the hearts of editors
sink in dismay and frustration.

The big ad budget has much less to do with selling the book
than with impressing the buyer for the chain and appeasing the
vanity of the author. Would five percent less make any real difference
to either of them? It can make all the difference to the author who
needs the recognition if he is to have a livelihood and career. You
don't even have to go back to the good publisher's formula of budgeting ten percent of anticipated net income to advertising and promotion; half of that would provide enough for the collection of poetry
that you expect will sell 4,000 copies in hardcover and paper, or
the novel or other prose work that you expect will sell 5,000 copies.

The big publishing house can afford to innovate. Less than
one percent of a typical annual ad budget would pay the salary of
a young publicist assigned to put his or her literary passion to work
in developing a program of readings, panels, book signings, and so
forth for quality authors. Such events would bring the authors
and their audiences together in bookstores, on the campus reading
circuit, and on college and listener-supported radio stations. Poets
have been selling most of the copies of their collections this way for
the past 15 years. Why not give them a hand in arranging readings
and other appearances, and do the same for serious fiction and nonfiction writers as well? Co-op advertising money that was allocated
more widely and flexibly would help too. A little seed money (little
in corporate terms) would go a long way, as would a slight realloca-
cation of priorities. It's shameful for an editor at a big house to
tell an author over a $60 lunch that there's no budget to advertise
his book. Give editors the free use of every dollar they save from
their entertainment budgets, matched by one from the house, to
promote their first novels and other budgetless books and see what
happens.

I once had an argument with an editorial director who believed
that the most exciting kind of publishing was to spot a writer you
wanted to publish, wait while another house did the first three or
four books, and move in for the killing. I made a list of authors
who were still with the house or the editor or both that had taken
on their early work. It included John Hersey, James Baldwin, Robert
Lowell, Allen Ginsberg, Susan Sontag, Robert Penn Warren, Reynolds
Price, J. D. Salinger, Samuel Beckett, Thomas Pynchon, Truman
Capote, Flannery O'Conner, John Updike, John Steinbeck. I remember stopping at 30 or so. It doesn't take much to make most quality
authors feel that they are appreciated and supported; such treatment
is what good writers mean by a good house, and if they receive it,

they're likely to remain loyal. All the rest is money and flattery and the aura of the big time. When these become the terms of appeal, the author loyalty over which publishers have been wringing their (slippery) hands collapses. Freedom, trust, and a voice in marketing decisions create the working conditions good editors need. When these depart, so do they.

The new unreality of publishing is reflected, too, in the way the business has come to honor its achievements. Until ten years ago, the National Book Awards were prizes of $1,000 given to the most distinguished work in each of six or seven major areas--fiction, poetry, science writing, current affairs, biography, history, and translation--as determined by a jury of three eminent figures in that area. The ceremony was generally held at Avery Fisher Hall in Lincoln Center, and most of the professional personnel of publishing turned out, to listen to a speech by a public figure that was usually respectable and to the remarks of the winners, which were often eloquent. All in all, it was an appropriate and even an inspiriting occasion. Then the big-timers moved in, notably the mass marketeers from the paperback industry and from one of the bookstore chains. Their idea was to make the National Book Awards just like the Academy Awards. So there came into being hosts of prizes for reprints (as well as original books), for jacket illustrations, book designs, and what-have-you, as chosen by jurors from all walks of the book trade and market; the event turned black-tie and was attended mostly by executives.

This circus was supposed to capture public attention, sell lots of books, and make the entire business proud of itself. When, within a few years, it collapsed of its own inanity, the sponsoring organization, the Association of American Publishers, cast about for alternatives. Soon only three prizes were awarded: for fiction, non-fiction, and, to show that everyone's heart was still in the right place, the first novel. Last year the awards for distinction were raised to $10,000 and reduced to two--fiction and non-fiction, with consolation prizes of $1,000 for the "short list" contenders. The celebration was held at the Starlight Room of the Waldorf-Astoria, and was financed by selling tables for $750 a crack. (The AAP sensibly decided to stop sponsoring the event.) This year the prizes will be even larger to attract more attention, which they won't. Thus the industry has turned its back on the ritual event that appropriately honored it, and instead has taken to making a pass at the Muses by flashing its money and glitz. It was predictable that the mood of the authors at the Starlight Room last year would be one of opposition (Peter Taylor) or self-irony (E. L. Doctorow); they realized that the real tribute that the publishing business was paying that evening was to its own hypocrisy. The Association of American Publishers should take back the National Book Awards and return them to their original format, as a competition and an event that enables it to remember its other mission.

And there's more to do if the AAP wishes to publicize serious books properly. American educational television has never had the type of serious book program that is taken for granted in England and France. The AAP should set to work to sponsor a really interesting program for PBS television, which can be rebroadcast on National Public Radio. It should have a lively, articulate bookperson as moderator, who can lead a spirited and informed discussion of a current provocative book. Such a program would accomplish the wide literary enlightenment of the reading public. It would show that the hand of commerce and the hand of culture can work together again. The trouble with having, say, Stephen King reading Dickens in a B. Dalton store (an idea that recently came out of a meeting of publishers and writers on the crisis in marketing serious books) is that, like the American Book Awards, it makes the book business more unreal. It integrates imagination and intellect not with their public, but with their nemesis: with hype.

I have been painting a bleak picture of the book business, because this bleakness is dominant and spreading. Of course many good books continue to be published in New York and Boston; some of them are marketed well despite the weak or negligible performance of the chain bookstores in their third of the market. Of course those editors who care about ideas and culture continue to find ways to function in the space where the margin of a publisher's risk meets the margin of a publisher's pride. And of course there are still publishers and editors (Robert Giroux, for example) who, whether they work in a big house or a small one, remain "the lords and owners of their faces." As models of high conduct, they enable the publishing business to honor its claim to being a profession.

Arthur Samuelson, one of the more astute younger editors, speaks of the benefits of learning the business at a small house, where the editor is close to the various phases of the publishing process, takes on diverse books, and is often left on his own to improvise. In big-time publishing, the editor tends to be more uncounseled by himself and others, to rely upon signals from the bestseller lists and the in-house authorities to counter a chronic lowgrade panic. This is one reason why many younger editors today know a great deal about market trends and promotional ploys, but are either glibly or poignantly at a loss when asked about their ideas for interesting books.

Samuelson makes the further point that the big-time house doesn't seem to have a memory, which limits its intelligence and distorts its will. In a small house, by contrast, all sorts of knowhow are retained and used, and memory is its guiding light. With its limited cash flow and credit, the house can't afford to forget either its mistakes or its right moves, and so they (rather than the round-robin derring-do of the agents' auctions and the elastic projections of sales and subsidiary income that the "heavy hitters" use in competing for a book) naturally become part of its mentality. Like a stable person, a good small house respects its experience.

Under Bennett Cerf and Donald Klopfer, Random House solved this problem brilliantly, by making its senior editors in effect publishers of their own books. Such a policy is virtually unthinkable in a comparable house today--with the exception of the handful of editors who have been given their own imprints. These editor-publishers (Helen Wolff, Seymour Lawrence, Elisabeth Sifton, James Silberman, the late Henry Robbins, and others) have been responsible for a disproportionate share of the distinguished books in the past 20 years of trade publishing. Like the small family farm and the small serious bookstore, imprint publishing is where the memory, the will, and the intelligence of a cultivating type of work can be found.

And there is; thank God, the alternative press. Much of the party of letters--particularly its experimental and traditional wings--has been moving to the campus. The literary and intellectual culture is finding in the university presses a home away from home. The campus-based publishers have been widely occupying territory that the trade houses have retreated from, in the arts and sciences, or all but abandoned, in foreign literature and thought. The small-press movement continues to lead its dispersed, precarious, seminal life. Like surprise witnesses at a trial, shrewd and reasonably well-funded presses such as North Point, Ardis, and David R. Godine testify that the future of independent trade publishing may well lie in regional centers like Berkeley and Ann Arbor, Atlanta and Cambridge. May all the publishers and editors of the alternative press, like their dwindling brethren in New York and Boston, continue to think small and ambitiously, to believe that a good book is an opportunity rather than a problem, to welcome the fine pens that need and confirm their work.

INSIDE BOOK REVIEWING*

Gail Pool

In a terse letter to the <u>New York Times Book Review</u> last winter, the poet Hayden Carruth complained about the negative review that the <u>Times</u> had given <u>The Selected Poems</u> of James Laughlin, founder of the venerable New Directions Publishing Corporation. Calling the review "a disgrace to us all," Carruth said that reviewer and book had been mismatched, that the reviewer had not understood the poems, and that this was especially unfortunate for a poet's final collection.

> "Most reviewers seem not only to dislike reading but to dislike writing, even when the task they set themselves is merely to express their disgust."
>
> Evelyn Waugh

Arriving at the heart of his objection, he concluded: "When the poet is someone who has given as much to writing in this country as Mr. Laughlin has, it seems even more distressing, though I know this is an extraliterary consideration. But I'm sure it will be prominent in the thoughts of most of your readers."

It did seem sad and somehow unjust that Laughlin, who had sponsored many of our finest poets, should have his own work panned. Yet the review was persuasive. Should the reviewer have toned down his judgment out of kindness or deference to the author? Should he have obscured his critical points to avoid attack? Would such treatment have been more "fair"? Or did responsibility lie with the editor: should he have sought out a reviewer more sympathetic to the poems? As Carruth implied, a different "match" might have yielded a more favorable reading. But is it any fairer to seek out a favorable judgment than a hostile one?

---

*Reprinted by permission of the author from <u>The Boston Review</u> 12:4 (August 1987) 8-10; copyright © 1987 by the author.

During ten years as an editor and reviewer for periodicals
as disparate as The Christian Science Monitor, Wilson Library Bulletin,
and The Nation, I have become increasingly aware of the moral
complexities of the field. In deciding which books to review, who
should review them, and how they should be treated editors and reviewers face choices that make unfairness hard to avoid. Yet surprisingly for a field so given to scrutiny, these ethical dilemmas
have seldom been addressed. Indeed, a National Book Critics Circle
"Ethics Questionnaire," distributed to members this spring, is one of
the few acknowledgements that a problem exists or that moral failures
occur.

"Whether written by fellow writers or professional reviewers,
the all-out assault is what every writer dreads. I have
heard it described in various ways--snide, dismissive, in-
sulting. Let us call it, for the sake of hyperbole, the
ground-zero review. In it, the writer is often urged to seek
another line of work."

Thomas Fleming

The extent of the problem was brought home last year by
A Mother's Work, a book that received wide attention because of its
controversial subject. Written by Deborah Fallows, a Radcliffe graduate with a Ph.D. in linguistics, the book explains her decision to
leave an administrative position and stay home with her two sons.
It also describes conditions in some daycare centers she visited in
the following years, discusses some problems of daycare, and makes
some suggestions for improving it.

The book first came to my attention when a writer asked to
review it for my column. From the book's dust jacket, it seemed
that Fallows felt a mother's work lay in the home, but I didn't take
the time to confirm this impression by reading the book before mailing
it off to the reviewer. To my surprise, her review praised Fallows
for moving "beyond the facile arguments for or against women working
outside the home." The dust jacket, I assumed, had been misleading.
Some weeks later, however, I found the book reviewed in The New
York Times Book Review: "I won't keep you in suspense," the reviewer began. "According to A Mother's Work, a mother's work is
to stay home and raise her children." Clearly, both reviews could
not be correct.

In the following weeks, I saw other reviews that gave contra-
dictory impressions about the book. The case began to intrigue me
and eventually I asked the publisher for all reviews the book had
received. Comparing them proved a fascinating exercise: not only
did they disagree in their evaluations of the book, they differed
in their assessment of its nature and basic message:

"She by no means urges that all moms stay home with their kids all day," said one reviewer. But another asserted that Fallows was maintaining that "if it is at all possible mothers should stay home and raise their children." Some reviewers characterized Fallows's observations of daycare centers as "objective research"; others (though they liked the book) described it as personal and "biased."

Some reviewers thought her research was thorough; others considered it so significantly limited that, broadly speaking, it wasn't valid. Some reviewers called the book "nonjudgmental"; others called Fallows "preachy" and said she felt everyone should make the same decision she had. Some reviewers gave the impression that the book contributed new information to an issue; others claimed it was a book that only articulated a position.

A lack of time may have led some reviewers to give the book a careless reading. A lack of space prevented almost all reviewers from developing an argument for or against the book's position: some merely stated the book was "important," without demonstrating why;

"Sweet, bland commendations fall everywhere upon the scene. A book is born into a puddle of treacle; the brine of hostile criticism is only a memory."

Elizabeth Hardwick

---

others gave a limited and somewhat distorted picture of its flaws.

But the main problem was that writers reviewed the issue of childcare rather than the book. Most reviewers were involved in the issue: almost all identified themselves as mothers. Some admitted they were measuring Fallows's ideas against their own experience; some even appeared to be working out their own guilt--or self-satisfaction--within the reviews. While the sensitive nature of daycare brought out a partisan emotionalism in some reviewers, it made others so cautious they handled the book with kid gloves. In the end, few reviewers seemed able to give the book a thorough, fair assessment.

Whether inspired by carelessness or bias, the discrepancies in these reviews point to an ethical failure in handling the problems of book reviewing. Although A Mother's Work may not be typical-- some books fare worse than others in the review media, and contro- versial books are hard to review--the problems the book posed were not unique. Nor were the solutions. Too often the book review industry fails to deal with the ethical problems involved in selecting books, matching them with reviewers and writing about them.

Of the thousands of books published each year, most editors can give attention to only a few. In choosing, some decisions are easy since much of what is published is recognizably trash, and dismissable. But in sorting through the rest, editors have many guidelines in common: the name of the author, the quality of the publishing house, the "relevance" of the topic, to name a few.

Most of the books that will end up discussed in newspapers and magazines are the lead books of major trade publishers. These are the books readers may expect to see reviewed--because they will have seen them advertised, because they are familiar with the authors. These are the books reviewers are most eager to be assigned--because they think they will be interesting or important. And these are often the best books that the editors of periodicals have on hand to review--because major publishers, unlike many university or smaller presses, send out hundreds of unsolicited advance copies.

One obvious result of these selection practices is that the same books are reviewed everywhere, leaving less space for books by lesser known authors, from smaller presses, or devoted to less topical subjects. Since the latest novel of Updike, however mediocre, "must" be reviewed, the first-rate fiction of Rachel Ingalls may have to be neglected.

A second, more subtle effect is that the disproportionate space given to books by famous authors or on controversial topics lends them an importance they don't necessarily possess. Even a negative review requires that the reviewer take a book seriously; a quantity of reviews make it seem that this is a book we need to respond to. If a modest book like A Mother's Work is selected because of its topic, it is logical that reviewers end up focusing on the topic, and the book comes to seem important when only its subject is.

If editors' methods of selecting books for review tend to yield an inaccurate picture of what books are being published and their relative value, the way they match books with reviewers distorts the picture further. It is unlikely that many editors deliberately

---

"Until one has some kind of professional relationship with books one does not discover how bad the majority of them are."

George Orwell

---

seek an unfair review, but they often turn to biased reviewers, with much the same effect.

For one thing, editors feel obliged to produce a lively book

page, and they want lively writing. As George Orwell observed in
his essay, "In Defence of the Novel," most books will fail to arouse
in the reviewer "even a spark of interest," and "the only truthful
review he could write would be, 'This book inspires in me no thoughts
whatever.'" A biased writer is at least an interested writer who is
likely to produce an interesting review.

Editors also want informed reviews. In specialized areas,
whether politics or education, editors may turn to experts. They
are likely to be supporters or opponents of authors' positions, they
may well have work to protect, and they will probably come up with
reviews that are biased but intelligent. The alternative is a general
reviewer who is bright, who writes well, who has no axes to grind,
and who may come up with a review that seems fair but is naive.

Third, editors often want reviews that reflect their own biases.
There are authors that editors think are outstanding, issues they
feel strongly about. Book review editors, after all, are as involved
with books as authors and reviewers; naturally they will use their
book pages to get their own values across.

From an editor's point of view, these choices are understandable.
Indeed, editors may feel they have sought out a definite interest or
taste, rather than a bias, and that it is the reviewer's responsibility
to treat the book fairly. But if the choices are understandable,
they often backfire, producing unfair reviews. Harold Bloom's scorn

---

"Reviewers have become rather pious toward the very
idea of writing, as if the mere fact of working up a book
constituted a virtuous act and a selfless public service...
When a reviewer has something disapproving to say
about a book, especially one by an established author,
it's often phrased in such euphemistic or circumlocutory
terms that it's difficult for the reader to know precisely
what is being said."

Anatole Broyard

---

for Thomas Wolfe as a writer was not intellectually irrelevant to his
New York Times February 8, 1987 review of David Herbert Donald's
critical biography of Wolfe; but the bias came so solidly between reviewer and book that it distorted the review. The choice of mothers
to review A Mother's Work made sense in terms of interest and expertise, but most had too much invested in the issue to evaluate
the book with detachment. And editors who select a reviewer who
shares their views on an author or issue often find it difficult to
leave the reviewer alone. Most writers can cite instances of editors
encouraging a negative or positive review, and even changing their
copy. The boundaries where an editor's influence ends can grow faint

In any case, editors can at best create the opportunity for fair reviews; the rest is up to the writers. Given the number of pitfalls along the path, a reviewer is almost certain to land in one, unless vigilant. As the poet and reviewer L. E. Sissman observed in "Reviewer's Dues," his essay on the ethics of reviewing, "...the sins and temptations of reviewers are legion."

In large part, a reviewer's problems derive from conflicting obligations. When I first began reviewing I imagined I would be alone with a book and my own taste and judgment. But no reviewer is alone with a book. Authors, readers, and editors all have some interest in the review and their claims are often at odds with the reviewer's. The reviewer wants to be lucid, witty, and right. The author might prefer a favorable review to an honest one. Readers want something that is interesting to read and tells them if the book is worth buying. The book section's editor wants a review that is lively, indicates the book is important (which justifies the space given to it in the periodical), and meets the specified deadline and word length.

In serving one audience, reviewers are often unfair to another. Out of kindness to the author, they may be so cautious that readers cannot tell if the book is being panned or praised. To please the editor, they may make the book out as more important and interesting than it is: readers go out to buy a "remarkable piece of work" and come home with a disappointingly ordinary book. To entertain readers, and perhaps themselves, reviewers may be witty at the author's expense. As a reader, I thoroughly enjoyed a review by Stephen Dobyns in which, referring to the many murders in the book, he concluded: "But these are the small deaths, the fictional ones. The deaths that bother me most are those of the trees that were cut down to make this book." As the author, I think I would have wept.

In serving their own values and taste, reviewers often fail to observe where biases distort their reviews. Recently, a writer sent me a review of some short stories. The review began: "The women in these stories are passive." I was astounded. When I had read--and liked--the stories, passive women had not struck me as a significant aspect of the fiction. Yet for the reviewer, this was the overriding factor; for her, a story about a passive woman could not be a good story. Clearly this was deeply felt, an honest point of view; but was it fair?

The two main causes of unfair reviewing are a lack of time and a lack of space. It is easy to see these as mechanical rather than ethical difficulties; but both impose choices that have ethical consequences. The first of these is inaccuracy. Reviews are filled with inaccuracies; indeed, it can be unnerving to read reviews of books one has actually read. In a recent New York Times Book Review roundup of some travel books with which I was familiar, I found the

reviewer had transformed one male author into a woman and had attributed another author's comment to the wrong person. In a rush,

---

"Most of the thousands of poets were bad, most of
the thousands of critics were bad, and they loved
each other."

                                        Randall Jarrell

---

and reviewers are often in a rush to meet deadlines, not only can
confusions like this occur but important aspects of a book may be
missed. Moreover, writers rarely have time to do the background
reading they should to evaluate fairly the book under review (especially for a $200 fee and with the press of other work).

Equally bad is the problem of space. In 700 words certain
criticisms cannot really be defended, and reviewers must decide
whether to raise them and leave them unexplained, or omit them altogether. Either way, without great care, the argument may be
inadequate or distorted. And as the reviews of A Mother's Work
made plain, reviewers are often not careful enough.

There is a misconception that book reviewing is easy. In fact,
it is hard to review books fairly. Indeed, given the scope of the
difficulties, perhaps it is not surprising that reviews should often
fail. But given the scope of the failures, it is surprising how little
analysis has been given to where reviewing fails, and why--and
whether, morally speaking, the field can be improved.

My impression is that reviewers and editors try to be fair; but
their concept of unfairness is often limited. They seem to reserve
the term for negative reviews, in particular those that seem unjustly
critical of a book, vicious, or mocking of its author. This kind of
unfairness is scrupulously avoided. Indeed, as Anatole Broyard
points out in his essay, "Fashions in Reviewing," critics tend to be
excessively gentle nowadays. It is hard to imagine finding in today's
reviews anything to compare with the nastiness of angrier eras, such
as Waugh's remark on Auden, "His work is awkward and dull, but it
is no fault of his that he has become a public bore"; or such epithets
as "slopbucket" and "rotten garbage of licentious thoughts" which
Broyard reminds us were hurled at Leaves of Grass.

But there is, after all, a great variety of ways for reviews to
be unfair, and it seems to me we are offhand about many. We are
reluctant to call books "terrible" when they may be just ordinarily
bad, but we are comfortable calling them "excellent" or "remarkable,"
when we know they are merely "good." We will not call an author's
ideas garbage, but we are willing to ignore them and proceed to
promote our own.

In "Reviewer's Dues," L. E. Sissman set forth his "moral im-
peratives" of reviewing, and I imagine many reviewers would be as
surprised as I was at their scope. Alongside the injunctions we would
expect, such as "Never review the work of a friend" or "Never review
the work of an enemy," are less obvious injunctions such as "Never
review a book in a field you don't know or care about," "Never read
the jacket copy or the publisher's handout before reading and reviewing a book," "Never compete with your subject," "Never neglect
new writers," and "Never fail to take chances in judgment." I expect most reviewers would accede to these injunctions; but I think
we do not tend to see them as moral, or their violation as unethical.
It seems to be we need to acknowledge more fully the moral nature
of the field--to view each book and each review as a moral challenge--
if we hope to resist the many temptations of reviewing and to avoid
its sins.

ETHICAL BEHAVIOR

The National Book Critics Circle recently sent a survey to its
members. Reprinted below, the questions indicate some of the common
situations which editors and reviewers encounter. A summary of the
responses will be available in September.

1. Should a book review editor assign a book to a casual
acquaintance of the author--e.g., someone the reviewer may have
met at a writing conference, party or on a panel, but who is not
a close friend?
2. Should a book editor assign a book to a friend of the author?
3. Should a book editor assign a book on subject A to a
reviewer who has also written a book on subject A, or a subject
extremely close to that?
4. The same question as number 3, assuming that the reviewer's book is more than a year old.
5. The same question as number 3, assuming that the reviewer's book will not be released until sometime in the future.
6. If authors Henry and James both have books coming out
around the same time on subject A, is it all right to assign each to
review the other's book?
7. Assuming the answer to 5 is yes, does the book review
editor have the right to keep the crossed assignments secret?
8. If the answer to 7 is yes, skip this question. If the answer
is no, it is presumed the book editor must acknowledge the assignment if asked about it. The remaining question becomes: Is the
book editor free not to reveal the crossed assignments if he is not
asked about it by either reviewer?
9. Is it all right for book editors to allow reviewers to request
a particular book, even though that practice occasionally leads to
backscratching and attempted set-ups?
10. Is it the book review editor's obligation to question a
prospective reviewer about potential conflicts of interest, rather than
the reviewer's to raise the subject?

11.   Is it ethical for a reviewer to decline to review a book he has already accepted for review, on the ground that he didn't like the book and doesn't want to say negative things in print?

12.   Should anyone mentioned in the acknowledgements of a book be barred from reviewing it?

13.   Is a book editor obligated to consult a reviewer before making significant changes in his copy?

14.   Is a book review editor obligated to consult a reviewer before making any changes in his copy?

15.   Should authors who publish with a particular house be permitted to review other books published by that house?

16.   Should a writer be allowed to review the book of someone who shares the same literary agent?

17.   Should an editor ever assign a book to a reviewer who is known to hold aesthetic, political or literary principles contrary to those of the author?

18.   Should an editor ever assign a book to a reviewer who is known to hold aesthetic, political or literary views similar to those of the author?

19.   Should publishers suggest reviewers of their books to book review editors, as university presses sometimes do?

20.   Occasionally, a person who has already accepted a review assignment from one publication is asked to review the same book by a more prestigious or attractive publication. Should the person accept the second assignment without receiving permission from the first editor to withdraw from the existing assignment?

21.   Should a person who has written an unpaid blurb for a book be allowed to write a fuller review of the book?

22.   Should an academic who has refereed a particular book for a university press be allowed to review it after publication?

23.   Should publishers urge writers to volunteer to review specific books for specific publications?

24.   Should book review editors be permitted to sell books they've decided not to review?

25.   Should freelance book reviewers be permitted to sell review copies?

26.   Should specialists on the staff of a book review's parent publication be allowed to have books in their fields of interest, for future reference, that have been passed over for review?

27.   Is it ethical for professional journalists to check off publisher request forms for large numbers of review copies that no individual could possibly review, then sell the large majority to used book stores for personal profit?

28.   Is it ever ethical to review a book without reading the entire book?

29.   Is it ethical for a writer to both a) review a book and b) interview the author and write a feature about him?

READING, INTERLIBRARY LOAN, AND OCLC:
A LETTER TO BILL KATZ*

Robert S. Bravard

Last week while looking for something else I found myself reading through my file of your letters. No matter what the letter started out being about, it eventually turned into a discussion of whatever you had just finished reading. I know my letters to you are the same; sometimes I finish a book and make a note to tell you about it in my next letter. Everybody I write to does this, but then how many people these days write letters? That is another matter altogether but let me keep on here about reading.

It is not at all uncommon in your letters for you to remark that you were glad to hear of such and such a book and that if the library there at SUNY Albany didn't have it you would have to order it up on interlibrary loan. That sounded familiar; I also do a lot of that here. Once I find a new-to-me author, I try to read all of his or her books, so I am a heavy interlibrary loan user. Not that long ago I finished reading everything by William Cooper and each novel came from a different library somewhere in the East.

I can easily remember when this would have been impossible. Back in 1964 when I wanted to read The Gentle Art of Murder, by Raymond Chandler, this library did not have a copy. There was also no staff member assigned to interlibrary loan; such responsibility did not exist even in many smaller academic libraries. Library policy stated in writing that ILL was available only to members of the faculty; well, I was a librarian and I had faculty status so I persisted.

I was given a copy of the A.L.A. form and typed it up, all except of course the name of the lending library. That was the eternal problem. It was a rare ILL patron indeed who knew where a particular book might be found. We went on instinct or intuition and trusted in blind luck most of the time. Yes, I eventually got

*Reprinted by permission of the author and publisher from Collection Building 8:2 (Summer 1986) 34-38; copyright © 1986 by Neal-Schuman Publishers.

the book and then had to put up with a lot of bad jokes about my intentions. I do not have a lot of nostalgia for those days.

I'll leave it to the library historians to work out the full impact that OCLC has made across our profession but I am certain of one area; those of us who read have entered into a golden age of interlibrary loan. Thanks to that familiar light grey box there is hardly a book beyond a reader's grasp. Somewhere, somebody has it and will, sometimes for a price, be willing to lend it.

It has also given us both a new term to befuddle our administrations and a new way to dazzle. I would guess by now that a lot of college and university presidents are a mite weary of having "retrospective conversion" tossed at them in conversation and in written reports. The first time a president hears it there is--especially at a public institution--a moment of stark terror that the director of library services has suddenly experienced a religious conversion that requires extensive and expensive ex post facto proselytization. Once it becomes clear that this is just another piece of library jargon the official relief is almost palpable.

The dazzling part is quite easy to attain, or at least it has been so far. All a library has to do is have the will to carry out retrospective conversion. Once between a fourth and a third of the collection is in the OCLC database, the library, no matter how small, will move from being a net borrower to being a net lender. I can assure you that there is nothing a senior administrator enjoys more than hearing from the library administrator that the campus library now loans out more than it borrows; the president will tell the board, etc., etc. For at least a month everybody will be glad to see you.

Yes, I've been through all this and found it both enjoyable, amusing, and professionally satisfying. But statistics, for all they seem to be telling, do not begin to tell everything. The operations of an interlibrary loan office tend to set their own routines and it becomes a bit difficult to tell just what it is that the library is lending. Such was the case here; we had a good time watching the totals swell. We really did not pay much attention to the titles that were going out.

Around 1979 or 1980, our Interlibrary Loan Librarian began to notice that one particular title was far and above our most frequently requested loan. On our campus the book sat quietly on the shelves without attracting much attention at all. Our all-time champion requested tome was The Anarchist Cookbook, by William Powell (New York: Lyle Stuart, 1971). Among other features, it has a considerable body of information about making one's very own bomb in the comfort of one's home. In many ways it seemed to be a relic of the final days of the sixties. Yet here it was in the beginning of the era of the Yuppie being requested by public libraries, academic libraries, and even a high school library or two. Each time it went out the ILL librarian would remark that we should note that particular city and wait to see if there would be headlines of any sort. There never were.

In several casual conversations, both the ILL librarian and I started to wonder out loud about just how all these readers had learned that such a book as The Anarchist Cookbook existed. The requests seemed to come fairly steadily; usually, as soon as the book was back it was requested again. There was no geographic pattern; one request would be from a college in eastern Pennsylvania and the next would be from a public library in an Ohio suburb.

One day I drafted a one-question questionnaire; my thinking was to make this as simple and as private as possible. (I'll send you a copy with this letter.) All I asked the individual who had requested one of our books on interlibrary loan was this: How did you find out that this book existed? I did give them some possible answers such as a bibliography, a fellow student, the librarian, or a teacher. Information not requested on the questionnaire included the name of the book, the name of the reader, and the name of the library.

I had 500 copies of the questionnaire run off. The ILL librarian agreed to include one in all requested books that we sent out. We sat back and waited to see what if anything would be returned.

This was our first surprise. Of the 500 questionnaires sent, we received 384 back. Our far-flung readers seemed to be as eager to tell us where they learned about the book as we were to find that out. Many just circled one of our possibilities or wrote in one or two words to indicate a source. A surprising number wrote anecdotes or tiny essays; at least one tried to convert us to a particular belief via the questionnaire. And to our distinct pleasure, a fair number included their personal thanks for our willingness to loan that particular title. We also think we may have accidentally learned something about the way OCLC has changed the way libraries operate.

So, you ask, how do readers find out that a specific book exists and accordingly might be borrowed? Let me just provide you with the raw statistics; then we can discuss them and their implications.

How Readers Become Aware a Title Exists

Source of Information	Number giving this source
Bibliography	113
Another person	63
Books	39
OCLC	34
Books in Print	28
Journals	26
Ads, catalogs, stores	19
Anecdotal	15
Book reviews	11

Source of Information	Number giving this source
Card catalog	11
Required/suggested reading	9
NUC	3
Television	3
Nonresponsive	10

TOTAL 384 Responses

I have to admit that the more I look at these the more I think I am learning. For example, look where television is; so much for the belief that TV can sell a book. I agree it can sell a diet book, but damn few of our ILL requests are for diet books. Two of the categories are broken down further and I'll get to that later on.

Before I attempt any analysis, perhaps I should indicate some additional factors that are present. Obviously these are all responses from highly motivated readers; it is a step beyond the routine to request a book in interlibrary loan. We know here from several past surveys that we loan about as much to public libraries as we do to academic libraries. There are a lot of small rural public libraries in Pennsylvania. One of the accomplishments of the State Library has been the distribution of OCLC terminals to about as many libraries in the Commonwealth as could use one. This library, for the record, has a collection of about 320,000 volumes; around 65 percent of this collection is in OCLC.

Some of the figures hardly require much analysis. I wasn't too surprised to see that "bibliography" led the list and perhaps as a co-author of a bibliography myself I was a bit pleased.

The category of "another person" did have some surprises when examined. The 63 responses could be broken down as follows in descending order: Teachers or professors-23; Friends and acquaintances -21; Librarians-11; Author-4; Relatives-2; and Others-2. I certainly expected teachers to rank first but I hardly expected my own profession, the keepers of the books themselves, to rank quite so distant a third; however, I will indicate further on how perhaps as many as 76 of the responses must have involved interaction with a librarian. There were four who had learned about a book directly from its author; in every case according to the response on the questionnaire, the reader had attended a lecture by the author wherein the book was heartily recommended.

The third largest category, books, could be broken into two areas: Books by or about the author-15 and a reference in another book -24. As near as we could tell, this did not refer to the bibliography in a given book. Mention was made of footnotes and of a specific title being mentioned in the text. In other words, our readers tend to be both curious and adventuresome and one book for them leads to another book.

One category made me a little sad. Eleven of our borrowers learned that a title existed from the card catalog in their local library. The book was found to be missing from the local library shelves and they then insisted that an interlibrary loan be placed. I am glad that the librarian was willing to place the loan and we certainly are pleased to help out.

The category I most dislike is the loans we made as the result of a review. Now we both know that a review in a professional or scholarly journal can be months or even years after publication so that isn't so bad. The requests that annoyed me were those for whatever title happened to be on the front page of the most recent New York Times Book Review section. Once in a while we have gotten the book early and the individual who had requested it was already done with it. Sometimes the request is for a book in processing; depending upon the circumstances we will probably send it out. I have some empathy for the intelligent reader being served by those small rural libraries. Every once in a while though, the request is for a title I have my eye on; I assume I don't have to tell you who reads the book first?

In describing our findings I indicated that my analysis showed that librarians were involved in at least 76 of the requests. I base this in large measure on my experiences in a small liberal arts college back in the early Sixties; I can recall vividly the struggle to provide any sort of bibliographic service. Anyhow, I think the previously indicated 11 listings for the librarian, 34 for OCLC, 28 for Books in Print, and 3 for the NUC should be totalled and be considered as sources used by the librarian to satisfy a user's request for book information. I say this because in that library of mine in 1960 there would have been no OCLC and many more indications for Books in Print, the NUC, and the CBI. Small libraries just didn't have such a range of bibliographic resources then. Further, it is a rare public library that has either its Books in Print or its NUC in an area generally open to the public. What I am fairly certain our questionnaire reflects is the reader asking a librarian for more books by this specific author or for information on a book on a specific subject.

I did not expect to have a category called "anecdotal" and I certainly didn't anticipate fifteen such responses. Each category of the questionnaire could easily provide quotable material, but this one had the full range of human emotions, ranging from pride to nostalgia.

Someone who borrowed a Loeb edition of Tertullian wrote in bold strokes of black ink, "As a Patristics scholar (Ph.D 1982) I am familiar with it!" A budding scholar informed us, "I became aware of this book's existence when I began to fill out an application for undergraduate admission to Notre Dame." Two others were reliving pleasant memories from childhood. An individual who borrowed one of the Five Little Peppers series (remember those?) wrote us, "My mother read these books to us as children. I remembered them and that there was a series of books." The other made me wonder about the outreach of libraries

as well as why this individual waited so long to try to get a copy: "When
I was sixteen back in the year 1943 I first read this book. It was given
to me as a gift. I've never forgotten it and since the 1950s, when it
was lost in a move from San Francisco to the Western part of Pennsylvania, I've searched flea markets, old book shops, etc. to get a copy to
reread and possibly purchase." I confess I haven't heard of this one:
Enchanted Vagabonds, by Dana Lamb.

Now I know you know I am something of a nut about the work of
Anthony Trollope. You certainly can imagine my delight when we turned
up this response: "I've been reading my way through Trollope's novels.
Some are hard to find. Happily, I've found quite a few through ILL
efforts made by the Allentown Public Library. I have read all but two
of the novels now."

In the end though, it is the 34 citations of OCLC that I keep coming
back to. At first when we started drawing this response I thought that
the reader had misunderstood the question and that we were getting
the procedure, not the source. Finally I called a couple of libraries
and asked about the response. The answer is an indication in a small
way of how OCLC has changed the way librarians do things.

The reader would ask the librarian if a given author had written
other books. The librarian would go to the OCLC terminal with the
reader and key up the author. I do this here with our terminal for my
own reading. To the reader, the source of the information was indeed
OCLC. It would not at all surprise me to be told that active readers
already have a fair amount of more than casual awareness of OCLC and
its potential for their further reading.

OCLC isn't just used to help readers. It is the first place to
check on just about any sort of bibliographic question. Is there a new
scholarly edition of Oliver Twist in the works? Try the terminal. Have
the new reprints of Jim Thompson become available? Let me at that
terminal. Hasn't Professor Rascal ordered this book by its subtitle?
Well, he usually gets the author right, so let's check the terminal.
There it is. This sort of quick and easy automated checking goes on
in every library in the country.

I write this with the first month's worth of "hit" charges for
casual use of the OCLC terminal being compiled. Oh yes, you get
credits, some for interlibrary loans and for retrospective conversion
activities. In other words, you get an infinite charge which is supposed
to be counterbalanced by a finite credit. I will not tell you what I
think of this, but it is exactly the sort of thing that I expected would
happen when librarians lost control of OCLC and the president was a
lawyer. We all know what Shakespeare suggested be done with lawyers.
The OCLC database has become the bibliographic source for first checking and now we will be charged for that use. I cannot resist the analogy
of the drug pusher; first he hooks you and then he raises his prices.
That seems to be the world we live in and I don't know any reasons why

librarians should expect their world and its utilities to be any better
or any worse than the so-called real world.

Anyhow, Bill, this is my latest fling with a questionnaire and I
think it might be my last. Unlike a lawyer, a librarian with a questionnaire really doesn't know the answer in advance. I like to think I was
surprised throughout this process. And, oh yes, there remained one
final surprise. We sent out The Anarchist Cookbook at least five times
during our study; five times we stuck in a copy of the questionnaire.
Not once did we receive back a response.

And what have you read lately?

P.S. Just for the record, our Interlibrary Loan Librarian here is Dr.
Esther Jane Carrier, who has written a couple of books herself. Mrs.
Carol Gehret put up with me looking over her shoulder while she tabu-
lated the returns. And my wife listened to me talk about it. I am grateful to them all.

AMERICAN LITERATURE--
WHO'S PUBLISHING IT?*

Leonard Kniffel

Claims for the significance of little magazines in contemporary American literature abound--most plentifully, in the magazines themselves. Little magazines and small literary presses, goes the theory, are where American literature is really happening. Citing a rapidly accumulating body of evidence, a 1984 article in the New York Times Book Review agreed, and announced that "small presses have finally come of age."

Legendary little magazines such as The Masses, The Pagan, The Dial, and The Fugitive, from the first part of this century, have secured positions in literary history for having published the early works of Carl Sandburg, Wallace Stevens, William Carlos Williams, Hart Crane, T. S. Eliot, and numerous others, while their high-circulation counterparts published the vapid and now-forgotten verse of writers like Fannie Stearns Davis and Anne Bunner.

Today, small presses and little magazines not only continue to pioneer literary talent, they present the works of established writers as well. When Jaroslav Seifert won the Nobel Prize for Literature in 1984, the Czech writer was well-known in Europe, but few Americans knew his work, though it had been translated and published in this country in the Hampden-Sydney Review. His only available book in English translation was published in a small press magazine in Iowa called The Spirit That Moves Us, the year before he won the prize.

Who Gets the Prizes

When a writer is said to publish in "the best" magazines, informed readers may have some idea which magazines these are, but librarians searching (as I did) for an objective ranking of magazines

*Reprinted by permission of the author and publisher of Library Journal 112:3 (February 15, 1987) 103-109; copyright © 1987 by Reed Publishing, USA, Div. of Reed Holdings, Inc.

that publish original fiction and poetry will be hard-pressed to find one. Most commentaries on little magazines separate them from mainstream periodicals, making it difficult to determine how their publishing records compare.

How can one determine which American magazines are publishing this country's best original fiction and poetry? Creative work which is collected and published by trade publishers, and which goes on to win America's major literary prizes, has almost always appeared previously in magazines. For this article, I chose nine major literary prizes and examined the books which won them, with the aim of determining which magazines consistently publish prize-winning fiction and poetry.

While the accumulation of awards and prizes may not be the best or only measure of a magazine's merit, it is one which is calculable and meaningful to librarians who need tangible measures of quality. The choice of which prizes to examine was based on the familiarity of the prize, its reputation and covetedness, and an effort to present a representative cross-section of awards.

The Awards, the Authors

For poetry, the American Book Award, the Pulitzer Prize, and the National Book Critics Circle Award are all nationally publicized and well established. The Yale Series of Younger Poets, the Lamont Poetry Prize, and the Walt Whitman Award are highly desirable awards because they include book publication in auspicious company.

Two annual story volumes, Prize Stories: the O. Henry Awards and Best American Short Stories, are the most widely known publications of their kind and have earned their standing over long periods of publishing excellence. The annual Pushcart Prize: Best of the Small Presses is the only publication of its kind known for consistent excellence and nationwide distribution.

In addition, recent story collections by a cross-section of 20 contemporary authors, ranging from a Nobel prize winner to acclaimed newcomers, were examined for this study. The authors, chosen for their range of styles and publishers, are: Max Apple, Louis Auchincloss, Donald Barthelme, Charles Baxter, Ann Beattie, Saul Bellow, Paul Bowles, Truman Capote, Raymond Carver, Stuart Dybek, John Gardner, Janet Kauffman, Joyce Carol Oates, Cynthia Ozick, Grace Paley, Isaac Bashevis Singer, John Updike, Alice Walker, Nancy Willard, and Richard Yates.

Novels were not examined because they generally do not contain significant numbers of credits for previous publication. In instances where prizes were given for collected or selected poems, especially in the case of the Pulitzer Prize, these credits were not tallied, as

The Big Picture—Citations per magazine for each award listed in the ten individual tables.

	Single-Author Collections	Best American Short Stories	O. Henry Awards	Pushcart Prize	Pulitzer Prize	National/American Book Award	National Book Critics Circle Award	Lamont Poetry Prize	Walt Whitman Award	Yale Series of Younger Poets	Total
The New Yorker	39	44	29		5	15	22	4	1	5	164
Poetry				15	3	15	21	4	6	9	73
Antaeus	6	6	8	21	1	10	1	2	1	2	58
The Atlantic	9	8	19		3	1	8	2	1	1	52
The American Poetry Review	1			18	1	7	8	5		1	41
The Iowa Review	2	2		17		8	2	1	3	2	37
Ploughshares	3	3	5	15		1	3	2		1	33
The Georgia Review		5	1	12	3	2		2	1	3	29
The American Review*	3	7	5		1	10	1			1	28
The Hudson Review	1	3	2	9			10	1		1	27
Kenyon Review	3	2	3	7				10	2		27
The Paris Review	2	2	2	12		1		3	2		24
The Massachusetts Review	1	7	6	6			1	1		1	23
Esquire	6	9	7								22
The Ohio Review		2	1	3	2	7	1		1	5	22
Shenandoah		4	7	5			2	1		3	22
The Southern Review	1	5	1	5	1	3		1	2	3	22
Triquarterly	3	4	2	12							21
Ironwood				4	1			1	13	1	20
Kayak*				3	1	13	1	1			19
Partisan Review	4	2	1	7		3	1	1			19
Chicago Review	1	1	1	8		5		1		1	18
Poetry Northwest				2	1	3	1	2		9	18
Michigan Quarterly Review	4	2	1	2			2	5	1		17
The Nation						1	6	7	1	2	17
Field				7		8				1	16
The North American Review	2	3	4	3		1		1	1	1	16
Mademoiselle	1	1	9				3			1	15
The Sewanee Review		5	8						2		15
Epoch	1	1	6			2			1	2	13
Prairie Schooner		3		1	1		1	1	4	2	13
The Antioch Review	3		4	2		1				2	12
The Missouri Review	1	1		3		4	1		1	1	12
Playboy	4	7	1								12
Salmagundi	1	1		7		1	1			1	12
Virginia Quarterly Review		2	3	2	1	1		2	1		12
Carolina Quarterly	1	2	4							4	11
New England Review	2			2	1	1	1	1		3	11
Ontario Review	1	2	2	6							11
Tendril				1				1	3	6	11
Ascent		5	3				1	1			10
Fiction International		3	2	4	1						10

	Single-Author Collections	Best American Short Stories	O. Henry Awards	Pushcart Prize	Pulitzer Prize	National/American Book Award	National Book Critics Circle Award	Lamont Poetry Prize	Walt Whitman Award	Yale Series...	Total
Harper's		2	5			2		1			10
The New York Review of Books				4		2	3	1			10
The Little Magazine		1	1	1		4		2			9
Kansas Quarterly		1	1	3				3			8
New Letters		1	1	4				1	1		8
Open Places				2		1	1			4	8
Southern Poetry Review				1		1	1	4	1		8
The Yale Review		1	1		1	1	1	1		2	8
Fiction	1		4	2							7
Southwest Review		3	2	1				1			7
Transatlantic*	1	1	2	1		1		1			7
The Carleton Miscellany		2	1			1		1	1		6
Choice		2				2	1	1			6
Hawaii Review		1	1							4	6
Mother Jones	2		2			1		1			6
Black Warrior Review		1		2						2	5
The Chariton Review			1	1				1		2	5
Cincinnati Poetry Review				1		1	1	1		1	5
Columbia				2	1			1		1	5
Crazyhorse				2		1		1		1	5
Ms.	3							1		1	5
Northwest Review	1	1		2						1	5
Pequod				1			1	2	1		5
Raccoon					1			2	2		5
The Agni Review		1		2				1			4
California Quarterly		2	1	1							4
Cutbank		1		1				1	1		4
Grand Street	1		2	1							4
The Greensboro Review		2	1	1							4
The Malahat Review		2		1				1			4
New American Review*					1	1	1	1			4
New York Quarterly						1	1	1	1		4
Seneca Review						1		1	2		4
South Carolina Review		2	1					1			4
Three Rivers Poetry Journal				1	1	1		1			4
The Threepenny Review	2		1	1							4
Caterpillar*					1	1		1			3
Darkhorse								1	1	1	3
The New Republic			1			1	1				3
A Shout in the Streets						1	1	1			3
Tar River Poetry				1		1	1				3

* Defunct

Single-Author Collections
Original Publishers Credited More than Once

The New Yorker	39
The Atlantic	9
Antaeus	6
Esquire	6
Michigan Quarterly Review	4
Partisan Review	4
Playboy	4
American Review	3
Antioch Review	3
Kenyon Review	3
Ms.	3
Ploughshares	3
Triquarterly	3
The Iowa Review	2
Mother Jones	2
New England Review	2
New York	2
The North American Review	2
The Paris Review	2
The Threepenny Review	2
Vanity Fair	2
The Writer	2

Best American Short Stories
Original Publishers Credited More than Once

The New Yorker	44
Esquire	9
The Atlantic	8
American Review	7
The Massachusetts Review	7
Playboy	7
Antaeus	6
Ascent	5
The Georgia Review	5
The Sewanee Review	5
The Southern Review	5
Colorado Quarterly	4
Shenandoah	4
Triquarterly	4
Fiction International	3
The Hudson Review	3
Ms.	3
The North American Review	3
Ploughshares	3
Prairie Schooner	3
Southwest Review	3
The Writer	2

O. Henry Awards
Original Publishers Credited More Than Twice

The New Yorker	29
The Atlantic	19
Mademoiselle	9
Antaeus	8
The Sewanee Review	8
Esquire	7
Shenandoah	7
Epoch	6
The Massachusetts Review	6
American Review	5
Harper's	5
Ploughshares	5
Redbook	5
The Antioch Review	4
Carolina Quarterly	4
Fiction	4
The North American Review	4
Ascent	3
Kenyon Review	3
Virginia Quarterly Review	3
The Writer	2

Pushcart Prize
Winners Three or More Times

Antaeus	21
The American Poetry Review	18
The Iowa Review	17
Poetry	15
Ploughshares	15
Triquarterly	12
The Georgia Review	12
The Paris Review	12
The Hudson Review	9
Chicago Review	8
Field	7
Kenyon Review	7
Partisan Review	7
Salmagundi	7
The Massachusetts Review	6
Ontario Review	6
Mississippi Review	5
Parnassus	5
Shenandoah	5
The Southern Review	5
Fiction International	4
Ironwood	4
New Letters	4
Gallimaufry	3
Kansas Quarterly	3
Kayak	3
The Missouri Review	3
The North American Review	3
The Ohio Review	3
Sun & Moon	3
The Writer	2

Pulitzer Prize
Original Publishers Credited More than Once

The New Yorker	5
The New York Review of Books	4
The Atlantic	3
The Georgia Review	3
Poetry	3
The Ohio Review	2
Parenthese	2
Saturday Review	2
The Times Literary Supplement	2
The Writer	2

National/American Book Award—Poetry
Original Publishers Credited More Than Twice

The New Yorker	15
Poetry	15
Kayak	13
American Review	10
Antaeus	10
Field	8
The Iowa Review	8
The American Poetry Review	7
The Ohio Review	7
Chicago Review	5
Workshop	5
Ambit	4
The Little Magazine	4
London Magazine	4
The Missouri Review	4
Marilyn	3
Partisan Review	3
Poetry Northwest	3
Samphire	3
The Southern Review	3
The Yale Review	3
The Writer	2

National Book Critics Circle Award
Original Publishers Credited More Than Twice

The New Yorker	22
Poetry	21
The Hudson Review	10
The American Poetry Review	8
The Atlantic	8
The Nation	6
The Hampden-Sydney Review	3
Mademoiselle	3
The New York Review of Books	3
The Paris Review	3
Ploughshares	3
The Writer	2

Lamont Poetry Prize
Original Publishers Credited More Than Once

Kenyon Review	10
The Nation	7
The American Poetry Review	5
Michigan Quarterly Review	5
The New Yorker	4
Poetry	4
Antaeus	2
The Atlantic	2
The Georgia Review	2
The Paris Review	2
Pequod	2
Poetry Northwest	2
Poets On	2
Virginia Quarterly Review	2
The Writer	2

Walt Whitman Award
Original Publishers Credited More Than Twice

Ironwood	13
Poetry	6
Cedar Rock	5
Prairie Schooner	4
Southern Poetry Review	4
The Iowa Review	3
Kansas Quarterly	3
Tendril	3
Texas Quarterly	3
Wind	3
The Writer	2

Yale Series of Younger Poets
Original Publishers Credited More Than Twice

Poetry	9
Poetry Northwest	9
Bamboo Ridge	8
Tendril	6
The New Yorker	5
The Ohio Review	5
Carolina Quarterly	4
Greenfield Review	4
Hawaii Review	4
Open Places	4
Ark River Review	3
Calyx	3
Dacotah Territory	3
The Georgia Review	3
Hapa	3
New England Review	3
Shenandoah	3
The Southern Review	3
The Writer	2

they were either too numerous or incompletely given, and they represent an entire career dating sometimes to the 1940s. Acknowledgements for previous publications appeared in every collection. The
tabulations include ten years of each award, 1975-1984.

High Marks for Storytelling

Of the 155 stories gathered in the 20 single-author volumes
examined, 39 (or 25 percent) of them were previously published in
The New Yorker. These 39 stories are by nine of the 20 authors:
Barthelme, Beattie, Bellow, Capote, Carver, Kauffman, Ozick, Paley,
and Singer.

The next highest number of credits went to The Atlantic which,
though credited for only nine stories, represented the work of eight
different writers: Apple, Auchincloss, Beattie, Baxter, Bellow, Carver,
Updike, and Yates. The next most frequently cited magazines are
Antaeus and Esquire with six credits each. Michigan Quarterly
Review, Partisan Review, and Playboy tied with four credits each.
American Review, Antioch Review, Kenyon Review, Ms., Ploughshares,
and Triquarterly published three stories each.

There is a surprising balance between the magazines--big and
little--which published the stories. While New York published two
(Auchincloss and Capote), so did The Iowa Review (Apple and Dybek). Vanity Fair published two (Bellow and Dybek), as did The
Threepenny Review (Bowles and Paley), and so on down the line.
In fact, of the 69 magazines mentioned in these books, almost two
thirds (42) are little literary magazines, in most instances publishing
the same authors as their commercial counterparts.

For The Best American Short Stories (Houghton), each year
a leading American fiction writer is invited to serve as guest editor
and select the some 20 stories to be included. Since its establishment
in 1915, the series has gained stature as one of the premier events
for writers of short fiction. Of a total of 68 magazines from which
stories have been selected over the past ten years, only six (roughly
ten percent) are high circulation. Topping the list of the 21 most
frequently cited is The New Yorker, with 44 stories to its credit,
followed by Esquire with nine, The Atlantic with eight, and American
Review, The Massachusetts Review, and Playboy with seven each.
The rest are little magazines with up to six credits apiece.

Prize Stories: the O. Henry Awards (Doubleday), a collection
of the year's best short stories published by American authors in
American periodicals, was first published in 1919 and continues to
be an important annual. In the last ten years, The New Yorker and
The Atlantic led in stories published that were subsequently republished in the O. Henry collections. Yet even in this prestigious anthology, Mademoiselle, Esquire, Harper's, and Redbook are the only

trade magazines which published significant numbers of the prize-
winning stories. Of the top 20 magazines, only six are trade magazines. In fact, of the 61 magazines that have had stories republished
in an O. Henry collection, the only other large-circulation magazines
mentioned are Cosmopolitan, The New Republic, Playboy (once each),
and Mother Jones (twice).

The Pushcart Prize (Pushcart Pr.; paperback, Avon) is an annual volume of stories, poems, and essays, culled from small press
publications, mostly little magazines. Since their inception in 1976,
the volumes have included material from 175 different magazines, 30
of which were winners three or more times. Antaeus leads with 21
separate inclusions. American Poetry Review and Iowa Review follow
with 18 and 17 inclusions respectively, then Poetry and Ploughshares
with 15 each. Edited by Bill Henderson, this prize collection reveals the solid publishing patterns of many little magazines which
supply stories and poems for the volumes year after year.

Prize Poetry

Since 1975, the Pulitzer Prize for poetry has gone to six poets
for individual volumes of poetry which do not constitute a retrospective
collection. The magazines most frequently cited in these collections
are split almost in half between high-circulation magazines (The New
Yorker, The New York Review of Books, The Atlantic, Saturday
Review, and The Times Literary Supplement) and littles (The Georgia
Review, Poetry, The Ohio Review, and Parenthese).

Original publishers of one poem in these Pulitzer collections
vary from the New York Times to such obscure journals as Kuksu,
Rogue River Gorge, and Clear Creek. John Ashbery's Self Portrait
in a Convex Mirror, which won the Pulitzer Prize, the National Book
Award, and the National Book Critics Circle Award in 1976, is one
of the few books which gives short shrift to little magazines, listing
only credits for first publication in The New Yorker, Poetry, The
American Poetry Review, The New York Review of Books, and "various
little magazines."

The American Book Award (before 1980, the National Book
Award) for poetry has been presented over the last ten years to six
books which are not collected works. Poetry previously published
at least one poem from every one of the six books--15 poems in total.
The New Yorker follows with 14 poems from four of the volumes, and
Kayak with 13 poems all from one volume. American Review and
Antaeus previously published nine poems each, and The Iowa Review
is close behind with eight. Others which published significant num-
bers of the poems are: The American Poetry Review, Chicago Review,
Field, and The Ohio Review.

Since it was established in 1975, the National Book Critics

Circle Award for poetry has gone to books which contain poems previously published in 44 magazines, of which six are high circulation. Five of them are credited more than twice for previous publication: The Atlantic, Mademoiselle, The Nation, The New York Review of Books, and The New Yorker. The list of publishers credited more than twice is over half little magazines: The American Poetry Review, Hampden-Sydney Review, The Hudson Review, The Paris Review, Ploughshares, and Poetry.

The Academy of American Poets, organized in 1934 to encourage the development of American poetry, recognizes and rewards poets of proven merit with awards from the income of a permanent trust fund. The Academy is governed by a board of 12 chancellors, representing various schools of poetry and the different regions of the country. Because they include book publication, two of the most coveted of the Academy's prizes are the Lamont Poetry Prize, given annually for the publication of a second book of poems by an American poet, and the Walt Whitman Award, given annually to an American poet who has not yet published a book of poems.

The magazine topping the credits in Whitman-winning volumes is Ironwood, and no trade magazine made the top ten. The Atlantic, The Christian Science Monitor, The Nation, and Mother Jones are mentioned once each. Kenyon Review published the largest number of poems in Lamont-winning volumes, followed by The Nation. The New Yorker and The Atlantic also appear in the top-14 list as well as ten little magazines, including the relatively obscure Pequod.

In ten years of the Yale Series of Younger Poets, only five high-circulation magazines published any of the poems in these books, out of 84 magazines that did so. That's less than six percent. Only one, The New Yorker, published poems by more than one poet in the series. The leading publishers of poems that subsequently appeared in the Yale volumes were Poetry and Poetry Northwest. The New Yorker is the only high-circulation magazine mentioned more than twice. Of the 84 magazines credited in Yale volumes, only four other trade magazines are mentioned: The Atlantic, Mademoiselle, Ms., and The Nation.

And the Winner Is...

A total of 426 magazines published poems and stories which subsequently appeared in the books examined for this study. Of those, 290 published material chosen for only one of the prizes examined. These range from such familiar names as Cosmopolitan, McCall's, New York, Rolling Stone, Vanity Fair, and Vogue to such unusual contenders as Big Scream, Boxspring, Buffalo Stamp, Clown War, Crawl Out Your Window, Dental Floss, Hearse, Holy Soul Jellyroll, and The Unspeakable Visions of the Individual.

One prize-winning story or poem, however, can be luck, a

fluke, or just beating the odds. The tales of how periodicals as varied as The National Jewish Monthly to the Berkeley Barb happened to publish poems and stories that ended up in prize-winning collections are undoubtedly as interesting and varied as the magazines themselves, but they do not reveal publication patterns.

An additional 52 magazines published eventual winners in two of the examined categories. These include familiar titles (Look, Redbook, and Saturday Review) as well as many university reviews and other curiously named magazines like Alcatraz, Chowder Review, Painted Bride Quarterly, and Shankpainter. The remaining 84 periodicals published stories and poems from three or more of the categories examined.

The resounding leader in this survey is The New Yorker, with a total of 164 stories and poems published in the collections examined. The next highest achievers are Poetry with 73 credits, Antaeus with 58, and The Atlantic with 52. Only 14 trade magazines appear among the top 84, 16 percent of the total, and that includes the now-defunct American Review and New American Review. These 14 published 28 percent, or 354 out of 1280, of the stories and poems in the chart of top scorers.

The only magazine with credits in every examined category is Antaeus. Though to some extent this is a matter of definitions (The New Yorker is not eligible for the Pushcart Prize for small presses, Poetry does not publish ficiton, and so forth), it nevertheless speaks well of editor Daniel Halpern's ability to consistently select work viewed as superior by a cross-section of judges.

This quality is also evident in The Atlantic, The New Yorker, and The Southern Review which are mentioned in nine out of ten categories, and in The Georgia Review, The Iowa Review, The North American Review, The Ohio Review, and Ploughshares which are present in eight. Magazines with credits in seven categories are: The American Poetry Review, The American Review, Chicago Review, The Hudson Review, The Massachusetts Review, Michigan Quarterly Review, The Missouri Review, New England Review, The Paris Review, Partisan Review, Poetry, Prairie Schooner, Virginia Quarterly Review, and The Yale Review.

In the three fiction categories, the biggest prize winners are: The New Yorker (112), The Atlantic (36), Esquire (22), Antaeus (20), American Review (15), The Massachusetts Review (14), The Sewanee Review (13), Playboy (12), Mademoiselle (11), Ploughshares (11), and Shenandoah (11). In the poetry categories, the leader is Poetry with a total of 58 credits, while The New Yorker is second with 42, followed by The American Poetry Review with 22, Antaeus and The Nation with 17 each, and The Atlantic, Iowa Review, Ironwood, Kayak, Michigan Quarterly Review, and The Ohio Review with 16 each.

"Basement and Garage" Publishing

There are an estimated 5000 little magazines published in the
United States today. The great majority of them are printed in runs
of less than 2000 copies, and many have fewer than a hundred readers, according to Michael Anania in The Little Magazine in America:
a Modern Documentary History. Our perception of quality in these
publications may have less to do with their records of publication
than with their advertising budgets.

Many literary magazines rely on universities for support, others
on grants, and a privileged few on benefactors. In any case, little
magazines are money losers. The sale of magazines and mass-market
paperbacks is accomplished through a system of distribution which
treats magazines as high-turnover merchandise with a fleeting shelf
life. Thomas Whiteside reasons that competition among publishers
"to acquire the greatest proportion of the available shelf space has
become intense."

It is virtually impossible for literary magazines to break into
this market. Most of them lack the capital, advertisers, and access
to distribution of their commercial counterparts. Many are so by
design, and it may be their fierce independence which ultimately accounts for their progressiveness and originality. This is not a new
phenomenon. The history of literary magazines in America is one
of basement and garage publishing, of literature made public with
little capital, of dedicated writers and readers.

The importance of literary magazines in presenting original
works of fiction and poetry, however, has not resulted in library
subscriptions. Even for well-established magazines like Poetry
and The Paris Review, the response from libraries is dismal--the
former with only about 4000 library subscriptions, the latter with
not even 1000. Others like Antioch Review and Partisan Review
average about 2000 library subscribers.

Antaeus, which has an outstanding showing in this survey,
has only 598 library subscribers (78 are public libraries), according
to Managing Editor Kate Bourne, despite the fact that they have
tried direct mail promotion and other sales techniques to attract
libraries. "Support from libraries has been minimal," says Antaeus
Editor Daniel Halpern. "Literary magazines do not have a wide
general readership. People don't go into libraries and ask for them.
When budget cuts come, less-used magazines are the first to go, and
we've had a drop-off in recent years."

He adds, "So many librarians are intimidated by the sheer
numbers of little magazines," and minimal effort has been made in
the library literature to identify which of America's 5000 or so little
magazines have proved the quality and durability of their publications.

The lack of indexing is often cited by librarians as a major
reason to exclude little magazines, and it is true that even the venerable Poetry was recently dropped from the Reader's Guide to
Periodical Literature. None of the little magazines mentioned in this
article are indexed in the Reader's Guide, though of course The New
Yorker, The Nation, Esquire, The New Republic, and other magazines
which publish original ficiton and poetry are.

John Updike said in a recent fiction issue of Esquire, "Most
of the people in the United States get along without reading fiction,
and more and more of the magazines get along without printing it.
Even Esquire, which used to run short stories as automatically as
he-men smoked unfiltered cigarettes, has to whip itself up and cheer
itself on to give us an issue like this one." The figures in this
survey indicate that American literature is indeed in the hands of
a few major magazines and a great many little ones. Librarians
must decide to what extent they will participate in the relegation of
fiction and poetry to what are now termed "special audiences."

Bibliography

Henry, DeWitt, "Literary Magazine Review," Wilson Library Bulletin,
    December 1980, p. 283-284.
Hoffman, Frederick J., Charles Allen, & Carolyn F. Ulrich. The
    Little Magazine: a History and a Bibliography. Princeton Univ.
    Pr., 1947.
James, Caryn, "14,000 Small Presses: Something More Than the
    Sum of Their Parts," The New York Times Book Review, December
    23, 2984, p. 3-4.
Literary and Library Prizes. 10th ed., rev. & ed. by Olga S. Weber
    & Stephen J. Calvert. Bowker, 1980.
The Little Magazine in America: a Modern Documentary History.
    ed. by Elliott Anderson & Mary Kinzie. Pushcart Pr., 1978.
Updike, John. "The Importance of Fiction," Esquire, August 1985,
    p. 61-62.
Whiteside, Thomas. The Blockbuster Complex. Wesleyan Univ.
    Pr., 1981.

Collections Analyzed

Single-Author Story Collections

Apple, Max. Free Agents. Harper, 1984.
Auchincloss, Louis. Narcissa and Other Fables. Houghton, 1983.
Barthelme, DOnald. Overnight to Many Distant Cities. Putnam, 1983.
Baxter, Charles. Harmony of the World. Univ. of Missouri Pr.,
    1984.
Beattie, Ann. The Burning House. Random, 1982.
Bellow, Saul. Him with His Foot in His Mouth and Other Stories.
    Harper, 1984.

Bowles, Paul. Midnight Mass. Black Sparrow, 1981.
Capote, Truman. Music for Chameleons. Random, 1980.
Carver, Raymond. Cathedral. Knopf, 1983.
Dybek, Stuart. Childhood and Other Neighborhoods. Viking, 1980.
Gardner, John. The Art of Living and Other Stories. Knopf, 1981.
Kauffman, Janet. Places in the World a Woman Could Walk. Knopf, 1984.
Oates, Joyce Carol. Last Days. Dutton, 1984.
Ozick, Cynthia. Levitation: Five Fictions. Knopf, 1982.
Paley, Grace. Later the Same Day. Farrar, 1985.
Singer, Isaac Bashevis. The Image and Other Stories. Farrar, 1985.
Updike, John. Too Far To Go. HBJ, 1979.
Walker, Alice. You Can't Keep a Good Woman Down. HBJ, 1983.
Willard, Nancy. Angel in the Parlor: Five Stories and Eight Essays. HBJ, 1983.
Yates, Richard. Liars in Love. Seymour Lawrence: Delacorte, 1981.

Anthologies

The Best American Short Stories. annual. Editor varies. Houghton, 1975-84.
Prize Stories: the O. Henry Awards. annual. Edited & intro. by William Abrahams. Doubleday, 1975-84.
The Pushcart Prize: Best of the Small Presses. Vols. 1-7. Edited by Bill Henderson. Pushcart Pr., 1976-84.

The Pulitzer Prize-Poetry

1984 Oliver, Mary. American Primitive. Little, 1983.
1981 Schuyler, James. The Morning of the Poem. Farrar, 1980.
1979 Warren, Robert Penn. Now and Then: Poems 1976-1978. Random, 1978.
1977 Merrill, James. Divine Comedies. Atheneum, 1976.
1976 Ashbery, John. Self Portrait in a Convex Mirror. Viking, 1975.
1975 Snyder, Gary. Turtle Island. New Directions, 1974.

National Book Award--Poetry

1983 Wright, Charles. Country Music. Wesleyan Univ. Pr., 1982.
1981 Mueller, Lisel. The Need To Hold Still. Louisiana State Univ. Pr., 1980.
1980 Levine, Philip. Ashes. Atheneum, 1983.
1979 Merrill, James. Mirabel: Book of Numbers. Atheneum, 1978.
1976 Ashbery, John. Self Portrait in a Convex Mirror. Viking, 1975.
1975 Hacker, Marilyn. Presentation Piece. Viking, 1974.
1974 Rich Adrienne. Diving into the Wreck: Poems, 1971-1972. Norton, 1973.

1974 Ginsberg, Allen. The Fall of America: Poems of These States,
1965-1971. City Lights, 1972.

National Book Critics Circle Award--Poetry

1984 Olds, Sharon. The Dead and the Living. Knopf, 1984.
1982 Pollit, Katha. Antarctic Traveller. Random, 1981.
1981 Ammons, A. R. A Coast of Trees. Norton, 1981.
1980 Seidel, Frederick. Sunrise. Viking, 1980.
1978 Lowell, Robert. Day by Day. Farrar, 1977.
1977 Bishop, Elizabeth. Geography III. Farrar, 1976.
1976 Ashbery, John. Self Portrait in a Convex Mirror. Viking,
1975.

Lamont Poetry Prize

1984 Schultz, Philip. Deep Within the Ravine. Viking, 1984.
1983 Olds, Sharon. The Dead and the Living. Knopf, 1984.
1982 Gibson, Margaret. Long Walks in the Afternoon. Louisiana
State Univ. Pr., 1982.
1981 Forche, Carolyn. The Country Between Us. Harper, 1981.
1980 Van Wallaghen, Michael. More Trouble with the Obvious.
Univ. of Illinois Pr., 1981.
1979 Seidel, Frederick. Summer. Viking, 1980.
1978 Ai. Killing Floor. Houghton, 1979.
1977 Stern, Gerald. Lucky Life. Houghton, 1977.
1976 Levis, Larry. The Afterlife. Univ. of Iowa Pr., 1977.
1975 Mueller, Lisel. The Private life. Louisiana State Univ. Pr.,
1976.

Walt Whitman Award

1984 Pankey, Eric. For the New Year. Atheneum, 1984.
1983 Gilbert, Christopher. Across the Mutual Landscape. Graywolf
Pr., 1984.
1982 Petrosky, Anthony. Jurgis Petraskas. Louisiana State Univ.
Pr., 1983.
1981 Rios, Alberto. Whispering To Fool the Wind, Sheep Meadow
Pr., 1982.
1980 Carter, Jared. Work, for the Night Is Coming, Macmillan, 1981.
1979 Bottoms, David. Shooting Rats at the Bibb County Dump.
Morrow, 1980.
1978 Snow, Karen. Wonders. Viking, 1980.
1977 Shakely, Lauren. Guilty Bystander. Random, 1978.
1976 Gilpin, Lauren. The Hocus Pocus of the Universe. Doubleday,
1977.
1975 Saner, Reg. Climbing into the Roots. Harper, 1976.

Yale Series of Younger Poets

(All published by Yale University Press in the year following the
award)

1984 Alexander, Pamela. Navigable Waters.
1983 Kenny, Richard. The Evolution of the Flightless Bird.
1982 Song, Cathy. Picture Bride.
1981 Wojahn, David. Icehouse Lights.
1980 Bensko, John. Green Soldiers.
1979 Davis, William Virgil. One Way To Reconstruct the Scene.
1978 Ullman, Leslie. Natural Histories.
1977 Ramke, Bin. The Difference.
1976 Broumas, Olga. Beginning with O.
1975 Forche, Carolyn. Gathering the Tribes.

TEENAGERS DO READ:
WHAT RURAL YOUTH SAY
ABOUT LEISURE READING*

Constance A. Mellon

Each time I teach my course on materials for young adults, I ask
students to list and discuss important issues in providing library
services to this age group. Almost invariably, the issue that tops
the list is "getting teenagers to read." Most of my students are
teachers or librarians who are returning to library school to fulfill
the state requirement for an advanced degree. They have daily
contact with young adults in the classroom, in the school media
center, in the public library. Some are parents of teenagers.
"Teenagers just aren't interested in reading," they tell me again and
again. Having raised three daughters, I was inclined to agree.

There can be no doubt that this is a media generation, seemingly
uncomfortable with silence. Television and tape players, boom boxes
and Walkmans provide background music to the leisure activities of
most young adults. Video games are readily available at teenage
gathering places and as inexpensive software for home computers.
With such sophisticated entertainment only a knob away, can the
printed word compete? Moreover, it is a complex time to be a teen-
ager. Easy access to drugs, to alcohol, and to methods of birth
control force adult decisions upon those who are not yet adults--
teenagers who are inadequately informed about the long-term effects
such decisions may have on their lives. Schools reverberate with
the current criticism, and administrators react by bringing more
pressure to bear upon students and teachers. Parents, meekly ac-
cepting the blame for everything, waver between permissiveness and
"tough-love" as they suffer through the increasingly long adolescence
of their children. Confused by too many choices and so much pressure, the suicide rate for young adults continues to escalate. With
teenagers faced with issues of survival as their daily fare, can we
expect them to be interested in reading?

*Reprinted by permission of the author and publisher of School
Library Journal 33:6 (February 1987) 27-30; copyright © 1987 by
Reed Publishing, USA, Div. of Reed Holdings, Inc.

The Setting

Eastern North Carolina is predominantly rural; many students live far from the small towns where they attend school. They depend on buses for transportation to school and, unlike their urban counterparts, they lack easy access to public libraries or to stores which sell reading material. Without the amusements and distractions of a city, it was expected that the teenagers of our region would have more leisure time. These and other factors unique to a rural setting might cause a difference in attitude toward reading between urban and rural teens.

Two of my graduate students were in unique positions to help explore these questions about reading and rural youth: Carroll Harrell is media specialist at Perquimans High School in Hertford, and Annette Privette is an English teacher at Bunn High School in Bunn. After a three-hour brainstorming session, we developed a questionnaire and, with the help of funding from the North Carolina Association of School Librarians and cooperation from the administrators and teachers of both schools, we designed a study to determine the leisure reading patterns of rural ninth-grade students.

Our focus was on "leisure reading" rather than "reading" because we were interested in what types of materials teenagers chose to read as opposed to what they were assigned to read. Ninth grade students were selected for preliminary study because they fall into a category described by G. Robert Carlsen in Books and the Teenage Reader (Harper, 1971) as "middle adolescence."

The two rural high schools mentioned are well-matched in all but one aspect--their proximity to a large city. While one school is located in a sparsely populated coastal area, the other is less than 35 miles from one of the state's largest cities. Both high schools are centrally located in the areas they serve and both include grades nine through 12. Over 90 percent of the student enrollment in both schools are classified "rural." Ethnic distribution is approximately equal, black and white, with no other group represented. Between one-third and one-half of the families have incomes at or below the poverty level; most are employed in agricultural occupations with little formal education beyond high school.

At both schools students are grouped for certain classes and courses of study. Five groups are designated: Academically Gifted; College Preparatory; General; Chapter I; and Special Education. These groups are defined as follows:

• Academically gifted students are identified by state guidelines, which include I.Q. and standardized achievement test scores and grade point averages.

• College preparatory students, planning to attend college, are determined by student choice.

• General students, those with no further academic plans, are determined by student choice.

• Special education students, determined by state guidelines, are those with limitations which may be physical, mental, or behavioral.

• Chapter I students are determined differently at the two schools. One defines them by reading scores below the 50th percentile on the California Achievement Test, while the other identifies them by using three criteria: C.A.T. scores below the 45th percentile; teacher recommendation; and performance in school.

Data Collection

The five-page, 28-item questionnaire we devised focused on factors related to reading by choice: whether or not teenagers read in their leisure time; if they do, what and where they read, and how they obtain their reading material; if they do not read, why not? The questionnaire is a modified checklist with space provided for comments and with several open-ended questions.

Questionnaires were duplicated in five colors for easy identification of the specific groups described above, and were administered to 20 English classes, 10 at each school, by their classroom teachers. A total of 362 questionnaires were administered: 22 Gifted: 156 College Preparatory; 72 General; 76 Chapter I; 32 Special Education.

Data was analyzed to determine what percentage of respondents, both overall and by groups, claimed they did or did not read in their spare time.   For non-readers, reasons they gave for not reading were examined.   For readers, factors relating to types of reading material chosen for leisure reading were analyzed: what types of reading material was purchased, and where and when they read for pleasure.

Data Analysis

A surprising 296 of the 362 respondents (82%) answered "yes" to the question: "Do you ever read in your spare time?"   By sex, 72 percent of the males surveyed and 92 percent of the females indicated that reading was a leisure activity.

Analysis by group was even more surprising.   It was anticipated that the Gifted and College Preparatory students would have a high percentage of spare-time readers, and they did: 100 percent of the Gifted group and 82 percent of the College Preparatory group responded "yes."   However 70 percent or more of the General and Chapter I respondents also indicated that they read in their spare time.

Less than 20 percent of all respondents claimed they did not read in their spare time. As might be anticipated, none of the Gifted, and only 10 percent of the College Preparatory students were included in this group. Twenty-five percent or less of the General and Chapter I students indicated no leisure reading activity, as opposed to 40 percent of the Special education students.

A breakdown by sex also revealed that twice as many males as females in each group did not read in their spare time. The two, most-frequent responses checked by non-readers (over 50 percent) were: they worked after school; or they hated to read. In addition, 75 percent of the General students who said they did not read in their spare time checked "reading is too hard." Among other reasons given for not reading were: "too much on my mind;" "too much to do;" and "[reading] bothers my eyes."

Leisure Reading Materials

On questions relating to types of materials chosen for leisure reading, a difference was observed between the responses of males and females. For males, the top three categories of reading materials across groups were magazines (72%), sports/sports biographies (68%), and comic books (54%). For females, the top three categories were romance (90%), mystery (73%), and magazines (73%). It's interesting to note that only 29 percent of the female respondents read comic books.

Specific magazines favored by boys included Hot Rod, Field and Stream, and Sports Illustrated. Girls favored Teen, Seventeen, Jet, Ebony, and Young Miss.

Twenty-two percent of each group, male and female, claimed to read non-fiction. Boys specified books on sports, hunting, and war. Girls chose biographies.

An interesting contrast in choice of leisure reading material is provided by science fiction. While 40 percent or more of students in the Gifted, College Preparatory, and General groups claim to read science fiction, 20 percent or less of the Chapter I and Special Education students selected it. Twice as many males read science fiction as did females.

Sources

The primary source of reading material is the school library. Almost 90 percent of the students, male and female, checked the school library in response to the question, "Where do you get the things you read?"

    Girls borrow books from friends (71%) more readily than do
boys (48%), while boys appear to read the magazines in their homes
(71%) somewhat more often than do girls (63%). More girls than boys
use the public library (66% as opposed to 41%). An equal percentage
(68%) of males and females read the books found in their home collections; over half of the respondents said they buy books at grocery,
drug, or discount stores.

    The major contrast across groups appears to be in the use
of the public library. Eighty-two percent of the Gifted and 59 percent
of the College Preparatory students use the public library. But
less than half of the remaining groups use the local library.

    In direct opposition to the image of the teenager as a non-reader
is the fact that 83 percent of both male and female respondents who
read in their leisure time spend their own money on reading materials.
Seventy-four percent of the boys buy magazines, their top choice of
purchased reading material; nearly 70 percent of the girls buy both
paperbacks and magazines.

    Across groups, the Gifted buy the most paperback books (77%)
and the fewest comics (5%). The greatest percentage of comics is
purchased by the General students (37%), while special Education
students buy the most newspapers. Most of the respondents who
spent their own money on reading material indicated that their
purchases were of the types listed above. A few respondents indicated
that they also spent money on hardcover and on book club books.

    The final factor studied was when and where leisure reading
occurs. Across categories, most leisure reading occurred in the
home (78% of the males and 94% of the females), usually in the bedroom
or living room. Slightly more than half the respondents, both males
and females, indicated that they also read for pleasure during school
hours. Approximately half of the girls and one-quarter of the boys
said they read on the school bus.

    Males read mostly on weeknights (89%), while females frequently
read both weeknights (97%) and weekends (84%). Summer vacations
were less popular leisure reading periods for boys (36%); however,
girls continue to read for pleasure during the summer months (85%).

Attitudes Toward Reading

    Some of the most interesting information we gathered was in
response to the question. "Tell us how you feel about reading for
fun." For the most part, the answers were positive, however, most
respondents felt they had too little spare time. "I would read for
fun, but I have other things to do," one student wrote. Another
explained, "I love it, but it's very seldom [that] I have the time to
go to the library and take the time to pick a book I know I won't
get bored with before I finish it."

While most of the responses to this question indicate a positive or a neutral attitude toward reading for fun, reading was rarely selected as the favorite use of spare time. One student explained that he didn't read much because, "[I] would rather live my life than read it."

Another respondent declared, "it's okay some of the time, but you don't want to spend all your spare time just reading." A third said, "I like it, but I almost never do it unless I'm bored to death." A girl echoed the thoughts of her peers when she wrote, "I guess I like reading for fun because there's really nothing to do in our small town and it takes up boring time."

Expanding on the reading "takes up time" aspect, several respondents described reading as a way "to get your mind off your problems for a while." Said one young man, "I think everyone should do it. Reading lets you escape the boredom and frustration of your normal life. Reading lets you be what you want to be."

In explaining why they liked to read, only girls discussed empathy with the characters about which they were reading. "It is fun," one declared, "because it can take you into another world and you feel what others feel." Another wrote "sometimes the same thing you are reading about happens to you and it helps." In careful, precise handwriting was one explanation that seemed typical of many:

> I like to read because a lot of time the characters I
> read about influence the way I act after finishing a
> book. I like learning new words and reading about new
> situations. I try to imagine myself in the character's
> shoes. I think about what would happen and what I
> would do if faced with the situations in the books I read.

One student appeared to get more excited about reading as she wrote. Her reply began in small, neat script which read, "It's okay if there's nothing else to do." Then, in script of steadily increasing size and illegibility, her thoughts flowed across the page:

"Reading for fun takes you to different places and lets you be who you want to be. You could go to the moon, to New York City, or be stranded on an island thousands of miles from nowhere. Or, you can be an old lady in distress from robbers, or a beautiful young lady in love with the finest guy you've ever seen. With reading, you could be anything or anyone or go anywhere. It's great!"

Independent Choice

Many of the respondents who expressed positive attitudes toward reading made a clear distinction between assigned reading and reading by choice. They didn't quite trust the questionnaire which stipulated "leisure reading" in almost every question. They had to emphasize that they felt good about reading by choice. For example, one young man said, "If I read on my own, it is fun. I don't like someone to tell me to read if I don't want to." Another insisted that if told to read something he "probably won't" although he liked to read. The matter of individual choice includes the right to select "something that interests me. Reading is fun if I can get involved in it." The respondents frequently seemed to consider things that interest them not quite legitimate categories of reading. Three comments: "I don't like reading except for comic books or magazines;" "I don't have time to read and plus I hate reading unless it's a magazine about something I like;" "I don't like to read too much except for romance, mystery, and scary books."

This last response is typical of an interesting inconsistency in self-proclaimed nonreaders. Sixty-six or 18 percent of the 362 questionnaires collected had "no" checked in response to the question, "Do you ever read in your spare time?" A closer analysis of these questions provides an intriguing insight into teenagers' definition of "reading" as "assigned reading." Seven of the respondents qualified their negative response by contributing statements such as "I will read a letter or a fun book or something like that." Forty-nine of those who said they never read in their spare time checked categories of leisure reading in response to the question asking what they liked to read and what things they purchased to read. Although the categories checked most frequently were newspapers, magazines, and comic books, other categories included science fiction, sports/sports biographies, mysteries, and teen romances. Of the 66 who said they did not read in their spare time, only eight consistently indicated throughout the questionnaire that they indeed never did.

Implications

One of the most compelling findings of this study is that teenagers, at least rural teenagers, are reading. Therefore, the issue librarians need to consider is what teens choose to read and how their choices should affect our practice of librarianship. Recently, I met a researcher from Wayne State University, Carole McCullough, who is exploring aliteracy, a term with which I was not familiar. She explained that it refers to those who can read but chose not to do so. This area is highly relevant to the practice of young adult librarianship. If young adults choose not to read, perhaps part of the cause is reflected in such statements as, "...most of the time someone else has the good books, so I don't read that much."

What are the "good books" that stimulate teenagers to read? Carroll Harrell called my attention to the popularity of the Sweet Valley High books in her library. "I can't keep them on the shelves," she said. Teenage series books, sports and sports biographies, magazines like <u>Seventeen</u>, <u>Ebony</u>, and <u>Sports Illustrated</u> are eagerly awaited and well-used. Yet these materials are the last to be considered when materials funds are allocated for school libraries. Perhaps it is time to reexamine the philosophy that library collections should consist of the "best" books, "best" being defined by selection guides and reviews rather than by readers' demands. Library educator Emily Boyce suggests that up to 50 percent of the materials budget for a school library be spent on materials that are considered ephemeral--magazines and paperback books. Boyce claims that the changing reading interests of youth, combined with increasing opportunities for networking and resource sharing among libraries, dictate the need to reevaluate traditional patterns of budget allocations for materials.

The provision of leisure reading materials preferred by young adults is especially relevant for school librarians working in rural areas. Our study revealed that almost all respondents borrow leisure reading materials from their school libraries. Moreover, they tend to purchase magazines and paperback books or to read the ones available in their homes rather than borrow them from the public library. This may be related to two factors: the distance many rural youth must travel to reach the nearest public library and the content of the collection. If school librarians in rural areas want to encourage reading as a leisure activity, they cannot depend solely on their colleagues in public libraries to provide the type of reading materials young adults prefer.

Popular magazines that can be circulated and a good selection of paperback books (including those series romances that are the despair of literary critics but the delight of teenage girls) should take their place among the hardbound copies of so-called "adolescent literature" that often collects dust on the shelf. And, if we place <u>The New Yorker</u> alongside <u>Seventeen</u> and <u>Sports Illustrated</u> or slip some good young adult authors (in paperback, of course) in among the series romances, who's the wiser?

LIARS AND TELL-TALES IN
EARLY CHILDREN'S BOOKS*

Samuel Pickering, Jr.

John Locke convinced the 18th century that childhood experience formed the adult, and in Some Thoughts Concerning Education (1690) provided the middle classes with what in effect became educational handbooks. Believing that "little, and almost insensible Impressions" made upon "tender Infancies" had "important and lasting Consequences," Locke declared that nine men out of ten were made "Good or Evil, useful or not, by their Education."

The influence of Locke's educational ideas upon the 18th century is incalculable. Not only did his thought help create belief in the importance of education but, in their emphasis upon early experience, his ideas contributed greatly to the success of the first English children's books.

Besides helping shape an educational climate in which children's literature thrived, Locke's thought also influenced the contents of children's books. In Some Thoughts Locke wrote that "Vertue" was "the first and most necessary of those Endowments, that belong to a Man." Without virtue, he said, a person would "be happy neither in this, nor the other World." As "the Foundation" of virtue, Locke explained "there ought very early to be imprinted" on a child's "Mind a true Notion of God," adding that this should be accomplished by "gentle degrees" and taking the child only "as far as his age is capable."

Aware of the potential abuses of religious instruction and interested in practical morality more than dogma, Locke spent comparatively little time on religion, and almost hurriedly moved on to lying. "The next thing to be taken Care of," he wrote, was to keep a child "exactly to speaking of Truth." Lying, he said, was "so ill a Quality, and the Mother of so many ill ones that spawn from it, and take shelter under it, that a Child should be brought up in the

*Reprinted by permission of the author and publisher of AB Bookman's Weekly 78:22 (December 1, 1986) 2233-2245; copyright © 1986 AB Bookman Publications, Inc.

greatest abhorrence of it imaginable." Let a child know, he continued, "That Twenty Faults are sooner to be forgiven, than the straining of Truth, to cover any one by an Excuse."[1]

In attempting to reach a broad audience, particularly the middle classes, who, nurtured on Locke's ideas, viewed their children's futures more in secular than religious terms, the leading publishers of early children's books usually avoided doctrinnaire religion and taught practical morality.

As Locke thought teaching children to be truthful was the most important moral lesson to be taught, so early children's books stressed the formative importance of truthfulness. Lying, Mr. Newton explained in Letters from a Mother to her Children (1780), "is a crime of so mean, so base, and dishonorable a nature, that people esteem it the greatest affront that can possibly be offered them, to be called by the approbrious name of a liar."

The seemingly insignificant lie always influence a child's character and led to unhappiness. "From an inattention to those trifles, which mark the rising character," Mrs. Pilkington wrote in The Disgraceful Effects of Falsehood (1807), "originate those imperfections, which cloud it with disgrace." In warning children against games of chance at a country fair in The Fairing (1788), Giles Gingerbread described the liar's family tree, stating "the gamester, the liar, the thief, and the pickpocket, are first cousins."[2]

School Stories

Before Felix left for school in Always Happy!!! (1814), his father urged him to remember his mother and sisters. "I would have you bear their remembrance clearly in your heart," he said; "the recollection of their virtues will soften and improve your character, whilst the claims they have upon you, will keep you steady in the path of rectitude. --Your name is theirs, do not, therefore, forget that by staining your character, you will also cloud theirs." Felix's father knew that a spirited boy would get into mischief, and he concluded tolerantly saying, "I will forgive any thing but a lie!"

In early school stories, moral lessons were more important than academic lessons. In The Academy; or A Picture of Youth (1808), Squire Scourhill described his expectations for his son Joseph in a letter to Mr. Macadam, the rector of a boarding school. "Make my son Joseph a scholar," he wrote, "but above all make him an honest man. I know little about your Latin and Greek, as being things very much out of my way; but this I know, that a man, if his heart be right, can look a fellow creature in the face; but without being an honest man, why he had better not live."[3]

As prosperity created the possibilities of financial and social

mobility and as numbers of people came to believe that education could
determine monetary as well as moral success, books which appeared
to promote moral and wordly success became popular. As a result
"godly" books like The Pilgrim's Progress which single-mindedly celebrated the other-wordly lost much of their appeal.

In contrast, however, the possibility of mobility invigorated
the metaphor of progress. In emphasizing early education, school
stories drew upon the metaphor, changing pilgrims into pupils and
transforming Bunyan's religious progress into a series of experiences
which shaped adults, certain to be "happy," in Locke's words, in
"this" and the "other World."

In The Academy as Scourhill instructed, one of the first lessons
taught was honesty. One day when there were no classes young
Scourhill and his friend Tom Standfast wandered into a village not
far from school. There they saw an old woman spinning in front of
a cottage. Nearby her grandson studied his alphabet and rubbed
a cat. This peaceful scene so impressed the boys that they were
about to present fruit to the little boy when suddenly they noticed
the old woman's hen on the village green, and the old Adam rose
within them. "A small stone," W. Mackenzie wrote, "lay at the foot
of Standfast; he took it up, and wantonly threw it at the unoffending
animal." The stone killed the bird, and the boys fled back to the
Academy. Seeing the incident, the woman sent her son to inform the
rector. Mr. Macadam then called the school together and preached
a sermon on the event. Although Scourhill was the only person who
could identify him as having thrown the stone, Standfast refused to
lie and admitted his guilt.

He then bought two hens which he gave, along with a copy of
Pilgrim's Progress, to the old woman. "I have not seen it this long
time," she said in thanking him; "often have I been amused with it
in my earlier years; would I had leisure just now to read it!" When
he learned that the old woman could not take time off from work to
read, Standfast volunteered to read to her; and while she spun, he
read. In doing so he became part of the almost paradisical village
world, showing that he had made true moral progress.[4]

Before becoming a successful adult, the honest boy was often
the most popular child at school. One day Peter James watched six
boys playing peg-top in The Entertaining History of Honest Peter
(1794). When a bag fell out of a player's pocket without his realizing
it, Peter Ball "resolved to make it his own," and since James had
observed his finding the bag, Ball offered to split the contents
with him. James "indignantly refused" and forced Ball to return the
bag. The other boys were so angry that they "turned Ball from the
party"; shortly afterwards when the rest appeared not to be looking,
Ball bloodied James' nose.

Peter would not reveal who hit him, but another boy who had

seen the affair informed the master. The master "severely chastised
Ball" and made him "go on his knees and ask Peter's pardon."
James readily forgave Ball and then told him "always to be honest,
and to do to others as he should like others to do to him, and then
added--God would love him." When Peter returned to the yard, his
schoolmates gathered around him and shouted "Honest Peter! Honest
Peter! play with me!" The name like formative childhood experiences
became part of James' character and from that time forward, he was
known as "Honest Peter."[6]

A Cardinal Fault

In school stories dishonesty was a cardinal fault. In stories
about boys, heroes frequently misbehaved. Indeed mischievousness,
if it were not calculated, was sometimes seen positively, as an indication of high spirits and energy. In contrast devotion to studies
occasionally appeared as a sign of the self-concern that led to dupli-
city and dishonesty.

In The Two Boys (1810), George and Henry Manship attended
a school run by their father, a clergyman. The characters of the
boys were "very different." "Glowing, passionate and fiery," George
was "quick and enterprising, with a great deal of volatility, and
great generosity of disposition." As a playmate, he "was courted"
but "among the steadier boys, he was rarely seen."

In contrast, although he had less shining abilities than George,
Henry made more scholastic progress. Patiently he watched "the slow
unfoldings of science, and his perseverance in conquering the difficulties of it, promised him a rich reward." Unfortunately Henry's
devotion to scientific study made him calculating and stripped him of
spontaneous, natural honesty. In his actions, "a certain subtilty
and closeness" was apparent, and he lacked George's "generosity
of spirit." Henry passed his free time in "sober walks with boys
like himself while George was flying over the play ground, at cricket
or ball, or some athletic game."

In most early children's books, and certainly those written
primarily for girls, Henry would have appeared as more admirable
than George. Disciplined as a child, Henry would have reaped financial and moral rewards as an adult. In contrast George's lack of
control would have prevented him from making educational and moral
progress, and he would have become an undisciplined failure as an
adult, most probably becoming the prey of sharpers and gamblers
and ending on the gallows. In The Two Boys, however, dishonesty
was the mother of other ills, and instead of undermining his progress,
George's "extreme fondness for play" was a sign of a spontaneity,
untainted by calculation.[7]

Because of the danger, Mr. Manship outlawed archery at school.

George and his close friend Frederick Fitz-Adam paid little attention
to school rules, and one day when they were in a group of boys
shooting arrows, Will Morris lost an eye. The accident so terrified
most of the boys that they disclaimed responsibility. In contrast
George and Frederick did the right thing and assumed responsibility.
"Mr. Manship," Fitz-Adam said, "may punish us for disobedience to
his orders, but shall not condemn us for want of humanity or falsehood; let us bind our handkerchiefs around Will Morris's eye, and
you and I George lead him in." Although Manship punished the boys,
their honesty impressed him favorably. When George tried to take
entire blame for the accident by claiming it was his arrow that struck
Will in the eye, Fitz-Adam responded that Will was standing in front
of his target and was extracting his arrow when the accident occurred.
[8]

Some months later, "several boys united in pilfering, not only
from the gardens and orchards of some neighbouring farmers, but
also from hen roosts and pigeon houses." "The prey, when obtained,"
they took to the house of Betty Simpson, "an old woman who not only
for a trifling emolument undertook to make it ready for these young
epicures, but also furnished them with drink." Deviation from strict
honesty had led to drink and the boys were well on the way to being
ruined. Like serpents, the author implied, they "used to steal from
their beds, and gliding softly through a back window," proceeded
to their "nightly carousel."

Local farmers reported their losses to Mr. Manship, and late
one evening when he was returning to school from a fair, he saw
boys in a lane. Hearing one say "it was a nice duck," Manship
jumped from the dark and grabbed the boy's coat. The coat tore
and the boy escaped, not, however, without leaving a piece of cloth
behind. The next morning, Manship called the school together, and
in examining their coats discovered that the piece came from George's
coat. When asked if he were the thief, George answered boldly, "I
abhor the character; I am no thief; I never took any thing which
did not belong to me." "I never," he concluded, "took even an apple
from a garden without leave." "You are a shameless, impudent young
rogue," his father said and grabbed him. When Manship seized him,
a note saying "Remember your appointment to night at nine; do not
fail--yours: F. F." fell from George's pocket. When George declined
to expose the author of the note, his father concluded that F. F.
was one of the thieves.[9]

Immediately he had George horsed and began to beat him.
George "bore it heroically"; and when his father stopped to rest
his arm and asked again if he were a thief, George denied it.
"George, George," his father began, sounding like Felix's father;
"the lie, more than the fault, hurts me." Suddenly he was interrupted
by the appearance of Betty Simpson in the grasp of Mr. Porter, a
farmer. His hen house had been robbed so often, Porter explained,
that he had stayed in his barn to catch the thieves. He had not been

quick enough to seize the boys, but in running away, one of the
boys, he said, had lost a pocket book, which he then gave to Mr.
Manship. Moreover, Porter continued, while chasing the boys, he
heard "the screaming of fowls" at Mrs. Simpson's, and after entering
her house, found birds which had earlier been stolen from him.

Upon examining the pocket book, Manship discovered it belonged to Henry. By mistake Henry had worn George's coat the
night before while the note written by Fitz-Adam had to do with
the plight of a poor widow and her family who had lost their goods
in a fire. "We immediately gave them all the money we had in our
possession," George explained, "and agreed to meet in my room this
morning, to send them additional relief."

Henry's dishonesty and refusal to confess his fault and prevent
his brother's unjust punishment disturbed Mr. Manship. At the
pleading of Mr. Porter and George, however, he forgave Henry,
and only banished him from school, sending him into the country
"without seeing your mother, to be deprived of all parental indulgence, for six months."[10]

Tempered by George's pleading, Henry's punishment was un-
usually light. In contrast the story of the Earl of Goodwin appeared
in several books. In the reign of Edward the Confessor, according
to Dorothy Kilner in The Adventures of a Pincushion (1788), when
the Earl of Goodwin was accused of being an accessory to the murder
of Prince Alfred, he seized a piece of bread and calling "God to
witness his innocence" stated "if he uttered any thing but the truth,
that the next mouthful he eat might choke him"--whereupon "the
bread stuck in his throat and he died immediately."

As Goodwin's lie was practically blasphemous, so in early
children's books, lying was often associated with the fall of man and
was seen as the precursor of deadly sins. Although Locke's ideas
shifted the focus of education from the next to this world, religion
and education were closely associated in early children's books.

In The Adventures of a Pincushion, the governess of a small
school was Mrs. Stanley, the widow of a clergyman. Among her
pupils was a sort of everychild, Eliza Meekly, who at thirteen was
approaching womanhood. One evening after Mrs. Stanley had put
her to bed, Eliza was so troubled that she confided her worries to
her cousin Harriet Una. Like Spenser's Una, Harriet served as
everychild's guide and intercessor with, if not the true God, then
the true educator. "What have you done, my dear cousin," Harriet
asked, "to make yourself so uneasy?" After saying that she did "not
like to confess my weakness," Eliza explained that while she was
away from school on a visit Charlotte Airy had invited her "to eat
some preserved plums, which she said had been made a present of
to her Mamma, and which came from Portugal."

Although the plums "were very sweet and luscious"--like the
apple in paradise, Eliza refused them at first, explaining that her
mother had forbidden her to eat "any thing of that kind." Like the
however, Charlotte was persuasive and moved Eliza to disobedience.
She "laughed at me so much for being so foolish," Eliza recounted,
"as to imagine any thing so innocent could hurt me," adding "that
she supposed, as I went to school, my mistress, for so she sneeringly
called Mrs. Stanley, would whip me if I did." "Overcome with her
persecutions, and vexed to be treated so much like a baby, and as if
I was afraid of punishment," Eliza said, she ate a plum. "Suppose
Mrs. Stanley," she asked Una, "should ask whether I have eat any
thing lately which I ought not; and if she does not put that question,
I feel so undeserving of her caresses, that she will see by my looks
that I have behaved improperly."[11]

Saying that she was sorry for what Eliza had done, "Miss Una
advised her that "the noblest reparation" she could make "would be
honestly to inform Mrs. Stanley of the crime and the sincerity of
your regret for having been guilty of it." Una's advice was well-
taken, and Eliza promised to comply the following morning.

However, like weak Christian man, she needed an intercessor
to plead for her, and finding herself too timid to approach Mrs.
Stanley, begged Una to plead her case. In "the mildest of terms,"
Una did so and engaged Mrs. Stanley's "compassion." Afterwards
Mrs. Stanley greeted Eliza "in the warmest terms" and after praising
her frankness and "generous confession" warned her "never to be
led into actions which you know are improper, because the company
you are with may ridicule your refusal." "It is best never to do
anything which you know to be wrong, though it may appear to be
in the smallest instance," she told Eliza, "since the desire of concealing
a trifling fault may lead you to hide it by a falsehood, which is one
of the greatest you can be guilty of."

Garden of Virtue

To emphasize her point she told Eliza the story of Betsey Lloyd.
One day, she began, Betsey visited her friend Hannah. After they
had played in the garden for some time, Hannah suggested that they
go to a nearby shop and buy gingerbread. At first Betsey demurred,
explaining she needed her mother's permission. Hannah ridiculed
what she called Betsey's "squeamishness" and eventually overcame
"her better resolutions."

Having left the garden and its protective hedge of rules in
pursuit of sweets, Betsey suffered. The shop was full of boys,
one of whom snatched Betsey's pocket book and ran off declaring
"he would see its contents, and know all the girl's secrets." Betsey
pursued the boy "until she was a good way from home" and until
he was joined by schoolmates who behaved in so wild a manner as
to terrify her greatly."

At 13, the same age as Eliza, Betsey had entered puberty,
that time in Dorothy Kilner's view, during which rules were essential
to protect one from wandering from home. Unfortunately Betsey
did not learn a lesson, and on returning home, she wandered farther
from the garden of virtue by lying and compounding her fault. She
told her parents that she had gone out with Hannah and Hannah's
maid and that a loose horse had so frightened her that she was unable to come home on time.

At first her "wicked deceit" made Betsey unhappy, but "at
length she grew reconciled as she found herself undetected." Shortly
afterwards, she reassumed her friendship with Hannah and went for
another unescorted walk. As childhood experience shaped the adult,
so disobedience led to lying and so tainted Betsey's character that
she was crippled. As she was crossing a road, a horse, much like
Betsey's own wilfulness or ultimately passions, broke "the bridle
which confined him" and galloping along the road trampled Betsey
and "broke her leg in such a terrible manner, as to occasion her
being a cripple ever after."[12]

Locke warned parents that punishment by "the Rod" was "the
most unfit of any to be used in Education." Only two faults, he
wrote, "must be master'd with Force and Blows": "an obstinate
Disobedience" and "a premeditated Lye" which after a child had been
warned "must always be looked upon as obstinacy." If not instructed
by warnings or mastered by force, the lying child became a morally
crippled adult.

In The Village School (1817), Jim Idle responded to Mrs. Propriety's asking what he and Sukey Giddy were laughing about by
saying, "Why, Ma'am, we were only talking of what Mr. Lovegood
said in his sermon last Sunday." Mrs. Propriety did not believe
Jim and calling Tommy Goodchild to her asked, "you sat next to
them: what did they say? You never told a lie." "Sukey," Tommy
responded like a good child, "was telling what droll things the Merry
Andrew did at the last fair."

"So," Mrs. Propriety said, turning to Jim, "you wicked boy,
you have told me a downright lie." "O! Jim," she preached, "how
often have you heard that liars must have their portion in that lake
which burns with fire and brimstone. As to you, Sukey Giddy, I
am very sorry that you should be running after every wake, or fair,
or dancing, and such foolish merriment. I wish your mother would
learn to keep you at home, to milk the cow, and mind your work.
It is the ruin of many young girls to be so fond of pleasure."

To break him of lying, Mrs. Propriety "fetched the birch rod"
and gave Jim "two or three sharp cuts." Then she made him stand
on a stool in the middle of the room with "a piece of paper round
his head, on which was written LIAR, in large characters." Since
she had not lied, Sukey was spared the paper and had only to stand
on a stool near Jim.

After the sudden death of her classmate Rachel Humble, Sukey, partly because her fault was less serious than Jim's lying, was able to reform and eventually became known as "Susan Serious." In Jim's case, however, lying was the mother of other ills, and the idle, dishonest youth became an irresponsible adult, ultimately dying in the workhouse.[13]

In warning parents against beating children, Locke wrote that it was "Shame of the Fault, and the Disgrace that attends it, that they should stand in fear of, rather than Pain." As Locke had urged making learning "a Play and Recreation of Children" and cozening them "into a Knowledge of the Letters," so in many children's books shaming children out of faults became a game.

In The Holiday Present (1787), two boxes were delivered to the Jennets' home. The first, the "naughty child's box," contained three rods, a fool's cap, and four silver medals on which were inscribed: "Whoever wears this, is a cross child;" "Whoever wears this, cannot be depended upon when out of sight;" "The wearer of this has told a lie;" and "This medal is a badge of sloth and idleness."

In "the good child's box" were books, hats, balls, kites, ninepins, marbles, workbags, housewives, dolls, and, as Charles Cheerful put it, "a variety of pretty things, which I do not now recollect." When the young Jennets were good they received rewards from the good child's box.

One day Miss Deborah the servant maid took Charlotte, Harriet, and "little Tom" for a walk in the field behind the Jennets' house. Harriet and Tom behaved well, but as soon as Charlotte reached the field, she darted from the path. When Deborah told her to come back, she threw clumps of dirt at her and called Tom and Harriet "tender chickens and foolish goslins."

When the group returned to the house, Mrs. Jennet asked Deborah why she had gone outside in "so very dirty a gown." On discovering that Charlotte had thrown dirt and run wildly about in the field, Mrs. Jennet forced her to wear the fool's cap. In the shape of a sugar loaf, the cap "had two long ears, like asses, hanging from the sides, and was painted red, blue, green, yellow, scarlet and black." Bits of ribbon hung about it and in the front was "the picture of a naughty child crying." When Charlotte put it on, she screamed so loud that her mother threatened to tie up her mouth.

At dinner Mrs. Jennet told Charlotte she could take it off after she apologized to Deborah and promised not to behave in such a manner again. Charlotte then left the table, but instead of seeking out Deborah, she went upstairs to her room. After remaining a few minutes, she returned and said she had apologized. Having heard Charlotte go upstairs and aware that Deborah was downstairs, Mrs. Jennet knew her daughter lied. As in Betsey Lloyd's history,

disobedience had led to lying and unless "mastered" augured poorly
for Charlotte's future.

To discourage her from lying, Mrs. Jennet whipped Charlotte
"as much as she deserved for being so wicked a girl" and made her
wear the liar's medal. She also refused to allow her to speak to her
brothers and sisters "for fear she should teach them to be as naughty
as herself, saying if she did not make the proper use of her tongue,
which was speaking the truth, she should not use it at all."[14]

The harsh treatment worked, and Charlotte reformed. The
main characters of many children's books, however, were not so
fortunate. As the story of Betsey Lloyd illustrated, disobedience
led to lying. Religious children's books often implied that lying and
mortal sins followed disobedience. Recalling Adam and Eve in the
garden, such books frequently taught that a child's first disobedience
was enough to maim not simply character of body for life but soul
for eternity.

The schoolmistress of York House (1820) Mrs. Martin was,
like Mrs. Stanley and Mrs. Teachum in Sarah Fielding's The Governess
(1749), the widow of a pious clergyman. Attending York House were
two sisters Emma and Maria Stirling. At 16 Emma had learned to
control her nature; at 13 Maria was entering adolescence and like
Eliza Meekly found it difficult to resist temptation, or the sweet plums
that life seemed to offer. Unlike Eliza who sought Una's intercession
with a higher power, Maria mocked Emma when she urged her to
take part in devotional exercises.

"I really think you will make an excellent parson," Maria said;
"if you chuse to be a mope, that is no reason why I should. Religion
is very well for old women, who must soon die, but girls have nothing
to do with it; give me a doll and a skipping-rope."

In its single-minded focus on the necessity of religion and its
celebration of eternal life, York House resembled the "joyful death"
books that had been popular among Calvinists at the beginning of
the 18th century. Such books usually consisted of short narratives
that culminated in providential deaths and glorious ascensions. Although numbers of such books, particularly religious tracts, continued
to be printed, they did not enjoy broad popularity among the middle
classes at the end of the 18th century.

With its emphasis on education and promises of success in this
world, Locke's ideas helped make the school story popular. As the
school tale gained readers and publishers, the popularity of the joyful death book with its narrow focus waned. In its blend of religiosity
and the school story and in its attempt to appeal to the middle classes,
York House was a hybrid, simultaneously behind and ahead of the
times. Behind it lay James Janeway's A Token for Children (1671)
while ahead lay Frederick Farrar's Eric, or Little by Little (1858).[15]

After Maria's refusal to pray, Emma warned that it was necessary "for us who are still spared, to seek without delay the pardon of our sins through Jesus, a crucified Saviour, lest we should be suddenly called to appear before God, and the door of mercy be forever shut against us."

Hearing this speech, Sophia Thompson, another school girl, told Emma that she went "too far" in calling her "sister's faults, sins," saying "I cannot think that so harsh a term is applicable to the foibles of school-girls."

Emma rejected Sophia's commonsensical statement--commonsensical at least from the point of view of the typical school story. "In the sight of a pure and holy God, all mankind are guilty, though all have not run equal lengths in sin; yet," Emma said, "we have the seeds of every sin in our hearts, and if they do not all spring up and appear in our conduct, it is not because we are naturally better than others, but because we have not been exposed to equal temptation, or restraining goodness has prevented their growth."

Because she prayed Emma avoided temptation; in contrast Maria was unable to resist it. At the bottom of Mrs. Martin's garden was a pear tree, and tempted by the fruit like Eve, she wanted "to strip one of the branches of its beautiful burden." One day she climbed the garden wall; just as she was reaching for a pear, the back door of York House opened. Frightened at being discovered, Maria tried to jump from the wall; unfortunately her foot slipped and she fell heavily, breaking her leg in two places and suffering a "severe contusion" on her head.

For several days she was unconscious. When she awoke, she was terrified. "My sister, where am I? where have I been," she exclaimed; "Emma, I feel that I am dying; but where, oh, where, am I going! O that I had hearkened to the voice of instruction! --pray for me, my sister! Jesus, have mercy!" As consolation, Mrs. Martin encouraged her "to look to him who heard the prayer of the dying thief."

Although Maria rapidly grew weaker, she had energy enough to preach to her schoolmates. "Ah, my dear young friends," she said, "you see me in the fatal consequences of disobedience and folly; let my death prove a salutary lesson to warn you of the danger of continuing in the path of sin, against the convictions of your judgment and conscience, and contrary to the affectionate advice of parents and teachers." "Had I enough strength," she continued, "I would earnestly entreat you to seek the Lord while he may be found, and to call upon him while he is near. Trust not to the repentance of a death-bed; I have done so, but would now give a thousand worlds to enjoy the reflection, that I had when in health desired savingly to know him whom in sickness I am constrained to seek, but fear he will not be found of me."

The sermon exhausted Maria, and shortly afterwards "the vital spark was extinguished," and she died, moaning "Hope--hope--mercy--Jesus."[16]

Since Maria had not actually lied, there was hope. For the liar, children's books taught, particularly to children from the lower classes, there was little chance of salvation. "I hope, Mary, you always speak the truth?" a teacher asked in Sunday School Dialogues (1784); "telling lies is one of the worst sins any one can be guilty of. God is very angry with those who tell lies: they will not go to Heaven when they die."

Addicted to Lying

Not only did liars miss their chance to go to heaven after death, but in books for the lower classes they missed opportunities for success on earth. The History of Mary Wood (1800) described the unhappy history of a girl addicted to lying. One day Mr. Heartwell, the clergyman of a country parish was sitting on the porch of his parsonage "when he saw a figure rather flying than running down a hill near his house, the swiftness of whose motion made it hard to distinguish what she was, much less could he guess who she was."

When she drew closer, Heartwell recognized Mary Wood, the daughter of Matthew Wood an honest laborer who had died some four years previously and for whose wife Heartwell had found a place at the alms house. Behind Mary followed a crowd of people. Seeing Heartwell, Mary ran to the parsonage and begged him to protect her, saying that she had been wrongly accused of robbery. Heartwell agreed to listen, and when the crowd arrived, he said he would investigate and be responsible for Mary.

The crowd explained that "sad doings" had occurred at their village. Squire Banks' gardener and dairymaid had robbed both the squire and Farmer Boucher, for whom Mary worked. Because "she had been telling a mort of lies about them," people suspected Mary of being in league with the thieves. A search of her trunk uncovered six silver teaspoons with the initials of the farmer, E. B., on them.

Although Mary "pertested they were none of his'n," she would not reveal where she got them, and since Mrs. Boucher, who was away visiting her father, had recently purchased teaspoons, circumstantial evidence was against Mary. Having been "detected in some falsehoods, that would make against her," Mary lost "all the comfort and confidence of innocence" and fled although she was not guilty of robbery. Farmer Boucher had pursued her, but "being fat and pursy, was not for running a race" so he gave the warrant to others. [17]

Mary's past told against her. After the death of Mary's father,

Lady Worthy helped her get a place at Mrs. Trueby's. On Mary's
second day at work, Mrs. Trueby sent her to dust the best parlor,
warning her not to touch the pier glass. Mrs. Trueby's six-year-
old son Edward accompanied Mary to the parlor.

Mary neglected Mrs. Trueby's instructions, and describing a
"balance-master" she had seen to Edward, she attempted to balance
the "long broom" on her palm. The broom toppled off and smashed
the pier glass. Hearing the crash, Mrs. Trueby hurried to the room
and seeing the damage exclaimed, "O Mary! My precious pier glass,
the best piece of furniture in my house, and a present from a dear
friend who is now no more, quite spoilt! I valued it above ten times
its price! Is this your awkwardness, Mary?"

Mary was frightened and she lied. "No, indeed, madame,"
she replied; and when Mrs. Trueby asked who broke the glass, she
expanded her lie, saying "A great bird, madame (I don't know whether
it was a pigeon) flew in at the window. I tried to drive it out, and
it dashed against the glass with its bill and cracked it as you see."

Her "invention and assurance" made Edward laugh; and when
his mother noticed it, Mary winked at him and said, "Master Edward
knows it is true, for he saw it as well as I."   "O, fye,
Mary," Edward said, "That's too much--I would not have
told upon you, but when you say I know it to be true,
you make me a liar as well as yourself, and my mamma says, if I
tell lies God Almighty will not love me."

"Wicked girl," Mrs. Trueby then said, "would you teach my
child to lie? Pack up and be gone out of my house." When Edward
pleaded for Mary, Mrs. Trueby was unyielding, explaining that she
would have forgiven the loss of the glass "but a girl that can so
readily invent a lie, and try to draw you into it, I cannot possibly
suffer to stay a day in my house."[18]

As a result of her daughter's shame, Mary's mother became
seriously ill. Her mother's sickness so upset Mary that she tried
to reform. Unfortunately "custom" proved too strong. Some time
later, a gentlewoman who had heard Mary's story took pity on her
and decided to give her a place. Before hiring her, however, she
asked Mary why Mrs. Trueby dismissed her. When Mary said it was
because she broke a pier glass, the woman asked "and was that the
only reason?" Again Mary lied and said, "I believe so." "Go," the
woman responded sternly; "you will not do for me. I see you are
not cured of your vile fault."

Eventually, Mary got a place with Farmer Boucher. Nearby
was the home of Mr. Banks, a gentleman who had gone on a tour
and had left his gardener and dairymaid in charge of his house.
The two servants were corrupt and not only did they make free with
their master's property "in every way," they also led Mary astray.

Whenever she passed Mr. Banks's house, the gardener gave her
fruit and the dairymaid cream for a syllabub.

One day when there was a great wash at Farmer Boucher's,
they invited Mary to accompany them to a fair, enticing her by saying
that a dwarf and a tall woman would be there. The temptation proved
too great for Mary, and she told Mrs. Boucher that her mother was
ill and asked if she could visit her. Although reluctant to let Mary
escape work, Mrs. Boucher allowed her to leave at five that afternoon.

That evening Mary's mother came to the farm to visit her.
When Mary returned from the fair and learned that her lie was discovered, she wept and promised to reform. After making Mary give
her word that she would not see Mr. Banks' servants again, Mrs.
Boucher gave her another chance. Unfortunately, Satan had Mary
firmly in his coils. The cream, the fruit, and "the civil things"
which the gardener said to her proved too strong, and Mary secretly
renewed acquaintance with the servants.[19]

One day when Farmer Boucher was out and Mrs. Boucher was
visiting her father, Mary invited the gardener and the dairymaid for
tea. Having already decided to rob his master, the gardener prowled
through Boucher's house. Boucher had recently sold grain and had
kept the money in the house to pay rent to his landlord. Aware that
the farmer's rent was due and having bought dung from him and
seen him put the payment in a bureau in the parlor, the gardener
guessed that the rent money was now in the bureau. While Mary
busied herself with tea, he examined the fastenings on the parlor
window.

That night he returned, broke in through the window and
robbed the farmer. When the farmer returned home the evening before the robbery, he asked Mary if anyone had come to the house.
Instead of revealing that she had entertained Banks' servants, Mary
lied and said no one had come. Later, during the investigation of
the robbery, a ploughboy said he had seen Mr. Banks' gardener
looking out the parlor window.

In conjunction with the spoons found in her trunk, which the
dairymaid had actually given to Mary to keep for her and which
belonged to Mr. Banks' housekeeper Elizabeth Bearcroft, the lie
convinced people that Mary was an accomplice. On the return of
Mrs. Boucher who found her teaspoons intact and on the capture of
Banks' servants, the truth came out.

It was, unhappily, too late for Mary. Boucher dismissed her,
and as a consequence, Mary's mother became "almost distracted" and
died. Then Thomas, a young baker who had wanted to marry Mary
but who had been prevented from doing so by his father who thought
he should marry a wealthy girl, now inherited a bakery. A "very
honest, sober, agreeable young man," Thomas now rejected Mary.

"Had she preserved a better character," he would have married
her. "I could not be happy unless I could make a friend of my
wife and depend on her truth and faithfulness," he explained; "her
pretty face and good humour would be nothing to me, without truth
and honesty. Next to a good conscience the best thing is a good
character. I bless God I have never forfeited my own; nor will I
ever marry a woman that has lost her."

As childhood experience irrevocably shaped the adult, so lying
destroyed Mary's character and hope of a successful life. After
Thomas' rejection, she decided to leave the village. Heartwell gave
her a letter to a clergyman 50 miles away, and she departed heart-
broken. As the lies had undermined her character, so unhappiness
now weakened her constitution, and although she got a place, the
labor was hard and "hastened on a decline which her sorrows had
begun." Mary died "at eighteen years of age," the tale concluded.
"May all," it urged, "who read this story learn to walk in the strait
paths of truth. The way of duty is the way of safety."[20]

Tell-Tales

Part of Mary's difficulty stemmed from her promise to the dairymaid that she would not reveal who had given her the teaspoons.
Despite the occasional appearance of a character like the dairymaid,
early children's books warned children against becoming "tell-tales."
In Always Happy!!! Felix's father advised him not to expose his
schoolmates' "faults nor cause their punishment, it will be enough
for you to guard your own conduct, and not disgrace yourself by
being a spy on other." Exception to this kind of advice appeared
for the most part in books about young children or children from the
lower classes and in books written primarily for girls.

In refusing to name the person who gave her the spoons, however, Mary protected a criminal. As lying had become so ingrained in
her character that it threatened her happiness and ultimately life
itself, her silence showed that she was unable to distinguish between
duty and as the author put it "false promises."

In books for girls, allegiance to schoolmates or to one's word,
when rashly or mistakenly given, was usually seen as inferior to
duty. Stories which emphasized duty frequently relied upon analogies
between a teacher's instructions to her pupils and God's instructions
to Adam and Eve. In such stories, the girl who informed upon
classmates or threatened to do so, was the voice of a rigorous and
life-saving morality, not a spy or tell-tale. In refusing to tolerate
disobedience or criminal activity, such heroines protected both gardens and childhood from corruption, and thereby, in Locke's words,
strengthened the "Foundation" of virtue, "the first and most necessary
of those Endowments, that belong to a Man."

In "The Exemplary Pupil," a story in <u>The Mother's Gift</u> (1787),
Mrs. Hammond, a governess, allowed her students into her private
garden. She let the children walk freely and except for telling them
not to eat strawberries, made no rules. As soon as Mrs. Hammond
left, however, two girls decided to taste the strawberries.

Recognizing her duty, Miss Johnson warned them. "I may depend upon it, if you touch any, I shall certainly acquaint my governess." When the girls said she would be a "telltale," Miss Johnson
answered that her actions were correct. "I should rejoice to prevent
your fault, and be very sorry to give a bad account of you," she
said; "she who deserves to be called a telltale, is one who is pleased
to speak ill of others; but call me what you like, I shall do what I
think right."[21]

In contrast to stories for girls in which duty often required
children to reveal truth, stories for boys taught that truth came out
on its own accord. Unlike stories for girls in which silence often
implied acquiescence or weakness, silence in tales for boys implied
self-control and strength. Frequently good boys were wrongly accused of crimes; instead, however, of revealing the truth, they en-
dured unfair punishment, thereby showing that they had character
enough to persevere against injustice and to overcome obstacles comparable to those which they would eventually face as adults.

Maria Edgeworth's <u>Tarlton</u> (1809) described proper behavior
for boys in school. Hardy, the hero of the story, was an admirably
strong character. "Beloved" by all the good boys, he did not
curry the favor of the bad and paid no need "when idle, mischievous,
or dishonest boys attempted to plague or ridicule him."

In contrast his friend Loveit wanted to be liked by everyone
and "his highest ambition was to be thought the best natured boy
in the school." Because he was afraid of offending other boys or
being laughed at, he lacked the "courage to say, <u>no</u>" and thus often
did "things, which he knew to be wrong."

One day after a game of battledore and shuttlecock, Tarlton
accidentally threw the shuttlecock over a hedge and into a nearby
lane. Forbidden to go into the lane, none of the boys volunteered
to retrieve the shuttlecock until Tarlton taunted Loveit. Hardy advised Loveit not to go into the lane, but after Tarlton called him
"Little Pando" and said he was under the thumb of Hardy, whom he
labeled "Parson Prig," Loveit duly fetched the shuttlecock.

This initial disobedience led to worse behavior. From the lane
Hardy saw a tree laden with apples, and on returning, described it
to Tarlton. That night and for two successive nights, a group of
boys crept out of school and stole apples. The tree belonged to an
old man who "had promised himself the pleasure of giving his red
apples to his grand-children on his birth-day."

Not wanting to inform the boys' master, Mr. Trueman, and get them flogged, the old man nevertheless knew that the boys had to be stopped. Childhood experience formed the adult, and stealing, the old man said, "would surely bring them to the gallows in the end." To prevent the theft, he borrowed the "fiercest mastiff in England," Farmer Kent's Barker, and chained him to the apple tree.

As in so many children's books, eating forbidden fruit led to worse actions, and although Loveit argued against such an act and indeed thought he had dissuaded him, Tarlton decided to poison Barker. For a sixpence Tom, a servant boy, obtained poisoned meat and agreed to give it to the dog. Looking out of the room he shared with Hardy, Loveit saw Tarlton meet Tom. He was so disturbed that he told Hardy what was occurring. Hardy dressed quickly and chased Tom down the lane. Although Tom threw the meat to Barker, Hardy arrived in time to seize a pitchfork and spear the meat, leaving Barker with only the handkerchief in which the meat had been wrapped.[22]

Returning to school, Hardy was met by Mr. Power, an usher. On Power's discovery of the meat, Hardy warned him that it was poisoned. "You wretch!" Power exclaimed and demanded that Hardy fall upon his knees, confess, name his accomplices, and beg for pardon. "Sir," Hardy said, "in a firm, but respectful voice, 'I have no pardon to ask, I have nothing to confess, I am innocent; but if I were not, I would never try to get off myself by betraying my companions.'"

Hardy's steadfastness angered Power, and he threatened Hardy, asking "how will you look tomorrow, Mr. Innocent" when "the Doctor comes home?" "As I do now, sir," Hardy responded; "ever since I have been at school, I never told a lie, and therefore, sir, I hope you will believe me now. Upon my word and honour, sir, I have done nothing wrong."

Power refused to believe Hardy and locked him in a small closet known as the "Black Hole."

The next morning Hardy refused to reveal anything about his actions the night before, and Power was preparing to beat him in front of the school when Mr. Trueman and the old man entered. After accusing Hardy both of being a thief and of trying to poison the dog, Trueman produced the handkerchief in which the meat had been wrapped. After Hardy denied ownership, Trueman said he would flog all the students beginning with Hardy if the owner of the handkerchief did not claim it. Although Hardy knew it belonged to Tarlton, he remained silent and "looked with a steady eye at the clue." He was spared punishment, however, when Trueman found Tarlton's initials on the handkerchief.

Unlike Hardy who remained silent even though innocent, Tarlton

tried to shift the blame to others, saying that Loveit first mentioned
the apples and that Tom suggested poisoning the dog. Not simply
a tell-tale but also a coward, Tarlton was dismissed from school,
and Hardy "not because you ask it," as Mr. Trueman said, was rewarded by being allowed the gratification of a wish. Generously,
he asked that the boys be pardoned, to which, after excluding Tarlton,
Mr. Trueman assented.[23]

Hardy's silence reflected not only strength of character but
also the sturdy individualism that an education based upon Locke
seemed to promise. Since adults were formed by childhood experience,
a child's education could be tailored to suit parents' expectations.

As prosperity spread during the 18th century, making society
more mobile and seemingly more Lockean, dreams became expectations.
Almost no success seemed beyond the grasp of the properly educated
child. As a result of the belief in the malleability of children and
the prosperity which made society less rigid, competition grew.

Instead of seeing a child as a member of a class or group with
whom he would always share common experiences, parents could reasonably expect the educated child to accomplish more than his peers
and advancing through society achieve individual success. To do
this, the child had to avoid Loveit's weakness and learn to say no
and to keep his own counsel.

In a mobile society in which wild success and dismal failure were
everyday occurrences, friendships which linked children to the behavior of others were potentially dangerous, and the successful child
had to become self-sufficient, trusting himself and often suspecting
others.

Although the assured and occasionally lonely individualism that
this attitude bred appeared more often in books for boys than in
those for girls, it occurred in books for girls. In the first school
story, Fielding's The Governess, Mrs. Teachum told her "little
Readers" that "Love and Affection" formed the "Happiness of all
Societies" and "what we should chiefly encourage and cherish in our
Minds."

In being affectionate and loving, however, she wrote, there was
"one Caution to be used, namely, that you are not led into many
Inconveniences, and even Faults, by this Love and Affection." This
"Disposition" led naturally "to delight in Friendships," she explained;
unfortunately, unless one were careful such delight could lead "into
all manner of Errors." The person, she said, who tempted "you to
fail in your Duty" or justified "you in doing so" was not a "real
Friend." "If you cannot have Resolution enough to break from such
pretended Friends," she warned, "you will nourish in your Bosom
Serpents, and that in the End will sting you to Death."[24]

Almost as if firmness were part of his character, albeit a
neglected part, Loveit shared a room with Hardy. Ultimately when he
confided in Hardy and relied upon him for direction, Hardy acted
swiftly. In drawing upon Hardy, Loveit lost his weakness, and if
Hardy is viewed as a potential for firmness within Loveit himself,
then Loveit had escaped the desire to be popular. In the future,
with a character as firm as Hardy's, he would do his duty and scotch
weakness or bosom serpents.

In many children's books, the desire for love and affection resembled telling tales. Unable to resist confidences, weak characters
gossiped and as a result occasionally undermined not merely their
social but also their economic futures. In First Impressions; or, The
History of Emma Nesbit (1814), Emma was so spoiled by her mother
that her father sent her to boarding school. Emma's bedfellow was
Miss Morgan, two years older than Emma. Morgan encouraged the
younger girl's habit of telling tales in confidence.

The most popular girl in school was Caroline Neville, a ward
of chancery. Although Caroline was not remarkably clever, she had
such "sweetness of disposition" and was such a good "friend of
those who were in grief or distress" that the other students preferred
her company to that of Morgan. Cleverer than Caroline, Morgan was
jealous and prejudiced Emma against her.

One day Emma suffered from a sore throat and slept near the
room of Mrs. Patterson, the schoolmistress. While resting she overheard Mrs. Patterson telling a teacher that Caroline's father had
begun work as a chimney sweep. He rapidly bettered himself and
enjoying enormous success was able to leave Caroline a fortune at
his death.

Although she heard Mrs. Patterson say that "she hoped no one
had the least idea of it" because "Caroline's greatest weakness was
her fear of it being known by her schoolfellows," Emma revealed
Caroline's secret to Morgan.

Sometime later when Caroline took out a dress to wear to a
dance, she discovered it was covered with soot. "It is certainly
very provoking," Morgan said; "but I dare say, Miss Neville, it is
not the first time you have had soot on your clothes, and perhaps
some years ago you would not have been so much surprised at it."

When the students speculated who had soiled the dress, Morgan
who was guilty, blamed a ghost and then revealed that Caroline's
father had been a chimney sweep. "I dare say," she recounted, "her
father hearing of the ball, and wishing to see his daughter's beautiful
frock, jumped out of his grave, to take a peep at it, and as I conclude, that the ghost would not part with what was through life
his constant companion, the soot-bag, I suppose he was, in his ad-
miration and surprise, let it fall on his child's frock."

Upset by her bedfellow's behavior, Emma accused her of acting "in a manner at once unkind and unfeeling." Morgan would have none of the rebuke and reminded Emma that she had revealed Caroline's past. "If reproof is the order of the day, I am sure you deserve it much more than I," she said; "you were so contemptibly weak as to mention to me, what you must have been sure I should take advantage of." [25]

Although Emma was repentant, she did not learn a lesson. As Lockeans believed the child to be mother of the woman, so Emma's weakness would undermine not merely happiness but opportunities for social and economic success. On a later occasion when Emma wanted a new dress to wear to a concert, her father refused to buy it. Although he warned her not to tell Emma, Mrs. Nesbit explained to Emma that Mr. Nesbit's bank was temporarily short of funds. Money from abroad was expected, but until it arrived, Mrs. Nesbit said the family would have to watch expenses, adding "be careful, I conjure you, Emma, to let no mention of this pass your lips."

Emma kept her counsel until the morning of the concert when a schoolmate Jane Turner asked if she were going to attend. When Emma said she was not, Turner was surprised and asked "what in the world is to prevent your going." On Emma's replying that her father would not buy her a dress, Turner accused him of being "most shamefully stingy." Emma loved her father, and unable to hear him wrongly criticized, she revealed the reason behind his refusal.

Immediately Turner left Emma's room and sent a servant with a message to her aunt, urging her to withdraw the money she had in Mr. Nesbit's bank. The withdrawal started a run on the bank and by late afternoon it failed. Mr. Nesbit was ruined, and blaming herself, Emma's mother "fell into a state of despondency, from which nothing could rouse her, and expired soon after in the arms of her husband." [26]

Living a Lie

Early children's books also criticized living a lie. Occasionally such a life resulted from lying in childhood, but for the most part children's books depicted it as reflecting educational and social corruption. Its outward sign was usually aristocratic or luxurious behavior which children's books frequently compared to a simple or natural style of life. According to Mary Wollstonecraft, aristocrats "raised above the common wants and affections of their race" shed "seeds of false-refinement" and scattered "corruption through the whole mass of society."

Written for and reflecting the aspirations of the middle classes, early children's books gave the aristocracy short shrift. In the ideal Lockean world, no person would inherit power or prestige but would

be educated to assume it. Attaining position and a proper morality
depended upon education and work, not privilege. Without a rigorous
education, a child could neither achieve success nor control his life.
Not educated for or even to maintain its position, the aristocracy was
usually depicted as morally weak and doomed.

Although education was seen as ultimately leading to the extinction of the aristocracy, luxurious and aristocratic behavior was
also seen as dangerously seductive. Instead of providing children
with an education which schooled them for life and eternity, parents,
critics believed, were misled by the promises inherent in Locke's
educational views. Dazzled by the possibilities for advancement in
society and then by the ornamental surface of aristocratic life, they
forgot the criticism of the aristocracy implied in Locke's educational
ideas and aping "their betters" provided children with educations
which taught the showy rather than the useful.

"Tradesmen and mechanics," Priscilla Wakefield wrote, "are fond
of bringing up their daughters in what they term a gentil manner;
that is, sending them, at a very inconvenient expense, perhaps as
half-boarder, to an elegant boarding-school, where they presently
imbibe a desire of emulating their superiors in dress, shewy qualifications, and fashionable folly." "Plain instruction in a plain garb,"
such things as "a thorough acquaintance with figures" and "a metho-
dical system of bookkeeping," she argued, would better suit these
girls who would eventually become tradesmen's wives.

Reflecting such a concern, writers of children's literature
roundly attacked, for example, Lord Chesterfield's Letters to His Son
which Francis Newbery published as a children's book in 1774. In
the Guardian of Education (1803), Mrs. Trimmer condemned it as "a
very dangerous book, unfit for the perusal of youth," teaching "a
system of artificial manners, devoid of religious or moral principle."
There was "no hope of educating young people to a love of integrity
in any family," Maria Edgeworth wrote, where "the Chesterfieldian
system" was adopted.[27]

Early children's books often depicted parents who admired
luxurious behavior and attempted to educate their children as aristocrats. As lies always came out in children's books, so such an education for what in effect was living a lie brought unfortunate results.
In children's books former servants often copied aristocratic behavior.
Newly-rich servants appeared in children's books almost as visible
emblems of the dangers of social mobility and wealth constituted
to people who had not received proper educations.

In Practical Education Maria Edgeworth observed that servants
"from their situation" and "from all that they see of the society of
their superiours" learned "to admire that wealth and rank to which
they are bound to pay homage." "The luxuries and follies of fashionable life they mistake for happiness," she continued, "and measure

the respect they pay to strangers by their external appearance."
"Want of education," she suggested, lay behind "their vices and ignorance."

In the first children's books, this want of education oftentimes
lay behind parents' educating children for aristocratic vices.   In
The Adventures of a Silver Penny (1794), "Miss Fanny's papa had
been a footman, and her mamma a cook-maid."   Going out of service,
they opened a shop to sell liquors and rapidly "got forward."   Since
both "had received very little education," they "determined to spare
no expense" to make Fanny "a most accomplished girl."

Unhappily as the goods they sold intoxicated purchasers and
made them behave foolishly, so Fanny's parents were intoxicated by
aristocratic life and provided Fanny with a poor education.   Instead
of being taught Wakefield's plain garb and plain acting, Fanny was
pampered.   Taught "false refinement," she had little respect for her
teachers and "would slap one in the face, tread on the toes of another,
and run a pin into a third."   She refused to go to bed until morning
and would not get up until noon.   At 12, she could hardly read and
could not write a letter or wristband a shirt.

As Maria Edgeworth argued that uneducated servants were
"doomed to ignorance, or degraded by inherent vice," so the mistaken
basis upon which Fanny's parents indulged their daughter undermined
all possibilities for solid moral growth and development of a capable,
happy adult.   Because she "took neither air nor exercise," she fell
into "a decline, that put a period to her life in the sixteenth year
of her age."[28]

Luxuries were costly.   In coveting them, people were led not
only to false, unnatural lives but to living beyond their means.
As aristocratic attitudes undermined morality, so the extravagant style
of life wrought economic failure.

Before Winifred Jones left home for boarding school in The
School Fellows (1818), her mother warned her to "be careful to speak
the truth" and to "be candid, but not too communicative."   Winifred
was the only surviving child of Sir David and Lady Jones.   Although
the Joneses were wealthy, their attitudes were middle class rather than
aristocratic.   With their expectations perhaps tempered by the loss
of their other eight children, they did not indulge their daughter,
as did Fanny's parents, and lay the seeds of physical and moral
decline.

Entering school with Winifred was Bridget Smith.   The only
child of wealthy aspiring parents, Bridget had been "spoiled by their
ill-timed indulgence."   Unlike Winifred who was a titular but not
spiritual member of the aristocracy, Bridget coveted the externals of
aristocratic life.

Not surprisingly this led first to lying and then to unhappiness and economic hardship. When her schoolmates asked Bridget where she got her Christian name, she told Winifred, "I am determined to say I was named after my grandmother, who left me a large fortune." Winifred could not dissuade Bridget, and Bridget lived a lie.

Eventually, however, the truth brought sad results. Bridget's father lost his money. If his creditors had been willing to settle, he would probably have been able to stave off financial disaster. Unfortunately Pry, the daughter of his principal creditor, was Bridget's schoolmate; and when she told her father about Bridget's wealthy grandmother, he refused to compromise and brought on Smith's total collapse.[29]

The Boarding School

As Priscilla Wakefield stressed that boarding schools only taught students to emulate "fashionable folly," so children's books criticized boarding schools, particularly those for girls. A "useful education," Kitty Bland's brother said in The Brother's Gift (1786) was "the basis of the chief happiness and enjoyment of this life." Unfortunately he thought, many subjects taught in boarding school were "chiefly ornamental" and instead of preparing girls for life sent "them into the world fit objects to be deceived and undone."

In stressing the ornamental such schools aped aristocratic leisure and instead of urging girls to be actively concerned with life taught false, and almost deceptive, posturing. Instead of learning to work, girls learned to be idle; instead of doing good girls talked well. Not only did idleness benumb the understanding, Kitty's brother said, but it corrupted the heart, for it was "inconsistent with a state of ease and indolence to have the strong, but fine affections of love, pity, compassion, sorrow, sympathy, and the life frequently awakened and excited in the breast."

The concerns voiced by Kitty's brother appeared in many early children's books. Words without deeds, declarations not followed by action, often typified the behavior of aristocrats, who were seen to be living what were in effect lies.

In Correspondence between a Mother and her Daughter at School (1817) Laura's mother sent her to school because she said, "our own insulated neighbourhood does not afford us the means of giving you some advantages we wish you to possess." Located in a village, the school was small and taught the useful rather than the ornamental. Not having embraced fashionable folly, the school had an honest, regular Georgian appearance. Almost as if it existed in an unfallen world--as in a sense it did because students were not encouraged to covet luxuries--the "red-brick house" stood "in a garden, a little way back from the road, with an immense row of tall poplars before it, looking like so many sentinals."

Into this protected garden two sisters who "had been at a high
school in London" were suddenly thrust. "Very gay, dashing girls,"
Laura wrote, they looked "down with contempt upon every thing,
and every body here."[30]

Shortly after their arrival, the sisters suggested to their new
schoolmates that they should donate money and form "The Juvenile
Ladies' Branch Bible Association." During the discussion, "Grace"
spoke, saying "there is a pretty little girl who calls here sometimes
with watercresses: I saw her this morning, as I was crossing the
hall, and asked her if she could read." When the little girl said she
could, Grace asked if she were able to read the Bible. "O, yes,"
she answered, adding, however, that although "she was a very good
scholar" neither she nor her mother owned a Bible. "Shall we give
her one, then?" Grace asked the group and turning to the older
of the sisters asked if she would bear half the expense with her.

The difference between words and deeds was great, and the
sister answered, "perhaps, I may; though I don't know why I should,
in particular: indeed, at the present I have very little to spare;
besides we are just now talking of something quite different." "If
our object is to give poor people Bibles," Grace responded; "it is,
you know, exactly the same thing: but if we are only wishing for
the fun, or the credit of having a Juvenile Ladies' Branch Bible Association, it is, certainly, as you say, quite different."[31]

Although Grace "was accused of a want of zeal about the subscription" to the society, the next time the girl called with watercresses she received a Bible.

In early children's books, right education, more than the
grace of God determined children's worldly and eternal futures.
Among the first lessons taught was honesty, not only of word but of
deed. In Memoirs of Peg-Top (1788), Mr. Heedmore, a shoemaker
lectured his son Charles on honesty.

"Those who are so wicked as to lie," Heedmore said, "will be
guilty (at least are to be suspected) of any crime, since to forfeit
your word, is to break every tie of honour; it is like the hemp with
which we sew shoes, Charles; if that fails, they will come up in
pieces, you know, and be rotten, and good for nothing."

In early children's books, liars became good-for-nothings while
those who lived lies like the sisters did nothing and, like the class
to which they belonged, were destined in the Lockean world to vanish
from society.[32]

References

1.   James L. Axtell, ed., The Educational Writings of John Locke

(Cambridge: Cambridge University Press, 1968), pp. 114, 239,
241-42, 244. For more on Locke's influence upon children's
books see my John Locke and Children's Books in Eighteenth-
Century England (Knoxville: University of Tennessee Press,
1981).

2. Dorothy Kilner, Letters from a Mother to her Children (London:
John Marshall, c. 1780), I, 156. Mrs. Pilkington, The Disgraceful Effects of Falsehood, and The Fruits of Early Indulgence
(London: J. Harris, 1807), vi. The Fairing (Worcester:
Isaiah Thomas, 1788), p. 34. The dates in the text refer to
editions I saw. In some case earlier editions exist. I also refer
to children's books published in both Britain and the United
States. Aside from a number of religious books, most early
American children's books were reprints of English books. For
the most part changes made by American publishers are themati-
cally insignificant.

3. A Mother, Always Happy!!! (London: J. Harris, 1814), pp.
60, 62. W. MacKenzie, The Academy (London: J. Harris, 1808),
p. 116.

4. Axtell, p. 241. The Academy, p. 67.

5. Nurse Truelove's New-Year's-Gift (London: Newbery & Carnan,
1770), title page, pp. 5-9.

6. The Entertaining History of Honest Peter (Boston: S. Hall,
1794), pp. 18-20.

7. The Two Boys; or, The Reward of Truth (Philadelphia: Bailey
for Johnson and Warner, 1810), pp. 5-8.

8. The Two Boys, p. 11.

9. The Two Boys, pp. 19-21, 23-27.

10. The Two Boys, pp. 27, 30, 32, 35-36.

11. Mary Ann Kilner, The Adventures of a Pincushion (Worcester:
Isaiah Thomas, 1788), pp. 30, 41-44.

12. The Adventures of a Pincushion, pp. 44-49.

13. Axtell, pp. 148, 177, 239. O. M., The Village School (Wellington,
Salop: F. Houlson and Son, 1817), pp. 24-25, 41.

14. Axtell, pp. 177, 255-56. Dorothy Kilner, The Holiday Present
(Worcester: Isaiah Thomas, 1787), pp. 82-86, 93-99.

15. Anna Kent, York House (London: Francis Westley, 1820), p. 19.

16. York House, pp. 22, 28, 180-85.

17. Sarah Trimmer, Sunday School Dialogues (London: John Marshall,
1784), p. 52. The History of Mary Wood (Philadelphia: B. &
J. Johnson, 1800), pp. 3, 7-8, 10.

18. Mary Wood, pp. 12-14.

19. Mary Wood, pp. 15-19.

20. Mary Wood, pp. 27-33.

21. Dorothy Kilner, The Rotchfords (Philadelphia: James Humphreys,
1801), I, 8. Always Happy!!!, p. 61. Mary Wood, p. 33. Axtell, p. 241. The Mother's Gift (Worcester: Isaiah Thomas,
1787), II, 14-15.

22. Maria Edgeworth, "Tarlton" in The Parent's Assistant (George-
town: Joseph Milligan, 1809), I, 51-52, 55, 64-65.

23. "Tarlton," pp. 76-78, 83.

24. Sarah Fielding, The Governess (London: A. Millar, 1749), xiii-xiv.
25. First Impressions; or, The History of Emma Nesbit (London: J. Harris, 1814), pp. 50, 55, 59-61, 66-67.
26. First Impressions, pp. 97-101, 118.
27. Mary Wollstonecraft, A Vindication of the Rights of Woman (London: J. Johnson, 1792), p. 5.   Priscilla Wakefield, Reflections on the Present Condition of the Female Sex (London: Darton & Harvey, 1798), pp. 58, 145, 147.   Guardian of Education, 2 (1803), 425.   Maria and Richard Lovell Edgeworth, Practical Education (Boston: T. B. Wait, 1815), I, 172.
28. Practical Education, I, 110-113.   Richard Johnson, The Adventures of a Silver Penny (London: E. Newbery, c1794), pp. 31-35.
29. The School-Fellows (London: J. Souter, 1818), pp. 12, 43, 65.
30. The Brother's Gift (Worcester: Isaiah Thomas, 1786), pp. 5-6, 23-24.   Mrs. Taylor and Jane Taylor, Correspondence between A Mother and Her Daughter at School (London: Taylor and Hessey, 1817), pp. 2, 6-7, 82.
31. Correspondence, pp. 92-93.
32. Correspondence, p. 93.   Mary Ann Kilner, Memoirs of a Peg-Top (Worcester: Isaiah Thomas, 1788), p. 76.

METAPHORS OF READING*

Catherine Sheldrick Ross

The traditional view of metaphor has been that it is a deviation from
a literal statement used to heighten style. This view holds that
metaphor is purely a lexical substitution, at the level of single words,
of a figurative expression in the place of a more straightforward
literal term. Therefore, as a way of decorating a literal statement
in a fresh and arresting manner, metaphors are ornamental, but they
have no cognitive value. Recently, however, work done by philosophers, literary critics, and linguists has suggested another account
that places metaphor at the very center of concerns of meaning and
epistemology. This new perspective recognizes metaphor as something
that permeates all discourse and structures our human conceptual
systems, thereby altering the way that we experience the world.[1]
It is not a stylistic flourish merely added on to an already existing
meaning but is instead a means of discovering new meaning. This
second understanding of metaphor, especially as developed in the work
of George Lakoff and Mark Johnson, is the one followed in the discussion here of metaphors of reading.[2]

Lakoff and Johnson have explored in particular the phenomenon
of "conventional metaphor." By this term, they do not mean tropes
used in heightened poetic style but rather metaphors that are so
much a part of how we think that we are normally unconscious of
them. One example that Lakoff and Johnson give of a conventional
metaphor is ARGUMENT IS WAR, which is disclosed in our everyday
language in common expressions such as:

> Your claims are indefensible.
> He attacked every weak point in my argument.
> His criticisms were right on target.
> I demolished his argument.
> I've never won an argument with him.
> You disagree? Okay, shoot!
> If you use that strategy, he'll wipe you out.
> He shot down all my arguments.[3]

*Reprinted by permission of the author and publisher of Journal of
Library History, Philosophy and Comparative Librarianship 22:2 (Sprin
1987) 147-163; copyright © 1987 University of Texas Press.

Lakoff and Johnson make the point that "the essence of metaphor is understanding and experiencing one kind of thing or experience in terms of another."[4]   In this example, the concept "war" provides a filter through which we perceive, talk about, and actually perform "argument."   The metaphor serves to highlight certain aspects of argument (the goal of victory) while it conceals or masks other (the goal of mutual understanding and consensus).   Normally, of course, we use conventional metaphors without being aware of them.   The conventional metaphors that structure our conceptual systems are largely invisible to us for the same reason that environments of un-examined values and tacit assumptions usually are invisible: we are like Marshall McLuhan's fish, who don't recognize water as the element that constitutes their environment because they have nothing with which to compare it and no reason to suppose that water is not the only reality there is.[5]   However, once attention is directed toward the problem of metaphor, then the ordinary language we use can be examined as a source of evidence about the nature of our conceptual systems.

An Introduction to Some Metaphors of Reading

The focus of this paper is the system of metaphoric conepts used to think about a subject historically of central importance to librarians: books and reading.   Examples drawn from late nineteenth century librarians' discussions of reading provide a convenient starting point, because metaphors are often easier to perceive in writings distanced by time.   The following description of the fiction reader (1877) by Noah Porter, president of Yale, provides a rich protocol of metaphors apparently chosen at random, but in fact forming a coherent system:

> The spell-bound reader soon discovers, however, that this
> appetite, like that for confectionary and other sweets is the
> soonest cloyed, and that if pampered too long it enfeebles the
> appetite for all other food.   The reader of novels only,
> especially if he reads many, becomes very soon an intellectual
> voluptuary, with feeble judgment, a vague memory, and an
> incessant craving for some new excitement.   It is rare that
> a reader of this class studies the novels which he seems to
> read....   He reads for the story as he says, and it usually
> happens that the sensational and extravagant, the piquant
> and equivocal stories are those which please him best.   Ex-
> clusive and excessive novel reading is to the mind as a kind
> of intellectual opium eating, in its stimulant effects upon the
> phantasy and its stupefying and bewildering influence, on
> the judgment.   An inveterate novel-reader speedily becomes
> a literary roue, and this is possible at a very early period
> of life.   It now and then happens that a youth of seventeen
> becomes almost an intellectual idiot or an effeminate weakling
> by living exclusively upon the enfeebling swash or the
> poisoned stimulants that are sold so readily under the title

of tales and novels. An apprenticeship at a reform school
in literature, with a spare <u>diet</u> of statistics and a hard bed
of mathematical problems, and the simple <u>beverage</u> of plain
narrative, is much needed for the recovery of such inane and
half-demented mortals. [my emphasis][6]

The metaphor that dominates this passage is READING IS EATING
However, a second implied metaphor, READING IS A LADDER, can
be seen as providing the spatial organization for the sets of contrasting values encompassed in Porter's metaphor of eating. The
up and down directions of the ladder are what bring into alignment
such pairs of opposites as good/bad, progress/retrogression, virtue/
depravity, healthy development/debility. If reading matter is food,
then nourishing food such as the "spare diet of statistics" and "the
simple beverage of plain narrative" are up on the ladder of up/down;
sugar and "confectionary" are down, as are "poisoned stimulants."
A reader with an "incessant craving" for fiction reading is under
a spell. Rational control and the cultivation of facts are up; surrender to fantasy or to a desire for pleasure is down. Since the reading
ladder can be seen as developmental, then maturity, health, strength,
and masculinity are all up; their opposites, such as, for example,
the "effeminate weakling," are down. This apparent miscellany of
images--spells, sugar, addictive drugs, poisons, roues, and so on--
is intelligible because these images form systematic groupings organized
by compatible metaphors for reading--up/down and kinds of food.
Furthermore, the passage will seem convincing as well as intelligible
if the metaphors structure the concept of reading in a way that fits
cultural values. The more detailed examination that follows of late
nineteenth century metaphoric statements about fiction and reading
suggests that the fit was so good that the metaphors themselves were
taken for granted--invisible to those who used them.

Reading Is a Ladder

It was a truism during the time when Noah Porter was writing
that the public library's role was to push people up the ladder, elevating reading taste and gradually leading the reader from lower to
higher sorts of books. Justin Winsor, the first president of the
American Library Association, told a conference of librarians in 1881
that he sometimes thought of the library "as a derrick, lifting the
inert masses and swinging them round to the sure foundations upon
which the national character shall rise."[7] This metaphor of the
ladder was so pervasive, perhaps, because it provided a way of
organizing ideas about reading that was compatible both with everyday physical experience and with culturally inherited dispositions of
thought. The ladder has had a long history in the conceptual structures of Western thinking. Jacob's ladder, which is the image of
Jacob's dream of ascent from earth to heaven, is typologically identical
with the journey of Israel through the desert wasteland to the
promised land. The ladder of Eros, as described in Plato's Symposium

and the Phaedrus, is the path for the ascent of the soul from attach-
ment to particular physical forms of beauty through successive levels
of refinement to the highest level of love for ideal forms and pure
ideas. The great chain of being, an idea that prevailed from Plato
and Aristotle through the Middle Ages to the late eighteenth century,
[8] is a conception of the universe as an immense unilinear hierarchy
from the lowest plant forms up by neat gradations through the animal
kingdom, thence to humans, and finally to angels and perfect being.
By the late nineteenth century, Darwinism and Social Darwinism had
been popularized as another form of ladder of evolutionary development and gradual progression. In this century, an example of an
originally theological version of the ladder metaphor's making its way
into popular culture is provided by the children's game Snakes and
Ladders: landing on a snake brings about a "fall," causing the
player to slide down and backward, while landing on a ladder allows
the player to climb upward toward victory.

In Western thought, then, it has seemed "natural" to think in
terms of a series of hierarchies in the individual, in society, and in
the world of nature. Moreover, this hierarchical construct carries
with it implications that are hard to resist and that have influenced
the way we think about things in a number of fields, including reading: upward climbing is a duty; backsliding is always bad; anything
that makes backsliding attractive, or more likely, is bad; once the
climber has reached the higher rungs of the ladder, he or she will
repudiate the lower.

Accordingly, the metaphor of the ladder provided librarians
with both a way of talking about reading and a rationale for recommending policies. As Lakoff and Johnson point out, metaphors have
entailments, and through these entailments "a metaphor may be a
guide for future action. Such actions will, of course, fit the metaphor. This will, in turn, reinforce the power of the metaphor to
make experience coherent."[9] When the ladder is used as a way of
organizing ideas about reading, then the entailments will include im-
peratives about climbing upward, avoiding backsliding, and repudiating
the lower in favor of the higher. The idea of unilinear gradation
sanctions the practice of classifying, from low to high, books on one
scale and readers on another. The twin assumptions are as follows:
a particular book can be more or less objectively assigned to one
particular level on the scale of reading quality; a particular reader
belongs at any one time at one level on the scale of reading maturity
(although under the obligation to progress to a "higher level"). As
I will be suggesting later, this is not the only available way to think
about reading, although it is the way most consistent with the ladder
metaphor. In the librarians' statements on reading that are shortly
to be examined, these metaphoric ways of thinking were tacitly pre-
supposed rather than formally expressed or explicitly examined.

Turning now to these statements (Esther Jane Carrier's Fiction
in Public Libraries 1876-1900 provides a convenient and thorough

compilation),[10] we find, not unexpectedly, that two propositions were considered beyond dispute. First, a unilinear gradation exists naturally in the books themselves. Second, librarians are called, as Justin Winsor put it, "to elevate the taste of their readers" by conducting them "from the ordinary society novel to the historical novel, and then to proofs and illustrations of the events or periods commemorated in the more readable of the historians."[11] "Let the attention be guided," he advised the First National Conference of Librarians in 1876, "from the poor to the indifferent, from this to the good, and so on to the best."[12] The main problem was where to draw the line between acceptable books and inadmissible books, or, as Ainsworth Rand Spofford put it, "between the good and improving novels, and novels which are neither good nor improving."[13] Everyone agreed that immoral and profane books should be kept out; many said that trashy fiction should be kept out; a smaller group said that all fiction ought to be excluded.

The stance taken on this matter depended on the commentator's view of human nature--whether human nature is active or passive and whether it tends toward goodness or toward evil. In the Lake Placid Conference of 1894, George Watson Cole, speaking at a session devoted to a series of papers on "the ruck of common novels," quoted F. B. Perkins in support of the idea that people are active agents seeking out the good:

> [What] is trash to some, is, if not nutriment, at least stimulus, to others. Readers improve; if it were not so, reading would not be a particularly useful practice. The habit of reading is the first indispensable step. That habit once established, it is a recognized fact that readers go from poor to better sorts of reading. No case has ever been cited where a reader, beginning with lofty philosophy, pure religion, profound science, and useful information, has gradually run down in his reading until his declining years were disreputably wasted on dime novels and story weeklies.... But the experience of librarians is unanimous to the contrary, that those who begin with dime novels and story weeklies may be expected to grow into a liking for a better sort of stories, then for the truer narrative of travels, of biography and history, then for essays and popular science, and so on upward.[14]

That is to say, if readers are active and inclined toward the good, they will make a ladder of even an inferior work.

But, if human beings are passive, they will need, as James H. Hubbard claimed, careful support so as to resist the "natural" tendency to sink:

> It is, therefore, in my opinion, a most pernicious error to encourage young people, of the lower classes especially, to

come to the library, and to give them poor stories in the
mistaken belief that, the taste for reading being developed,
they will naturally and surely rise from these to better books.
Such a belief is contrary to our experience of human nature.
With careful guidance and restraint a boy may be brought
from the dime novel to read Scott and Macaulay. But without
this restraint and guidance, where one will rise, a hundred,
a thousand rather, will remain at the level from which they
started, or more naturally sink to still lower depths.[15]

And finally, if human nature is not merely passively susceptible
to harmful impressions but is of a decidedly fallen character, then
readers must be thoroughly hedged about by deterrents, restraints,
and punishments. Just such a view of fallen human nature and a
sinful world may have been the basis for the sermon preached in 1896
by the Presbyterian minister Reverend J. A. Milburn, in which he
attacked the Indianapolis Library for providing "debasing, meretri-
cious, immoral, pernicious, and destructive fiction."[16] Similarly,
in the belief that at least the uneducated are fallen, Mr. William M.
Stevenson explained, in his annual report of 1896, why he had rooted
out from the Carnegie Free Library of Allegheny, Pennsylvania, works
by such authors as Horatio Alger, Bertha M. Clay, May Agnes Fleming,
E. P. Roe, and Mrs. E.D.E.N. Southworth:

> As to the overworked who need fiction, the observation of
> your librarian is that the most inveterate readers of fiction
> are anything but the overworked, but are, on the contrary,
> the most idle class in the community. It is certainly not the
> function of the public library to foster the mind-weakening
> habit of novel-reading among the very classes--the uneducated,
> busy or idle--whom it is the duty of the public library to
> lift to a higher plane of thinking.[17]

In the examples just considered, commentators, all starting with
their own particular views of human nature, came to differing conclusions about the proper treatment of fiction. But, given their
different premises, their conclusions are the ones called for within
the paradigm of the reading ladder.

It has probably not escaped attention that, in some of the
passages quoted, there is a tacitly assumed correspondence between
the scale of book quality and the scale of readers, where the unit
of measurement implied is economic. At the very bottom of the scale
of book quality are "trash," "shoddy" books, "cheap" books, "light"
books, dime novels, and penny dreadfuls. These cheap, worthless
books are thought to be read by people lowest on the scale of readers
--low-brows--who are also, William Stevenson seems to imply, lowest
on the socioeconomic scale: the "idle" and the "uneducated."[18]

Most commentators of the period, however, probably would
have said that the measure used to create the scale was not economic

but something else: the moral or literary quality of the book or
alternatively the maturity of the reader. The passages by Justin
Winsor and F. B. Perkins quoted above imply that books can be arranged on a unilinear scale from low to high according to their genres.
Presumably the original audience would not need to be told explicitly
why proceeding "from the ordinary society novel to the historical
novel" or from "the better sort of stories" to "the truer narrative
of travels, of biography and history" should be considered evidence
of improvement. Genres, it seems, are to be placed higher on the
scale as they move away from imaginative and fictional material.
At the lowest level of all are works of popular romance--sensation
novels, Beadle's dime novels, Horatio Alger's fables of industrious
apprentices, Mrs. E.D.E.N. Southworth's domestic melodramas of
calumniated wives, and other popular works sharing the following
characteristics of romance: folklorish and conventional plot elements
such as hairbreadth escapes, deliverance from death or dishonor,
revenge, amnesia, miraculous cures, mysterious births, identical
twins, and recognition scenes; and emphasis on incident rather than
on character; characters that are stylized figures resembling psychological archetypes; a strongly marked dialectic of good and evil;
and a greater emphasis on design than is normally possible in works
of realism. Realism was seen as belonging on a higher level because
of its emphasis on content, its portrayal of social concerns, and its
greater fidelity to what Hawthorne has called "the probable and ordinary course of man's experience."[19] Works on the next step
up--travel, biography, and history--are purified of fictional elements
but are still informed by the principles of narrative and storytelling.
And finally, at the top, are genres of nonfiction and nonnarrative
writing such as reference tools, accounts of scientific research, essays, sermons, and other discursive forms.

     This classification scheme seems clear enough, but turned out
to be hard to apply. Difficulties arose with works such as those
influenced by the French realist writers like Zola and the Goncourts:
their realism and their preoccupation with social concerns put them
relatively high on the scale, but in moral value they were judged
sadly debased.[20] Such difficulties point to a source of confusion
in thinking about reading. The assumption has been that there is
a single unilinear scale for books in themselves--in other words, one
ladder. Reflection, however, suggests a number of ladders, each
one organizing the scale according to a different standard. Books
can be graded variously according to their genre, their literary
quality, their moral value, or the degree of specialized knowledge
and training required of their readers. These last two scales may
purport to measure objectively the moral value or the difficulty of
the "work in itself," but it is undeniably harder here to eliminate
from consideration the role of the reader in relation to the work being
read. Hence the ladder metaphor, as it is used in everyday language
with respect to reading, can be found to mask the following possibilities. There may be not one scale for books but many. The same
reader may, to suit different moods and needs, quite legitimately

read at very different levels of so-called maturity and quality (in
which case the charge of backsliding is inappropriate). And, finally,
it may not be possible to leave out of account the transactional
nature of reading as a process that occurs between a text and a
reader whose individual and creative acts of reading can be said to
make sense out of texts.

Reading Is Eating

A metaphor grounded in physical relationships such as up/down
(or in/out, forward/backward, etc.) is a basic orientational metaphor
of great importance in our conceptual system. However, there is
another kind of metaphor--what Lakoff and Johnson call a "structural
metaphor"--that is richer in its possibilities for elaboration. Structural
metaphors allow us "to use one highly structured and clearly delineated concept to structure another."[21] Usually the more abstract
concept is structured in terms of a concrete, well-understood concept,
as is the case in the second metaphor under examination, READING
IS EATING. Here the defining concept is a particularly rich domain
of common everyday experience, capable of considerable elaboration:
there are different kinds of foods, various cooking styles, and many
kinds of eaters and ways of eating. For example, some readers are
gluttons for detective stories, or voracious (vorare, Lat.--to swallow),
avid (avere, Lat.--to crave), or hungry for books. Some readers
have refined, discriminating palates. Others have no stomach for
reading. Many enjoy browsing among books.

READING IS EATING has the advantage of being compatible
with the orientational metaphor of the ladder, so that the two metaphoric systems are congruent and can be used together, as they
are in the term "elevated (or debased) reading taste." We have seen
that, on the ladder of up/down, the following are all up: nonfiction,
utilitarian information, realism, factuality, and rationality. Fiction,
pleasure, "escapism," fantasy, and irrationality are all down. The
domain of food and eating is compatible with this hierarchical organization, having its own contrasting values: wholesome food (information
and facts) vs. debilitating food (escapism and fantasy), high taste
vs. low taste, and so on. Various levels of foods/books can thus
be said to be consumed by different levels of eaters/readers. As
readers digest what they read, they experience predictable bodily
effects, from beneficial to "pernicious." Certain books are tough
meat or good protein; others are spices, relishes, or sauces; others
pap, pabulum, or milk; and still others are sugar or addictive drugs.

It was agreed among the librarians whose statements we are
examining that readers should be "weaned" from the poorer sort of
book. As the term "weaned" suggests, one aspect of reading highlighted by the metaphor of eating is developmental. The immature
reader is someone at an early (or low) developmental stage, who needs
a diet of wholesome, but suitable, nutriment. E. S. Willcox developed

this analogy for the benefit of the Illinois Library Association in
1900:

> The good public is a great baby, and must be fed spoon
> victuals at first, not boiled into concentrated extracts, as
> Walter Pater does it; their weak stomachs will not bear it;
> it must be thin, with a plenty of cheap filing and sweetening
> in the way of sentiment and moonlight and hairbreadth
> escapes and impossible heroes and impossible villains and es-
> pecially impossible young ladies.[22]

In other words, the sugary "spoon victuals" suitable "at first" are
works of romance. The hierarchy of genres, considered above, which
stretches from romance at the bottom to realism to travel, biography,
and history and finally up to nonnarrative prose, is thus brought
into alignment with a hierarchy of foods. The counterpart to the
work of romance is the sugary confection. Just as one climbs the
hierarchy of foods by leaving behind the sugary dishes and the milk
puddings in favor of "stronger foods" and pure meat, so one climbs
the ladder of genres by successively leaving behind the fictional
and narrative elements that give delight rather than instruction. To
quote William J. Fletcher, "Let the library, then, contain just enough
of the mere confectionary of literature to secure the interest in it
of readers of the lowest--not depraved--tastes; but let this be so
dealt out as may best make it serve its main purpose of a stepping
stone to something better."[23]

The acceptance of this equivalent between types of books and
types of foods in the context of discussions of the development of
the individual strengthened the position of those who, like the trustees
of the Boston Public Library, argued that the library should provide
materials suitable for all capacities:

> Some readers will always demand this class of book [books
> uninteresting to highly educated people, but reflecting ...
> the lives of those who enjoy them], and if they are happily
> led to choose stronger food, their places should be filled by
> new-comers, who are only fit to begin on a milk-and-water
> diet. Some may never get beyond it, but should they, there-
> fore, be starved or turned away, to seek stimulants offered
> by the private circulating library or the news-stands?
> [my emphasis][24]

However, observers who felt that firm restraints were needed
to keep readers from sinking did not talk about popular fiction as
milk puddings and candy; they talked of poisons, spirits, and
narcotics. To the argument that it is better that "unformed readers"
read poorer books than none at all, Ainsworth Rand Spofford,
librarian-in-chief of the Library of Congress, answered, "You might
as well say that it is better for one to swallow poison than not to
swallow anything at all."[25] Romance was the genre most often

associated, if not with actual poisons, then with alcohol and addictive drugs. Romances, it was claimed, put readers under a "spell," made them crave sensation, and gave them "false views of life." Addicted readers become "fiction-vampires" or, as William Stevenson put it, "fiction-fiends,"[26] the term "fiends" emphasizing the demonic aspects of reading. In this context of drug addiction, the terms "reading habit" and "hooked by books" also acquire sinister connotations. "Once the [reading] habit is formed," continues Stevenson, "it seems as difficult to throw off as the opium habit."

The entailments of the metaphor READING IS EATING may be summarized as follows. Since a balanced diet is crucial to healthy development, it is harmful to consume too much of the same kind of thing. Librarians are therefore justified in policies such as "the two-book system" (readers were allowed to withdraw two books, but the second book had to be nonfiction). As with eating, there is a sensual pleasure in reading, but also a danger that this pleasure may be a cause of harmful immoderation. The pleasurable aspect of reading is therefore morally ambivalent. On the one hand, it is suspect, because the sources of pleasure too often turn out to be escapist, sensationalist, addictive, and connected with sexuality. On the other hand, the pleasure of reading can be useful, as Herbert Putnam put it, to attract the reader as a first step toward "wheedl[ing]" him "into something better."[27] The real content of a book, its ideas or information, is thought of as a thing that can be swallowed. The relationship between the librarian who knows which books are healthful and the passive reader who is wheedled into swallowing resembles that existing between a doctor and a patient. As Charles A. Cutter put it, the librarian has a new role that is not just a "book-watch-man" but a "mental doctor for his town."[28] These entailments, as I'll be arguing in the next section, can be expected to shape policy and influence decisions along lines that fit the metaphors.

Stories of Reading

So far, the argument goes that late nineteenth century librarians saw the complex phenomenon of reading through the filter provided by the familiar concrete metaphors of ladders and eating. These metaphors may be said to provide a language that librarians can use to talk about and think about reading. With this language, it is clearly easier to tell certain kinds of stories about readers and harder to tell others. Jonathan Culler, discussing accounts of reading provided by recent literary critics, has pointed out some important variables, relevant here, concerning the way that stories of reading get told.[29] There is the issue of control: does the text provoke certain responses in a passive reader or does the reader actively take charge in the creative, productive role of making meaning? There is the related question of what is "in" the text: is the text a determinate structure that has an objective meaning in itself apart

from any reader? Or is the text a set of indeterminate marks upon
which the reader confers meaning, attributing significance to signifiers
on the basis of personal experience or of previously learned literary
and cultural codes? And finally there is the question of the ending:
does the reader's encounter with the text end triumphantly in discovery and new knowledge or does the story of reading have the unhappy ending of causing the reader harm? Within the conceptual
frame provided by the metaphors of ladders and eating, it is easier
to tell a story of active texts and passive readers. In this story,
the text, as we have seen, is a thing to be swallowed. Because
meaning is fixed in the text itself, all the reader can do is to swallow
it whole and incorporate its content in unaltered form. Texts, therefore, have an objective status. They can be objectively assigned to
particular levels of quality from low to high. And they have predictable effects on readers, with fiction, especially romance, leading
to downfall and nonfiction fostering an upward climb.

Conversely, the metaphors we have been examining make it
harder to tell other kinds of stories--stories of active readers whose
activity of making meaning from black marks on a page occurs in
the context of the readers' own lives. In this second kind of story,
the focus of interest shifts from the effect of texts on readers to
the relationship between the readers and the text. Now readers--
not librarians, teachers, or other experts--become the judges of the
value of materials, and readers make this judgment in the context of
their own lives.

However, a quick survey of librarians' treatment of fiction in
this century suggests that the first story of reading is the one that,
until quite recently, has prevailed. Moreover, librarians who tell
themselves this story get caught in a dilemma: most of their work
involves materials, readers, motives, and satisfactions that are "down"
on the scale, while librarians measure their own success by the
degree to which they push people up the reading ladder.[30] A
footnote in Dee Garrison's Apostles of Culture illustrates the trouble-
some and persistent gap between the officially declared educational
mission of public libraries and the evidence of circulation records:

> In 1878 the Mercantile Public Library in San Francisco re-
> ported 71.4 per cent of its circulation was fiction, while
> .6 per cent was religious works. In the same year the In-
> dianapolis library crowed that its fiction circulation had
> dropped from 80 to 72 per cent, after heroic efforts had been
> made by the librarian to reduce fiction reading.[31]

Thematic in this story is the crucial choice that the librarian
is forced to make between high/low, duty/expediency, objectives/
practice, quality/popularity, or what people should have (nonfiction)/
and what people want (fiction). In the 1920s and 1930s, the Reader's
Advisory Service was developed, not to promote leisure reading or
reading in general, but to promote a self-disciplined, educational

course of "reading with a purpose" on socially significant topics.[32]
The publication in 1924 of William S. Learned's The American Public
Library and the Diffusion of Knowledge gave weight to the idea that
the public library should be primarily an educational institution or
"community intelligence center." When Douglas Waples and his colleagues at the University of Chicago undertook their substantial
research on reading in the 1930s, the reading assumed to be valuable
was nonfiction, particularly nonfiction treatments of subjects of contemporary social concern.[33] By 1950, the Public Library Inquiry
made the discouraging discovery that, while librarians still endorsed
educational objectives for the library,[34] the presumed beneficiaries
reported almost unanimously that they "never thought of" the library
as a source of information.[35] In the Forum on the Public Library
Inquiry, Bernard Berelson drew specific attention to "the split between
the professed and the practiced objectives for the public library,"
[36] Ralph Munn's proposed solution to which was "radical" change
to bring practice into alignment with educational objectives: "the
change can be gradual. If a library has been on a life-long cheap
novel spree, it may be better to sober up gradually than to take
the Keeley cure and try to reform over night."[37] And finally,
to conclude this quick survey, there is the response of librarians
to the findings of three large-scale national surveys on reading conducted in 1978[38]--the Statistics Canada-based Leisure Reading
Habits, the ALA-sponsored Book Reading and Library Usage, and the
Book Industry Study Group-sponsored Consumer Research on Reading
and Book Purchasing. Summarizing librarians' responses to these
last two surveys, Michael H. Harris and James Sodt claim: "Either
library professionals could accept the data, admit the failure of their
broad-based cultural uplift mission, and succumb to popular demands
for recreational services deemed decidedly low culture in emphasis,
or they could distort the findings to suit their professional requirements. The latter, not surprisingly, has always been the standard
reaction."[39]

This either/or choice is made necessary in a story of reading
that polarizes as opposites pleasure and information, fiction and
nonfiction, and so on. It might be asked whether the library profession's dilemma here, with all its attendant guilt, evasion, and
splitting in consciousness, is not the necessary price of telling this
particular story of reading. The question may soon be answerable
because new stories of reading are recently being told. Challenges
to the authority of the older story are coming from various quarters,
such as structuralism, which is antihierarchical,[40] the new field
of popular culture, which rejects the claim to monopoly by elite
culture,[41] and the reader-response school of literary criticism,
which has undermined the concept of the objectivity and autonomy
of the text.[42] The library field itself recently has been hearing
another kind of story of reading. Some advocates, for example, have
been recommending a shift from studying books as autonomous objects to studying the relation between books and readers or between
library materials and users. Once this shift is made, it seems

appropriate not to classify a book in itself as high or low, good or
bad, but to consider the book as helpful or not helpful to a particular
reader in a particular situation. Hence Gordon Stevenson suggests
that there be "more emphasis on the function [of cultural objects]
in people's lives."[43] Similarly, Douglas Zweizig and Brenda Dervin
say that the old emphasis on studying library use (circulation of
materials) or library users (demographic surveys) should be replaced
by a study of library uses (the way that people use materials in
the context of their own lives).[44] Such shifts in emphasis, it is
worth repeating, are hard to make because they go against assumptions
carried in the metaphoric language that we use.

    Identifying as such the entailments of metaphor has the effect
of changing the status of these entailments from unassailable truths
to debatable propositions. Hence, now open to question is the status
of the notion of a hierarchical ordering of the verbal universe into
distinct levels and the related imperative of leaving behind the lower
in favor of the higher. Metaphors, as we have seen, give coherence
to our picture of the real. They function as a kind of filter, telling
us what is important and what can be safely ignored. It follows, then,
that it might prove fruitful to reexamine those things that the reading
metaphors have indicated are unimportant: fiction, reading for
pleasure, fantasy, romance, "escapism," and "trash" (which would
probably have to be renamed). In summary, the recognition that
seeing is metaphoric--that all seeing is seeing-as--has implications
for our understanding of the stories of reading that the library profession has told itself. Identifying the "metaphors we live by" may
perhaps also make it easier to envisage calling into use new metaphors
and telling new stories of reading.

References

1. For a historical overview of work on metaphor, see Mark John-
    son (ed.), Philosophical Perspectives on Metaphor (Minneapolis:
    University of Minnesota Press, 1981). This volume is a collection
    of thirteen central articles on metaphor and includes a 23-page
    annotated bibliography of key sources.
2. George Lakoff and Mark Johnson, Metaphors We Live By (Chi-
    cago: University of Chicago Press, 1980). A condensation
    of the ideas in this book can be found in Lakoff and Johnson's
    article "Conceptual Metaphor in Everyday Language," in Johnson,
    Philosophical Perspectives, 286-328.
3. Lakoff and Johnson, "Conceptual Metaphor in Everyday Language,"
    288.
4. Johnson, Philosophical Perspectives, 289.
5. "One thing about which fish know exactly nothing is water,
    since they have no anti-environment which would enable them to
    perceive the element they live in," in Marshall McLuhan and
    Quentin Fiore, War and Peace in the Global Village (New York:
    Bantam Books, 1968), 175.

6. Noah Porter, Books and Reading: or, What Books Shall I Read and How Shall I Read Them? 4th ed. (New York: Scribner, Armstrong and Co., 1877), 231-232.

7. Justin Winsor, "Free Libraries and Readers," Library Journal 1/11 (30 November 1876): 63-67. Quoted in Esther Jane Carrier, Fiction in Public Libraries 1876-1900 (New York and London: Scarecrow Press, 1965), 24.

8. Arthur O. Lovejoy, The Great Chain of Being: A Study in the History of an Idea (Cambridge, Mass.: Harvard University Press, 1936).

9. Johnson, Philosophical Perspectives, 321.

10. Carrier, Fiction in Public Libraries 1876-1900.

11. Justin Winsor, "Reading in Popular Libraries," Public Libraries in the United States of America, part I (Washington, D.C.: Government Printing Office, 1876), 432; quoted in Carrier, Fiction in Public Libraries, 50.

12. Winsor, "Free Libraries and Readers," Library Journal 1/11 (30 November 1876): 65; quoted in Carrier, Fiction in Public Libraries, 51.

13. Ainsworth Rand Spofford, A Book for All Readers (New York: G. P. Putnam's Sons, 1900), 19.

14. George Watson Cole, "Fiction in Libraries: A Plea for the Masses," Library Journal 19/12 (December 1894): 20.

15. James H. Hubbard, "How to Use a Public Library," Library Journal 9/2 (February 1884): 28; quoted in part in Carrier, Fiction in Public Libraries, 213.

16. "Pulpit vs. Library Again," Library Journal 21/3 (March 1896): 106. The article goes on to quote an editorial in the Indianapolis Sentinal by Mr. J. P. Dunn in defense of the library: "As a matter of fact, the Indianapolis Library is one of the best selected libraries in the country, and one of the most carefully guarded. ...It is continually elevating the taste of the people, even in the line of pushing them on from 'fiction' to purer literature."

17. Seventh Annual Report of the Librarian (Allegheny, Pa.: Carnegie Free Library, n.d.), 10; quoted in Carrier, Fiction in Public Libraries, 258.

18. An interesting example of the use in research of this assumption that fiction can be ranked on a scale of quality and aligned with readers, who are ranked on a socioeconomic scale, can be found in Jeannette Foster's "An Approach to Fiction through the Characteristics of Its Readers," Library Quarterly 6/2 (April 1936): 124-174. Foster distributed 254 authors of fiction on six "quality levels" and validated her scale by recourse to what she called a "new and more objective angle--the nature of the readers who choose given types of fiction" (p. 125). Essentially this meant that the place of certain authors on the low end of the scale of quality was confirmed if these works turned out to be the ones read by readers ranked low on the "readers' maturity index": younger readers, those with less education and lower-status jobs, and those who didn't read much non-fiction.

19. Nathaniel Hawthorne, "Preface," The House of the Seven Gables
    (New York: Signet Classic, 1961), p. vii.
20. See Carrier, Fiction in Public Libraries, 133.
21. Lakoff and Johnson, Metaphors We Live By, 60.
22. E. S. Willcox, "Annual Address Extract," Public Libraries 5
    (April 1900): 122.
23. William I. Fletcher, "Public Libraries in Manufacturing Communi-
    ties," in U.S. Bureau of Education, Public Libraries in the United
    States of America (Washington, D.C.: Government Printing
    Office, 1876), 410-411.
24. Boston Public Library, Forty-first Annual Report of the Trustees
    of the City of Boston (Boston: Rockwell and Churchill, 1893),
    11; quoted in Carrier, Fiction in Public Libraries, 255.
25. Spofford, A Book for All Readers, 20.
26. William M. Stevenson, "Weeding Out Fiction in the Carnegie
    Free Library of Allegheny, Pa.," Library Journal 6/3 (March
    1881): 133.
27. Herbert Putnam, "Fiction in Libraries," Library Journal 15/9
    (September 1890): 264. Putnam went on to say: "Our American
    public hardly needs to be wheedled into the reading habit; it
    reads too many books, not too few."
28. Charles A. Cutter, [editorial], Library Journal 6/3 (March 1881):
    39-40.
29. Jonathan Culler, On Deconstruction: Theory and Criticism after
    Structuralism (Ithaca, N.Y.: Cornell University Press, 1982),
    69-80.
30. For a discussion of what she calls the "schizophrenia" of trying
    both to give the public what it wants and to "assemble a collection
    that might inspire some readers to scale a ladder, the rungs of
    which are marked good, better, and even best," see R. Kathleen
    Molz, "The American Public Library: Its Historic Concern for
    the Humanities," in Robert N. Broadus (ed.), The Role of the
    Humanities in the Public Library (Chicago: American Library
    Association, 1979), 30-49.
31. Dee Garrison, Apostles of Culture: The Public Librarian and
    American Society; 1876-1920 (New York: Collier Macmillan, 1979),
    68.
32. See John Chancellor, "Helping Readers with a Purpose," ALA
    Bulletin 25/4 (April 1931): 138. "I believe we should emphasize
    conscientious reading. ...Let us emphasize thoroughness as
    much as we can, the getting of a whole and complete view....
    Let us not just urge people to read--read haphazardly--but to
    'read with a purpose,' a very apt slogan." Unfortunately, in-
    dividuals presenting themselves for this purposive library
    guidance turned out, observed one reader's advisor from Portland,
    to have minds "made lazy by ... easy victories over popular
    magazines, light fiction and moving pictures." See Virginia
    Cleaver Bacon, "Possibilities of Informal Education under Library
    Guidance," ALA Bulletin 21 (1927): 317.
33. Stephen Karetzky, in Reading Research in Librarianship: History
    and Analysis (Westport, Conn.: Greenwood Press, 1982), 107,

comments on what he apparently considers to be curious limitations in Waples's approach to reading. Significantly, these limitations match the entailments of our metaphors for reading--
the privileging of nonfiction over fiction, the dismissal of products of the imagination, the intense suspicion of "escape literature," and so on:

> Throughout the thirties, Waples considered non-fiction reading
> on subjects of contemporary social concern to be far more
> important than any other kind of reading. His dismissal of
> literature, art, and the humanities was a bit high-handed....
> He thought that reading was sometimes associated with mental
> illness, as an effect and possibly as a cause, and he seemed
> especially suspicious of the effects of "escape literature."
> Waples's ideas on these matters (as well as on some others)
> appear to have stemmed from his intellectual shortcomings,
> shortsightedness, prejudices, and fears.

34. Robert D. Leigh, The Public Library in the United States
     (New York: Columbia University Press, 1950), 22. Leigh re-
     ported that the majority of respondents who were asked their
     opinion of a statement of library objectives approved, but
     a small and discredited minority of dissenters challenged "the
     whole tendency of the document to limit library materials to
     those dealing with serious and significant personal and social
     interests."
35. Ibid., 97.
36. Bernard Berelson, "Reply to the Discussants," in A Forum on
     the Public Library Inquiry (New York: Columbia University
     Press, 1950), 61.
37. Ralph Munn, "Summarizing of the Conference," in A Forum, 260.
38. Kenneth Watson, Leisure Reading Habits: A Survey of the
     Leisure Reading Habits of Canadian Adults with Some International
     Comparisons (Ottawa: Infoscan, 1980); Gallup Organization, Inc.,
     Book Reading and Library Usage: A Study of Habits and Per-
     ceptions (Chicago: American Library Association, 1978); Yanke-
     lowich, Skelly, and White, Inc., Reading and Book Purchasing
     (New York: Book Industry Study Group, 1978).
39. Michael H. Harris and James Sodt, "Libraries, Users, and
     Librarians: Continuing Efforts to Define the Nature and Extent
     of Public Library Use," in Michael H. Harris (ed.), Advances
     in Librarianship, vol. 11 (New York: Academic Press, 1981),
     112.
40. Hayden White, "Structuralism and Popular Culture," Journal
     of Popular Culture 7/4 (Spring 1974): 759-775.
41. Ray B. Browne, "Up from Elitism: The Aesthetics of Popular
     Culture," Studies in American Ficiton 9/2 (Autumn 1981):
     217-232.
42. Jane P. Tompkins (ed.), Reader-Response Criticism: From Forma-
     lism to Post-Structuralism (Baltimore, Md.: Johns Hopkins
     University Press, 1980); Susan R. Suleiman and Inge Crosman
     (eds.), The Reader in the Text: Essays on Audience and In-
     terpretation (Princeton, N.J.: Princeton University Press, 1980).

43. Gordon Stevenson, "Popular Culture and the Public Library,"
    in Melvin Voigt and Michael H. Harris (eds.), Advances in Li-
    brarianship, vol. 7 (New York: Academic Press, 1977), 222.
44. Douglas Zweizig and Brenda Dervin, "Public Library Use, Users,
    Uses," in Advances in Librarianship, vol. 7, 251.

BRITTLE BOOKS IN OUR NATION'S LIBRARIES*

David C. Weber

> The statement submitted by ARL and ALA before the Sub-committee on Postsecondary Education, Committee on Education and Labor, U.S. House of Representatives, March 3, 1987.

I am David C. Weber, director of the Stanford University Libraries, member of the Association of Research Libraries and chair of its Committee on Preservation of Research Library Materials, also a member of the American Library Association and past president of its Association of College and Research Libraries.

While you have heard of the frightful rate of which valuable cultural records are becoming embrittled, this "brittle books" challenge must be faced and corrections made over the next two to three decades or we all shall have lost a good deal of who and what we are.

To put it in a local context, I shall describe the situation in my home town, Palo Alto, California--a city of some 60,000 people, including many scientists, engineers, teachers, government officials, students and writers.

An individual interested in a current political issue and con-cerned with its antecedents, causes, and past corrective attempts has available the following:

- A fine public library with over 230,000 volumes.

- The nearby Stanford University Libraries and the Hoover Institution, together having 5.5 million volumes, also nearly 3 million microtext sheets and large numbers of maps, motion picture films, photographs, prints, slides, sound recordings and data sets.

*Reprinted by permission of the author and publisher of College & Research Libraries News 48:5 (May 1987) 238-244.

- And within 20 miles there are a state university library,
  two private college libraries, four community college libraries,
  and a dozen other public libraries linked by a State Library
  inter-system service.

A richness for that individual pursuing a political issue? Yes
and no.

The resources for study are, at 6 million volumes and upwards
of 60 million manuscripts, far greater than in most communities for
60,000 people. The Hoover Institution alone has more archival records
of social action than many entire states. However, over a quarter
of these resources are now so fragile that use is perilous, and in
little more than a decade any use will be problematic due to the rapid
decay of paper. Most of those resources are housed in quarters
where temperatures bake the materials several months of the year,
a situation gradually being corrected at Stanford and elsewhere.

Resources in the West amount to only a fraction of what they
are in the East and Northeast, even the Midwest. The hinterlands
are in fact most of these United States. Requests for interlibrary
loan increasingly result in no availability because the owning library
indicates its book is too fragile to loan, and a microfilm does not
exist, or by policy original letters and archival documents do not
circulate outside the building, and again no film copy exists.

How frustrating for the individual researcher! How limiting if
one does not live in Washington, New York, Philadelphia, or Boston!
How frightening to realize that the condition is nationwide, of awesome
proportions, and getting worse every year!

Concerning interlibrary loan of microfilms, there is a significant
traffic of this type, though it is much less than of books or photo-
copies provided in lieu of the volume. An institution like Stanford
University lends to all kinds of libraries--public and school libraries,
county and state libraries, agencies of government, commercial and
not-for-profit research organizations, as well as community colleges,
four-year colleges and universities. In a recent year, Stanford has
lent microfilms to institutions as far away as the State University of
New York at Buffalo, Columbia, Florida, Johns Hopkins, Princeton,
Rutgers, Virginia, and Yale. Libraries are experienced in lending
this type of material. All academic and most public libraries have
reading machines available for 35mm film. Pre-filming activities,
including collation and creation of film captions (targets), and technical specifications for filming, including quality control procedures,
have been well established by national and international professional
and standards organizations, with major contributions over the past
40 years by the Library of Congress.

The production of preservation microfilms is, in fact, one of
long standing. Starting in the early 1930s there have been programs

in some university libraries, and other research libraries such as
the New York Public Library, to make archival master film copies
of brittle material, copies from which public reading copies are made,
thereby archivally assuring availability of the original text for future
generations.

This preservation filming, sometimes the by-product of an interlibrary loan request, is in the interest of the nation as a whole. It
is true that the institution making the negative film is protecting its
own investment in the original. But it is every bit as important
to readers, students and scholars elsewhere throughout the country
that the content be archivally preserved. Otherwise it may be lost
... permanently.

Let me use one example. In the early 1950s at the Harvard
University Library, I was responsible for a foreign newspaper microfilm
project that had been originated in 1938 with Rockefeller Foundation
funds. One of the challenges that was undertaken was to prepare
a complete master microfilm of every issue of Pravada and Izvestia.
The first of these Russian newspapers began publishing March 18,
1917, and the second on February 28, 1917. The task was to complete
the file for the first 20 years. This required obtaining negative
film from copies of individual issues held at Columbia, the New York
Public Library, the Hoover Institution, Harvard, the British Museum
Library, the Bibliothèque Nationale, the Bibliothèque de Documentation
Internationale Contemporaine in Paris, and a few issues found only
in Moscow itself. Even so, the master archival film still lacked 24
issues from 1917, nine in 1918, one in 1919, four in 1920, and one in
1921.

One can reflect, however, on how important was that preservation effort, as just one example of this ubiquitous "brittle books"
problem. Copies of that film have now been sold to many libraries
here and abroad. It is the only nearly complete record of these
primary sources, regardless of where in the world an individual
may be working.

Brittle books reside in libraries of all sizes and types. How
any one library addresses the brittle book problem depends on a
number of factors including but not limited to the number of brittle
books to be treated, the filming and processing equipment, trained
staff, and financial support available to the library. There is general
agreement within the library community that it is unrealistic for every
library to develop in-house facilities capable of producing archival-
quality microfilming of brittle books. Reformatting is an expensive
undertaking and in-house facilities are difficult to justify unless a
library anticipates a significant volume and steady flow of brittle
books to be treated. While there are a few exceptions, only the
larger libraries have developed in-house programs to treat brittle
books. Such operations serve their own institutional needs as well
as serving the needs of other libraries as a source of microfilm to

replace brittle books. Libraries without in-house preservation facilities, with just as serious a problem but with fewer numbers of
brittle books, face an extra hurdle of identifying a laboratory or
service agency where their unique materials may be treated.

Smaller libraries facing this special problem might take a number
of different approaches. In some cases, a nearby library that has
developed an in-house facility might provide preservation services
for other libraries. A few commercial firms can handle archival
microfilming. In addition, regional non-profit preservation laboratories
have been established as cooperative and "mutual help" projects.
One regional center is the Northeast Document Conservation Center
(NEDCC) in Andover, Massachusetts; developed with funds from the
Council on Library Resources, the National Endowment for the Humanities, and private sources, the Center has evolved into a full-service
treatment facility for preservation of research materials. Another
center is the Mid-Atlantic Preservation Service, based at Lehigh University. Each of these options has its limitations.

Some commercial facilities that have traditionally provided filming
services mainly for business records have developed or are developing
new services to film brittle books for libraries to exacting archival
standards. In this regard, considerable effort has been made from
California to Virginia by individual librarians and library associations
to educate people operating such commercial facilities about the special
requirements for the filming of brittle books, as well as educating
librarians as potential customers of such services to the information
filmers need from them.

By way of example, I would like to note that the Association
of Research Libraries, in partnership with NEDCC and with funding
from the Andrew W. Mellon Foundation and the National Historical
Publications and Records Commission, has developed a comprehensive
instructional manual to assist in preservation microfilming. We expect
publication of the manual by the American Library Association this
year.

The majority of libraries will seek services outside their own
organization to treat their brittle books. They will require many
of the same things as libraries with an in-house program:

- Staff trained to assess the extent of the "brittle book problem" in a library collection, to develop a strategy for addressing the problem, and to coordinate the work.

- An internal process to identify, insure completeness of and
  prioritize the material needing treatment, within the context
  of a national strategy.

- Management support, e.g. operational models, guidelines,
  instructions, manuals, public information programs and staff
  workshops for continuing education.

- Bibliographic information within a national network to determine whether the brittle materials in library collections are unique, whether the item has already been reformatted and the microfilm available, or whether the item has been selected for filming but not yet treated elsewhere. (As noted elsewhere in my statement, the availability of such bibliographic information is absolutely essential for using our limited resources most effectively.)

- Funding to support staff to identify brittle materials that require reformatting and to pay for archival preservation filming, entering of the revised bibliographic data into a national database, and storage locally or elsewhere of the archival master file under archival conditions.

Libraries without in-house preservation facilities have one urgent need, however: more regional and cooperative centers. The number is slowly growing but most of the country is still unserved in this regard. Encouragement as well as financial support is necessary.

A survey of scholars by the National Humanities Alliance revealed that their high priority in the area of humanities scholarship was the preservation of research library material. Members of the American Library Association and the Association of Research Libraries have been aware of this crucial need. It was therefore most welcome news in 1985 when the National Endowment for the Humanities expanded its response to this national need by establishing the Office of Preservation. I could hardly exaggerate how important this NEH Preservation Program will be to libraries, though the funding has yet been much too small. Grants available from the Department of Education under the Higher Education Act, Title II-C, constitute another source of funding of extreme importance to a national preservation effort. Fortunately foundations such as the Andrew W. Mellon Foundation have also provided significant support. The State of New York has budgeted an exemplary statewide preservation program, and individual libraries have also built into their basic operating budgets a substantial commitment of financial resources.

As examples, some college and a few university libraries have found that they could commit 1% to 3% of their operating monies to their preservation effort. A substantial number of ARL libraries have made major efforts to increase this and are now committing 3% to 5% of their budget. A few libraries, all too few, have been able to budget as much as 6% to 8% of their total expenditures for preservation activities. The very significant effort libraries have made to address this problem is clear when a comparison is made between the amounts they have spent on preservation activities and the amounts spent on acquisition of new materials for the collection. From 10% to 25% of their entire materials budget is spent for binding, microfilming, or other preservation treatment. This can be regarded as a measure of the problem, the urgency with which the need is viewed by the administrations of these libraries.

One might ask how priorities can be set when libraries are able to spend limited sums on the preservation of materials and yet the problem is of awesome dimension. Let me cite a hypothetical example, based on a program designed for the Association of Research Libraries. ARL has used a documentary conspectus to provide a descriptive map of the strength of existing collections and current collecting efforts in specific subject fields. That data could provide the basis for selecting which members of ARL could best be asked to undertake preservation responsibility in this or that subject. Since library collections are not duplicates, two or even three libraries may need to pool their resources for adequate coverage of one subject. That sum of archival microfilm will then function as the representative collection of record for that subject field.

The Research Libraries Group of institutions has followed the same strategy. (RLG is a Connecticut corporation formed and supported by about three dozen research universities and libraries, with services used by many libraries scattered from Maryland and Florida to Colorado and California.) One of its long-standing programs is dedicated to the preservation of research library materials. Its members, nearly all of whom are also members of the American Library Association and the Association of Research Libraries, have for four years been pursuing a focused and carefully worked out program of preservation microfilming. A conspectus of comparative collection strengths has been assembled. Libraries with special strength in a discrete subject field have undertaken filming of those items, concentrating first on U.S. imprints between 1850 and 1920. A computer database records decisions to film and lists resultant master films. Masters are stored archivally by a Pennsylvanian commercial firm. A broader cooperative attack on a similar prioritization basis, extended to foreign imprints and more recent publications is now being fashioned by RLG. For an example, Chinese language materials of 1880-1949 are now being filmed.

While national standards would be used for a national program of preservation filming, the processes and priorities used to identify items for preservation would be left to the discretion of subject experts in the individual institution. In the interest of cost-effectiveness, all variants of a popular history or text would not be filmed, though all variant editions of a literary work would be. Also excluded would be, e.g., offprints and facsimiles. Within the subject designation assigned to a particular library, funds would be used to concentrate on the materials identified as being in the most brittle or physically deteriorated state. Once preservation copies have been made of those that are most endangered, one would then turn to those that will be in a similar state in another five or ten years, and so on in a progressive conversion effort.

The need to preserve representative rather than exhaustive
collections for all subject areas requires that scholars and librarians
plan within a national context and use limited resources in a coordinated fashion. Thus a "national collection" consisting of individual
collections of discrete subjects at different institutions will be formed
with minimal duplication and with future access assured for everyone.
Later there may be the chance to supplement that national collection
where other libraries can fill in significant gaps. But only in this
systematic way can we guarantee that a balanced national collection
of materials in all subject fields will be available in the next century.

I do not mean to suggest that all of the procedures and methods
have been agreed to; quite the contrary. Yet the objective is uni-
versally supported. The standards are well understood. The de-
pendability of preservation microfilming is well established. The
longtime value of this investment is assured by storage of the master
negative in secure vault-like quarters with suitable atmospheric conditions.

As the ARL testified in March 1986 before the House Subcommittee on Appropriations for the Interior Department and Related
Agencies (including funding for the National Endowment for the
Humanities), libraries also recognize an absolute requirement for a
national bibliographic record, or catalog, which records when the
preservation copy has been made, where it exists, and thereby publicly records where use copies may be purchased or borrowed. "Given
the enormous amount of material to be preserved, the urgency to
move ahead as quickly as possible, and the limited funding available,
duplication must be avoided. Technology provides a reasonable solution: register local decisions to preserve a book, newspaper or
any research material in a widely available database to alert others
that the title need not be treated elsewhere and that the title is, or
will be, available for use. Reasonable access to information about
what titles have already been preserved or identified for treatment
is a basic element of the infrastructure necessary to move this national
objective ahead in a cooperative and expeditious manner. In short,
we require a basic bibliographic structure in place to make wise
preservation decisions."

Since that hearing, I am very pleased to report that the Mellon
Foundation and NEH have awarded the Association of Research Libraries $1,200,000 in funds to convert all monographic records in
the National Register of Microform Masters (located in the Library of
Congress) into a machine readable database, one that will be available
two years from now in the RLG database, the OCLC database, the
Western Library Network database and others. This project will
be a grand achievement, providing a basic building block for the
national bibliographic network necessary for economical preservation
of brittle books.

Since we know the magnitude of the problem and since we have

a methodology for selecting how and where to begin our attack, it
is apparent that a solution to the problem is at hand if we act together.
Let me add to its solution by providing the answers to three other
key questions.

1. What are the appropriate Federal, State and private sector
roles in efforts to address this problem? Each sector plays a key
role, as I have suggested in the picture described above. Essential
cooperative planning is provided by such organizations as ALA, ARL,
RLG and the Council on Library Resources. The new National Commission on Preservation and Access can play a lead role. The Library of Congress has for years done us all a great service with
its research and development work and its publicizing and prosely-
tizing of the state of the preservation art--including international
coordination work. The National Agricultural Library and the National
Library of Medicine have also initiated preservation programs of value
nationally and internationally. The Government Printing Office should
be encouraged to work with librarians, archivists and paper companies
to establish and apply standards for acid-free paper and binding as
appropriate for a good part of government publications. The Higher
Education Act Title II-C program and the National Historical Publications and Records Commission program are modestly funded but make
significant contributions to the national preservation strategies.
The program of the Office of Preservation in the National Endowment
for the Humanities should be greatly strengthened.

2. What procedures are necessary to ensure public access to
preserved materials? Part of the answer is easy, since public, academic and independent research libraries have a long-standing commitment to access. In addition, it requires that individual institutions,
professional associations and funding agencies insist that bibliographic
data be currently maintained on what is in the queue for filming,
what has been completed and by whom. It requires that reading copies
of the master films be readily available and publicized, and that the
interlibrary services staff and users consider films as routine rather
than exceptional loans. There is a role here for ALA, ARL, and
consortia such as RLG.

3. And what are the costs and who should bear them? The
Council on Library Resources has made fair estimates of the total
cost. The total effort we face is daunting, perhaps on the order
of tens of millions of dollars. While each group might like some other
to pay full costs, that is patently unrealistic. A consensus exists
among libraries that costs must be shared; some costs must be covered
locally. Start up costs in particular need government and foundation
help. Ongoing costs require local budgeting for at least a significant
share, with endowment support for preservation programs in research
libraries to the extent possible.

Yet one must recognize that libraries generally are so meagerly
financed that there is little budgetary potential for dealing with

problems of ten or fifty years hence when current book budgets and
clientele services are severely beleaguered. The brittle books
problem is a national concern, and indeed worldwide. Recognizing
that, Federal support for a few decades is essential. A major share
of start up costs should be a Federal responsibility, as should a
strong portion of local operating costs.

Just as the Federal highway system is financed as being in
the nation's interest, for both civilian and national defense purposes,
exactly so should the "brittle books" system be financed as in the
nation's interest: Students, scholars, our defense structure, our
very civilization demands no less protection against the now recognized
seeds of cultural destruction.

Thus it seems evident that there must be a Federal role, sharing
the effort with state, local and institutional authorities.

Resolutions supporting a second White House Conference on
Library and Information Services for 1989 have been introduced in
the House and the Senate (H.J. Res. 90 and S.J. Res. 26). I call
attention to this proposal on this occasion because we anticipate such
a forum could provide an opportunity to focus national attention on
the catastrophic consequences of the deterioration of printed material
in the nation's libraries. As this hearing demonstrates, Congress
is aware of the problem and is actively engaged in defining an appropriate federal role to contribute toward a solution. But we all
acknowledge that Congress cannot solve the problem alone--nor can
any other single agent. The enormity of the problem and the costs
associated with developing and implementing programs to preserve
brittle books dictate a responsibility within every sector of the nation.
Therefore, while the proposed White House Conference on Library
and Information Services will not "solve" the brittle book problem
we consider here today, it would provide a forum to continue to raise
the level of understanding about the scope and seriousness of the
challenge we all face. We appreciate the support members of the
Subcommittee showed in the past for the Conference and hope we
may count on that support continuing again this year.

To sum up: We recognize the urgency and magnitude of the
library materials preservation problem. We have a plan whereby
decisions can be made as to what material needs preservation and in
what priority. We have a rough idea of the costs involved. We
accept the concept of reasonable cost sharing. And we are rather
well equipped--except for the lack of a federal policy of commitment
to help resolve the problem of brittle library materials, and except
for sufficient funding.

To improve access to cultural resources and safeguard our own
future, the Congress must act, providing leadership and help with
financial aid. On behalf of the Association of Research Libraries
and the American Library Association, I request your support.

THE RAILROAD, THE COMMUNITY,
AND THE BOOK*

Ronald J. Zboray

The completion of the northeastern rail network in the 1850s has
long been recognized as an event of great significance for American
publishing history. Rail opened a mass market of national dimension
for books and assured an easy dissemination of literature from publishers in New York, Philadelphia, and Boston. In the first of these
cities particularly, American book production centralized, largely
at the expense of smaller publishing centers scattered across America.
As the publishing industry boomed in the 1850s, American literary
life seemed well on its way to becoming nationalized and not just a
little homogenized.

Such a general view of the interaction between the book and
the railroad, however, all too easily loses sight of the personal impact
of rail upon the common reader and his or her community. For the
coming of rail not only dramatically improved the distribution of
literature, it changed the very context in which it was read. Before
rail, information from the outside world came into most communities
bit by bit, unpredictably, depending upon the weather, the season,
the state of the roads, or the dispositions of drivers and canalmen.
Those limitations looked back to an agrarian age, when time intertwined
with nature's cycles. The shriek of the locomotive, long before the
first factory bell tower, signalled to many communities the arrival
of so-called industrial time, wedded to the clock. Indeed, many
local railroad stations had their own bell tower to announce the arrival
of a train: "The bell on the roof" on the Medford, Massachusetts,
stationhouse was viewed by local inhabitants as "a public convenience"
that allowed them to keep track of time (Francis B. Bradlee, The
Boston and Maine Railroad: A History of the Main Road, with Its
Tributary Lines [Salem, Mass.: private printing, 1921] 33).

Printing played an important role in the altered sense of time
brought about by rail. The passengers at Medford and other stations

*Reprinted by permission of the author and publisher of Southwest
Review 71:4 (Autumn 1986) 474-487; copyright © 1986 by Ronald
J. Zboray. This essay first appeared in the Southwest Review.

on hearing the bell could guess the time without looking at a time-
piece; for the scream of the whistle, the clang of the bell coincided
with the arrival times of trains listed in the mass-produced schedule.
"Men are advertised that at a certain hour and minute these bolts
will be shot to particular points of the compass," Thoreau observed
in his Walden and Civil Disobedience (Sherman Paul, ed. [Cambridge:
Riverside Press, 1960], 82). Learning to read a timetable conferred
a certain mastery over an event as locally important as the arrival
of a train. A quick look at a watch or clock would tell of the im-
minence of the event. So great was the faith placed in the printed
schedule, that if the event failed to occur as predicted in it, a
moment of personal confusion inevitably ensued: Was the watch off
or the train late? Few ever thought to question whether the schedule
was correct.

Rail had indeed brought a new temporal accuracy to America.
The trains "come and go with such regularity and precision, and their
whistles can be heard so far," Thoreau reported, "that the farmers
set their clocks by them.... Have not men improved in punctuality
since the railroad was invented?" (ibid). Although timepieces of all
sorts existed well before the coming of rail, they seldom, in America
at least, followed any common time standard. As late as the 1830s
Harriet Martineau discovered Americans "very imaginative ... in
respect of the hour" (Society in America [London: Saunders and
Otley, 1837], vol. 2, 206). In New York she "found a wide difference between the upper and lower parts of the city," and a full
half-hour separated Canadaigua and Buffalo. Though she chided
Americans for their temporal laxity, she failed to realize that in the
period she visited they did not need to keep better track of time.
Most pre-industrial communities required only an approximate appointment time measured by the stroke of an hour of local church bells--
not necessarily synchronized to any time standard but to the rising
and the setting of the sun.

The printed rail schedule, published in some metropolis far
from the community, would destroy, after first attempting to adapt
to, this sense of locally determined appointment time. A Boston and
Portland 1841 time schedule, for example, announced not the arrival
times of Dover trains in Boston, but only the departure times from
Dover; the trains arrived at whatever time the locale determined it
to be. Only four years later, the same road issued an elaborate
timetable showing more stops, more trains, and time figured in minutes
rather than hours. For both safety and schedule maintenance, time
had to be standardized. "Conductors will daily compare their watches
with the clock in Boston Depot," the Boston and Maine's "Rules for
Running Trains" enjoined, "which is the standard by which clocks
at the Station-houses, and all the watches of men employed must be
regulated" [Bradlee, 8, 12-13]. Thus a new time sense, publicized
in the printed schedule, governed by minutes, and accurately standardized all along the rail line, came to many agricultural communities
long before the toll of the first factory bell.

As Hawthorne realized while visiting the isolated village of
Sleepy Hollow in 1844, this time sense intruded into the consciousness
of everyone within earshot of the whistle or bell. His own intro-
spective reverie interrupted by the harsh locomotive whistle, he is
moved to write: "No wonder it gives such a startling shriek, since
it brings the noisy world in the midst of our slumberous peace"
(The American Notebooks, Randall Stewart, ed. [New Haven: Yale
Univ. Press, 1932], 104). A single small town, such as Ballardvale,
Massachusetts, heard the whistle and bell at 7:16, 8:07, 8:53, and
11:31 a.m., and at 12:22, 3:22, 3:35, 4:22, 5:52, and 7:01 p.m.
(Bradlee, 13). The bell signalled not the remembrance of the hour
to people engaged in face-to-face communications, but rather an
intercity (town) communication event. "How much life has come
into this lonely place," Hawthorne remarked, watching a train come
and go on the very same line in 1850. "The stationhouse ..., for
an instant, has thus been put in communication with far off cities"
(Passages from the American Notebooks, Sophia Hawthorne, ed.
[Boston and New York: Houghton, Mifflin, 1900], 468-470). After
the train departed, new faces appeared on the street, letters and
messages were rushed to homes and businesses to be opened, packages
were carted to be delivered--all bearing witness to the outside world.
In this way, time became more than something shared with the local
community; it linked that community to the outside world. No longer,
as in the days before rail, would the friendly book peddler stroll
into town at the optimum time to integrate his information with the
flow of local events. The community now had to adapt its time sense
to the alien rhythm of the train schedule, which promised information
and contact with no concern or consideration for local conditions.
The community was required to reorient itself outward, toward family,
friends, and business contacts well beyond the boundary of the town
or county.

The strengthening of these extra-community social networks
brought about by improved transportation was largely effected through
correspondence. As the rail network was completed in the 1850s,
the volume of domestic correspondence increased dramatically, from
27,536,000 letters carried by the postal service in 1840 to 161,802,000
in 1860, or, based upon the population census, from 1.61 letters
per capita to 5.15 on a yearly basis (Allan Pred, Urban Growth and
City Systems in the United States, 1840-1860 [Cambridge: Harvard
Univ. Press, 1980], 189). The correspondence that arrived in isolated
communities wherever transportation had improved inspired a heightened awareness of national economic currents. That New York City
in 1852 received roughly nine million letters from outside the city
limits while sending twelve million out suggests that information
clearly flowed from the industrialized areas in the urban North, more
than from anywhere else. A greater part, by far, of the information
sought from the developed areas by the rest of the country had a
commercial character.

Even farmers in the North sought information on agricultural improvements from periodicals issued from the major cities. Wherever communications improved, a running battle between traditional agricultural methods and so-called book farming ensued. "Book farming won't pay," The Northern Farmer reported a farmer saying [in "Book Farming," The Northern Farmer, 2[1855]:636). "My father and Grandfather farmed without these new lights." "Do you intend to say that because knowledge is put in print, it is no longer good for anything?" another farmer responded. "If you can learn a thing from a book is it therefore of less value than if you received it from a neighbor?" Thus the book competed with community-based knowledge. The modern farmer challenges the traditional one to submit whatever special knowledge he had acquired to the "city fellows" who produce the agricultural periodicals so that, if found sound, that knowledge could be broadcast. The traditional farmer's value would no longer be measured by his progress on the ancestral line stretching back far into the past, but rather on the rail line running to the northern cities, acting as clearinghouses for agricultural information. With every agricultural periodical that came down that line, he moved his farm that much closer to modern agrarian capitalism.

The books, periodicals, and letters the rail brought into isolated agricultural communities helped those communities turn from tradition to modernity. Literacy rates improved, farming methods became more efficient, and event-consciousness expanded beyond the confines of the community. The new literature that came down the rail lines oriented communities outward in a specific direction, from whence the rail lines came, to the cities of the Northeast. Because the West and South lagged far behind the North in economic development, the rails, and, indeed, the roads and waterways, served as avenues through which the ideas, responses, and approaches of the more mature capitalism of the North penetrated into the interior of the country to compete with existing regional cultures. Thus the distribution of northeastern literature of all sorts--whether newspapers, magazines, or books--played no small part in bringing about a more homogenous national cultural life.

The railroad's encouragement of reading went beyond the dissemination of literature to be read in isolated communities. The passenger car itself provided a new scene and an ideal opportunity for reading. "This [the railroad] has got to be the ne plus ultra of luxury, and railroad cars the flying palaces of Aladdin," an editorial in The Flag of Our Union attested (in "Railroad Travelling," The Flag of Our Union, 4 [28 April 1849]:3). "People read, sleep, and eat ... at the rate of twenty miles an hour." So common was reading on trains, that the physician J. Henry Clark in his Sight and Hearing (New York: Charles Scribner, 1856) inveighed against the practice, citing the damage it did to the eyes:

> Observe the passengers in the train, on any of our public routes. A shelf of popular novels is passed before the eyes of every individual; next, a pile of popular magazines, then,

illustrated newspapers, while advertisements, guidebooks,
newspapers with long, narrow, closely printed columns are
distributed or purchased, until all tastes are suited, and
before all eyes, young and old, spectacled and otherwise,
there oscillates some kind of printed page. Opportunity for
fresh air is lost at stopping-places, while the eyes are eagerly
strained and worried over the plot of some novel.(208)

Whatever new hazards reading in rail cars brought, the railroad freed travellers from the old ones they experienced on earlier
modes of transportation. The low bridges under which canal boats
passed required a constant watchfulness that made reading all but
impossible. "A solitary person, reading or in reverie, is really in
danger," Martineau commented on her trip on an American canal;
"We heard of two cases of young ladies reading, who had been crushed
to death and we prohibited books on deck" (Martineau, vol. 3, 194).
Frances Trollope found her Sunday on an Ohio steamboat "dull enough
for there was no creeping into the corner with a book"--partly because of the sabbatarian hostility to light reading and partly because
there was, on a crowded steamboat, simply no vacant corner to be
found. Even "colporteurs, who brought on a collection of devotional
books," observed Ann Archbold in her book "especially designed for
steamboat passengers," "met an entire repulse, if not an open insult"
(A Book for the Married and Single, the Grave and Gay: And Especially Designed for Steamboat Passengers [East Plainfield, Ohio:
The Practical Printer, 1850], vi). On both canal boat and steamboat,
lighting below deck remained minimal for fear of fire, preventing
reading even in bed. "When the light failed to shew us the bluffs,"
Trollope recounted, "we crept into our little cots, listening to the
ceaseless churning of the engine, in the hope it would prove a lulla-
by till morning." Travellers, however, reserved their harshest
criticism for the stage coaches that bumped mercilessly along America's
long, ill-developed, and badly maintained roads. Going by private
coach from Columbus to Tiffin, Ohio, Charles Dickens recalled: "At
one time we were all flung together in a heap at the bottom of the
coach, and at another we were crushing our heads against the roof"
(American Notes [Gloucester, Mass.: Peter Smith, 1968], 222).
With travel in America's coaches similar to "attempting to go up to
the top of St. Paul's in an omnibus," no wonder few instances of
reading in them have been recorded.[1]

Although Dickens experienced on an American railroad "a great
deal of jolting, a great deal of noise, a great deal of wall," he carefully noted that at the beginning of his journey "a great many newspapers are pulled out, and a few of them are read" (ibid., 79-80).
On the Boston and Maine line, Hawthorne saw four or five long cars,
"each, perhaps, with fifty people in it, reading newspapers, reading
pamphlet novels" (Passages 468). If reading matter was not purchased
in the station prior to boarding, it could be bought on board by
the ubiquitous news vendor, as Charles Lyell found:

Although we had now penetrated into regions where the
schoolmaster had not been much abroad, we observe that
railway cars are everywhere attended by news-boys, who,
in some places, are carried on a whole stage, walking up
and down the "middle aisle" of the long car. Usually, however, at each station, they and others who sell apples and
biscuits, may be seen calculating the exact speed at which
it is safe to jump off....
   One of them was calling out, in the midst of a pine barren
between Columbus and Chehaw [Ohio], "A novel by Paul
le [sic] Koch, the Bulwer of France, for twenty five cents--
all the go! More Popular than the Wandering Jew" &c. Newspapers for a penny or two pence are bought freely by the
passengers. [Charles Lyell, A Second Visit to the United
States of North America [New York: Harper and Brothers,
1849], vol. 2, 40-41]

Indeed, Lyell wrote of Eugène Sue's Wandering Jew: "It had
been so often thrust into my hands in railway cars, and so much
talked of, that, in the course of my journey, I began to read it in
self-defense: (ibid., 253). That Sue's book was published by the
Harpers shows that as early as 1849, that house's publications rode
the Western rails. So successful was the national marketing of the
book, that James Harper told Lyell he had sold "80,000 [copies]
in different shapes, and at various prices" (ibid.). The twenty-five
cent "railroad book," in paper, represented the bottom end in terms
of shape and price, and no doubt contributed a large share of total
sales. So lucrative was the railroad book market that, in the 1850s,
a publisher as prominent as George P. Putnam issued an entire line
of "Railway Classics ... in neat and compact volumes for travellers,"
which included Irving's Sketch Book and his Tales of a Traveller.
"They are small enough to be put in the pocket," Putnam's advertisements claimed "while the print is large enough to be read without
damaging the eyes." (American Publishers' Circular, 3[1857]:258;
and Norton's Literary Gazette, 2[1852]:80)

   The American railway journey encouraged reading in many ways.
Most obviously, trains provided a smoother ride than stagecoaches;
while America's roads generally followed the undulations of the land,
its rails had to be either level or smoothly graded for the train to
keep on the track. Also, the noisiness of American rail cars put a
damper on conversation. The long distance between destinations in
the United States meant that the traveller faced long stretches of
time with little else to do but read. The small windows in the cars
made watching scenery difficult. Observing one's fellow passengers
was only a little easier; unlike British rail cars in which the seats
ran lengthwise, American coaches had two-passenger seats running
crosswise and facing forward, separated by a center aisle. As Alexander Mackay observed during his visit in the forties, the American
car "was like a small church upon wheels" and its "row of seats
want[ed] only book boards to make them look exactly like pews"

(The Western World, or Travels in the United States in 1846-47
[New York: Negro Universities Press, 1968], vol. I, 31).

The religious connotations of the American rail car are not
surprising. During an age when large civic gatherings rarely occurred in farming communities, the church provided a model for
public conduct among a mixed, 'democratic' crowd. The chapel-like
railway coach offered a familiar setting in which an individual could
feel comfortable amid strangers and the all-too-common dangers from
fire and accidents. The open setting promoted public order as Thomas
Low Nichols observed: "There is no danger of robbery, murder,
or other outrage, as in the small, locked, and inaccessible compart-
ments of European roads" (Forty Years of American Life [New York:
Negro Universities Press, 1968], vol. 2, 8-9). Few antebellum public
institutions except for churches and railroads could boast the maintenance of such order.

As a natural outgrowth of the ordered, church-like rail coach
environment, reading was encouraged. For in America, reading and
Protestantism always went together; the book in the rail coach was
as logical as a hymnal in a chapel. Moreover, the very idea of
travelling long distances on a regularly scheduled route hearkened
back to the days when itinerant preachers and Yankee peddlers were
the chief suppliers of information about the outside world for isolated
towns. Some individuals like Mathew Carey's famous agent, Parson
Weems,combined itinerancy, preaching, and book peddling. Too, the
conservative voice in the Northern Farmers should be remembered;
it equated "book farmers" with "new lights," again summoning up
images of the religious schisms accompanying the second Great Awaken-
ing of the early nineteenth century. The farmer who spoke for
modernity, in response, gives as the rationale for following the "new
lights" that it was the age of the rail car; horses and coaches, like
traditional farming methods, belonged to the past.

Clearly, improved communications challenged a sense of community that had long managed to control and interpret the influx of
information about the outside world within a local context. However
much the interior of rail coaches evoked a traditional religious setting, the change in the human perception of life brought about by
rail was inescapable. "Who will deliver us from these annihilations
of time and space?" bemoaned an editorial in the Yankee Blade on
the relationship of the railroad and the telegraph to modern authorship ("Modern Authorship," The Yankee Blade 4[26 Sept. 1849]:2).
The railroad quickened the pace of life and interrupted its flow. If
the railroad whistle could be predicted to the minute, the information,
the people, indeed, the events with which the railroad confronted
the individual could scarcely be predicted at all. Experience could
seem to rush at the individual much as the "wild, startling, and inflated" were jammed into the popular novels of the time. "People
read now for excitement, and hence the more artificial stimulants
and intoxicating ingredients crowded into a raw-headed and bloody-

bones novel, the better." The Yankee Blade could not see that it was witnessing much more than a change in reading taste. Literature was merely attempting to cope with the new, seemingly disjointed experiences that accompanied the destruction, wrought by the railroad, of locally determined time and space.

Hawthorne, once again aboard the Boston and Maine in 1850, sensed this psychological dislocation. He wrote in his journal:

> The passenger, stepping from the solitary station into the train, finds himself amidst a new world all in a moment. He rushes out of the solitude into a village; thence through the woods and hills, into a large town; beside the Merrimack, which has overflowed its banks, and eddies along, turbid as a vast mud puddle, sometimes almost laving the doorstep of a house, and with trees standing in the flood halfway up their trunks. Boys with newspapers to sell, or apples or lozenges; many more passengers departing and entering, at each new station; the more permanent passenger, with his check or ticket stuck in his hat band, where the conductor may see it. A party of girls, playing at ball with a young man. Altogether it is a scene of stirring life, with which a person who had been long waiting for the train to come might find it difficult at once to amalgamate himself. (Passages, 468-470)

Obviously in that flow of disjointed images, Hawthorne truly did have trouble collecting himself. That the unexpectancy, the disconnectedness of those sights bothered him enough to make note of it, demonstrates the great cultural distance separating his time from our own. The modern individual is constantly surrounded by events too numerous to digest, too unpredictable to control, and, ultimately, too meaningless to engage the self. Those who grew up during the early nineteenth century experienced a much more constricted universe of limited, albeit predictable and meaningful, social events. Those events formed a causal web against which the individual defined and located himself. The centrifuge of localism, supported by family, community, and church, kept that web closely knit--that is, until the rail line unravelled it. Then suddenly, faced with an unprecedented flow of information about distant events, a super-community of national dimension presented itself as a challenge to traditional, local self-definitions.[2]

The adjustment of the self to this new sense of community would not be easy, as the social life of the American railway car makes plain. Visitors to America could not but help note the lack of social connection between railroad passengers. "Although nearly three-score people were packed closely together, the utmost silence pervaded the car," Alexander Mackay wrote; "everyone seems as if he were brooding over some terrible secret, with which he would burst if he dared" (The Western World, vol. 1, 36). Shocked by "the

publicity of the railway car," Charles Lyell, on his 1841 trip, reported: "As the Americans address no conversation to strangers,
we soon become reconciled to living so much in public" (Travels in
North America [New York: Wiley and Putnam, 1845], 37). Dickens
found that while on an American railroad, "everyone talks to you,
or to anyone else who hits his fancy," he could hardly converse
with anyone (American Notes, 80).

Dickens records an encounter that amply illustrates the difficulty one American had in coming to grips with this new experience,
this anomaly, this Englishman whom the railroad had thrown in his
perceptual path. He generalizes the experience to include all American
rail passengers:

> If you are an Englishman, he expects that the railroad is
> pretty much like an English railroad. If you say "No," he
> says "Yes?" (interrogatively), and asks in what respect they
> differ. You enumerate the heads of difference one by one....
> Then he guesses that you don't travel faster in England;
> and on your replying that you do says "Yes" again (still
> interrogatively), and, it is quite evident, doesn't believe it.
> After a long pause he remarks partly to you, partly to the
> knob on the top of his stick, that "Yankees are reckoned
> to be a considerable of a go-ahead people too;" upon which
> you say "Yes" and then he says "Yes" again (affirmatively
> this time); and upon your looking out the window, tells you
> that beyond that hill and some three miles from the next
> station, there is a clever town in a smart lo-ca-tion, where
> he expects you have con-cluded to stop. Your answer in
> the negative naturally leads to more questions in reference
> to your intended route...; and wherever you are going,
> you invariably learn that you can't get there without immense
> difficulty and danger, and that all the great sights are some-
> where else. (Ibid.)

For all the fun Dickens pokes, he fails to see the pathetic attempt
this man made to gain some mastery over a world alien to him. The
man tries to share the similarity of experience on rail lines with
Dickens, which the author frustrates. Uneasy, he looks at his cane,
and resorts to uttering the cliché about the "go-ahead people," a
phrase which had become a mainstay of English traveller accounts
of America. Upon Dickens' recognition of this phrase, the man,
encouraged, attempts to show off his knowledge of local business
prospects and the state of transportation--an attempt Dickens inter-
prets as boorishness. So, Dickens counterattacks by thoroughly
frustrating the man, withholding from him even the destination of
his journey. Such fumbling encounters not only on railways, but
everywhere strangers gathered in America, abound in the travel
accounts of English-speaking writers of the period. For all of them,
the disconnection between the self and community experienced by
Americans on the whirlwind of the transportation revolution rings
clear.

This perspective makes evident the deep, cultural ramifications of the relationship of the book to the railroad. For it was largely through the printed word in books and periodicals that the railroad carried information about the outside world on such a scale that standing local community structures could not contain it. The massive expansion of the printing industry made it certain that information would indeed flood down the rail lines, with little regard for the needs, hopes, or the very ways of life of local communities.

But the destruction of the traditional relationship between the self and community tells only half the story. The railroad and the printed word laid the foundation for an entirely different sense of community, one writ on a national scale and within what would become an increasingly integrated and rationalized economic system. The self and the local community would not only have to make peace with this larger structure, but indeed, redefine themselves in relation to it. The printed word would become the primary tool that the individual would, through his buying power, have some hand in fashioning. The individual reader's taste, expressed through his book purchases, represented a single, small consumer decision in a large market; yet those decisions had the collective impact of encouraging specific types of literature, published in response to the tastes of different readers all over the country. A national community of taste was thus formed. In addition to providing an ideational surrogate for a concrete yet disrupted community life, that literature would also help the individual cope personally with the immensity, unpredictability, and apparent meaninglessness of this new world order. Reading during the period of national rail expansion thus had a greater personal impact along a wider spectrum of society than it ever had before, or ever had since modern cultural forms evolved to deal with the exigencies of industrial capitalism. It must be remembered that those cultural forms have their foundations in this period, so that they undoubtedly bear traces of the genetic development of the national transportation system, for example the strong northeastern urban biases in book and periodical distribution.

Given that the book and the railroad mediated in such an important way between the self and the community in antebellum America, it seems remarkable that the dominant genre of literature at midcentury was fiction. Certainly, factual knowledge would seem to have been called for to help Americans cope with the industrialization of their nation, from the personal level of teaching skills necessary for social mobility to the political level of urging government protection of workers. And of course, a more realistic assessment of the nation's past and present may well have cooled down the sectional tempers of the heated 1850s. Nevertheless fiction obviously supplied some need or had some purpose or played some role that nonfiction failed to.[3]

Perhaps some part of the answer lies in the nature of the transformation of American community life during the age of rail. For as the individual redirected the self from the local to the national community, that larger community had to supply some of the affectional needs formerly fulfilled locally. If, as one definition has it, the sense of community is based upon the mutuality of relations (see Thomas H. Bender, Community and Social Change in America [New Brunswick: Rutgers University Press, 1978]), how could the cold, printed word reciprocate the full dimension of human experience invested in it by readers? While nonfiction can, of course, evoke emotional responses from the reader, fiction, insofar as it attempted to create the illusion of life, was far more efficient at the task. "Useful reading is that which goes to make the heart and the head equally wise, that will cultivate the flowers of the soul in conjunction with those of the mind," the True Flag opined ("Useful Reading," The True Flag 3 [21 Oct. 1853]:3). Fiction, moreover, in a telic manner, pointed the way toward self-construction, in an era when the railroad and the information it brought persistently negated community-defined truths: "If a character is beautiful and possible in a novel, it may be no less beautiful and no less possible in actual life" ("Fiction in Life," The True Flag 5 [23 Aug. 1856]:3). Above all, fiction transcended local realities to such a degree that it could sell widely to the scattered and heterogeneous antebellum reading public. Because fiction to a large extent ignored local sensibilities, it could hardly offend them.

The antebellum American reader, thus, with respect to cultural participation, possessed something of a dual citizenship. In books, and in novels particularly, the reader found what seemed to be the totality of human expression that he formerly found only in his local community. Yet the integuments of tradition within the local community continued to exist; kin, community, and church continued to make their demands upon the individual, even though their monopoly of the process of self-definition had been lost. Between the ideational world of the printed word (and beyond, the national community, the republic of letters) and the concrete world of local exigencies, the reader had to engineer his or her existence. One world looked toward boundless futurity, the romance of self, and the self's intimate participation in an expansive national culture; the other looked toward the so-called old fogeyism of the past, the responsibilities of life, and the constrictions of life's possibilities by local conditions. Little wonder that the book on the mantelpiece may well have grown emotionally closer to the reader than the family among whom he sat, or the neighbor whose fence he shared. The book, and the railroad that brought it, had transformed the very nature of American community life.

References

1. Obviously some books could be read aboard steamboats, as attested by the existence of several shipboard libraries advertised with steamboat schedules, although Harry R. Skallerup, Books

Afloat and Ashore: A History of Books Libraries, and Reading during the Age of Sail (Hamden, Conn.: Archon Books, 1974), 47, claims that there was nowhere aboard to store any sort of large collection.

2. My use of the concept of self here and below draws from Quentin Anderson, The Imperial Self: An Essay in American Literary and Cultural History (New York: Alfred A. Knopf, 1971).

3. Fiction's domination of the marketplace finds treatment in: Samuel G. Goodrich, Recollections of a Lifetime (New York: Miller, Orton, and Mulligan, 1856), 380-398; Lyle H. Wright, "A Statistical Survey of American Fiction, 1774-1850," Huntington Library Quarterly, 2 (1939): 309; and Susan Geary, "The Domestic Novel as a Commercial Commodity," Papers of the Bibliographical Society of America, 70 (1976): 370.

Author's note: Support for this study was provided by the Albert Boni Fellowship (1983) of the American Antiquarian Society; the author personally extends his thanks to the staff there, particularly John Hench, Kathleen Major, and Nancy Burkett, for their encouragement and help. Due gratitude goes out also to Kenneth Silverman, John Tebbel, Thomas H. Bender, Richard Sennett, and Paul R. Baker, who read and commented upon this material as presented in original dissertation form.

Editor's note: This article won the DeGolyer prize for the best nonfiction essay in American Studies submitted in 1986 to the DeGolyer Institute, Southern Methodist University. The DeGolyer prize was established in 1977 by Everette Lee and Nell DeGolyer and consists of publication in the Southwest Review and a cash prize of five hundred dollars.

Part III

THE SOCIAL PREROGATIVE

THE NEW ETHICS*

Norman D. Stevens

Librarians must distinguish clearly in their actions and their statements between their personal philosophies and attitudes and those of an institution or professional body.

Librarians must avoid situations in which personal interests might be served or financial benefits gained at the expense of library users, colleagues, or the employing institution.

On 30 June 1981 the Council of the American Library Association adopted a Statement on Professional Ethics that concludes with the two provisions cited above. We have, for the most part, dismissed those provisions from our thinking and ignored them in our actions. A front-page article in The Chronicle of Higher Education for 6 February 1985 calls our attention to the fact that many professional associations are considering, revising, or writing codes of professional ethics and developing procedures for the enforcement of those codes. The publication of Ann E. Prentice's and Jonathan A. Lindsey's Professional Ethics and Librarians (Oryx Press 1985), which is the first full-length monographic treatment of the subject, reminds us that we do have what appears to be a reasonable code of ethics in place, although there is no means of enforcing it other than our own attention to proper behavior.

As a long-time observer of librarianship, I am concerned by the increasing number of practices that seem to be regarded as normal yet clearly conflict with those provisions of our Statement of Professional Ethics that address our personal behavior. We librarians seem to have adopted a new code of ethics that enables us to represent multiple views with one voice and to advance our own personal financial interests in any way possible. We have not yet approved the clearly illegal practices, such as the misappropriation of funds or the outright theft of materials, that make the news. But we have accepted and adopted marginal practices that we somehow regard as

*Reprinted by permission of the author and publisher of Library Hi Tech Consecutive Issue 16, 4:4 (Winter 1986) 49-51; copyright © 1986 Pierian Press.

normal, but should not. Apart from the question of whether or not
a particular practice violates our Statement of Ethics, institutional
policies and procedures, or the law, there is the simple question of
whether or not that practice is appropriate. We need to avoid both
real and apparent conflicts of interest. Too much of our current
behavior is no better than that of politicians and other public figures
whose tendency to be less than honest, and to use their position to
advance their personal welfare, we roundly condemn.

We have moved, in recent years, from a rather leisurely, somewhat isolated, professional body with a limited role to play in the
collection and dissemination of information, to one that is participating
in a more active environment where we are competing with other organizations for a role in the "information society." As we and others
see, for the first time, that information has a substantial economic
value (as does much of our work), we seem to become more concerned
with the prospect of financial gain and less concerned with ethical
practices. The profusion of settings in which we serve, along with
the way that librarians are moving into profit-making organizations
while maintaining their ties with the profession, contributes further
to our problem in deciding what is right or wrong. We participate
in so many activities and organizations that it is no longer necessarily
clear whom we represent, other than ourselves, in our professional
dealings. The situations in which we find ourselves may make it more
difficult for us to adhere to the personal provisions of our Statement
of Ethics, but do not absolve us from doing so.

Are the following practices ones that we wish to·accept as reasonable, ethical behavior?

1. Individuals who have produced library products, systems,
    or services that are for sale, either by them or by their
    institution or organization, publish articles in major pro-
    fessional journals, or present papers at professional meetings,
    that describe their product, system, or service and how
    it will serve library needs.

2. Librarians who serve on the boards of major library networks
    (or other library organizations that actively market services
    to libraries) give speeches, write articles, or otherwise
    offer as objective statements descriptions of how their own
    organizations offer solutions to library problems, or other-
    wise take official actions in another role that advance that
    network's views.

3. Material distributed or published by one organization clearly
    promotes the interests of another organization with which
    the first organization has a direct financial relationship.

4. A librarian on the staff of a commercial firm that specializes
    in producing information services for sale to libraries serves
    as the review editor for a major professional journal.

5. A library publisher prints unsigned reviews of its own publications in a reference tool marketed to libraries.

6. Meetings of library associations include, as part of the official program, presentations by commercial vendors of their products and services.

7. Commercial vendors offer an assortment of mechanisms for financial support, some of which are directed to individuals, for the activities of professional associations whose members represent a major portion of the vendors' potential market.

8. Librarians who have gained experience with a commercial vendor's product, system, or service through its adoption in their library, leave that library to work for the vendor.

9. Librarians serve as paid directors on the boards of commercial firms or other organizations that are marketing goods and services to libraries, including those of their directors.

This small sample of existing dubious practices represents a real challenge to us. Caveat emptor is, of course, one response. We are, one might argue, mature professionals who can recognize situations in which the vested interests of an organization or individual are presented to us as an objective evaluation of a situation. We can judge for ourselves the actual quality of a system, the value of a publication, the marvelous thing that some organization will do for us, or the individual's assurance that he or she is presenting us with an honest, personal view of a situation. Unfortunately many of us are not sophisticated enough to make those distinctions, especially when the available biographical information makes no reference to the affiliation of the person with the cause that is being advanced. These practices are ones that we can no longer accept.

The solutions are not simple. The first step is personal action. I would urge each of us to think carefully about our motives in situations in which we are asked to undertake some new activity, especially if there is an element of financial gain involved either for us or for our library organization. I would urge each of us to think carefully about whose cause we are advancing when, if we are involved in a variety of library organizations, we are asked to speak or take some action on an issue. I would urge each of us not to present our views on subjects in which we have a vested interest, in settings that make it appear as though we are presenting an objective view of a situation. I would urge each of us, whenever possible, to separate our personal actions from those of our institutions or organizations and to make those distinctions clear. I would urge each of us to think about our motives, and the motives of others, as we, or they, promote or advance a particular product, system, or service. Above all I would urge each of us to pay particular attention to the two provisions of the American Library Association's Statement on Professional Ethics

that are expressly directed to our personal behavior. We should ask
ourselves if our actions meet the intent of those provisions.

The second step is professional action. The article in The
Chronicle of Higher Education on the renewed interest in professional
ethics cites a number of associations, such as the American Political
Science Association, which have established some kind of committee
empowered to investigate complaints of ethical violations. In her
statement in Professional Ethics and Librarians, Caroline Arden makes
a strong case for the establishment by the American Library Association of a due-process ethics tribunal with the authority to recommend
sanctions. This approach, which may seem drastic, is not likely to
be adopted. However, the present nature of our profession, and the
commercial nature of the environment in which we work, make it
worthy of consideration and debate. Even if this approach were not
adopted, the process of considering such a tribunal and the kinds
of issues it might address, would surely call attention to, and help
eliminate, the many dubious practices in which we now engage.

In our frantic efforts to deal with change, adopt new technologies, promote library cooperation, and otherwise enhance library and
information services, we must not lose sight of broader professional
concerns and issues. Much of what we now do will change. The
technology that we are seeking to use will change. The nature of
our profession will change. If we can establish and maintain a sound
ethical basis for our professional practices we will have done much to
ensure that, despite all of those changes, librarianship will have a
continued independent role to play, and will be respected for that
role, in the development of a strong information society.

RESEARCHERS, ARCHIVISTS, AND THE ACCESS CHALLENGE OF THE FBI RECORDS IN THE NATIONAL ARCHIVES*

James Gregory Bradsher

The National Archives presently has custody of some 300 cubic feet of Federal Bureau of Investigation (FBI) records, mostly predating 1924.[1]   These records are completely open for research.   During the next decade the National Archives will accession a substantial volume of FBI case files, mostly pre-dating 1945, and many case files pre-dating 1965.[2]   These files will provide researchers with a wealth of information about the individuals and subjects of investigation.   The files contain much information about American political, social, criminal, and economic life, as the FBI, during the course of its investigations, has touched almost every aspect of American life.   The FBI's investigations, filed under over 200 categories, include cases covering civil rights, treason, espionage, domestic security, Selective Service violations, White Slave Trade, mail fraud, interstate transportation of stolen cattle, foreign counterintelligence, racketeering, gambling, extortion, election laws, crimes on government reservations, bank robberies, involuntary servitude and kidnapping.

According to Judge Harold H. Greene, of the U.S. District Court for the District of Columbia, the records of the FBI "perhaps more than those of any other agency, constitute a significant repository of the record of the recent history of this nation, and they represent the work product of an organization that has touched the lives of countless Americans."[3]   But, in making the FBI archival records available, access challenges will be faced by both archivists and researchers.   What follows is an analysis of the access problems associated with the FBI's records once they are accessioned by the National Archives.

FBI Organization and Records

FBI records are created and accumulated in four types of offices.

*Reprinted by permission of the author and publisher of The Midwestern Archivist, XI:2 (1986) 95-110; copyright © 1987 The Midwest Archives Conference.

First is the FBI headquarters in Washington, D.C., which establishes policies and oversees the operations and activities of the bureau. The bulk of the FBI's investigative work is conducted by the fifty-nine field offices located in all the states, Puerto Rico, and Washington, D.C. Each field office has one or more resident agencies, i.e., sub-offices, reporting to it. There are over 470 of these resident agencies in all the states, Puerto Rico, Virgin Islands, and Guam. Overseas the FBI maintains liaison offices, termed Legats, in a dozen embassies, including Paris, London, Mexico City, and Hong Kong.[4]

Today there exist in the FBI headquarters over six million criminal, civil, security, applicant-loyalty, and administrative case files. These files contain a variety of documents, such as reports: teletype messages; prosecutive summaries; accounts of interviews and physical surveillance; letters; memorandums; lab reports; logs, transcripts, and summaries of electronic surveillance; informant reports; photographs; and newspaper clippings and other public record material. The source of this information includes foreign governments, federal and state agencies, agents, electronic surveillance, informants, and confidential sources.[5] There are also over sixty-five million index cards in headquarters relating to case files. In the field offices there are over five million case files, and well over 100,000 million index cards. For security reasons the volume of records maintained in the legats and resident agencies is kept to a minimum.[6]

Appraisal

As a result of a lawsuit in 1981, the National Archives assigned seventeen archivists, including the author, to appraise all of the FBI's records.[7] This appraisal, described by Robert M. Warner, former Archivist of the United States, as "the most expensive and elaborate appraisal project" in the history of the National Archives, resulted in about twenty percent of the FBI's records being determined to have sufficient value to warrant permanent preservation as archives.[8] To many researchers this may not seem like a significant percentage. It is, however, a higher percent than retained from most federal agencies. About one percent of federal records have sufficient value to warrant their continued preservation as archives. One percent may seem a low figure, but one percent of the six million cubic feet of federal records created annually is 60,000 cubic feet.[9] That is a large volume of records.

The Access Challenge

Researchers and archivists will both be faced with a myriad of access challenges once the post-1924 FBI records are accessioned by the National Archives. Before discussing them, two general observations need to be made. First, besides not keeping all FBI files, many files will not be accessioned until fifty years after a case is

closed because of security and privacy reasons. Second, researchers
and archivists must keep in mind the expungement process. Under
the Privacy Act individuals, under certain conditions, can request
that part or all of the documents relating to them be destroyed. Thus,
certain documents or portions of documents, appraised as permanent
may be legally destroyed by the FBI before the records are accessioned
by the National Archives. This procedure will certainly be frustrating
to researchers, but this is an instance where the right to privacy
takes precedence over the right to know.[10]

Filing System and Indexes

The first challenges to researchers will be knowing what to
ask for and understanding what they receive. These challenges can
be met by understanding the FBI's filing and indexing systems. This
is not as easy as it sounds, for as one researcher noted, "Understanding the FBI's extensive and complicated filing system is no easy
task. Quite probably no one outside the Bureau fully grasps its in-
tricacies."[11] Despite some truth in this observation the filing system
is very straightforward. Each type of investigation or activity is
given a classification number. Then records are arranged numerically
by type of classification number. Then records are arranged numerically by type of investigation or activity. For example, 7 means kidnapping, 44 means civil rights, and 175 means assaulting the president.
Altogether there are 256 classification numbers.[12] Then comes a
sequential case number. So, 7-978 means the nine hundred and
seventy-eighth kidnapping case file opened. Next, in most instances,
each document in the case file is sequentially numbered. Thus, the
last number in 7-978-75 indicates the seventy-fifth document in the
file. Corresponding case files relating to 7-978 in each field office
participating in the investigation will have different sequential case
file numbers beginning with 7.[13]

This arrangement means that one cannot gain access to the FBI
records without an index. The basic index to the FBI's's files is arranged alphabetically by the name of the subject. Generally this is
the name of a person, but also included are names of groups, events,
projects, and publications. The index has two types of cards which
are interfiled. They are "Main" cards and "See Reference" cards.
The former lists the main file number or numbers where a person,
place, or thing is the subject of an investigation, and the latter lists
the file number or numbers where they are mentioned in a case. Not
every name mentioned in the files is indexed. The only names indexed
are those believed important enough to note for future reference.[14]

When permanently appraised case files come to the National
Archives, either from headquarters or the field, the related index
cards will also be accessioned. During the appraisal of the index,
some questions were raised about keeping index cards for cases that
were identified for destruction. Two factors precluded keeping all

the cards. First, their bulk. In headquarters alone there are over 10,000 cubic feet of them. Second, and more important, is the privacy issue. If a name turned up on an index card relating to an inter-state transportation of obscene material case that was destroyed, without the case file one would never know what role the named individual played in the case. Such a situation would be open to mis-interpretation and unfair to that individual.

Archivists, the FOIA, and National Archives Access Procedures

Once researchers understand the FBI organization and record keeping systems, and thus are able to know what to ask for and interpret what they receive, they will then be faced with the possibility of not receiving all the information in the files they request. Operating under laws and regulations, archivists are required to review the files and withhold information that is restricted or exempted from public inspection.[15]

In deciding what information must be withheld from researchers the National Archives' archivists will be guided by two sets of access restrictions. The first are the National Archives access regulations, which provide for general restrictions that are based on the Freedom of Information Act (FOIA), and specific restrictions that agencies have requested be imposed in conformance with the FOIA. [16] The second set of restrictions are those imposed under the Freedom of Information Act, when reference requests are made under it. It provides that any person has a right to records of federal agencies, except to the extent that such records, or portions thereof, are protected from disclosure by one of nine exemptions.[17] The Act was adopted in the belief that an informed citizenry is vital to the functioning of a democratic society, and to be informed, the public needed to know what their government was doing and thus be able to hold their governors accountable. However, in achieving an informed citizenry is counterpoised society's interest in protecting personal privacy and preserving confidentiality of national defense and criminal investigative matters, among other things.

Archivists and researchers will find that the application of these restrictions and exemptions will be the major challenge to the FBI's records in the National Archives. This task, especially with investigative files, is difficult. Because of the nature and age of the information, several of the exemptions will not apply to the FBI's records.[18] The ones that do, to varying degrees, will present a challenge to archivists in determining whether or not certain information should be withheld.

Once archivists have identified the files researchers want, they will review the files to determine if anything should be withheld. Normally, archivists first review the files for things that must be withheld, such as classified information and information restricted by statutory provisions, and then they review the files for information, relating to law enforcement and privacy matters, that may have to be withheld.[19]

Classified Information

The first question archivists will be faced with is determining whether information in the files is classified, because information that has been properly classified in accordance with the substantive and procedural requirements of an appropriate executive order is not releasable.[20] Fortunately, the criminal, civil, and applicant investigative files, which will come to the National Archives fifty years after the close of a case, normally are not security classified. Other files, including counterintelligence and internal security, will be fifty years old, which means there is a good chance the records can be-- or are already--declassified.

Statutory Exemptions

Certain information cannot be released because, by a specific statute, it must be withheld. For example, income tax returns and certain types of Central Intelligence Agency and National Security Agency material are not to be made available to the public.[21] Ensuring such material is not released will not be an easy task, primarily because there is no official compilation of the statutes mandating nondisclosure.

Administrative Information Exemptions

It is likely that the FBI will want the National Archives to impose restrictions on certain administrative information contained in the files, which, if released, would allow the circumvention of federal laws or would impede the effectiveness of the FBI's law enforcement activities.[22] The courts have ruled a wide variety of administrative information, including informant symbol numbers, computer codes, law enforcement manuals, studies of FBI practices and problems concerning undercover agents, teletype routing codes, and sensitive instructions regarding administrative handling and dissemination of documents and intelligence information, protectible from disclosure.[23] The courts have even found protectible file numbers, routing stamps, and other administrative markings.[24] Fortunately, most FBI files will be so old that these concerns will not be applicable, however, in some cases they will be, and therefore great care will have to be exercised to assure that certain information is not released.

Law Enforcement Information Exemptions

Investigatory records compiled for law enforcement purposes can be released unless one or more of six specific harms would follow the release of the information.[25] Two of these harms, interfering with law enforcement proceedings and depriving a person of a right to a fair trial or an impartial adjudication, will be moot by the time the National Archives receives the records. A third harm, unwarranted invasions of personal privacy, is discussed below in the context of the privacy exemption.

Before discussing the harms, we need to define what kinds of records are "law enforcement records." The legislative history indicates they are records of investigations leading to enforcement of the criminal laws, and investigations that enforce the laws by means of civil suits.[26] The courts have held that investigations involving criminal and civil violations are included, but internal administrative investigations are not.[27] Thus, FBI investigations of the manner in which it accomplishes its mission are not considered to be actions taken for investigatory law enforcement purposes.[28] Thus, FBI investigations of the manner in which it accomplishes its mission are not considered to be actions taken for investigatory law enforcement purposes.[28] However, an investigation into possible illegal actions taken by FBI special agents meets the test.[29] Also meeting the test are background security investigations conducted by the FBI.[30]

Several courts have adopted a per se rule that qualifies all investigative records of criminal law enforcement agencies for protection.[31] Other courts have held that the government must demonstrate some nexus between the records and a proper law enforcement purpose, that is, a rationale for the activities being investigated and violations of federal laws.[32] Political surveillance records, such as those created by the FBI under its COINTELPRO program, which some people may not consider as truly law enforcement records, have been held by the courts to be such.[33] Additionally, even though some records might have been improperly created--documenting people exercising their first amendment freedoms--the improperly acquired information cannot, usually, be released while the subject of the file is still alive.[34]

Archivists will have to face the question of whether releasing certain information will disclose investigative techniques and procedures because the law provides for withholding such information if it is "generally unknown to the public."[35] The legislative history makes it clear that the exemption only applies to secret techniques--not things like fingerprinting, spectrographic analysis, ballistics tests, and "bait money."[36] The courts have held that "mail covers" are not protectible.[37] But, they have held that the layout and security devices of a bank are.[38] Undoubtedly there will be some debate on this issue, as it is difficult to determine what is "generally unknown to the public."

Archivists will have to decide whether the release of information will endanger the life or physical safety of FBI personnel because disclosure of information in investigatory records, which would "endanger the life or physical safety of law enforcement personnel," is protected.[39]   Since most files will be fifty years old when they come to the National Archives, this provision will not present a major problem.   However, some people hold grudges--for a long time.   Releasing the names of FBI agents involved in a case when they were thirty years old, and having that case file accessioned by the National Archives when it is thirty years old, might subject them to harm if their names were released.   Thus, the courts have held that certain protections remain applicable even after a law enforcement officer has retired.[40]

Archivists will also have to decide about releasing confidential information or information about individuals furnishing such information. The law provides protection for confidential sources in all law enforcement investigations, and in case of criminal or national security investigations it permits withholding of all information provided by a confidential source.[41]   The legislative history of the 1974 Amendments to the FOIA indicates that the term "confidential source" was chosen by design to encompass a broader group than would have been included had the term "informer" been used.[42]   In the context of this exemption, "confidential" means that the information was provided in confidence, with the assurance that it would not be disclosed. [43]   No balancing test is required because this exemption hinges on the circumstances under which the information is provided, and not exclusively on the harm resulting from disclosure.[44]

The first clause of FOIA Exemption 7(D) protects the identity of confidential sources in records of any law enforcement investigation, civil or criminal, but not, directly, the information furnished.   The legislative history, however, shows Congress' intention to protect absolutely and comprehensively the identity of anyone who provided information in confidence.[45]   The courts have recognized that the first clause of the exemption safeguards not only the identity of a confidential source, but also information which would "tend to reveal" the source's identity.[46]

The identities of the sources are protected whether they have provided information under an express promise of confidentiality or "under circumstances from which such an assurance could be reasonably inferred."[47]   With respect to the FBI, the courts have generally ruled that there is an implied assurance of confidentiality, "as any other interpretation would jeopardize its ability to obtain information in [the] future."[48]   Entities which the courts have qualified as confidential sources include citizens providing unsolicited allegations of misconduct, citizens who respond to inquiries from law enforcement agencies, state and local law enforcement agencies, commercial or financial institutions, and foreign law enforcement agencies.[49] Non-human sources, however, cannot be considered confidential sources.[50]

The second clause of FOIA Exemption 7(D) protects all confidential information furnished to law enforcement authorities in the course of a criminal investigation or a lawful national security intelligence investigation. The courts have ruled this clause protects all information provided by a confidential source because the disclosure of such information would jeopardize the system of confidentiality that ensures a free flow of information from sources to investigatory agencies.[51] The courts have permitted the withholding of information provided by anonymous sources; sources even when the identity of the source is known; information provided by a source, some of which has been the subject of testimony in open court; and information provided by now-deceased sources, some of whom also testified at a trial.[52]

The National Archives' General Restriction No. 5 permits the Archivist of the United States to release information in law enforcement records, if in his judgement, "the passage of time is such that the safety of persons is not endanger[ed], and the public interest in disclosure outweighs the continued need for confidentiality."[53] The courts, in dealing with two cases involving FBI files over twenty-five years old, have noted that the protections afforded by FOIA Exemption 7(D) are not lost through the mere passage of time.[54] Thus, case files accessioned when they are thirty years old will have to be carefully screened to ensure the protection of confidential sources and the confidential information the sources supplied.

Privacy Exemptions

The FOIA (5 U.S.C. 552(b) (6) and (b) (7) (C)) provides for withholding certain information because of privacy reasons. In general terms, "personnel and medical files and similar files the disclosure of which would constitute a clearly unwarranted invasion of privacy," are protected from release. Until 1982 much FOIA litigation in the courts centered around the term "similar files." In that year the Supreme Court ruled that Congress intended a broad rather than a narrow meaning of the term, so now all information which "applies to a particular individual" qualifies for exemption consideration.[55] With respect to law enforcement files the word "clearly" does not appear in the exemption clause. Therefore, a lesser burden of proof is needed by archivists to withhold personal information in the FBI files.

In deciding if personal information is releasable, archivists will be confronted with a variety of questions relating to whose privacy is involved. They must determine what information is actually personal and private; and they must answer the question, does the public's interest in knowing the information outweigh the subject's interest in personal privacy?

The first question to be answered relates to whose privacy is

being protected. Political and religious groups, or businesses and
other organizations are not granted the right to privacy. "Personal
privacy" interests only apply to people. Although the question of
whether deceased persons remain possessed of privacy rights has
not been entirely settled, generally the courts have ruled that privacy
protection is only afforded to living persons.[56] The courts have
generally held that public figures lessen their expectations of privacy
by placing themselves in the public eye.[57] Nevertheless, the courts
have held that public figures are entitled to privacy protection and
that disclosure of sensitive personal information about them is appropriate "only where exceptional interests militate in favor of disclosure."
[58]

The next question is what kind of information should be protected. It must be of an intimate and personal nature.[59] Courts give
a broad interpretation to these terms.[60] Generally, in handling
requests from someone who is not the subject of the records, several
criteria are used to determine whether data is in fact intimate and
personal. As a rule, the courts have found that information relating
to marital status, legitimacy of children, medical condition, welfare
payments, alcohol consumption, family rights, reputation, and religious
and philosophical beliefs is protected from disclosure.[61] And the
Privacy Act specifically protects data about an individual's exercise
of First Amendment rights, which include political and religious association, beliefs and activities.[62]

Archivists must determine whether disclosure of certain information constitutes an unwarranted invasion of personal privacy. This
requires a balancing of the public interest in disclosure, if any,
against the privacy interests which would be threatened by disclosure
of the file.[63] The "public interest" must truly be in the interest
of the overall public, not individuals seeking information for their
own benefit, particularly if it is only to satisfy their curiosity.[64]
Even if a requester has identified a specific and tangible disclosure
interest, but one which is peculiar to the requester, the courts have
ruled there is no "public interest" compelling disclosure.[65]

The courts have found that some public interest factors should
be taken into consideration and accorded great weight. For example,
disclosure is favored when the requested information would inform the
public about proven violations of public trust.[66] On the other
hand, the courts have found there is also a public interest in nondisclosure.[67] This is especially true with respect to protecting the
public's interest with regards to law enforcement activities.[68] The
courts have held that identities of individuals who provide law enforcement agencies with reports of illegal conduct, particularly where
they reasonably fear reprisals for such assistance, should be protected.[69] Additionally, the names of and information about FBI
personnel and other law enforcement personnel mentioned in the files
are generally not released if it could conceivably subject them to
harassment and annoyance in the conduct of their official duties and
in their private lives.[70]

Archivists, in the balancing process between disclosure and non-disclosure, will be called upon to decide if the release of personal information will actually harm someone. This means determining whether the risks to personal privacy go beyond the realm of abstract possibility and have some concrete likelihood of happening.[71] This will be a difficult task because the courts have generally held that privacy protection is not diminished with the passage of time.[72] Since most FBI case files will be fifty years old when they are accessioned by the National Archives, the balancing will not be so difficult a task. However, in those instances when the records are accessioned when they are thirty years old, archivists will have to screen them carefully, remembering that the courts have held that when a person's name is mentioned in an investigative file there is a stigmatizing connotation.[73]

Releasing Part But Not All

Even if some information in a particular FBI case file is withheld, archivists must make the remainder of the information available because the FOIA requires that "any reasonably segregable portion of a record" must be released after appropriate application of the nine exemptions.[74] However, where non-exempt material is so "inextricably intertwined" that release of it would "leave only essentially meaningless words and phrases," such material, according to the courts, need not be segregated.[75]

As I have indicated, some information in the FBI records in the National Archives will not immediately be available for research, and determining what to withhold will be a difficult, time-consuming, and often aggravating task. However, substantial numbers of case files will be, in toto or in part, made available to researchers. Once researchers obtain access to the files, they will still be faced with the challenge of understanding what they are reading.

Understanding the Contents

On the surface the contents of the FBI files appear straightforward. Actually, they are not so simple to understand. A Department of Justice senior attorney, investigating illegal break-ins in the mid 1970s, reported that his staff had been on the case more than a year, and "they still didn't know how to read an FBI file."[76] Part of the problem is the language used in the files. Like any agency, the FBI has its own terminology and euphemisms that researchers will have to learn in order to understand what they are reading. First are the abbreviations. There are scores of them throughout the files, and researchers will have to decipher these abbreviations if the information in the files is to make sense.[77]

Then there are the euphemisms. Former Attorney General

Nicholas Katzenbach told Congress in 1975 that "the Bureau constantly resorted to terms of art, or euphemisms, without bothering to inform the Attorney General that they were terms of art. I don't think it is excessively naive to assume that a 'highly reliable informant' is precisely that, and not a microphone surveillance."[78] For example, when reporting break-ins, agents sometimes used such terms as "special techniques" or "sensitive investigative techniques." When included in the files, information from break-ins was reported often as having come from an "anonymous source," a "highly confidential source," "a highly confidential informant," or a "confidential inform- ant." The term "confidential informant" was also used to disguise the source of illegally obtained information from a wiretap, bug, mail cover, or mail intercept.[79] According to former special agent, G. Gordon Liddy, if a field office submitted a plan for headquarters approval and it contained the words "'security guaranteed,' it meant we did it last night and got away clean--approve it so we can send you the results officially."[80] Often in a report you will see "T-1, a usually reliable informant whose identity cannot be disclosed" or "T-2, a reliable informant who is not available for reinterview." These may relate to human informants, but occasionally they denote electronic eavesdropping.[81]

Conclusion

Making the FBI's records available and using them will be an access challenge to archivists and researchers. This is as the former Director, J. Edgar Hoover, would have wanted. Hoover, particularly after the Judith Coplon case in 1949, was adamant about keeping the contents of the Bureau's files closed to outsiders, even the courts and Congress.[82] He did so for a variety of reasons, including fear of disclosure of illegal activities; fear of embarrassment, both per- sonally and to the Bureau (which, of course, he considered the same); and, if we can believe him, because of all the unsubstantiated deroga- tory information in the files. Now, with the FOIA and Privacy Act these records are being made available. With patience and knowledge, the access challenge of the FBI's records should be met in a manner which makes substantial quantities of information available while at the same time protecting the privacy of individuals and the legitimate security and law enforcement concerns of the government.

After reading this article, the reader should have a greater appreciation of the complexities and difficulties involved in making the post-1920 FBI records available to researchers. In some respects, the same complexities and difficulties are encountered by federal ar- chivists in making records of many other federal agencies available. At times, the task can be a frustrating experience. As Trudy and Gary Peterson have noted recently, "It is the tension between the two ideas--to provide access to research materials and to protect confi- dentiality--that creates the frustration archivists feel when confronted with access problems."[83] It is not only the federal archivist who

feels frustrated with access problems. All reference archivists dealing
with records created this century, to one degree or another, are
subject to frustrations.

"Every archivist," the Petersons have written, "wishes there
was a nice little checklist that could be followed to determine whether
a particular record or set of records must be restricted." But, they
state, "the plain fact is that there isn't." "Restricting records,"
they correctly maintain, "is making judgments" based on knowledge
of laws and knowing when the "access problem involves a law and
when it involves ethical or practical issues."[84] Indeed, knowledge,
experience, and a good dose of common sense are the reference archivist's best tools in deciding whether to release information or not.
These only come with time and study. So, to conclude, let me urge
all reference archivists to take the time to study, to be knowledgeable
about the applicable laws, institutional regulations, and the contents
of their records. This will contribute to reducing the level of frustration inevitably encountered in making modern records available to
researchers.

References

1. Copies of FBI records are also found in many Department of
    Justice case files and those of military intelligence agencies. They
    are also to be found in the various presidential libraries operated
    by the National Archives, in the records of the Warren Commis-
    sion, and the Watergate Special Prosecution Force that are in
    the National Archives. The FBI's electronic surveillance material
    on Martin Luther King, Jr. was sealed by a court order and
    placed in the National Archives where it will be opened in 2027.
    Timothy S. Robinson, "FBI Tap Data on King to Go to Archives,"
    The Washington Post, 1 Feb. 1977, p. A5.
2. Most case files will be accessioned by the National Archives when
    they are fifty years old. Records from seventeen obsolete FBI
    file classifications, as well as some selected files, will be ac-
    cessioned once litigation relating to the National Archives' ap-
    praisal of the FBI's records has been resolved. Records from
    the following file classifications will be accessioned when they
    are thirty years old: (7) Kidnapping; (25) Selective Service
    Violations; (26) Interstate Transportation of Stolen Motor Vehicles
    and Aircraft; (42) Deserters; (44) Civil Rights and Civil Rights
    Election Laws; and (91) Bank Robberies. For a detailed dis-
    cussion of when FBI records will be accessioned by the National
    Archives see the two-volume appraisal report entitled "Appraisal
    of the Records of the Federal Bureau of Investigation: A Report
    to Hon. Harold H. Greene United States District Court for the
    District of Columbia Submitted by the National Archives and
    Records Service and the Federal Bureau of Investigation. No-
    vember 9, 1981, Amended January 8, 1982." (hereafter cited as
    NARS, "FBI Appraisal Report").

3. American Friends Service Committee v. Webster, 485 F. Suppl
    222 (D.D.C. 1980). Athan G. Theoharis, who has used the FBI's
    records extensively, has described them as constituting "a written
    record of incomparable scope and richness." See his article,
    "The FBI and the FOIA: Problems of Access and Destruction,"
    The Midwestern Archivist 5, no. 2(1981):62.
4. Investigative case files are begun in a field office responsible
    for an investigation. These offices become known as the "office
    of origin" of the case. Other field offices providing information
    to the office of origin on a particular case are known as "auxili-
    ary offices," and they also create a case file. Periodically, when
    appropriate, the field offices send reports on the investigation
    to headquarters, which also creates a case file. The headquar-
    ters file, besides containing documents received also has docu-
    ments created at headquarters related to the case, such as in-
    structions sent to the field and decision-making memoranda.
    Resident Agencies create documents, but do not normally maintain
    them. They send them to their field office to be incorporated
    into their files. Legats, most often, create case files as "aux-
    iliary offices," providing the "office of origin" with information
    related to their investigations. For major cases, there may be
    dozens of case files in the different field offices, with the office
    of origin having the bulk of the documentation. For information
    about the organization and functions of the FBI, see Sanford
    J. Ungar, FBI (Boston and Toronto: Little, Brown and Company,
    1975), and Steven A. Stinson, "The Federal Bureau of Investi-
    gation: Its History, Organization, Functions and Publications,"
    Government Publications Review 6, no. 3 (1979): 213-39.
5. For listings of and discussions about the types of FBI documents,
    see Ann Mari Buitrago and Leon Andrew Immerman, Are You
    Now or Have You Ever Been in the FBI FILES: How To Secure
    and Interpret Your FBI Files (New York: Grove Press, Inc.,
    1981), 22-23, 113, 116, 118, 122, 125, 128, 132, and Research
    Unit, Office of Congressional Affairs, Federal Bureau of Investi-
    gation, "Conducting Research in FBI Records" (Federal Bureau
    of Investigation/Department of Justice, Washington, D.C., 1986),
    12. The latter also provides guidance for researchers in citing
    FBI documents, see pages 11-12. Informants are individuals
    whose activities are under the direction of the FBI, and are often
    paid. Confidential sources are individuals who provide informa-
    tion to the FBI on a confidential basis, often regularly, who are
    not paid. U.S Congress, Senate, Hearings Before the Select
    Committee to Study Governmental Operations with Respect to
    Intelligence Activities, 94th Cong., 1st sess., Volume 6, Federal
    Bureau of Investigation, November 18, 19, December 2, 3, 9,
    10, and 11, 1975, 109 (hereafter cited as U.S. Cong., Senate,
    Intelligence Hearings).
6. After documents were stolen from Media, Pennsylvania Resident
    Agency on March 8, 1971, and subsequently made public, the
    FBI began tightening its rules on records maintained in the
    resident agencies, restricting them to documents related to

current investigations. W. Mark Felt, <u>The FBI Pyramid From</u>
<u>the Inside</u> (New York: G. P. Putnam's Sons, 1979), 88-99;
Ungar, <u>FBI</u> 136-40. Legats generally keep case files on hand
for a year, at which time they are forwarded to headquarters
for safekeeping. Ibid., 239.

7. For discussions of the lawsuit and appraisal, see Athan G. Theo-
    haris, "The National Archives and FBI Records," <u>Government</u>
    <u>Publications Review</u> 10 (May-June 1983): 251-55; Theoharis,
    "The FBI and the FOIA," 70; John Anthony Scott, "The FBI
    Files: A Challenge for Historians," American Historical Associa-
    tion <u>Newsletter</u> 18 (March 1980): 1-2; Susan D. Steinwall, "Ap-
    praisal and the FBI Files Case: For Whom Do Archivists Retain
    Records?" <u>American Archivist</u> 49 (Winter 1986): 52-63; F. Gerald
    Ham, review of the National Archives' "FBI Appraisal Report,"
    <u>American Archivist</u> 45 (Fall 1982): 475-77.

8. Robert M. Warner, "The National Archives: A Memoir, 1980-
    1985," in <u>Guardian of Heritage: Essays on the History of the</u>
    <u>National Archives,</u> ed. Timothy Walch (Washington, D.C.: Na-
    tional Archives and Records Administration, 1985), 84. A con-
    servative estimate is that 50,000 cubic feet of the FBI records
    existing in 1981 would eventually be accessioned by the National
    Archives. NARS, "FBI Appraisal Report," Vol. 1, p. 2, 4. The
    appraisal of the FBI's records cost the National Archives upwards
    of one million dollars when salaries, staff and consultant travel,
    and clerical, legal and computer support are considered.

9. James Gregory Bradsher, "When One Percent means a Lot: The
    Percentage of Permanent Records in the National Archives,"
    Organization of American Historians <u>Newsletter</u> 13 (May 1985):
    20-21.

10. The courts have found that expungement of records is, in proper
    circumstances, a permissible remedy for an agency's violation of
    the Privacy Act (5 U.S.C. 552a), Hobson v. Wilson, 737 F.2d
    126 (D.C. Cir. 1984). Two cases have expressly held this to
    be true when an agency has violated the Act's prohibition on
    maintenance of records describing an individual's exercise of
    rights guaranteed by the First Amendment, contained in 5 <u>U.S.C.</u>
    552a (e) (7). Clarkson v. Internal Revenue Service, 678 F.2d
    1368, 1376-1377 (11th Cir. 1982); Albright v. United States, 631
    F.2d 915, 921 (D.C. Cir. 1980). It is equally well-established
    that expungement of records is, in proper circumstances, a
    proper remedy in an action brought directly under the Consti-
    tution. Paton v. La Prade, 524 F.2d 862 (3d Cir. 1975); Chas-
    tain v. Kelley, 510 F.2d 1235 (D.C. Cir. 1975); Matadure Corp.
    v. United States, 490 F. Supp., 1368 (S.D.N.Y. 1980). Ex-
    pungement procedures for FBI records are provided for in 28
    <u>C.F.R.</u> 16.50 and 16.51. For an excellent account about an
    individual having his FBI file expunged, see Penn Kimball, <u>The</u>
    <u>File</u> (San Diego, New York, and London: Harcourt Brace Jovano-
    vich Publishers, 1983). For a recent interesting case relating
    to expungement see Hobson v. Wilson, 737 F.2d 123-130 (D.C.
    Cir. 1984). It should be noted that archives in the National

Archives are exempted from the expungement process by 5
U.S.C. 552a(1) (3). As the House report notes, "A basic archival rule holds that archivists may not remove or amend information in any records placed in their custody. The principle
of maintaining the integrity of records is considered one of the
most important rules of professional conduct. It is important
because historians quite properly want to learn the true condition
of past government records when doing research; they frequently
find the fact that a record was 'inaccurate' is at least as important as the fact that a record was accurate." U.S. Congress,
House of Representatives, Report together with Additional Views
to Accompany H. R. 16373, 93d Cong., 2d sess., 2 October 1974,
H.R. Rept. 93-1416, 21.

11. David J. Garrow, The FBI and Martin Luther King, Jr.: From
'Solo' to Memphis (New York and London: W. W. Norton & Company, 1981), 10.

12. For a complete listing of the classification numbers, see FBI,
"Conducting Research in FBI Records," 13-17. For a discussion
of what information is contained in each classification, up through
214, see NARS, "FBI Appraisal Report," Vol. 2.

13. For discussions of the FBI filing system, see NARS, "FBI Appraisal Report," Vol. 1, pp. 2.1-2.7; U.S. Congress, Senate
Committee on the Judiciary, FBI Statutory Charter-Appendix to
Hearings before the Subcommittee on Administrative Practice and
Procedure, pt.3, 95th Cong., 2d sess., 1979, 33-73; U.S. Congress. House of Representatives, Inquiry into the Destruction
of Former FBI Director J. Edgar Hoover's Files and FBI Record-
keeping. Hearing before a Subcommittee of the Committee on
Government Operations, 94th Cong., 1st sess., 1 December 1975,
passim.

14. There are also ninety indexes for special collections of records
or information, such as those relating to electronic surveillance.
For more thorough discussions about the general and specialized
indexes, see Buitrago and Immerman, Are You Now or Have You
Ever Been in the FBI Files, 11-13, 19-22, and NARS, "FBI Appraisal Report," Vol. 2, Appendix.

15. Before attempting to use federal archives, including the FBI's
records, researchers should be familiar with the regulations
for the public use of records in the National Archives, which
are contained in 36 C.F.R. 1250 thru 1264.74. Researchers will
be informed of what information, if any, is being withheld and
under what specific authority, and their right to appeal.

16. By law, 44 U.S.C. 2108(a) the Archivist of the United States
establishes, under certain conditions, restrictions on access to
records transferred to his custody. These General Restrictions
are found in 36 C.F.R. 1256.1 thru 1256.18. The FBI, under
the above cited law, in transferring records to the National Archives may, with the concurrence of the Archivist, impose restrictions if such restrictions appear "to be necessary or desirable in the public interest." These Specific Restrictions have
not yet been specified by the FBI.

17. The nine exemptions, found in 5 U.S.C. 552(b) (1)-(9), relate
    to (1) information that is security-classified; (2) information re-
    lated solely to internal personnel practices or rules of an agency;
    (3) information specifically exempt from disclosure under other
    federal legislation; (4) information considered to be confidential
    business information such as trade secrets or confidential finan-
    cial data; (5) information dealing with interagency or intra-
    agency communications that form a part of the decision-making
    process; (6) information that permits a clearly unwarranted in-
    vasion of personal privacy; (7) information about investigatory
    matters collected to further law enforcement, that would inter-
    fere with law enforcement, deprive a person of a fair trial,
    cause an invasion of privacy, expose the identity of a confiden-
    tial source, disclose investigative techniques, or endanger lives
    of law enforcement personnel; (8) information concerning financial
    institutions held by agencies that regulate or supervise such
    institutions; (9) information about wells of a geological or geo-
    physical nature such as oil.
18. They are those covered by 5 U.S.C. 552(b) (4), (5), (8), and
    (9) discussed above.
19. 36 C.F.R. 1250.14 provides that "except when a record is classi-
    fied or when disclosure would violate any Federal law, the au-
    thority to withhold a record is permissive rather than mandatory.
    NARA will not withhold a record unless there is a compelling
    reason to do so. In the absence of a compelling reason, NARA
    will disclose a record although it otherwise is subject to exemp-
    tion."
20. 5 U.S.C. 552(b) (1) and the National Archives' General Re-
    striction No. 1 (36 C.F.R. 1256.10) restrict access to matters
    that are specifically authorized under criteria established by an
    Executive Order to be kept secret in the interest of national
    defense or foreign policy, and are in fact properly classified
    pursuant to such Executive Order. Presently the federal govern-
    ment is operating under Executive Order 12356 (3 C.F.R. 166)
    (1982 comp.), which replaced predecessor Executive Order
    12065, on August 1, 1982. For discussions of this exemption
    see Christine M. Marwick, Your Right to Government Information
    (Toronto, New York, London: Bantam Books, 1985), 67-75;
    Buitrago and Immerman, Are You Now or Have You Ever Been
    in the FBI Files, 53-63; and U.S. Department of Justice, Freedom
    of Information Case List, September 1985 Edition (Washington,
    D.C.: U.S. Government Printing Office, 1975), 272-79.
21. 5 U.S.C. 552 (b) (3), as amended in 1976, provides for the with-
    holding of information prohibited from disclosure by another
    statute only if that statute "(A) requires that the matters be
    withheld from the public in such a manner as to leave no dis-
    cretion on the issue, or (B) establishes particular criteria for
    withholding or refers to particular types of matters to be with-
    held." The National Archives' General Restriction No. 2 covers
    records containing information which is specifically exempted
    from disclosure by statute." 36 C.F.R. 1256.12(a). For income

tax returns and Central Intelligence Agency statutory exemptions, see 26 U.S.C. 1603 and 7213; 50 U.S.C. 402, 403g, and 403(d) (3).

22. 5 U.S.C. 552(b) (2) exempts from disclosure records "related solely to the internal personnel rules and practices of an agency." It has been interpreted to include internal matters which if disclosed would allow circumvention of a statute or agency regulation. Department of the Air Force v. Rose, 425 U.S. 369 (1976); Founding Church of Scientology v. Smith, 721 F.2d830n.4 (D.C. Cir. 1983); Crooker v. Bureau of Alcohol, Tobacco & Firearms, 670 F.2d 1073 (D.C. Cir. 1981).

23. Lesar v. Department of Justice, 636 F.2d 472, 485 (D.C. Cir. 1980), Rizzo v. FBI, Civil No. 83-1924, slip op., 3 (D.D.C. Feb.10, 1984); Cox v. Department of Justice, 601 F.2d 1, 4 (D.C. Cir. 1979), Cox v. Levi, 592 F.2d 460, 462-463 (8th Cir. 1979), Cox v. Department of Justice, 576 F.2d 1302, 1306-1309 (8th Cir. 1978); Cox v. FBI, Civil No. 83-3552, slip op. 1, 1 (D.D.C. May 31, 1984); Wightman v. Bureau of Alcohol, Tobacco & Firearms, 755 F.2d 979, 982 (1st Cir. 1985); Moody v. Drug Enforcement Agency, Civil No. 83-2582, slip op., 3 (D.D.C. June 18, 1984); and Founding Church of Scientology v. Smith, 721 F.2d 831 (D.C. Cir. 1983), Meeropol v. Smith, Civil No. 75-1121, slip op., 1 (D.D.C. Feb. 29, 1984).

24. Scherer v. Kelley, 584 F.2d 170, 175-176 (7th Cir. 1978); Nix v. United States, 572 F.2d 998, 1005 (4th Cir. 1978); Maroscia v. Levi, 569 F.2d 1000, 1001-1002 (7th Cir. 1977).

25. 5 U.S.C. 552(b) (7). See for example, FBI v. Abramson, 456 U.S. 615, 622 (1982). The National Archives' General Restriction No. 5 relating to law enforcement records is similarly worded. 36 C.F.R. 1256.18.

26. U.S. Congress, House of Representatives Committee on Government Operations, Clarifying and Protecting the Right of the Public to Information, 89th Cong., 2d sess., 1966, H.R. Rept. 1497, 13.

27. Rural Housing Alliance v. Department of Agriculture, 498 F.2d 81 & n.46 (D.C. Cir. 1974): Williams v. Internal Revenue Service, 479 F.2d 317, 318 (3d Cir. 1973).

28. Stern v. FBI. 737 F.2d 89 (D.C. Cir. 1984).

29. Stern v. FBI, 737 F.2d 89 (D.C. Cir. 1984).

30. U.S. Congress, Senate, Conference Report on the 1974 Amendments to the Freedom of Information Act, 93d Cong., 2d sess., 1 October 1974, S. Conf. Rept. 1200, 12; Block v. FBI, Civil No. 83-0813, slip op., 14-15 (D.D.C. November 19, 1984).

31. Williams v. FBI, 730 F.2d 882, 884-885 (2d Cir. 1984); Kuehnert v. FBI, 620 F.2d 666 (8th Cir. 1980).

32. Binion v. Department of Justice, 695 F.2d 1189, 1193-1194 (9th Cir. 1983); Malizia v. Department of Justice, 519 F. Supp. 338, 347 (S.D.N.Y. 1981).

33. Williams v. FBI, 730 F.2d 882, 884-885 (2d Cir. 1984); Pratt v. Webster, 673 F.2d 408, 416-418, 420-421 (D.C. Cir. 1982).

34. Irons v. Bell, 596 F.2d 468 (1st Cir. 1979).

35. Malloy v. Department of Justice, 457 F. Supp. 543, 545 (D.D.C. 1978).

36. U.S. Congress, House of Representatives, Conference Report to Accompany H.R. 12471. 93d Cong. 2d sess., 25 September, 1974. H.R. Rept. 93-1380, 12.

37. Dunaway v. Webster, 519 F. Supp. 1059, 1082-83 (N.D. Cal. 1981). Mail Covers involve reading the addresses on the cover of an envelope.

38. Malloy v. Department of Justice, 457 F. Supp. 543 (D.D.C. 1978).

39. 5 U.S.C. 552(b) (7) (F). Maroscia v. Levi, 569 F.2d 1000, 1002 (7th Circuit, 1977) held that FBI special agents are "law enforcement personnel."

40. Moody v. Drug Enforcement Agency, 592 F. Supp. 556, 559 (D.D.C. 1984).

41. 5 U.S.C. 552(b) (7) (F).

42. U.S. Congress, Senate, Conference Report of the 1974 Amendments to the Freedom of Information Act, 93d Cong., 2d sess., 1 October 1974, S. Conf. Rept. No. 1200, 13.

43. Shaw v. FBI, 749 F.2d 58, 61 (D.C. Cir. 1984).

44. Lame v. Department of Justice, 654 F.2d. 917, 923 (3d Cir. 1981).

45. U.S. Congress, Senate, Conference Report on the 1974 Amendments to the Freedom of Information Act, 93d Cong., 2d sess., 1 October 1974, S. Conf. Rept. No. 1200, 13.

46. Pollard v. FBI, 705 F.2d 1151, 1155 (9th Cir. 1983).

47. U.S. Congress, Senate. Conference Report on the 1974 Amendments to the Freedom of Information Act, 93d Cong., 2d sess., 1 October 1974, S. Conf. Rept. No. 1200, 13.

48. Nix v. United States, 572 F.2d 998, 1003 (4th Cir. 1978); Diamond v. FBI, 707 F.2d 78 (2d Cir. 1983); Miller v. Bell, 661 F.2d 623, 627 (7th Cir. 1981), found that confidentiality is "inherently implicit" in FBI criminal investigation interviews.

49. Pope v. United States, 599 F.2d 1386-1387 (5th Cir. 1979); Miller v. Bell, 661 F.2d 627-628 (7th Cir. 1981); Lesar v. Department of Justice, 636 F.2d 489-491 (D.C. Cir. 1980); Abrams v. FBI, 511 F. Supp. 758, 763 (N.D. Ill. 1981); Biberman v. FBI, 528 F. Supp. 1140, 1143 (S.D.N.Y. 1982); Malizia v. Department of Justice, 519 F. Supp. 338, 350 (S.D.N.Y. 1981); Founding Church of Scientology v. Regan, 670 F.2d 1158, 1161-1162 (D.C. Cir. 1982).

50. U.S. Congress, House of Representatives, Conference Report to Accompany H. R. Rept. 12471, 93d Cong. 2d sess., 25 September 1974, H.R. Rept. 93-1380, 12. More than likely, a "confidential source" providing information about both sides of a telephone conversation is a non-human source, and cannot be considered a confidential source.

51. Shaw v. FBI, 749 F.2d 62 (D.C. Cir. 1984).

52. Mitchell v. Ralston, Civil No. 81-4478, slip op., 2(S.D. Ill. Oct. 14, 1982); Radowich v. United States Attorney, District of Maryland, 658 F.2d 964 (4th Cir. 1981); Cohen v. Smith, No. 81-5365, mem. op. 4 (9th Cir. Mar. 25, 1983); Kiraly v.

FBI, 728 F.2d 273, 279 (6th Cir. 1984); Stassi v. Department
of Justice, Civil No. 78-0536, slip op., 9-10 (D.D.C. Apr. 12,
1979).

53. 36 C.F.R. 1256.18(b) (6).

54. Diamond v. FBI, 532 F. Supp. 216, 227 (S.D.N.Y. 1981); Dia-
     mond v. FBI, 707 F.2d 76-77 (2d Cir. 1983); Abrams v. FBI,
     511 F. Supp. 762-763 (N.D. Ill. 1981).

55. Department of State v. Washington Post Co., 456 U.S. 595,
     599-603 (1982).

56. Tigar & Buffone v. Department of Justice, Civil No. 80-2382,
     slip op., 9-10 (D.D.C. Sept. 30, 1983); Diamond v. FBI, 707
     F.2d 75 (2d Cir. 1983); Sims v. CIA, 642 F.2d 562 (D.C. Cir.
     1980); Providence Journal Co. v. FBI, 460 F. Supp. 778, 785
     (D.R.I. 1978). The National Archives' General Restriction No.
     4 covers "records containing information about a living individual."
     36 C.F.R. 1256.16(a).

57. Common Cause v. National Archives & Records Service, 628
     F.2d 179, 184 (D.C. Cir. 1980); Lamont v. Department of Jus-
     tice, 475 F. Supp. 761, 778 (S.D.N.Y. 1979).

58. Fund for Constitutional Government v. National Archives &
     Records Service, 656 F.2d 856, 865, 866 (D.C. Cir. 1981).

59. The National Archives' General Restriction No. 4 covers "records
     ...which reveal details of a highly personal nature that the in-
     dividual could reasonably assert a claim to withhold from the
     public to avoid a clearly unwarranted invasion of privacy, in-
     cluding but not limited to information about the physical or mental
     health or the medical or psychiatric care or treatment of the in-
     dividual, and that contain personal information not known to
     have been previously made public, and relate to events less than
     75 years old." 36 C.F.R. 1256.16(a).

60. Department of State v. Washington Post Co., 456 U.S. 595
     (1982).

61. Rural Housing Alliance v. Department of Agriculture, 498 F.2d
     73, 77 (D.C. Cir. 1974).

62. 5 U.S.C. 552a(e) (7).

63. Department of the Air Force v. Rose, 425 U.S. 352, 372 (1976);
     Heights Community Congress v. Veterans Administration, 732
     F.2d 526, 530 (6th Cir. 1984); Public Citizen Health Research
     Group v. Department of Labor, 591 F.2d 808, 809 (D.C. Cir.
     1978).

64. Fund for Constitutional Government v. National Archives &
     Records Service, 656 F.2d 856. 866 (D.C. Cir. 1981); Tarnopol
     v. FBI, 442 F.Supp. 5, 8 (D.D.C. 1977).

65. Committee on Masonic Homes v. National Labor Relations Board,
     556 F.2d 214, 220 (3d Cir. 1977).

66. Stern v. FBI, 737 F.2d 84, 93-94 (D.C. Cir. 1984); Columbia
     Packing Co., Inc. v. Department of Agriculture, 563 F.2d
     495, 499 (1st Cir. 1977); Congressional News Syndicate v.
     Department of Justice, 438 F.Supp. 538, 544 (D.D.C. 1977);
     Tax Reform Research Group v. Internal Revenue Service, 419
     F. Supp. 415, 418 (D.D.C. 1976).

67. Fund for Constitutional Government v. National Archives & Records Service, 656 F.2d 865 n.22 (D.C. Cir. 1981).
68. Miller v. Bell, 661 F.2d 623, 631 (7th Cir. 1981); Church of Scientology v. Department of State, 493 F. Supp. 418, 421 (D.D.C. 1980); Flower v. FBI, 448 F. Supp. 567, 571-572 (W.D. Tex. 1978); Freeman v. Department of Justice, Civil No. 85-0958-A (E.D. Va. March 12, 1986).
69. Holy Spirit Ass'n v. FBI, 683 F.2d 562, 564-565 (D.C. Cir. 1982); Kiraly v. FBI, 728 F.2d 273, 278-280 (6th Cir. 1984).
70. Nix v. United States, 572 F.2d 998, 1006 (4th Cir. 1978). The 7th Circuit Court of Appeals in 1981 observed that "it is not necessary that harassment rise to the level of endangering physical safety before the protections of 7(C) can be invoked." Miller v. Bell, 661 F.2d 630. The District of Columbia Circuit Court ordered that the name of a high-level FBI employee who engaged in intentional wrongdoing be released, but ordered withheld the name of two mid-level employees whose negligence furthered a cover-up. Stern v. FBI, 737 F.2d 84, 94.
71. Department of the Air Force v. Rose, 425 U.S. 352 (1976); House of Representatives Committee on Government Operations. Clarifying and Protecting the Right of the Public to Information, 89th Cong., 2d sess., 1966, H.R. Rept. 1497, 11.
72. Diamond v. FBI, 707 F.2d 75, 77 (2d Cir. 1983); King v. Department of Justice, 586 F. Supp. 286, 295 (D.D.C. 1983); Dunaway v. Webster, 519 F. Supp. 1059, 1079 (N.D. Cal. 1981).
73. Miller v. Bell, 661 F.2d 631-632 (7th Cir. 1981). See also Congressional News Syndicate v. Department of Justice. 438 F. Supp. 538, 541 (D.D.C. 1977); Iglesias v. CIA, 525 F. Supp. 547, 562 (D.D.C. 1981).
74. 5 U.S.C. 552(b). The National Archives' access regulations states that "NARA makes available any reasonably segregable portion of a record after the restricted portion has been deleted." 36 C.F.R. 1254.30(a).
75. Neufield v. IRS, 646 F.2d 661, 663 (D.C. Cir. 1981).
76. Anthony Marro, "FBI Break-in Policy," in Beyond the Hiss Case: the FBI, Congress, and the Cold War, ed. Athan G. Theoharis (Philadelphia: Temple University Press, 1982), 84.
77. Abbreviations are listed and discussed in Buitrago and Immerman, Are You Now or Have You Ever Been in the FBI Files, 159-215.
78. U.S. Congress, Senate, Intelligence Hearings, 218.
79. Marro,"FBI Break-in Policy," 85, 101-102; Percival R. Baily, "The Case of the National Lawyers Guild, 1939-1958," in Beyond the Hiss Case, ed. Theoharis, 138, 165n.15; Athan G. Theoharis, "In-House Cover-Up: Researching FBI Files," in Beyond the Hiss Case, ed. Theoharis, 33-34. Mail intercepts and mail covers involve reading the covers and contents of mail.
80. G. Gordon Liddy, Will: The Autobiography of G. Gordon Liddy. (New York: A Dell-St. Martin's Press Book, 1980), 109.
81. Victor S. Navasky, Kennedy Justice, (New York: Atheneum, 1977), 15-16.
82. Judith Coplon, a Department of Justice employee, was arrested

by FBI agents in March 1949 and charged with attempting to pass FBI documents to a Soviet official in New York City. During her trial she requested that the documents be made public to prove they contained no secrets. Attorney General Tom Clark overruled Hoover and permitted government attorneys to place in evidence the documents. The documents, many of which related to political surveillance of New Deal liberals, Hollywood personalities, and financial supporters of Henry Wallace's 1948 presidential campaign, gave evidence of the Bureau's intrusive investigative techniques. They were ridiculed by the press as a storehouse of gossip and trivia. Hoover, embarrassed by having "raw files" made public, began a campaign to ensure they were never made public again. Don Whitehead, The FBI Story: A Report to the People (New York: Random House, 1956), 287-90; Kenneth O'Reilly, Hoover and the Un-Americans: The FBI, HUAC, and the Red Menace (Philadelphia: Temple University Press, 1983), 133-34.

83. Gary M. Peterson and Trudy Huskamp Peterson, Archives & Manuscripts: Law, SAA Basic Manual Series (Chicago: Society of American Archivists, 1985), 39.

84. Ibid., 60.

THE NAZI PUBLIC LIBRARY
AND THE YOUNG ADULT*

Margaret F. Stieg

Before 1933 Library service to young adults in Germany ranged from
incidental to nonexistent. In a country with a proud tradition of
scholarly libraries, public libraries in general attracted little interest
and less respect. Most large cities could claim a public library, but
usually they were shoestring operations maintained by voluntary,
often denominational, charitable organizations and supported by contributions and fees. In smaller towns, the libraries were even less
substantial, and rural areas were virtually unserved. A brief statistical comparison with a few comparable American libraries of the
period shows their relative weakness (see table 1).

German public librarianship was not innovative and looked to
American and British models for inspiration. Services were limited
to traditional collecting and making books, magazines, and newspapers
available. Large urban public libraries had begun to develop children's collections and rooms, and some youth libraries existed, but
they remained the exceptions. Thanks to the German fondness for
music, city libraries often had music libraries, but only Erwin Ackerknecht, librarian of Stettin, saw the potential of films and advocated
an auditorium in the public library. Hours were short and, except
in children's rooms, the stacks were closed.

Philosophically, public librarians in Germany were divided into
two schools of thought. One school led by Walter Hofmann, librarian
of Leipzig, stressed the educational role of the public library; readers
were to be guided, if necessary under protest, to the classics of
German literature. This was the more widely accepted view. The
other, which is identified with Erwin Ackerknecht, recognized that
the reality of public library service was a readership interested in
entertainment, not cultural improvement. The two groups agreed that
the public library had two essential political functions: to keep citizens informed and to strengthen national bonds.

*Reprinted by permission of the author and publisher of Top of the
News 43:1 (Fall 1986) 45-57; copyright © 1986 American Library Association.

TABLE 1
German and American Public Libraries:
Selected Comparative Statistics 1933*

	Berlin	Chicago, Illinois
Population	4,236,416	3,376,478
Volumes	840,332	1,628,248
Circulation	2,939,100	13,100,826
Borrowers as percentage of population	3.12	19.5
Circulation per borrower	22.32	19.86
Budget	1,689,757.-RM	$1,306,681.98
Expenditure per capita	0.40RM	$0.39

	Hamburg	Los Angeles (City), California
Population	1,125,025	1,238,048
Volumes	158,881	1,409,922
Circulation	796,422	13,498,718
Borrowers as percentage of population	3.25	31.8
Circulation per borrower	21.76	34.24
Budget	242,329.-RM	$1,155,713.94
Expenditure per capita	0.22	$0.64

	Leipzig	Milwaukee, Wisconsin
Population	712,475	725,263
Volumes	106,671	952,388
Circulation	318,823	6,102,919
Borrowers as percentage of population	3.48	22.2
Circulation per borrower	12.86	37.87
Budget	279,785.-RM	$391,630.70
Expenditure per capita	0.39RM	$0.54

	Hannover	Birmingham, Alabama
Population	438,922	399,713
Volumes	183,736	203,563
Circulation	239,781	1,776,864
Borrowers as percentage of population	1.98	
Circulation per borrower	27.53	
Budget	198,200.-RM	$111,249.54
Expenditure per capita	0.45RM	$0.28

Table 1 Continued

	Braunschweig	Nashville, Tennessee
Population	156,840	153,866
Volumes	17,304	155,572
Circulation	50,486	397,955
Borrowers as percentage of population	1.42	20.6
Circulation per borrower	22.71	12.52
Budget	40,500.-RM	$58,008.00
Expenditure per capita	0.26RM	$0.37

	Würzburg	Duluth, Minnesota
Population	100,937	101,463
Volumes	13,840	142,928
Circulation	50,577	761,796
Borrowers as percentage of population	2.9	30.57
Circulation per borrower	17.27	24.55
Budget	16,250.-RM	$81,226.00
Expenditure per capita	0.16RM	$0.80

RM = $0.238

*The German statistics are from "Die Volksbüchereien in den deutschen Grossstädten," in Die deutschen Volksbüchereien nach Ländern, Provinzen und Gemeinden, 1933/34, Statistik des Deutschen Reichs, Band 471 (Berlin: Verlag für Sozialpolitik, Wirtschaft und Statistik, 1935), p. 54-55. The U.S. statistics are from "Comparative Statistics for 1933 of Public Libraries in Cities of More than 200,000 Population," Bulletin of the American Library Association 28:248-49 (May 1934) and "Comparative Statistics for 1932 of Public Libraries in Cities of 75,000-199,000," Bulletin of the American Library Association 28:98-99 (Feb. 1934).

Library statistics show that German public libraries had young adult users before 1933, although they made little effort to serve their needs. For the entire Reich in that year only 6.1 percent of the collections and 12.1 percent of the circulation in public libraries were categorized as youth materials. (Youth included both children and young adults.)[1] Societal patterns made it easy for the librarian, who already had quite enough to do with the limited resources available, to ignore this area. The German school day was long and rigorous, leaving students little time or inclination for serious recreational reading. The vast majority of youth left school at age fourteen to work. A strong youth movement offered middle-class youth, the very group most likely to be public library users, an attractive outlet for their energies. It was difficult for libraries to compete with the kind of total experience the movement afforded--outdoor rambles, trips abroad, and an ethos that included close group ties, songs, and philosophical camp-fire discussions.

The school libraries could have offset this bleak picture, but they were as weak as German public libraries. The Prussian decree of 1928 on school libraries began with the admission that school libraries were not fulfilling their responsibilities. In 1933 there were approximately 25,000 school libraries. That the Nazis founded some 55,000 more shows that there was room for improvement.[2]

January 30, 1933, the day on which Adolf Hitler became chancellor, inaugurated a period of far-reaching changes. The Nazis had promised a revolution, and although they may have failed to bring about the fundamental societal reorganization which that term signifies, few would deny that the transformation was drastic. Within a few short months they had eliminated political opposition and taken over all levels of government. They began the process of remaking all institutions in the Nazi image, whether orchestras, labor unions, or churches. Their values and ideas became the only acceptable ones. Racism; unquestioning obedience; a virulent, expansionist nationalism; the exaltation of brute strength; militarism; and the glorification of all things German were the new order of the day.

To the world of public librarianship the Nazi takeover brought both ideological and organizational change. Many old leaders were set aside; others joined the party with indecent haste in an effort to preserve their careers. The profession's philosophy was reworked and new, Nazi-oriented goals were proclaimed. New programs were implemented, the most visible being the removal of thousands of newly unacceptable books from collections. Between 1933 and 1940 an administrative hierarchy was created that reached from the smallest village library to new national organizations with responsibility for public libraries, the Reichsstelle für Volksbuchereiwesen (National Institute for Public Librarianship, [RV]) and the Reichsministerium für Wissenschaft, Erziehung und Volksbildung (National Ministry for Science, Education and Adult Education, [RWEV]). Most important of all, the public library was at last defined as a public agency and therefore a public responsibility to be supported by localities out of tax revenue. No longer was it a stepchild, maintained by charity with an occasional handout from city authorities. Librarians could enjoy a new sense of importance and feel that they were participating in the national renewal.

The Nazi public library was an instrument of the state; its mission was now political education. It was described by the first director of the RV as a "political library" and by the ministerial

adviser for public libraries as a "political weapon." Underlying it
and incorporated in its very name was the idea of the Volk--a word
central to Nazism and variously translated as folk, people, race, or
nation--and to both Volk and state the library was to orient itself.
The ideal of reader self-fulfillment was noticeably absent, and liberal
individualism was explicitly rejected. As set forth in the national
guidelines published in 1937, the library was "to care for the inheri-
tance of the folkish tradition, to keep itself ready with the writings
appropriate for political and values education and job training, and
to disseminate folkish entertaining reading and good youth writings."
[3]

Despite insistent pressure for conformity to new values and a
pervasive anti-intellectualism, public librarianship managed to maintain
its essential identity. The redefinition of purpose, which was imperative for survival, altered its traditional educational function,
although it did not eliminate it. Energetic efforts failed to obtain
jurisdiction over public libraries by the Propaganda Ministry. They
remained instead under the Education Ministry--a significant symbol
of continuity and of the primacy of education.

Nazi attitudes toward youth contributed to the remodeling of
young adult services. Most societies acknowledge that their young
people will inherit the future; they also recognize that youth is the
time to mold and shape individuals. The Nazis made youth a religion.
They idealized it and at the same time assigned to the young the
responsibility and privilege of fighting the battles that would bring
about the Nazi millennium. In the musical Cabaret the group of Hitler
Jugend (or Hitler Youth) singing "Tomorrow Belongs to Me" as they
march in perfect unison conveys with accuracy the aggression and
mindless obedience the Nazis were trying to inculcate. The Nazis
described themselves as "the organized will of youth" and their victory
in 1933 as a triumph of youth over age. It became commonplace to
include in speeches on quite unrelated topics such paeans as this,
from the speech of Wilhelm Schuster, president of the Verband deutscher Volksbibliothekare (Association of German Public Librarians),
to the 1933 annual conference:

> We experience with joyful astonishment how German youth,
> apparently without effort, gives birth to the new model of
> man for which we strive. A biological rejuvenating process,
> arising out of the unknown depths of the race and the blood,
> encounters the political and intellectual revolution and gives
> the nation the readiness of this new youth, its bold and pure
> will, its simple straightforwardness, its steadfast following
> of the chosen Führer, its solidarity over all the separating
> barriers, and the caste spirit it has achieved.[4]

Unlike many Nazi promises, the focus on youth was translated
into policies and influenced the activities of many different institutions.
Not only were young adults identified as a distinctive clientele with

a legitimate claim upon the public library (a crucial precondition to the improvement of service) but they were important. They were also numerous. After the low birth rates during World War I, the number of fourteen-year-olds was suddenly increasing. In 1935 a librarian wrote what would have been inconceivable three years before: "We all know today that the youth library is an important part of public librarianship everywhere. A public library which is supposed to serve the entire populace and forgets or handles only inadequately the children's room and youth library is an organism that is not functioning rationally."[5]   Symptomatic of the new trend was the choice of theme for the 1935 conference of large city public libraries held in Frankfurt am Main: "Youth and the Public Library."

The attention produced concrete results. By 1937-38 there were a total of 144 youth libraries. Almost every town of more than 100,000 people had at least one youth library, and the capital and largest city, Berlin, had twelve. Towns too small to have a separate youth library or libraries too small to have a separate youth collection augmented what they did have. Lack of young adult materials had become a very serious matter; a major factor in the recommendation by the director of the provincial library commission for Westphalia not to reopen the library at Lübbecke after its 1939 reorganization was the absence of young adult books.[6]

Young adults took advantage of their new opportunities. A number of small towns in the Upper Palatinate and Upper Franconia in 1942-43 recorded young adult readers ranging from a low of 13.5 percent in Waldsassen to a high of 45.7 percent in Neustadt. Young adults composed 15.9 percent of Hamburg's readers in 1936, and in Berlin 46.6 percent were under eighteen in 1937-38. Where breakdowns by sex are available they indicate that young men were far more likely to be readers than young women. The few towns for which there are earlier and later statistics available confirm that the figures given represent significant increases. The young adult categories in Hamburg were the only ones to show an increase between 1935 and 1936. The young adult component of the Upper Franconian city of Hof was 17.6 percent in 1942-43; in 1936 all readers under eighteen had accounted for only 3.1 percent.[7]

The idea that a special kind of librarian was needed to administer the youth library began to appear. As described by Irene Graebsch, a librarian at Breslau with a special interest in youth work, he or she had to have a natural inclination for young adult work, a basic education in all its aspects, and a lively affinity with the young. Membership in the Hitler Youth was highly desirable. The librarian had to be able to reassure a small boy and persuade him to tell his wishes. The librarian also had to be able to say to a large boy with dirty hands "With such unwashed paws one doesn't come into the library," to make girls stop giggling, and to control the natural inclination of young boys to attack their peers. Most important, the librarian had to know the collection inside out. How could a librarian gain the confidence of a small reader if he or she offered the wrong book? Knowledge of the collection was even more important than in adult work because younger readers, especially girls, were totally dependent upon the librarian for advice. Allowing for differences in style and detail, this description of the young adult librarian is very similar to the concept of the young adult librarian emerging in the U.S. during this period.[8]

The goal of young adult work was to open the world of books to the young adult, and the librarian's principal activity was advising readers. As elsewhere, this was marked by perennial conflict between the values of the librarian and the reading interests of young adults, but special circumstances made it even more difficult in Nazi Germany. The Nazi state had rapidly developed an extensive system of censorship and literary control that determined what was available for the librarian to recommend. To be published, an author needed to be a member of the official writers' union. Books had to be approved by party and state agencies before publication, and after publication other agencies reviewed and endorsed them. Numerous basic lists were developed to guide librarians, such as Die ersten hundert Bucher für nationalsozialistische Büchereien (The First Hundred Books for the Nazi Library). In a very real sense the librarian was at one end of a continuum that regulated publication, from inception to dissemination.

This elaborate structure was created to prevent the spread of unwanted ideas and to propagate Nazi views. Charles Beard accurately described Nazi intentions in 1936. "If the Hitler regime continues for several years, the German people will be a people almost totally ignorant of the outside world and indifferent to all ideas and interests not contained in the Nazi creed."[9] Recreational reading was simply one more way to inculcate values of national unity, self-sacrifice, and racial purity, and these political standards were now grafted onto the librarian's traditional concern for the humanistic literary qualities of style and depth. The good youth book, in Nazi terms, was the book that aroused an enthusiasm for the heroes of sagas, legend and history; for the soldiers of the great wars; and for the Führer and the new Germany. It might show the beauty of the German landscape or focus on the fate of the children of German ethnic groups living abroad. It might deal with the love of nature and promote nature crafts. It could relate old German myths, folktales, and legends or give practical advice and help to the Hitler Youth in their recreational and educational activities.[10]

Some older materials remained acceptable by the new standards. Folktales, legends, and sagas were given a prominent position both in school curricula and recreational reading, subject to some revision to serve Nazi objectives more pointedly. Odin, for example, became the protoype of the Führer and the barbaric Thor a noble defender of the peasant community. Heimat literature, a minor literary form featuring peasants and the rural life, was encouraged, and such

authors as Hermann Löns, Peter Rosegger, Theodor Storm, and
Annette von Droste-Hülshoff were recommended. Older historical
novels, like the influential Volk ohne Raum of Hans Grimm, a plea
for living space that portrayed the struggles of German colonists in
Southwest Africa, were advocated for older children.[11]

   A whole new genre of Nazi-oriented youth novels began appearing
to compete with the older, less hortatory boys' and girls' stories.
One librarian described the less-than-subtle intentions of the girls'
books: "Frequently political or other kinds of events are disguised,
so that the girl is unknowingly led out of her small world and learns
that in addition to her concerns and duties, there is something much
greater and more important." The best known and most popular overall was Alois Schenzinger's Hitlerjunge Quex, the uplifting tale of
Heini Völker, a working-class Berlin youth who found salvation and
adventure through the Hitler Youth and eventually died a martyr to
the cause. Innumerable novels like Juttas Pfichtjahr (Jutta's Year
of Duty), a story with a self-explanatory title and Die Wolgakinder
(The Volga Children), one of many tales proclaiming the longing of
ethnic Germans outside Germany for the Reich, spread the new values.
[12]

   The abundance of rules and directions greatly circumscribed
the professional independence of librarians in the Third Reich. Nowhere is this more apparent than the numerous book lists published
during the period either prohibiting or recommending. Young adult
books were subject to the same restrictions as adult; no books by
Jewish, Marxist, or pacifist authors could be held, nor any on unacceptable themes. One example of a banned book was Rudolf Frank's
story of a young boy who, although considered a hero by the soldiers
of World War I, ran from the chance to be honored by the kaiser
because he had decided that nothing about war was honorable. It
has recently been translated into English as No Hero for the Kaiser.
Recommended lists were strong on works such as Baldur von Schirach's
book on the Hitler Youth, Helke's Der junge Reichsbürger, a book
rejoicing in the subtitle What Every Young German Should Know about
His Duties to the State and Party, and President von Hindenburg's
memoirs. Novels receiving the official accolade tended to be extremely
nationalistic, such as Beumelberg's World War I story Sperrfeuer
um Deutschland (Barrage against Germany) or Die Wolgakinder.
Hitlerjunge Quex was, of course, ubiquitous. For light relief there
were sagas and folktales or the Nazi-oriented young adult novels.
The notable absence of one of the most popular youth books, the
charming, apolitical Die Biene Maja, bears silent witness to the fact
that the guiding principle of these lists was political, not professional.[13]

   How wholeheartedly individual librarians cooperated in guiding
young adults to officially approved reading cannot be known. Undoubtedly some were more enthusiastic than others. Betty Schladebach
the assistant director of the provincial library commission in Lippe,

wrote to the Reichsstelle zur Förderung des deutschen Schrifttums
objecting to Max Mezger's Monika fährt nach Madagaskar (Monica
Travels to Madagascar). It seems that Monika, a German Nancy
Drew, and her father committed the sin of staying with Sally Mendel,
a Jew. Although Sally was portrayed unfavorably, this was not acceptable behavior, and Schladebach was concerned that the book had
earlier been on recommended lists. (A 1940 reprinting of Monika
shows that the Reichsstelle considered her scruples somewhat ex-
cessive.) Schladebach clearly had a keen eye for what was being
read and what wasn't. On an inspection of the village library in
Brake in 1941 she noted that although Karrasch's Stein gibt Brot had
not yet been read once, Hitlerjunge Quex was "very well read."[14]

Several surveys suggest that the exertions of the regime to
direct the reading preferences of children and youth had only limited
impact. Folktales and legends were very popular, but a considerable
part of the popularity must be attributed to the natural inclinations
of the young. The old standbys were not superseded; Karl May,
the prolific writer of much-disparaged Wild West and other adventure
tales, and the numerous series novels for girls remained unwelcome
favorites. Particularly disconcerting was the indestructible appeal
of one such series, the Nesthäkchen books, by Else Ury, a Jewish
author. Although these were banned because of her Jewish ancestry,
girls continued to prefer them to more ideological modern stories.[15]

In the 1930s young adult work both expanded and diversified.
One highly visible and much advertised activity was the creation of
two model libraries, the Reichsjugendbücherei (National Youth Library)
and the Dietrich Eckart Library. The Reichsjugendbücherei had been
founded as a scholarly library to preserve youth books and enhance
appreciation for their role in transmitting culture. The Dietrich Eckart
Library was opened in 1935 as the model library of the Nationalsozialistische Lehrerbund (National Socialist Teachers' Association).
Both offered extensive lectures, discussions, and exhibits aimed at
young people. Some exhibits attracted as many as 6,000 visitors.
The Reichsjugendbücherei sponsored poetry readings. Baldur von
Schirach, head of the Hitler Youth, was one of the featured poets.

Both libraries reached beyond their immediate neighborhood with
other programs. The Reichsjugendbücherei took an important part
in censorship, printing lists of both banned and recommended books.
Beginning in 1934 the Dietrich Eckart Library distributed duplicate
copies of every book it cataloged to ten school libraries in border
areas. It also sponsored nationwide essay contests on themes such
as "The Greater German Reich."[16]

Other libraries were not able to work with young adults on the
same scale as did these two national youth libraries, but almost all
did something. Exhibits were frequent; issues of Die Bücherei, the
official public library journal, regularly announced yet another exhibit. Not all exhibits, of course, were aimed exclusively at youth,

but many were designed to appeal both to young adults and adults.
An account of the 1936 Spandau exhibit on youth and the library
indicates how these exhibits attempted to indoctrinate visitors. The
exhibit's title was "Peasant and Soldier," and it celebrated the official rejection of the last limitations imposed by the Treaty of Ver-
sailles on the armed forces of Germany and the rebuilding of the
German army. The Führer was featured prominently; at the entrance
he was pictured eye to eye with Walter Darré, the Reichsbauernführer
(national peasant leader). Every effort was made to identify Hitler
with the past glories of German arms and to portray him as a modern
version of Frederick the Great. In addition to displaying recommended
books like those published by the Blut and Boden Verlag--Blut und
Boden (blood and soil) was a Nazi slogan--numerous book lists were
available without cost on such topics as "Blut and Boden," "Rassen-
kunde und Rassenpfleg" (racial knowledge and care), and "Junge-
und Mädelbucher" (boys and girls' books).[17]

       Some young adult work was done through schools. Several
decrees from Rust, the minister for education, whose jurisdiction included both schools and public libraries, mandated cooperation between
the two. The provincial library commissions were given formal responsibility for school libraries in 1937. A year later Franz Schriewer,
the director of the library commission for Brandenburg, could write
an article describing his work with schools, but few commissions did
much to fulfill this responsibility. The tours of the library for school
classes and posters distributed for display in the schools listed in
the Hamburg library's annual report were probably more than most
libraries offered.[18]

       Most youth work was done in cooperation with the Hitler Youth;
they were natural partners. The public library had always been an
educational institution outside the hierarchy of formal education. As
the Nazi state evolved, the role of the Hitler Youth changed from that
of the neglected junior branch of the party to an important instrument
for the political socialization of future citizens. The 1936 Law for
German Youth decreed that the whole German youth was organized
in the Hitler Youth; in other words, all young people, aged ten to
eighteen, were supposed to join. "The whole of German youth is to
be educated, outside the parental home and school, in the Hitler
Youth physically, intellectually and morally in the spirit of National
Socialism for service to the nation and community." The Hitler Youth
could thus, at least in theory, offer the public library access to the
entire population of young adults; the public library offered the
Hitler Youth much-needed support for its activities.[19]

       Work with the Hitler Youth began on an ad hoc basis; individual
Hitler Youth leaders would contact a library or provincial library
commission. In the early years efforts apparently were made to con-
fine relations to an institution-to-institution basis. Readers' cards
in Hamburg, for instance, were issued to members through the group
leader. Only in 1937 could members get their cards directly from the
library by showing their Hitler Youth membership cards.[20]

Efforts became increasingly systematic, especially after the Youth Law of 1936. Many provincial library commissions concluded agreements with their provincial youth authorities. A typical agreement, concluded early in 1937 and covering the provinces of Westphalia, Lippe, and Schaumburg-Lippe, provided that the three provincial library commissions and the Hitler Youth leadership would jointly prepare a list of youth books and magazines to be made available in public libraries. Local Heimat literature was to be featured. The Hitler Youth was to encourage active library use by its members, and the public library was to attempt to satisfy the reading needs of the group by appropriate acquisitions. To provide the additional financing necessary, their leader was to encourage localities to increase public library appropriations.[21]

An agreement between the RV and the Reichsjugendführung (National Youth Leadership) of the Nazi party later in 1937 supplemented these provincial agreements and set forth general principles. The RV and Reichsjugendführung were to produce national lists of suitable books. The regional director of the Hitler Youth and the director of the provincial library commission were jointly responsible for library-related youth activity in their province. Cooperation was to be close, and the Hitler Youth was to use public libraries whenever possible rather than establishing its own.[22]

For the local library, cooperation with the Hitler Youth was almost always necessary when preparing reading lists. The provincial library commission of Lippe, for instance, prepared a list of Heimat literature for the Hitler Youth summer school of Hörste in 1937. Many reading lists were tied to the Heimabend, originally simple weekly meetings, but gradually evolving into a carefully coordinated educational series with radio broadcasts and discussion on a set theme. Each member was supposed to have prepared beforehand by reading books from the list of recommended titles.[23]

Libraries often placed small collections at the disposal of local Hitler Youth groups, sometimes to support a particular course, sometimes simply for general recreation. The provincial library commission of the Saar made such a collection available to the Hitler Youth camp in Scheidt, as well as for weekend courses. Block loans were particularly helpful in producing praiseworthy statistics. Mein Kampf, although virtually unreadable, could be considered circulated if it went out in one of these group loans along with more popular books, even if no member actually read it.[24]

The extent of work with the group depended on the enthusiasm of the local youth leader for reading and the eagerness of the library. Schneidemühl, directed by Richard Kock, was considered a model. It pioneered the practices of group loans and participation in Hitler Youth lectures and developed formal guidelines for the selection of books especially for them. There, Hitler Youth members statistically accounted for 55.8 percent of the library's readership and 51.9

percent of its loans. The librarian at Altenstadt, a village in the
jurisdiction of the Bayreuth Beratungsstelle, on the other hand, was
quite happy to leave all young adult work to the school library.[25]

The work of public libraries with the Hitler Youth had one important and quite unintended side effect. Because work with youth
was given such high priority during the Nazi period and libraries
were under pressure to demonstrate significant cooperation, many
public libraries waived the customary readers' fees. In most cases
this was the first time libraries had dispensed with their fees on a
regular basis. It was a significant first step toward general access
without charge. Together with the Nazi affirmation that the public
library was to be tax supported, it marked a major shift in the basic
philosophy of the public library.

Young adult work in Germany made tremendous strides under
the Nazis. There is a sense of excitement and enthusiasm that cannot
be missed. Although the rest of the population might be completely
uninvolved with books and reading--as they apparently were in the
rural Upper Palatinate--young adults were eager to read, and librarians responded with equal eagerness.[26]

Young adults benefited from the great expansion of library
service in all forms. For the first time, young adult materials were
available in many rural areas. Nazi emphasis on youth obtained recognition for young adult work as a responsibility in its own right.
Libraries began devoting time and money to such work. Creative
programs and services were developed to reach youth.

At the same time this progress had its darker side. Young
adults were receiving such attention because they were prime targets
for influence. The spirit that infused library work was iniquitous.
Instead of serving humanistic and democratic values, the public library
served a totalitarian state dedicated to some of the most unsavory
and destructive principles the human mind has yet devised. Nazi
young adult work was the result of an all-too-successful accommodation
by the profession to a creed and program that were essentially evil.

References

1. "Deutsches Reich," Die deutschen Volksbüchereien ... 1933/34,
    p. 8-9. The category "young adult" is no easier to establish
    in German terms than in American. In compiling statistics many
    public libraries only used the categories "youth" and "adult."
    Youth probably meant everyone eighteen years old and younger.
    More detailed breakdowns usually distinguish between children
    and youth, the latter usually including those fourteen to eighteen
    years old.
2. "Die preussische Schülerbüchereierlass für Volksschulen, 1928,"
    in Die Schulbibliothek: Texte zu ihrer Geschichte und Theorie,

ed. Klaus Hohlfeld (Bad Honnef: Bock und Herchen, 1982),
p. 156; Christa Kamenetsky, Children's Literature in Hitler's
Germany: The Cultural Policy of National Socialism. (Athens,
Ohio, and London: Ohio Univ. Pr., 1984), p. 265-67.

3. [Heinz] Dähnhardt, "Weg und Ziel deutscher Volksbüchereiarbeit,"
Die Bücherei 4:1-5 (1937); [Rudolf] Kummer, "Nationalsozialismus
und Volksbüchereiwesen," Die Bücherei 1: 319-24 (1935); "Richt-
linien für das Volksbüchereiwesen," Die Bücherei 5:39-44 (1938);
Franz Schriewer, "Die Volksbücherei," Die Bücherei 2:193-202
(1935); Wilhelm Schuster, "Bücherei und Nationalsozialismus,"
Die Bücherei 1:1-9 (1934).

4. Otto Dietrich, Mit Hitler in die Macht (Munich, 1934), p. 135,
quoted in Karl Dietrich Bracher, The German Dictatorship, trans.
Jean Steinberg (Penguin Univ. Bks., 1978), p. 188; Schuster,
"Bücherei und Nationalsozialismus," p. 1.

5. Irene Graebsch, "Jugendbücherei und Kinderlesehalle," Die
Bücherei 3:357 (1936).

6. Tables 2-5, Handbuch der deutschen Volksbüchereien, 1940,
V. 6, (Leipzig: Einkaufshaus für Büchereien, 1940), p. 172-83;
Nordrhein-Westfälisches Staatsarchiv, Detmold, D 14, Nr. 149
Staatliche Volksbüchereistelle für die Provinz Westfalen, Hagen
to Herrn Regierungspräsident, Minden, 6. Juni 1939; Elfriede
Blister, "Was wird am liebsten gelesen?" Jugendschriften-Warte
48:60 (Oct. 1943).

7. Bayreuth, Staatliche Beratungsstelle für öffentliche Büchereien
in Oberfranken und in der nördlichen Oberpfalz. Files: Coburg,
Helmbrechts, Hof, Neustadt, Schwarzenbach/Saale, Waldsassen,
Weiden; Senat der Freien und Hansestadt Hamburg, Staatsarchiv.
Hamburger Offentliche Bücherhallen, File 13, Statistikzahlen;
Handbuch der deutschen Volksbüchereien, 1940, V.6, p. 182.

8. Graebsch, p. 364-465; Hiltraut Heiderich, "Das Mädelbuch in
der Jugendarbeit der Volksbüchereien," Jugendschriften-Warte
47:52 (July/Aug. 1942).

9. Charles A. Beard, "Education under the Nazis," Foreign Affairs
14:452 (Apr. 1936).

10. Kamenetsky, p. 55-56.

11. Ibid., p. 70-135.

12. Ibid., p. 119-35; Heiderich, p. 53.

13. "Grundliste für Schülerbüchereien der Volksschulen," Die Bücherei
4:221-23 (1937); Reichsstelle für das Volksbüchereiwesen.
Reichsliste für kleinere städtische Büchereien, 2. Ausgabe.
(Leipzig: Einkaufshaus für Büchereien, 1939); "Banned by
Hitler," News from Lothrop, Lee & Shepard Books, Spring 1986,
p. 6.

14. Nordrhein-Westfälisches Staatsarchiv, Detmold, D 14, Nr. 169,
Dr. B. Schladebach to Reichsstelle zur Förderung des deutschen
Schrifttums, 18.2.38; D 14 Nr. 185 Besichtigungsfahrt am 13.
Mar. 1941.

15. Kamenetsky.

16. Karl Hobrecker, "Die neue Reichsjugendbücherei," Das junge
Deutschland 27:252-55 (Sept. 1933); Kamenetsky, 284-94.

17. Max Wieser, "[Die Ausstellung "Jugend und Buch" der Volks-
    bücherei in Spandau]," Mitteilungen und Arbeiten für das Berliner
    Stadtischen Büchereiwesen, 1936. Reprinted in Volksbücherei
    und Nationalsozialismus, comp. Friedrich Andrae (Wiesbaden:
    O. Harrassowitz, 1970), p. 160-64.

18. Peter Aley, Jugendliteratur im Dritten Reich. Schriften zur
    Buchmarkt-Forschung, 12:35-41 (Hamburg: Verlag für Buchmarkt-
    Forschung, 1967); Franz Schriewer, "Leistungszahlen der Schü-
    lerbüchereien," Jugendschriften-Warte 42:49-51 (July 1938);
    Senat der Freien und Hansestadt Hamburg, Staatsarchiv. Hambur-
    ger Offentliche Bücherhallen, File 13, Tätigkeitsbericht vom
    Sept. 1934-Sept. 1936.

19. "The Law for the Hitler Youth, 1 December 1936," in The German
    Youth Movement 1900-1945: An Interpretative and Documentary
    History, ed. Peter Stachura (New York: St. Martin's, 1981), p. 180.

20. Senat der Freien und Hansestadt Hamburg, Staatsarchiv. Ham-
    burger Offentliche Bücherhallen, File 12, Rundschreiben der
    Bücherhallenleitung, Rundschreiben Nr. 2, 10. Jan. 1935.

21. Nordrhein-Westfälisches Staatsarchiv, Detmold. D 14, Nr. 169,
    Abkommen zwischen den Staatlichen Beratungsstellen für Bücher-
    eiwesen der Provinz Westfalen, der Länder Lippe und Schaum-
    burg-Lippe, und der Gebietsführung Westfalen der Hitler-Jugend.
    Enclosure in letter of Fritz Reuter to Lippische Landesberatungs-
    stelle für Volksbüchereien, April 15, 1937.

22. Vereinbarung zwischen der Reichsstelle für das Volksbüchereiwesen
    und der Reichsjugendführung der NSDAP, 28. Die Bücherei
    4:558 (Oct. 1937).

23. Staatliche Volksbuchereistelle, Detmold. Jahresbericht 1937/38.

24. Stadtarchiv, Saarbrucken. G Nr. 6419/1. W. Koch to Dr. Gaudig,
    16. Feb. 38.

25. Waldemar Wenzel, "Das Gesicht einer Jugendbücherei," Die Bücher-
    ei 6:355 (1939); Richard Kock, "Bericht uber die Zusammenarbeit
    der Städtischen Volksbücherei Schneidemühl mit der HJ," Die
    Bücherei 4:488-91 (1937); Erik Wilkens, "Vorlesestunden für
    die Hitler-Jugend," Die Bücherei 3:351-57 (1936). Bayreuth,
    Staatliche Beratungsstelle für Offentliche Büchereien in Ober-
    franken und in der nördlichen Oberpfalz. File: Altenstadt.
    Frau Schönberger to Staatliche Volksbüchereistelle, 28.V.42.

26. Bayreuth, Staatliche Beratungsstelle für öffentliche Büchereien
    in Oberfranken und in der Nordlichen Oberpfalz. File: Flossen-
    bürg. Uberprüfungs-Bericht, 24/25. Sept. 1942, I. Bruns.

INFORMATION TECHNOCRACY: PROLOGUE
TO A FARCE OR A TRAGEDY*

Carolyn M. Gray

> A popular Government without popular information, or the
> means of acquiring it, is but a Prologue to a Farce or a
> Tragedy; or perhaps both. Knowledge will forever govern
> ignorance: And a people who mean to be their own Governors
> must arm themselves with the power which knowledge gives.--
> James Madison, letter to W. T. Barry in 1822.

Information technology is transforming American society, providing expanded opportunities, and presenting new challenges. Recognizing the significant challenges these technological innovations present
to society and the library community, in 1983 the American Library
Association created a Commission on Freedom and Equality of Access
to Information. The commission was charged with the dual task of
analyzing technological trends in the production and dissemination of
information and of recommending policy development. [1]

Government information is among the eight major themes around
which the commission's recommendations centered. The commission
calls upon local, state, and federal governments to "raise library and
information services to a much higher place on the societal agenda.
Specifically because access to the full range of both print and electronic information technologies is so essential to effective participation
in a modern democratic society and a free economy," librarians must
assume an active political role to ensure that libraries are assigned
a higher place on the societal agenda. [2]

Since the days of Madison and Jefferson, Americans have recognized freedom of information to be an essential component of the democratic process. Freedom of information implies that access to government information shall be both unrestricted and free of charge. For
groups as diverse as environmentalists, scientists, librarians, labor
unions, human-service advocates, and consumer rights organizations,

*Reprinted by permission of the author and publisher of Information
Technology and Libraries 6:1 (March 1987) 3-9; copyright © 1987
American Library Association.

as well as private citizens, freedom of information is relevant. A lack of concrete information may have adverse effects upon the ability of any such group to bring about change, to conduct research and accurately report findings, and to advise the public of potential danger, or good.

Information policy formulated to support the basic principles and values of American society can help us examine issues in relation to (1) the stewardship and control of resources upon which we are dependent; (2) the organization of work in society; (3) the exchange and distribution of the products of that work; and (4) the governance of decision making. Citizen involvement in the democratic process must be based on knowledge of the workings of the federal government. Information policies that ensure citizen access serve also to ensure that decisions and policies will not be left solely in the hands of bureaucrats and interest groups.

As the Commission on Freedom and Equality of Access to Information found, it is becoming increasingly difficult for citizens to gain access to government information. This paper (1) reviews some information technology trends that relate to collection, transfer, and dissemination of information and the subsequent implications for information policy; (2) examines the roles of government and both the public and private sectors in information policy formulation; and (3) draws some conclusions to suggest a broad course of action for citizen involvement in information policy formulation.

Emerging Problems of Information Technology

"As a result of information technology, man's power over his environment will increase greatly and his susceptibility to manipulation will rise proportionately."[3] As a nation, we are faced with important policy issues related to developments in information technology being implemented by the federal government. As librarians, we need to involve citizens in policy formulation relating to the collection, transfer, and dissemination of government-held information through public awareness campaigns and other educational programs. Issues involved include the right to privacy, the freedom of information, First Amendment rights, Fourteenth Amendment rights, and the provision of information by the government.

Some recent developments illustrate the importance of addressing these issues in relation to information policy formulation. The free flow of information about the workings of the American government is being restricted by three trends:

1. the privatization of public information;

2. the reduction in the number of government documents printed; and

3. the subversion of both the Freedom of Information and the
    Privacy Acts by government agencies.

The trend toward privatization of public information is the
process whereby information gathered at the public's expense is sold
to a private company, which in turn markets the information for its
own profit. Access is thus limited to those who can pay. Citizen
access to public information is a right that is being threatened by
the very nature of the technology that has led to the "information explosion." The 1966 Freedom of Information Act (FOIA), as amended
in 1974, clearly defines the right to access information collected at
government expense. That right includes access to any document,
file, or other record in the possession of an executive agency of the
federal government (subject to nine specific exemptions).[4]

The following, taken from the March 1984 Congressional Record,
illustrates the trend toward the privatization of public information.
"The Patent and Trademark Office has signed agreements with private
companies for the automation of agency records at no cost to the
Government. One aspect of these agreements requires the agency to
deny Freedom of Information Act requests for the records in automated
form."[5] Another example of the privatization concerns the U.S.
census. Unlike past practice, the 1980 census data is being held
in the private sector, without comprehensive documents having been
placed in the nation's depository libraries.

Another significant trend is the reduction in the number of
documents put out by the Government Printing Office (GPO), documents that serve as important sources of information. According to
the American Library Association's Washington office, one in every
four government publications has been eliminated since President
Reagan took office.[6] Though electronic technologies promise great
opportunities, they carry with them the triple specters of monopoly
control, invasion of privacy, and limitation of access to government-
held information. Valuable public information services are being dis-
continued. Under the Reagan administration, information is being
treated as an economic commodity.

Americans have always viewed information as having public
value. One of the chief methods of insuring a free flow of information
has been through a strong nationwide network of depository libraries
dating back to the middle of the nineteenth century. Today there
are more than 1,380 depository libraries, with at least one being
located in each of the 435 congressional districts.

The federal depository library system requires that one copy
of each unclassified document published by the executive, judicial,
and legislative branches be placed in each of the depository libraries.
Depository libraries receiving government documents in printed form
free of charge must grant free access to these materials. No provisions requiring free access are made for documents published in

electronic form. Technological advances allow for electronic storage
and retrieval of information, intensifying the complexity of information
access for an open democratic society. Members of the library community have requested that the scope of the depository program be
expanded to include access to electronic databases created by the
government. Maintenance of "free" access to government information
regardless of the format is the key issue. In response to pressure
from librarians, professional associations, and individual citizens,
Congress appointed an Ad Hoc Committee on Depository Library Access
to Federal Automated Data Bases. The final report of that committee,
published in 1984 and entitled Provision of Federal Government Publications in Electronic Format to Depository Libraries, presents a good
overview of the issues, as well as providing specific recommendations.[7]

     The other significant trend affecting access to information is
the subversion of the Freedom Of Information Act by executive orders,
directives of the Office of Management and Budget, and the curtail-
ment of funds to federal agencies to support FOIA compliance requirements. Looking back over the twenty years since the FOIA was
passed, we see that its implementation has gone awry. When hostile
to a particular concept, an administration can subvert a law which
promotes that concept. Not until 1966 did citizens win the statutory
right of access to federal agency documents with the passage of the
FOIA. (The FOIA passed with broad bipartisan congressional support.)
However, agencies of the executive branch showed little regard for
the bill either when it was enacted or during the seven years following
passage. Congress expressed displeasure with the treatment of the
FOIA by government agencies and moved to strengthen the bill in
1974.[8]

     The 1974 amendments to the FOIA require agencies to furnish
information either without charge or at a reduced rate when the agency
determines waiver or reduction of the fee to be in the public interest.
Research shows that federal agencies have unclear or nonexistent
fee-waiver regulations, and in fact, that fee waivers are seldom
granted. For example, when the National Farmers Union asked for
a listing of payment-in-kind (PIK) participants and amounts of the
PIK commodities each received, the union was met with a request from
the U.S. Department of Agriculture for $2,284.87.[9]

     Contributing to the trend of fewer government publications
being accessible is the simple fact that fewer publications are being
issued. The Paperwork Reduction Act places federal agencies under
the directive from the Office of Management and Budget to reduce the
number of publications.

     Access to unclassified government information has decreased
as well. In a 1984 series in the Boston Globe, Ralph Gelbspan found
that, "the Reagan Administration, while denying it is pursuing any
formal policy, has moved systematically over the last three years

to restrict or cut off access to a wide range of traditionally public information."[10] Gelbspan cites three broad areas of concern: (1) the reclassification of previously open information as secret; (2) restrictions seeking to control communications by scientists under government contract; and (3) the noncompliance by federal agencies with Freedom of Information requests.[11]

Government agencies have gathered much informaiton about individuals. The nature of the technologies being used makes monitoring more difficult and increases the danger for invasion of an individual's privacy. Burnham, writing in the New York Times, reports that, "the Reagan Administration has sharply reduced the number of Federal employees working to protect individuals from improper use of public and private records, according to a report by the Government Accounting Office."[12]

The privatization of public information, the reduction in printed government documents with a related limitation on access to electronic information, and the subversion of laws enacted to protect both access to public information and individual privacy are trends that prompt this author to suggest the need for increased public involvement in information policy formulation.

Public Policies and Information
Technology: Implications and Consequences

The convergence of print media with the electronic media and computer technology is creating an environment that allows bureaucrats to limit the public's access to government-held information. There may no longer be printed documents for some types of information.   With the installation of word-processing, text-editing, and electronic-photocomposition equipment in government agencies, the creation and storage of government documents is becoming electronic in nature.

We must have an understanding of information technology issues if we are to retard the forces that can prevent the maintenance of an environment where informed, timely debate about critical policy issues can take place. One of the issues of policy formulation is the traditional economic conflict between equity and efficiency. The stakes are high for companies in the information processing field. Information entrepreneurs stand to make a good deal of money in the purchase, repackaging, and sale of government information. In the development of information policy we must develop a strategy that balances equitable access with the need to encourage private sector investment in information technology.

With the convergence of print media, computer technology, and communications technology, information policy issues become

critical to the maintenance of an informed, free democratic society.
The three-way division of power in the federal government has provided a system of checks and balances; until recently, a network of
safeguards had protected the collection, transfer, and dissemination
of information in American society. Regulations differed because of
the nature of the media and the development of technology. In the
past, the print media, especially newspapers, were separated from the
electronic communications media. Even with the emergence of broadcast journalism, there were still fundamental differences in the media
and healthy competition among them. The limited spectrum for broad-
casting dictated some forms of regulation. The Communications Act
of 1934 established the Federal Communications Commission (FCC)
that, in the public interest, was empowered to regulate interstate
and foreign communication by wire and radio. The fundamental differences between printed sources and broadcast media have been
blurring ever since the establishment of the first data communications
network. Ithiel de Sola Pool expressed this convergence in the following manner:

> No longer can electronic communications be viewed as a special
> circumscribed case of a monopolistic and regulated communi-
> cations medium which poses no danger to liberty because there
> still remains a large realm of unlimited freedom of expression
> in the print media. The issues that concern telecommunica-
> tions are now becoming issues for all communications as they
> all become forms of electronic processing and transmission.[13]

The consequence of doing nothing about information policy formulation
threatens the very fiber of the democratic process, because, "how
information is handled in this country determines, to a large extent,
the quality of the decisions which our people make."[14]

The Justice Department has estimated that the cost of adminis-
tering freedom of information requests was $47.1 million in 1984. The
administration has given this seemingly high cost as the reason for
imposing severe budget cuts for FOIA administration. The question
arises as to what taxpayers are willing to support to meet the public's
request for information through the FOIA.

For good or ill, the fragmentation of information policy formulation strengthens the role of private industry. We must develop a
mediated agreement between the varied private interests and the
public welfare in the development of information policy. Rapidly
changing technologies and the concomitant emergence of new economic
interests serve to create a diversity of interests resulting in a frag-
mentary approach to the formulation of information policy.

To understand policy directions for the future it is helpful to
examine some of the information policies developed by the federal
government in the past twenty years.

During the mid-sixties, issues of privacy relating to government-collected information came to the national attention with the Griswold v. Connecticut case. With that case, the Supreme Court began the process of developing a new legal definition of privacy. Nine years of Senate hearings, House hearings, and public debate regarding the invasion of privacy by government agencies ensued before the Privacy Act of 1974 was enacted. The development of computerized data banks by the federal government made potential abuses so threatening.

In 1966 the Freedom of Information Act was enacted under pressure for more open government. Amendments in 1974 clarified the scope of the act and the requirement for compliance by federal agencies.

The Paperwork Reduction Act of 1980 established the Office of Information and Regulatory Affairs and the Federal Information Locator System (FILS) within the Office of Management and Budget (OMB). FILS is intended to be used by federal agencies to determine whether data sought has already been collected. The act requires all agencies to have a senior-level official who coordinates information activities, including: (a) an inventory and review of information systems; (b) a check for duplication of functions within agencies; and (c) an impact assessment of the burden of paperwork for proposed legislation affecting the agency.[15]

A directive from the OMB, entitled Improving Government Information Resources Management, has as one of the stated objectives a review process to determine if federal information centers perform a necessary government function, duplicate a private-sector service or another government operation, and/or operate on a full cost-recovery basis. "The Paperwork Reduction Act has provided a framework through which information, broadly defined, is viewed as an economic resource to be managed effectively and efficiently."[16]

These are only a few examples that show the piecemeal approach to information policy formulation through laws, agency regulations, and directives.

The OMB review process is a policy that encourages, and even under certain economic conditions mandates, the privatization of public information. To eliminate duplication of services offered by the private sector, reviews have concentrated upon information centers of the Department of Education, the National Library of Medicine, and NASA and federal information centers of the Department of the Interior and the Department of Labor's Occupational Safety and Health Administration Technical Data Center. In 1982 alone, 26 federal agencies were targeted for the review process. No provision for free public access to the information once it has been transferred to a private sector provider is made.

Under the OMB review policy in 1985, the Securities and

Exchange Commission (SEC) issued a request for proposal for a pilot
test of an electronic filing, processing, and dissemination system.
The SEC is seeking a system to handle the multiple disclosure forms
that publicly held companies are required by law to file. These forms
represent some of the most heavily used information collected by the
government at public expense. The SEC has said that the company
chosen to run the system will be required to make a certain amount
of basic information available at low cost.[17] As in the case of the
Patent and Trademark Office, there is no assurance of reasonable
access to the forms by individual citizens or public interest organizations.

The Role of Government and Citizens

     No legislative action has tied together the laws and regulations
regarding the print, communications, and electronic media. The only
indication by Congress of a need for coordination of issues regarding
information policies that have been developed occurred ten years ago
with Senate Bill 3076, introduced on March 4, 1976, which would have
required that all reports accompanying proposed legislation include
an information impact statement; the bill was never passed.

     Public laws continue to bring into existence commissions that
relate to specific aspects of information policy. Laws have covered
privacy, wiretapping, electronic funds transfer, federal paperwork,
and the records and documents of federal officials. The executive
branch has responded in much the same way as Congress when faced
with information policy issues. Our government does not seem equippe‹
to meet the immediate pressures generated by technology and citizen
demands.

     Broad input into the policy-making process is desirable. "Our
challenge is to ensure that the changes in society, caused by changes
in technology, are consistent with the principles that have framed
our society for the last two centuries."[18] Librarians, along with
citizen groups, should take the lead by informing the public of the
problems and offering constructive solutions to the legislature. State
groups should develop model information policy programs, which may
in turn be adopted by other states, for the new technologies affect
more than just federal information. These model state programs could
serve to put information policy formulation on the national agenda.

     Taking into account the pluralistic nature of our political process
we must frame an agenda with two very broad policy categories:
(1) the legal foundation of information dissemination and access and
(2) the economics and management of information. An independent
commission should be established to coordinate activities, work with
Congress to create the necessary legal foundation, and work with the
private sector to resolve conflicts arising from competing interests.
The National Commission on Library and Information Science (NCLIS),

an independent agency that advises the executive and legislative
branches of government on policy, though having a more narrow focus,
has served some of the functions being proposed. At this writing,
the commission has an uncertain future because of federal funding
cuts. Given adequate funding and support, NCLIS could be charged
with the coordinating role of establishing a national information policy
agenda.

Congress must readdress itself to the issues of collection, transfer, and dissemination of information to ensure a comprehensive legislative approach. A broad information policy agenda is proposed in the
Rockefeller Report, which calls for the

1. formulation of information collection policies to balance
   governmental needs against economic, political and social
   costs;

2. establishment of principles that promote efficiency and provide adequate safeguards for the intragovernmental transfer
   of information; and

3. continuance of progress toward a more rational disclosure
   policy.[19]

Actions by the executive branch are shaping national information
policy without any rational plan or public input.

Despite the advances in consumer rights practices in recent
years, decisions on the consumption of communications and information still tend to be the exclusive province of the
bureaucracies--public and private--involved. At a time when
we need to take actions to strengthen communications and information patterns in this country through the end of the
century, an important element in the decision process is often
missing--the views of the individual consumers.[20]

The complementary nature of government and the private sector
can exist only through a spirit of cooperation that will lead to the
achievement of the overall objectives of an open information society.
Dizard proposes an information grid that will deal with public needs,
available technology, and economic resources. The information grid
gives the private sector responsibility for the development of technology in a competitive market. Society develops a set of social goals
to establish information technology needs. The public sector's role
is limited to providing fiscal incentives for applications of technology
to meet the social goals that could not otherwise be met on economic
grounds. Within this construct, the public sector must also assure
the availability of communication and information services. This cannot
be provided equitably in a competitive marketplace without the establishment of an information elite.[21]

As librarians, we must perfect our political and technological skills, so we may fully participate in the ongoing debates and help frame a rational information policy agenda to insure that citizens and politicians understand the importance of these issues for the maintenance of an open democratic society. Careful study of the recommendations of the Commission on Freedom and Equality of Access to Information coupled with an action-oriented response by the library profession is a constructive place to begin to frame such an agenda.

References

1. American Library Association, Commission on Freedom and Equality of Access to Information, Freedom and Equality of Access to Information (Chicago: ALA, 1986), p. xi.
2. Ibid., p. 101.
3. Theodore Lowi, "The Information Revolution, Politics and the Prospects of an Open Society" in Government Secrecy in Democracies (New York: New York Univ. Pr., 1977), p. 49-60.
4. Freedom of Information Guide. (Washington, D.C.: WANT Publishing, 1984), p. 9-13.
5. "Electronic Filing of Documents with the Government: New Technology Presents New Problems," Congressional Record House, Mar. 14, 1984, H1614-H1615.
6. Patricia Schuman, "Social Goals vs. Private Interests: Players in the Information Arena Clash," Publishers Weekly 226, no. 21:56-58 (Nov. 23, 1984).
7. Ad Hoc Committee on Depository Library Access to Federal Automated Data Bases, Provision of Federal Government Publications in Electronic Format to Depository Libraries (Washington, D.C.: Joint Committee on Printing, United States Congress, 1984), p. 10-14.
8. Tom Riley and Harold C. Relyea, eds., Freedom of Information Trends in the Information Age (London: Frank Cass, 1983), p. 54-79.
9. Schuman, p. 57.
10. Gelbspan, Ralph, "U.S. Tightening Access to Information," Boston Globe 225, no. 22:1, 20 (Jan. 22, 1984).
11. Ibid.; "When Scientists get Aid from U.S.," Boston Globe 225, no. 23:1, 20 (Jan. 23, 1984); "Reagan's Revised Information Act under Scrutiny," Boston Globe 225, no. 24:1, 16 (Jan. 24, 1984).
12. David Burnham, "Cuts Found in U.S. Work on Privacy Issues," New York Times 134. no. 46, 176:28 (Sept. 23, 1984).
13. Ithiel de Sola Pool, Technologies of Freedom (Cambridge, Mass.: Belknap, 1983). p. 42.
14. U.S. Domestic Council, Committee on the Right to Privacy, National Information Policy, Report to the President of the United States submitted by the staff of the Domestic Council Committee on the Right to Privacy. Honorable Nelson A. Rockefeller, chairman (Washington, D.C.: National Commission on Libraries and Information Science, 1976), p. 4.

15. Dennis D. McDonald, "Public Sector/Private Sector Interaction in Information Services," Annual Review of Information Science and Technology. V.17 (White Plains, N.Y.: Knowledge Industry, 1982). p. 88.
16. Ibid., p. 89.
17. Schuman, p. 57.
18. Michael Rogers Rubin, Information Economics and Policy in the United States (Littleton, Colo.: Libraries Unlimited, 1983), p. 312.
19. U.S. Domestic Council, p. 25-46.
20. Wilson P. Dizard, Jr., The Coming Information Age: An Overview of Technology, Economics, and Politics (New York: Longman. 1982), p. 134.
21. Ibid., p. 137-38.

ECONOMIC HARD TIMES AND PUBLIC
LIBRARY USE: A CLOSE LOOK AT
THE LIBRARIANS' AXIOM*

Stephen E. James

Literature in the field of library and information science has tended
to support the theory that public libraries prosper whenever the
country is experiencing economic stringency. An example of such
writing is an article by Murray L. Bob in the February 15, 1985
issue of Library Journal in which the author wrote, "The conventional
wisdom, not so much wrong as inadequate, is that public library
circulation varies inversely with the economic cycle: rising when the
latter is at ebb tide; declining when it crests."[1] In that article
Bob presented the results of a sociological study by Warr and Payne
in which those investigators found that, in England, middle-class men
are likely to report increased use of books and libraries during
periods of unemployment.

In reviewing the literature for their research Warr and Payne
found that during the 1930s book and library use among the unemployed in Great Britain decreased as those who had lost their jobs
became increasingly apathetic. In the report from their 1983 study
these authors suggest that, contrary to the 1930 findings, contemporary middle-class males reported significantly greater increases in
book reading and library use during periods of unemployment. The
investigators note that this increase in reading is an unexpected
finding, given the level of book use during the 1930s, and they sur-
mise that raised educational standards may account for the change
in user behavior.

Bob's findings indicate that recent circulation figures from
American libraries show increases in the use of library resources,
and that "unemployment remains relatively high by historic standards."
Based upon the study by Warr and Payne, and given the unemployment figures in this country, Bob writes, "we can provisionally infer

that the rise in public library circulation is probably due in some significant measure to increased unemployment..."

The purpose of this article is to present additional information
on this topic based upon an investigation of American libraries. The
results of this study demonstrate that there is still much to learn
about the relationship between economic hard times and public library
use. Because the data gained from the American study present
findings that are not supportive of the Warr and Payne results, it
appears premature to posit any correlation between the local or national
economy and user behavior on the part of American library patrons.

The suggested relationship between library use and economic
conditions has been discussed for more than one hundred years.
One of the first references to the linkage is in a statement made by
William Poole in his 1880 Annual Report from the Chicago Public
Library. In that report Poole referred to the decline in use of the
library which he associated with a revival in local business activity.
Later economic fluctuations in Chicago (particularly the depression
of 1893) brought similar observations as user interest appeared to
respond to the vagaries of the economy. More recently, in the 1949
report by Bernard Berelson (The Library's Public) it was stated that
libraries are used "less in good times than in bad" (pp. 129); and in
1981 Rep. Dale Kildee (D.-MI) is quoted as saying "It's true there
is greater use of libraries when the economy is bad."[2]

There is ample evidence from the period of the Great Depression
in America to substantiate the assertion of a linkage between business
cycles and public library use patterns during that era. In 1930
there were 6,524 public libraries in the United States and Canada.
Collectively these libraries owned 68,653,275 volumes. They circulated
237,888,282 volumes that year and spent $37,094,303. Viewed in per
capita figures the libraries owned six-tenths of a book per capita, circulated two books a year per capita and spent thirty-two cents per capita
in 1930. These relatively low per capita figures for collection size and
expenditures are offset by extraordinary increases in library use during
this period.

The American Library Association estimated an increase of four
to five million registered borrowers during the years 1929-1933, and
reported an increase in national circulation figures of nearly forty
percent. During these same years individual libraries across the
country were reporting record library use levels. Documents from
the Chicago Public Library indicate the belief that one of the first
effects of the Great Depression was to "increase book circulation
markedly."[3] Public libraries in Detroit, Indianapolis, Louisville,
Knoxville, Richmond, and New York all reported increased library
use figures. The Enoch Pratt Free Library provides a concise overview of conditions during the thirties: "While Baltimore's book-buying
fund was dropping fifty percent the public demand for library books
was going up thirty-seven percent--the latter figure being about the
average for the libraries of the United States during this period."[4]

Given this information it is apparent that the British findings
from the 1930s are not comparable to similar data from America. If
it is true that library users in Great Britain reduced their reliance
upon libraries during the years of the Great Depression, Americans
during that period appeared to respond to economic stringency in a
decidedly different fashion. While one can consider such variables
as institutional responses to the national crisis, differential effects
of national welfare systems, and other potential explanations for the
differences in patron behavior, the fact is that while England reported a decline in public library use during the depression of the
1930s, American libraries reported measurable increases in patronage.

With this knowledge regarding the assumed relationship between
American library use vs. economic conditions in the past, what do
we know about contemporary correlations between these factors? A
recent study indicates that the increased use reported by Warr and
Payne for middle-class male users in England could not be identified
in American public libraries during our most recent bout with economic
stringency.

In 1983 an investigation was completed which included twenty
public libraries in fifteen states.[5] The cities and states targeted
in this study were as follows: Atlanta, Georgia; Baltimore, Maryland;
Boston, Massachusetts; Chicago, Illinois; Cincinnati, Ohio; Cleveland,
Ohio; Detroit, Michigan; Houston, Texas; Kansas City, Missouri;
Los Angeles, California; Minneapolis, Minnesota; New York, New York;
Philadelphia, Pennsylvania; Pittsburgh, Pennsylvania; Portland, Ore-
gon; St. Louis, Missouri; San Francisco, California; Scranton, Pennsylvania; Seattle, Washington; and Washington, D.C. The purpose
of the study was to determine whether or not public library use in a
community increased or decreased as adverse economic conditions in
that community increased or decreased.

The research included the years 1960 through 1979, and the
cities designated were chosen for analysis because those were the
cities which composed the 1960 Consumer Price Index list of selected
metropolitan areas. This group of cities represented approximately
forty-five percent of the nation's 1960 population, and tracing these
subjects across time provided reliable economic data from a single
source upon a large segment of the national population. For a more
contemporary understanding of what these cities represent, this list
includes: all of the American cities with a 1980 population of one
million persons or more; eleven of the nation's thirteen cities with
Black populations of 200,000 or more; ten of the nation's twenty
most heavily populated cities; ten of the nation's thirteen public
libraries with 1982 book collections of two million volumes or more;
and ten of the nation's fourteen public libraries with 1982 expenditures
of ten million dollars or more.

The twenty years chosen as the time period of interest in this
study met several criteria: (1) A time period of sufficient length

to show economic and library use trends; (2) a period from which much of the needed library use data would still be available; (3) a period close enough to the present for this research to be of interest to currently practicing librarians. In addition, the years chosen for the study include some of the harshest economic times observed in America since the Great Depression. In 1982 economists Paul and Ronald Wonnacott wrote about those twenty years in the following manner:

> The history of the last two decades is disconcerting. The 1960s began with optimism and high hope that the Phillips curve dilemma [high employment and high inflation] could be solved with wage price guidelines. Yet the opposite has happened. Rather than move to a point of high employment and low inflation, we have gotten the worst of both worlds during the seventies. [6]

Because it was felt that national economic conditions would have different influences on different cities, and because individual localities would show economic trends unique to those specific locations, only local measures of the economy were used in the study. The chosen indicators of local economic conditions were the local unemployment rate, the local inflation rate, and a combination of those two commonly referred to as the Discomfort Index. Thus, "economic hard times" was defined as an increase in the number of persons unable to find work in a city, an increase in the average level of prices in a city, or the sum of those two economic factors.

In order to measure library use three variables were studied: book circulation per capita, total library cards in force per capita, and annual registrations per capita. These sets of data were chosen because each one measures an attempt by the patron to establish a library/client relationship, and it was this patron-initiated activity that was of interest in the study rather than library efforts to increase patron use of library resources (i.e., increased staff size, increased budget, increased collection size, etc.). In addition, these use statistics are routinely recorded in public libraries and could be traced through trustee reports, annual reports of state libraries, and other official primary documents.

In an attempt to avoid drawing conclusions from spurious relationships between measures of the economy and measures of library use the investigation controlled the effects of five extraneous variables which might also have influenced variations in library use. Reports from previous research had shown that total population of the city, book collection size, the number of volumes added to the collection per year, library expenditures, and staff size could account for changes in the measures of library use. Annual population estimates were calculated through straight line interpolation using decennial census figures as boundaries. Population data were then used to convert raw library statistics into per capita figures. Library specific extraneous variables were held constant over the twenty-year period of interest through regression analysis. The result was that the effects of the extraneous variables were removed from the final measurements of library use during the investigation.

The analysis of the collected data followed an eight step process: (1) convert raw statistics into per capita figures; (2) regression analysis to remove the effects of extraneous library variables upon the measures of library use; (3) correlation analysis to obtain co-efficients for the relationships between the local economy and library use; (4) calculation of averaged correlation coefficients to determine overall trends in the data; (5) t tests to obtain probability values for the averaged correlations; (6) repetition of the above steps using one, two, three, four, and five year time lags to test for delayed library use responses to economic influences; (7) multiple tests adjustment to calculate the p value for the group significance levels; (8) individual assessment of averaged correlations against multiple tests adjustment p value to assess significance of correlation figures.

The results from this investigation could be interpreted using either of two methodologies. The most strict interpretation of the data (that is, using the multiple tests adjustment) indicated that there was no statistically significant correlation between any of the tested measures of library use and the tested measures of economic conditions. There was, in addition, no evidence that the time-lagged data produced a relationship between these variables. In other words, the research indicated that neither unemployment, inflation, nor a combination of these two factors could be linked with increases or decreases in book circulation, annual library card registrations, or the numbers of total library cards active in any given year. Also, if the economy of one year was matched against library use of suc-ceeding years there was no evidence of delayed influence of the local economy upon patron use patterns.

It is also possible to interpret the data without the use of the multiple tests adjustment, so that the possible spurious results caused by 684 individual and 54 averaged correlations are not addressed statistically. When considered in this manner the findings are some-what different. This method of analysis reveals no statistically sig-nificant correlations from the zero and five year time lags. However, the following significant correlations are in evidence for the remaining lagged correlations: one year lag--a negative correlation between total cards in force per capita and inflation; two year lag--a negative correlation between book circulation per capita and inflation, and a positive correlation between total cards in force per capita and un-employment; three year lag--a negative correlation between book cir-culation per capita and inflation, and a positive correlation between total cards in force per capita and unemployment; four year lag--a positive correlation between total cards in force per capita and the Discomfort Index.

Using this approach to analyze the study, one can find no correlation between any of the tested measures of economic conditions and annual library card registrations. There is, also, no positive correlation between any of the measures of library use and the local rates of inflation. There are, however, negative relationships between local inflation rates and measures of library use. In other words, whenever the rate of inflation rises the evidence suggests that library use will decrease. The area of probable decrease will be book circulation, as opposed to the other tested use variables. The evidence suggests that book circulation requires two to three years to respond to an inflationary period. There is no indication of increases in circulation during an inflationary economic cycle.

There is an indication of increased library use in the measurement of total library cards in force during a period of increased unemployment. Therefore, when unemployment rises, the study suggests that public librarians should expect an increase in the total number of persons registered to use the library. However, there is no evidence that variations in local unemployment results in increased or decreased circulation figures.

Overall the investigation suggests that when one uses the most rigorous statistical standards no relationship can be shown between local economic conditions and the use of public libraries. When those standards are relaxed the relationship between the economy and library use is as follows:

1. During a period of inflation public libraries can expect book circulation to decrease beginning the second or third year following the onset of the inflationary cycle. Annual library card registrations and the total library cards in force at a public library will remain largely unaffected by the local rate of inflation.

2. During a period of unemployment public librarians can expect total library cards in force to increase at the library. This increase will probably begin during the second or third year of increase in the unemployment rate. Annual library card registrations and book circulation do not appear to respond to fluctuations in the unemployment rate.

3. When both inflation and unemployment are in evidence the influence upon library use patterns should be as shown above. There is no evidence of conflicting results from the multi-variate analysis over time.

It is not suggested that the results of this study be considered without the multiple tests adjustment. In the opinion of this writer the very best assessment of the data is that there is no relationship between the economy (as measured) and public library use (as measured). The data do not suggest that a liberal interpretation, using the multiple tests adjustment, would reveal a significant correlation. Interpreting the data without the inclusion of the recommended adjustment forces one to accept an unnecessarily high level of probable error; thus, the safest assessment is "no relationship."

If there is no relationship between the local economy and public library use in America how, then, does one account for the many reports of increases in circulation during the Great Depression? While a comparison of these two time periods was not a focus of this study, some possible explanations do occur when the two sets of results are examined.

1. The reports of increased usage during the 1930s are reports of "raw data." There was no attempt during this period to control for extraneous variables which might influence the findings in undetermined ways. For example, if the population changed from one year to the next this factor was not considered in the reports of increased use. Neither were changes in collection size or staff size considered in any consistent way. The reports from that period state in a straightforward manner, "... our money went down, unemployment is up, circulation is up ... there must be a relationship between these things." Because the data were not subjected to more thorough analysis, perhaps the assumed relationship between the economy and library use (primarily circulation) was simply in error.

2. An alternative explanation is that there may, in fact, have been a relationship between unemployment and library use during the period of the Great Depression, but that the nature of unemployment (and the unemployed) in America may have changed over time. Differences in the number and kinds of welfare aid, changes in the level of education and the resulting changed career expectations within the labor force, the increase in the number of females working outside of the home, and the changes in the kinds of work performed by the majority of American workers may all influence user response to the library. In short, an attempt to compare the 1930s with the 1960s and 1970s may be difficult because the conditions governing library patron behavior have changed so drastically.

There is the need for further research if the library community wishes to pursue the question of causes for the difference in reported findings between these two time periods. What seems apparent presently is that research results from the later dates do not mirror anecdotal reports from earlier years.

This study did not attempt to examine the demographics of library use; therefore, reports of library use by gender, economic status, education, etc. were not recorded. This was a study to examine actual library use rather than reports of such use by library clientele. Therefore, direct comparison between the results of this study and the Warr and Payne report cannot be easily made. However, it would appear on the surface that the American study is not in support of the study from England. Assuming that middle-class males were included among the total number of users of the public libraries studied in America, the finding of "no relationship between the economy and library use" applies to middle-class males as well as to other library users. It is possible that if this specific group of users could be isolated from other users of American public libraries they would show behavior patterns different from the others, but isolation of user groups cannot occur using the data from this study. Therefore, speaking in a general sense only, the results from England do not appear to apply to libraries in this country.

In the final analysis I am in agreement with Bob when he states, "...without an informed theory on the subject, intelligent planning of services, collections, and buildings is nearly impossible. Economic determinism may be as inadequate to this analysis as it is anywhere else. All manner of cultural and technological determinants come into play."[7] Although we have believed for more than one hundred years that the relationship between economic conditions and public library use exists, there is no tightly constructed, contemporary evidence to support that assumption. Even a rather liberal interpretation of the data reveals no increase in circulation during "hard times." If library administrators are seeking an intelligent method for planning library services, reliance upon the librarians' rule of thumb seems inadvisable given the results of this investigation.

References

1. Murray L. Bob, "Library Use, Reading, and the Economy." Library Journal 110 (February 15, 1985), pp. 105-107.
2. Dale Kildee, "Oversight Hearing on Federal Library Programs," Washington Newsletter 33 (April 21, 1981), p. 1.
3. Carleton B. Joeckel and Leon Carnovsky, A Metropolitan Library in Action (Chicago: University of Chicago Press, 1940), p. 50.
4. Robert L. Duffus, Our Starving Libraries: Studies in Ten American Communities during the Depression Years (Boston: Houghton Mifflin, 1933), p. 102.
5. Stephen E. James, An Investigation of the Relationship Between Public Library Use Patterns and Local Economic Conditions in Twenty Urban Areas: 1960-1979 (Ann Arbor, Michigan: University Microfilms, 1983).
6. Paul Wonnacott and Ronald Wonnacott, Economics Second Edition (New York: McGraw-Hill, 1982), pp. 276-277.
7. Murray L. Bob, "Library Use, Reading and the Economy," Library Journal 110 (February 15, 1985), p. 107.

THE FISCAL IMPACT OF PAY EQUITY*

Helen Josephine

For most working women, being in the job market doesn't pay. Women earn the most in professions where men predominate--operations research, law, engineering, medicine--but they earn less than their male colleagues. Women predominate in the low-paid occupations-- clerical, retail sales, health services--and yet, even in these lower- paid occupations, they still earn less than men.

Stanford University economist Victor Fuchs in an article on sex differences and economic factors concludes that "for women to earn as much as men they would have to behave like men with respect to subjects studied in school, choice of jobs, post-school investment and commitment to career."[1]

The major changes in public policy that would help narrow the earnings gap between men and women--subsidized child care, allow- ances for women who have children, comparable worth programs, and paid maternity leave--have not been fully implemented. Comparable worth programs are probably the most controversial. And, it is in the professions where women predominate--like librarianship--that the issues are most crucial.

Pay equity, comparable pay for work of comparable value, and comparable worth are all terms used interchangeably to describe the concept of setting salaries not by the predominant gender of workers in a field, but by the experience, responsibility, education, and skill required to perform the job.

What are the choices for those who have already invested them- selves and their education in a career in librarianship? How much does it really cost to implement comparable worth? How much does it cost not to?

To realize the full fiscal implications of pay equity, costs must

*Reprinted by permission of the author and publisher of The Bottom Line 1:2 (1987) 18-21; copyright © 1987 Neal-Schuman Publishers Inc.

be calculated in three ways to determine: the actual dollar amount
needed to raise salaries to equitable levels; the cost of litigation, back
pay adjustments, and possible union actions if pay equity is achieved
through legal channels; and the loss to the profession of the best
and the brightest as qualified professionals seek employment in other
fields.

The earnings gap between women and men persists despite
enactment of the Equal Pay Act of 1963 and subsequent executive
orders. The problem is the result of gender-based occupational
segregation and sexually discriminatory salary-setting procedures.
The Equal Pay Act covers only those positions where men and women
are doing exactly the same work but are being paid differently. Occupational segregation and gender bias in salary setting are much
more subtle and much more difficult to document. But their effects
are not germane to women alone. They are felt as much by men as
by women in librarianship because the wages of all workers in female-
dominated professions are lower than those where males have historically formed the bulk of the workforce.

Legislate, Litigate, Negotiate

The three main methods for achieving comparable worth are
litigation, legislation, and negotiation. It takes an average of five
years for a lawsuit to be heard by the courts; before any salary
adjustments are made, one side usually appeals the decision, adding
another three to five years to the process.

In those cities and states where comparable worth is part of a
negotiated contract, the time between the introduction of the concept
into the collective bargaining process and the implementation of adjustments is usually less than two years. Historically, when comparable worth has been legislated, the time between the introduction of
legislation and its implementation is also less than two years.

Regardless of the jurisdiction, the process of achieving pay
equity in the public sector has some common elements. The first
step often involves conducting a job evaluation. This kind of study
is frequently spearheaded by a state commission on the status of
women, or by a labor union or employee association. (The state of
New Mexico is an exception. There, $23 million was appropriated to
upgrade the lowest paid job titles in the state government workforce
without first having completed a job study.)

One of the first steps in designing a job evaluation study is to
set up a joint labor-management advisory committee to monitor the
process and review the results. The second step is implementation,
which usually requires that employees pressure management to accept
the results of the study and to negotiate for salary adjustments. In
some cases, litigation (Washington State, Los Angeles, and Connecticut)

and union actions (San Jose, California) have been used as pressure
tactics.

In general, comparable worth adjustments are phased in over
a period of several years. Gradual budget adjustments provide time
for program review and allow for changes in the implementation process. Further negotiations for subsequent adjustments can be made
once the contract term expires.

The Comparable Worth Project has estimated that 19 cities and
school districts and 37 states have initiated some form of comparable
worth action.[2] In many cases lengthy job evaluation studies were
performed, in other cases lawsuits or EEOC actions were filed, and in
still other cases labor union strikes were called or the issue was part
of collective bargaining.

Laws have been passed, court decisions have been rendered--
but are we any closer to comparable worth as an accepted principle?

A study sponsored by the National Committee on Pay Equity
(NCPE) attempted to assess the cost to public and private employers
of implementing pay equity; it shows that, for the most part, private
industry has adopted a wait-and-see attitude.[3] The NCPE identified
six private employers who have implemented pay equity as a result of
lawsuits or law-suit-related settlements and 56 companies that have
implemented pay equity as a result of collective bargaining. None of
the six private employers were willing to cooperate with the NCPE
study, and only one company representative of the collective bargaining settlements was included. Based on interviews with 15 private
employers, this report shows that companies are committed to paying
fairly as a good business practice only if they can remain "competitive"
in the marketplace.

The report also shows that in some instances, private employers
don't want to admit that a bias exists in their salary-setting policies
for fear of future litigation. Others are concerned about internal
equity--paying fairly within the organization, and external equity--
paying fairly in the context of the marketplace. Some believe that
comparable worth will be federally legislated eventually, but prefer
to achieve equity in salaries by fully integrating job classes through
recruiting and training of women and minorities. Overall, accurate
cost estimates for pay equity implementation in the private sector are
not available because companies are unwilling to share information about
salaries and salary-setting policies.

Led by women, workers in the public sector have been organizing and demanding salary adjustments based on comparable worth
for over ten years. The comparable worth issue made front page
news when city employees in San Jose, California, went on strike in
1981. After the state of Washington lost a comparable worth case
to the American Federation of State, County and Municipal Employees

(AFSCME) in 1983, and was ordered to pay back-wages as well as make salary adjustments, comparable worth became a well-known phrase. With less notoriety, Minnesota passed legislation in 1982 that included a timetable for implementation of comparable worth and a process for increasing salaries. And in 1985 the city of Los Angeles negotiated a precedent-setting agreement which used comparable worth as a basis for setting wages for city employees.

The Minnesota Example

The history of Minnesota's success in achieving pay equity begins with the studies and reports on the status of working women issued by the state's Commission on the Status of Women. In 1981 the commission became an official legislative advisory body--the Council on the Economic Status of Women--and included state legislators, representatives of employee unions and associations, and prior to 1983, the public. The pay equity recommendations made by the council resulted in passage of comparable worth legislation in 1982 which included a timetable and process for implementation. Documentation for the wage disparities came from a job evaluation system developed by Hay and Associates and the state's Department of Employee Relations.

The procedure established by law for making the required pay adjustments involved four steps. [4]

1. By January 1 of odd-numbered years, the Commissioner of Employee Relations submitted a list of female-dominated classes in which salaries are less than other classes with the same number of Hay points. Also submitted was an estimate of the cost of full salary equalization.

2. The Legislative Commission on Employee Relations recommended an amount to be appropriated for comparability adjustments to the House Appropriations Committee and the Senate Finance Committee.

3. Funds for comparability adjustments were appropriated through the usual legislative process. These funds were within the salary supplement, but were only used for salary equalization according to the job classes on the list submitted to the commissioner. Any funds not used for this purpose reverted back to the state treasury.

4. The funds were assigned to bargaining units based on the number of underpaid classes they represented. The actual distribution of salary increases was negotiated through the usual collective bargaining process.

Implementation of pay equity in Minnesota was phased in over four years by increasing the state's payroll budget by one percent

each year. Initially $21.7 million was appropriated to cover the first
two years. In addition, the usual cost-of-living increases were given
to everyone.

Inaction in Washington

In contrast to Minnesota's efforts, inaction by the legislature
in Washington has cost the state more than four percent of its annual
payroll budget to correct salary inequities. In 1974, the state com-
missioned a comparable worth study of 121 selected job classes. Performed by an outside consultant, Willis and Associates, the study found
that employees in classes where women are predominant were paid
about 20 percent less than those in comparable predominately male
classes. Each time the study was updated (1974, 1979, and 1980)
the findings were reconfirmed. However, no steps were taken by
the state legislature to correct the inequities. In 1983, nine years
after the completion of the original study, and only after AFSCME
had filed a lawsuit against the state under Title VII of the Civil
Rights Act, the state legislature appropriated $1.5 million to begin
wage corrections and gradual implementation over ten years. Workers
whose jobs paid at least 20 percent less than the average rate of com-
pensation received $100 ($8.33 per month) for the year July 1984-
July 1985. [5]

In September 1983, Federal District Court Judge Jack Tanner
found Washington State guilty of "direct, overt, and institutionalized"
discrimination against employees in the predominately female job classes.
Judge Tanner further ruled that the court could not adopt the 1983
action by the Washington state legislature as the appropriate remedy.
[6] In its appeal, the state estimated the decision could cost $838
million to cover immediate wage corrections to employees, pay adjustments retroactive to September 1979, and increased costs for pensions
and other benefits that vary with pay levels.

While Judge Tanner's decision was under appeal, AFSCME
prodded the state legislature into appropriating $42 million in June
1985 for implementing pay equity. After the judge's decision was
overturned and AFSCME decided to appeal, the state agreed to begin
negotiation. A $106.5 million settlement was agreed to on December
31, 1985--12 years after comparable worth was first raised as an
issue in Washington State. Under the terms of the settlement, employees in specified classifications will receive $46.5 million between
April 1986 and July 1987 and an additional $10 million each year there-
after through 1992.

Negotiation in Los Angeles

The struggle for pay equity in Los Angeles began in 1981 when
EEOC charges were filed by AFSCME alleging wage discrimination

against female employees in the city's salary structure. The union
did a preliminary study of salaries in 1982 which documented a high
level of sex-segregation and wage disparity in the city's workforce.
After a year of negotiation, the city and AFSCME reached an agreement
in May 1985 on pay equity adjustments averaging 26 percent over a
three-year period.

The contract includes pay equity adjustments for clerical classifications ranging from 10 percent to 15 percent, to be paid in four
adjustments: April 1, 1985; July 1, 1985; July 1, 1986; and July 1,
1987. Annual salary increases for clericals averaged $5,000 per year
and for librarians $6,000 per year. The salary increases cost the
city $12 million--one-half of one percent of its annual $2.1 billion
budget.[7]

The Cost to Implement

The costs of salary adjustments based on comparable worth vary
considerably depending on differences in numbers of employees, recommended adjustments, and the timetables for implementation. However, the overall figure is clearly higher if a lawsuit is filed and
employees are awarded back-pay as well as future salary adjustments.
For example, Minnesota's implementation costs are an estimated 1.25
percent of the personnel budget for the 1983-85 biennium, while in
Washington State, the cost for back-pay and current adjustments is
estimated at over 25 percent of the state's payroll. Implementation
costs for Los Angeles are .05 percent of the city's total annual budget.[8]

The costs of achieving comparable worth in libraries is similar
to those for jobs in other classifications. Most library employees--
both professional and support staff--are women. Wages in these
classes are 20 percent less than comparable classes where men predominate. Once established, comparable worth policy must remain part
of the salary-setting process or all gains will be lost when negotiated
contracts expire.

Pay equity adjustments are usually negotiated as an addition to
cost-of-living adjustments. In the public sector, they have ranged
from 14 percent (Berkeley Public Library) to 19.2 percent (Chicago
Public Library). Adjustments are occasionally made over a two-year
period ranging from 12 percent (Los Angeles Public Library) to 15
percent (San Jose Public Library).

Events at the University of Connecticut illustrate pay equity
adjustments in academic libraries. Librarians there are among the non-
faculty professionals' bargaining unit, represented by the University
of Connecticut Professional Employees Association. Library assistants,
archivists, computer programmers, student service personnel, nurses,
and other employees are included in this unit. A job classification

plan was first proposed in 1979 to create an entirely new system of
payroll titles and an equitable pay system. The study, completed
in 1983, was based on recommendations outlined by Douglas MacLean
in "Development of a Classification Plan and a Related Pay Plan," and
the criteria established by Hay Associates--skill, responsibility, effort,
and working conditions.[9]   After further adjustments, including
a review of library positions, equity salary increases were announced.

In July 1984, almost half of the library staff received an equity
increase; other library staff were reclassified or promoted. Most
increases ranged between $1,000 and $2,500, although some were
as high as $3,500. A total of 131 employees received equity adjust-
ments. The university's new salary schedule has 12 groups; library
classifications fall between group one, University Library Assistant
1 (starting salary $14,000) and group ten, University Assistant of
Associate Librarian (starting salary $27,026). Group ten also includes
computer programmer analysts and engineers.

To alleviate the problem of salary compression--employees with
years of experience but now at the minimum level of their salary
group--an additional $200,000 in salary increases was distributed.
Those with more than 10 years of service received 69.1 percent of
the total money available. In all, 130 women and 29 men received adjustments, with maximum increases of $2,000.

The bargaining power of UCPEA and the inclusion of all non-
teaching faculty in the same unit to create a larger base for the
study accounts for the success of the university's salary adjustment
and job reclassification plan. Helen Lewis, president of the UCPEA,
noted that during the scoring of library positions for reclassification,
librarians had to explain the nature of library work and overcome the
stereotypes and assumptions associated with libraries and librarians.
[10]

Based on prior cases in public and academic settings, we can
come up with a scenario for a comparable worth salary adjustment in
a large library with a total operating budget of about $5 million (ex-
cluding expenditures for acquisitions). By increasing the total operating budget by $600,000--less than 10 percent--the salaries of 200
professionals and classified staff could be raised. All staff members
would receive a $1,000 comparable worth adjustment added to their
base salaries, bringing salaries closer to comparable job classifications.
An allocation of $300,000 would allow for a $500 cost-of-living adjustment and a $1,000 comparable worth adjustment; or the implementation
could be phased in over two years.

The cost of not implementing pay equity is growing daily. In
most areas librarians are receiving cost-of-living increases, but these
are added to a base salary that does not reflect the education, experience, or expertise required in the position. The result is a continued depression of salaries for librarians. Increasingly, library

administrators are finding it difficult to hire qualified candidates, and enrollments at many library schools are down.

In Library Journal, Herbert White poses the question, "Why don't we get paid more?"[11] Although he is not convinced that achieving pay equity through legal action or threat of legal action is the best strategy, he does concede that "if the drive for legal solutions to our pay dilemma has a particular positive emphasis it is that it disposes once and for all the myth that we are paid so little because our employers cannot afford to pay us more." White goes on to say that while "nobody is required to hire librarians, or for that matter to have libraries ... if they do, then those with fund-raising authority have the responsibility for finding the money."

The responsibility for convincing those with fund-raising authority to raise salaries lies with librarians--we must work to change the perception of libraries and librarians. As White says, "We will change the perception when we take ourselves and our roles more seriously, and when we concentrate on economic issues just as other professions do."

Librarians are beginning to discuss the shortage of professionals in their field in articles and letters to the editors of the library literature. Librarians who once filled the ranks of children's specialists have found that other fields are now open to them, most of which pay $2,000 to $5,000 more per year if they invest in a master's degree. Catalogers, science reference/subject specialists, and business reference/subject specialists are becoming more difficult to find for the same reason. The special expertise required in these positions is liberally rewarded and valued in other institutions where the jobs no longer have the title of librarian attached to them.

As positions remain unfilled, what are the options? Will administrators tough it out until a candidate is found or will they, as White suggests, lower their requirements and hire whoever they can get for the salary offered? What must we do to improve the salaries of librarians?

As administrators, we should make equitable salary ranges our first priority. As librarians, we must bring the issue of salary inequities to the public and make them aware that attracting the best and brightest to library service is to their advantage. How much an institution--whether public or private--is willing to pay librarians is directly influenced by the value they assign to their services, which in turn is influenced by the value librarians place on their professional worth. How willing are we to make equitable salary treatment a priority for action?

References

1. Victor Fuchs, "Sex Differences in Economic Well-Being," Science

232 (25 April 1986), pp. 449-464.

2. Who's Working for Working Women?: A Survey of State and Local Government Pay Equity Initiatives (Washington, D.C.: National Committee on Pay Equity, 1984).

3. The Cost of Pay Equity in Public and Private Employment (Washington, D.C.: National Committee on Pay Equity, n.d.).

4. Pay Equity and Public Employment (Minnesota Council on the Economic Status of Women, Task Force on Pay Equity, 1982).

5. Helen Remick, "An Update on Washington State," Public Personnel Management Journal 12 (Winter 1983), pp. 390-394.

6. Pay Equity and Comparable Worth (Washington, D.C.: The Bureau of National Affairs, 1984).

7. Helen Mochedlover, "Special Issue on Pay Equity," Communicator 18 (May-June 1985).

8. Karen Shallcross Koziara, "Comparable Worth: Organizational Dilemmas," Monthly Labor Review 108 (December 1985), pp. 13-16.

9. Douglas MacLean, "Development of a Classification Plan and a Related Pay Plan," Journal of the College and University Personnel Association (Feruary 1968).

10. Helen Lewis, "Job Evaluation: The University of Connecticut Experience," Connecticut Libraries 27 (October 1985), pp. 1-7, and other documents from the University of Connecticut Professional Employees Association.

11. Herbert S. White, "Why Don't We Get Paid More," Library Journal 111 (March 1, 1986), pp. 70-71.

Pay Equity Resources

Comparable Worth Project
Center for Labor Research and
    Education
University of California, Berkeley
Berkeley, CA   94720

National Committee on Pay
    Equity
1201 Sixteenth St., N.W., Rm. 422
Washington, DC   20036

Office for Library Personnel
    Resources, American Library Association
50 E. Huron Street
Chicago, IL   60611

Pay Equity Trends
A National Newsletter on Pay Equity
    Developments
Hubbard & Reno-Cohen, Inc.
1810 Michael Faraday Dr., Suite 101
Reston, VA   22090

Part IV

COMMUNICATION AND LIBRARIES

THE UN-AUTOMATED LIBRARIAN'S DICTIONARY
--AN IRREVERENT AID TO FAKING IT IF
YOUR LIBRARY DOESN'T HAVE A COMPUTER YET*

Carol Hole

Are you one of the great silent majority of un-automated librarians?

Have you given up reading library periodicals because you don't understand the articles? At conventions, do you hide in the bar all day, afraid to attend meetings lest someone discover that your library doesn't even own a word processor? Do you blush when forced to divulge your ghastly secret? Have you abandoned all hope of entering the inner circles of your profession?

Take heart. To make it in the library biz, you don't actually need to own a computer. You only need to talk as if you do. The secret: use computer language to talk about the same old library system you've always had.

Who's gonna know, when they hear you bandying about terms like "kludge" and "baud rate," that you're not talking about a system so advanced, even they haven't heard of it yet? After all, everybody knows all computer systems are obsolete before they're installed.

This dictionary will enable you to hold up your head and sling jargon with the best of them. Just keep smiling. They won't understand a word you say, but they'll be too intimidated to admit it, and you can get on with talking to your peers about libraries without fear of humiliation.

-A-

Access time: hour when library opens.

---

*Reprinted by permission of the author and publisher of THE U*N*A*B*A*S*H*E*D LIBRARIAN,™ Consecutive Issue 56 (1985) 5-8; copyright © 1985 THE U*N*A*B*A*S*H*E*D LIBRARIAN,™ the "How I Run My Library Good"ˢᵐletter, G.P.O. Box 2631, New York, New York 10116. $20 for 4 issues.

Acoustic coupler: intercom.

Accumulator: patron who has 43 overdue books.

Algol: what Caesar said was divided into 3 parts. In public library usage, usually divided into: 1. Reference patrons, 2. Children's patrons, 3. Outreach patrons. Academic library usage prefers: 1. Students, 2. Faculty, 3. Staff.

Assembler: staff member trying to arrange a meeting around five people's schedules.

Assembly language: abusive terms heard during heated exchange at staff meeting.

Automatic interrupt: 1. what happens when you try to catch up on work. 2. a telephone.

-B-

Back up: condition of patron who got overdue notice for books he already returned.

BASIC: mysterious ickky substance on bases of steel bookends, which causes them to stick together.

Batching: lifestyle of single staff.

Baud rate: percentage of sex scenes in a bestseller.

Binary: place you send books to be rebound.

Bipolar: hire a consultant to make a user survey.

Bit: your last pay raise.

Bit slice: tax withheld from your pay raise.

Black box: malfunctioning copy machine.

Boolean operator: staff member who is constantly in the soup.

Boot: article given to obstreporous patrons.

Bootstrap programming: storyhour conducted without advance preparation.

Bottom-up testing: ordeal of Reference staff retrieving periodicals from sub-basement.

Breadboard: library board which controls funding.

Breakpoint: 1. maximum number of phone lines Reference staff can stand to have blinking at once. 2. coffee and doughnut time.

Bring up the system: to inject Branch grievances into discussion of Headquarters policies.

Bug: effect of problem patrons on staff.

Byte: 1. budget cut. 2. Tax paid to support a library.

-C-

Central processor: typist in Main Library Cataloging Department.

Channel priority: urgent item requiring signatures of Department Head, Assistant Director, Director, and Head of Purchasing.

Chip: object worn on shoulder by irate patron.

Code: disease frequently transmitted to staff by patrons, and vice/versa.

COM: condition of Children's Room when no children are present.

Console: what Assistant Director does for Director after budget cut.
Controller: Director's secretary.
Core memory: boring reminiscences of ex-marine patron.
CPU: warning that nonbathing patron has been spotted entering
    library.
Cross assembler: staff member attempting to put together new shelv-
    ing unit with piece missing.
Cross simulator: harassed Director pretending to be Reference
    Librarian during staff shortage.
CRT: to meet with editor of American Libraries.
Cursor: abusive patron.
Cycle time: period required to route a journal through all depart-
    ments.   Usually 3-6 months.

-D-

Data base: day library cornerstone was laid.
Data bus: day new bookmobile arrived.
Data capture: day the mad book slasher was caught by staff.
Data control: imaginary future day when Circulation Department will
    know where all the books are.
Data processing: day a book is made ready to circulate.
Debug: to remove insect life from box of gift books.
Decomposing: condition of paperback after 25 circulations.
Dedicated: basic character of library staff.
Depletion load: amount of work routinely assigned each staff member.
Development cycle: period of time from inception of new fad or trend,
    until LC condescends to give it a subject heading.
Digital system: to compute fines on fingers.
Direct digital system: traditional method of pointing out location of
    biography section to patron.
Direct memory access: method used by staff to locate information
    without having to break down and consult catalog.
Disk drive: campaign to retrieve overdue records.
Documentation costs: person-hours required to keep government docu-
    ments approximately in order.
Dot Matrix: former head of Tech Services who quit to have quad-
    ruplets.
Download: to delegate onerous tasks to subordinates.
Downtime: period immediately after announcement of next year's
    budget.
Drivers: bookmobile staff.
Dump: staff work area.

-E-

Error party: point at which % of books not returned by due date =
    % of inaccurate overdue notices sent to patrons.
Exorcizer: 1. one who attempts to purge dirty books from library.

2. staff member addicted to jogging.
External interrupt: phone call on outside line.

-F-

Feedback control action: to "load" the questions on a user survey
    so as to ensure "correct" answers.
Fetch instruction: overdue notice.
Floppy disk: spinal condition induced by unloading book drop.
Front-end processor: person who pastes in book pockets.

-G-

GIGO (Garbage in/garbage out):   staff comment on number of paper-
    back romances in circulation.
Graphics: to "adjust" a statistical chart so that it appears to support
    your budget request.

-H-

Handshaking: condition of Children's Librarians at end of Summer
    Reading Program.
Hard copy: non-paperback book.
Hardwiring: method of fastening boxes of new books so that Acqui-
    sitions Clerk is unable to open them.
Hardware: what patrons give to car repair manuals.
Head crash: nervous breakdown of Library Director.
High level language: style used in writing memos you'd prefer to have
    misunderstood.
High level programming: schemes thought up by Director. (See Low
    Level programming.)

-I-

IBM-PC: condition of main floor men's room after busy Saturday.
I/O packages: COD book deliveries.
I/O section: bookkeeping department.
Information retrieval: process of coaxing patron to reveal what he
    really wants.
Input device: book drop.
Input-output module: checkout machine.
Inserted subroutine: total screwup of system by hapless substitute.
Integrated circuit: bookmobile route covering both Black and White
    neighborhoods.
Interface: place staff heartily desires to punch abusive patron.
Interrupt priorities: staff pecking order.
Interrupt program: main activity of mothers awaiting end of story-
    hour.

-K-

K: character in novel by Kafka.
Keyboard: condition of staffer after typing 300 overdues.
Kilobyte: federal income tax withheld from your paycheck.
Kludge: unknown substance often found on covers of returned books.

-L-

Laser scanner: staff member eyeing sleeping patron.
LED display: spectacle presented by staff when asked to volunteer
   to work holiday weekend.
Linking loader: branch delivery driver.
Load-and-go: main activity of bookmobile staff.
Low level programming: schemes thought up by staff (See High level
   programming.)

-M-

Machine language: writing style found in most library literature.
MARC: unsuspecting Page about to be accosted by stack creep.
MARC record: to note fine owed on patron's registration.
Master/slave configuration: demanding patron's idea of his relation-
   ship to staff.
Memory: compact storage unit in skull of staff member with most
   seniority.
Menu: male patrons with upper-class English accents.
Microfiche: small fish in large pond: usually applied to Library Pages.
Microprogramming: toddler story hour.
Modem: polite term of address to female patron.
Module: new-fashioned staff Christmas party.
Multiminis: many story hour attendees.
Multitasking: Director's solution to understaffing.

-N-

Network: total amount accomplished.

-O-

OCLC: remark of visiting Librarian on seeing the Library of Congress.
Offline: out-of-order telephone.
On-line: where patron signs registration form.
On-line operators: telephone Reference staff.
Operand: what YA Librarian attempts to keep over teenagers.
Operator Interrupt: copier breakdown due to klutz user.
Optical scanners: eyeballs of staff member watching suspicious be-
   havior of patron.
Output: traditional method of dealing with rowdy teenagers.

-P-

PASCAL: famous author and inventor of early computer.
Power dissipation: participatory management as seen by administra-
tion.
Preprogram: story hour for three- to five-year-olds.
Printout: what patron should do on registration form.
Printed circuit: routing slip.
Printer: juvenile applicant for library card.
Program: in favor of metric system.
Prototyper: novice clerk.
Pseudocode: disease suffered by some staff on beautiful Spring days.
Pushdown list: stuff you'll get around to eventually.

-Q-

Queque: 1. checkout line. 2. letter after P.

-R-

RAM: method used by Page to wedge book onto overcrowded shelf.
Random access: what staff grind during gripe sessions.
Read time: 1. time when shelves are hopelessly out of order.
    2. commodity not possessed by library staff.
Reader: operator of traditional information retrieval system.
Real time: non-working hours.
Reentry: first act of unruly child after being expelled from library.
Relative time: period used by staff in taking phone calls from family
members.
Response time: lag between overdue notice and return of book. May
be indefinitely prolonged.

-S-

Semiconductor: Acting Director.
Sensors: book burners.
Shared system resources: reserve books requested from Branches.
Silicon: attempt by delinquent patron to convince you that he re-
turned 25 overdue books in book drop.
Slave: average staff member's view of self.
Software: usual condition of paperback covers.
Software stack: paperback rack.
Software support: magazine binder.
Stack overflow: what happens when building of new library is delayed.
Subproblem: difficulty caused by illness of staff member.
Subroutine: system of providing staff to cover for sick co-workers.
Systems files: shelf list.

-T-

Terminal: condition of Reference staff just before finals at local
  schools.
Time sharing: 1. giving up some of your staff to cover the Reference
  Desk on weekends. 2. staff gossip session.
Top-down approach: to keep one's place in a book by dog-earing
  pages.
Top-down design: 1. library organization chart. 2. typical library
  building design.
Turnkey system: method of securing library when it is closed.

-U-

Up: disposition of staff after pay raise comes through.
User friendly: fanny-patting patron.
User interface: confrontation between two patrons who both want the
  same book.
Utility program: power company plan for outage at height of weekend
  rush.

-V-

VDT's: symptoms displayed by problem patrons.
Videofax: erroneous author and title of new book which patron saw
  on TV, s/he thinks.
Visual control system: method of making sure all parts of library are
  supervisable from main desk.
Visual display: 1. method of holding picturebook so all storyhour
  children can see it. 1. usual behavior of library flashers.

-W-

Wand Reader: good fairy patron who leaves $4 million to library.
Wire wrap: personal phone call on work time.
Worst case design: 1. book with covers that fall off after two circu-
  lations. 2. scheduling two story hours at busiest time of week.

THE INVISIBLE DRIP ... HOW DATA
SEEPS AWAY IN VARIOUS WAYS*

Although certain forms of computer memory may be superior
to paper and print for long-term storage, information in a
computer memory remains vulnerable. It remains vulnerable
because it may exist in only a single copy or, with backup
capability, in a very limited number of copies. In this respect,
an electronic environment resembles a nonliterate society,
where the society's vital religious myths, literary creations,
and genealogical traditions may be preserved in complete
form in the minds of a handful of individuals. Just as a nonliterate society takes great pains to ensure that these individuals survive to pass on their knowledge to the next generation, it will be necessary in an electronic environment to
pay special attention to the protection and care of computer
memories. Otherwise, a single disaster could destroy a portion of the stock of knowledge.[1]

> May whoever steals or alienates this book,
> or mutilates it,
> be cut off from the body of the church
> and held as a thing accursed,
> an object of loathing.[2]
> --A popular Medieval anathema

As scribes we may assume that the action of inscription, be it on clay
tablet, marble, vellum, or paper, has permanence according to the
apparent durability of the material onto which we write. We have
always understood the nature of writing materials--that they must be
protected from fire, water, or corrosive elements in order that the
information they contain remain legible. In general, barring natural,
recognizable disaster, when we write we trust that our inscription
will endure of its own accord.

*Reprinted by permission of the author and publisher of ONLINE:®
The Magazine of Online Information Systems 11:2 (March 1987) 15-26;
copyright © 1987 Online, Inc.

The advent of electronic inscription has changed the nature of
committing thoughts to written words. Those words are initially represented as lights on a terminal screen, as easily erased as they are
produced. Their permanence is not as apparent, not as literal, as
it was before. With this in mind it can be chilling to note that many
of the most important of our documents including civil records, financial transactions, and government documents, are initially inscribed
not onto paper but onto magnetic media, and that some are never
converted into printed form.

The reason that this thought may prove chilling is the inherent
vulnerability of electronic data. While the conversion to electronic
information processing allows for far more facile retrieval, editing, and
storage, there remains a risk of losing stores of data through lack
of foresight in electronic information management.

THE ACTIVE DESTRUCTION OF DATA

Much has already been written on the active destruction of
electronic data, especially as it concerns electronic publishing. As
Gordon B. Neavill points out, "the malleability of information that
is one of the major advantages of computer-based electronic systems,
has as its corollary the potential transience of information. Nothing
inherent in the technology of computer-based electronic systems ensures that information in the system will survive."[3]

Since electronic publishing allows for information sources to be
produced online, it also allows them to be edited online. Online editing
can blur the distinction between editions in cases when an earlier
text never saw the light of day, and can cause bibliographic citation
problems in cases when an earlier edition was purged while the information contained therein was cited elsewhere as a source.

Further, online editing in electronic publishing has long-term
historical implications. "Because of erasures of electronic records,
future historians may know less about the Reagan Administration's
1985 arms control initiatives than about those of 1972 which led to
SALT I or, for that matter, those of 1921 which led to the Washington
naval treaties."[4] As a result of online editing of government documents, historians will also be denied the study of legislative processes
through the analysis of preliminary drafts of documents. To continue
the illustration above, we shall know more about the political phil-
osophies--those accepted for publication, and those rejected--behind
the creation of the Declaration of Independence than we shall about
key documents created in the 1980's.

Data are also submitted to "active" destruction due to lack of
archival storage practices. Just as a print publisher pulps unsold
volumes to avoid costly storage, so may an electronic publisher purge
unsold works from a database. The difference, of course, is that

such works may never have been printed or preserved anywhere.
Further, electronic publishing allows for the unfettered purging of
past issues of indices, price lists, and the like; and lastly, it allows
for data stores to vanish when a publisher goes out of business.
Repercussions of this loss of material span all disciplines of intellectual
endeavor including literary, scientific, philosophical, and historical.

The intent of this article is not to assess blame for the winnow-
ing of our cultural and scientific heritage. Nor could the author hope
to propose solutions to the questions regarding what should be retained and who should pay for it. The above examples are cited to
illustrate part of a much discussed subject in the field of library and
information science--preservation of the content of electronically-
produced data. This article is intended to present a very seldom
mentioned issue in information management: the lack of proper care
in the storage of that information, i.e., the passive destruction of
data.

Following a definition of the issue of passive destruction of
data, three case studies involving the long-term retention of machine-
readable data will be presented. Two of the studies, those concerning OCLC (Online Computer Library Center), and the National Aeronautics and Space Administration (NASA), involve the retention of
data on specific media: magnetic tape and compact disk--read only
memory (CDROM). The third describes the transfer of data from one
hardware system to another, as completed by the Research Libraries
Information Network (RLIN).

THE PASSIVE DESTRUCTION OF DATA

Poor planning and insufficient research on the part of information managers can cause data to disappear without our being aware
of the loss. In the first place, hardware dependence should be taken
into consideration. Will the data processed on the computers used
today be transferable to the machines put in place when equipment
is upgraded? Software dependence is another issue. Are we in-
sisting on the proper documentation and, if possible, the standardization of software so that fifteen years from now researchers will
be able to decode data? Third, we must be aware of the life span
and the vulnerability of the media on which we archive. Are we providing optimal conditions for the data retention, and are we transferring the data to fresher, or more durable media within an appropriate time frame?

Hardware Dependence

Hardware upgrades are common as organizations follow the progress of the computer industry's meteoric growth, and buy accordingly.
Such upgrades can have negative effects on the data that have already

been produced and archived, if old data cannot be read by new
machines. Much governmental material, for example, has a permanent
retention schedule, and so will very likely outlive the hardware on
which it was produced. This can be dangerous, as can be seen in
the statement that "by the mid-1970's, when computer tapes for the
1960 census came to the attention of archivists, there remained only
two machines capable of reading them. One was already in the Smith-
sonian. The other was in Japan."[5]

A second example illustrates how this problem might affect
smaller institutions. In the early 1980's, the directors of Casalini
Libri of Florence, Italy decided to automate their international book
distributorship by purchasing an integrated system from Digital Equipment Corporation (DEC). After two years of inputting and extreme
dissatisfaction with the system, the directors made the difficult and
costly decision to sell the Digital ensemble. They decided to continue
operations on an IBM 3600 with software generated in-house. Although
operations now run smoothly at Casalini Libri, the fact remains that
two years' worth of business records including bibliographic entries,
orders, claim responses, and client information, are effectively lost
because those data are stored on magnetic tape readable only by a
machine that the company has sold.

An even more pervasive problem lies in the unmonitored acquisition of microcomputers. As of 1983 there were approximately 18,000
mainframe computers in use by the United States Government, but the
Government Services Agency reports that "no one has yet been able
to estimate accurately the number of word processors and micro-
and minicomputers used by federal agencies."[7]

The government is not the only institution in this situation.
Unchecked hardware acquisition on the microcomputer level pervades
institutions of every kind, since microcomputers are well within the
budgets of small businesses, small libraries, or, in many cases, individual departments of larger entities.

Often one institution supports different types of hardware in
the same office. For example, The Bank of Boston runs half of its
central operations on Wang computers and the other half on IBM PCs.
In another more dramatic instance described in a 1984 issue of Harvard
Business Review "in one division of a major manufacturing company
the data processing budget is $25 million. Managers knew about the
proliferation of personal computers inside the company, but they did
not realize that the small, single expenditures added up to $14 million
and that there is a strong likelihood of unmanaged end-user investment and operating expenditures exceeding the central computing resource by 1985."[8]

In cases such as these, part of the problem lies in the fact
that data produced on one type of machine are difficult to transfer
to others. Another resides in the hidden costs of stand-alone systems.

Authors of the article quoted above note that "if software, extra disk storage, printers, modems for communications, and so on are added, the cost of $3,000 per unit may grow as high as $6,000 to $10,000. If the machines are incompatible with the company's main computing communications equipment, much of the investment may have to be written off."[9]

As a solution to the problem of haphazard microcomputer procurement, the authors recommend that managers form a policy for information management. Such a policy would emphasize coordination of hardware for all computing and word processing tasks institution-wide. This mandate also would describe the decisions which have been made about the "longer term technical architecture for the company's overall computing resource, with personal computers as one component."[10]

Software Dependence

Even more frequent than one institution's operating with a number of different computer systems, are cases in which one section of an operation might produce data on its preferred software, and another section might carry on with a different package. Should record keeping of the disks or tapes fail to reveal the type of software used to produce the data, even well-preserved data will be inaccessible without the software key.

A more technical, and perhaps a more profound problem involves software produced for specific tasks within an organization. Problems of accessibility may arise due to poor or non-existent documentation for software produced in-house. "Instructions for processing the tapes may not exist or definitions of the codes may be missing. In racial codes, for instance, B, W, O might stand for black, white, other or black, white, oriental."[11]

Prevention of missing or misunderstood software support material may lie in the establishment of library procedures by which a piece of software and its accompanying documentation should be fully catalogued and cross-referenced. It also may lie in the establishment of standards which would affect how software is produced. The recommendations of the Committee on Data Management and Computation (CODMAC) include clear suggestions that space science software be produced according to standards for "documentation, development methodologies, languages, protocols, libraries, and portability."[12]

That final issue of "portability" also deserves special consideration:

> The issue of software portability must be addressed by any group that sees itself in existence even five years in the future. Major software projects are a large, and necessary

expenditure that must be protected like any other investment.
Software must be derived in such a way that it is portable
across operating systems. This ensures the ultimate longevity
of the software as well as easing the transition across local
operating system upgrades. [13]

VULNERABILITY OF STORAGE MEDIA

Magnetic Media

Magnetic media, on which the bulk of machine-readable data
are stored, are susceptible to heat, sunlight, humidity, extreme dry-
ness, magnetism, dirt, cosmic rays, and accidental erasure. The
most common instructions to preserve data stored on computer tape,
for instance, dictate first that care be taken to keep the tape in an
environment which promises 60-70 degrees Fahrenheit and 50 percent
humidity, and second that the tape be refreshed by rewinding on a
semi-annual basis.

This type of care proves to be only part of that which is imperative for the long-term retention of data on magnetic tape. Other
safeguards involve constant attention to the cleanliness of the drives
on which the tapes are read, and necessitate the production of back-up
copies of data sets, all of which would be stored in a separate, en-
vironmentally correct, storage facility.

Following interviews with a number of tape managers, it has
become evident that there is relatively little concern with the loss of
data from, or eventual deterioration of, magnetic tape. Most tape
managers interviewed for this study seemed to trust magnetic tape
implicitly, regardless of the environment they provide for it. The
only exception was Mike Martin at NASA's Jet Propulsion Laboratory,
a person who over the years has had to reckon with much older tape
in much more critical situations than managers connected with shorter-
term storage.

The fact remains that even when conditions and refreshment
procedures are ideal, the nature of magnetic media allows for mishaps.
One such case involved the tape on which raw data from the Mariner
9 spacecraft were stored. After the 1971 mission was completed,
data managers at Jet Propulsion Laboratory copied the original tapes
in order to make back-ups, and subsequently found that after having
been copied the originals were unreadable.

No data were lost because they had been successfully copied.
Nevertheless, what originally seemed to be viable tape had a fundamental defect. If the tape had been archived and left unread for
several years, then occasionally rewound as is the common practice,
invaluable data would have been lost.

Further, even when the product used is of the highest archival quality, magnetic tape simply wears out over time. "The National Bureau of Standards has judged the longevity of modern magnetic tape to be about twenty years under ideal storage conditions."[14] The same time frame applies to other magnetic media such as floppy disks and magnetic hard disks.

Optical Media

Contrary to popular computing folklore, even digitally encoded disk media--optical disks and compact disks--cannot be expected to last forever. The National Bureau of Standards has yet to complete longevity testing for optical media currently on the market. Research done by the producers themselves, however, estimates that write-once optical disks on a twelve-inch format have a lifespan of ten years.[15] This shorter life expectancy is thought by some to be due to the action of writing onto the disks, which may destabilize the surface in a way that makes it prone to deterioration.

Much less concrete evidence exists to reveal the life span of the compact disk--read only memory (CDROM). At a recent meeting of CODMAC held in Pasadena, California, Mike Martin of the Jet Propulsion Laboratory suggested a life expectancy of no less than forty to one thousand years for the disk. He cautioned, however, that although we know the medium to have superior longevity, no one knows exactly how long the CDROM will last because of the lack of longevity testing results from both the National Bureau of Standards and from the producers.[16]

The reason for the long life expectancy of CDROM involves the fact that it is pressed from a master, forming microscopic pits on the disk surface, each of which represents a fraction of digitally-encoded data. (This impression of data on a surface, Martin noted, likens CDROMs to the books produced on the earliest printing presses, or, for that matter, to earlier inscriptions on clay or stone.) The result is that the pressing of pits into the disk represents a transfer from one stable medium to another, increasing the longevity of the medium.

It should also be noted that although optical media of any type do wear, they do so far less rapidly than other storage media. This is due to the fact that optical media are read by the passing of laser beams over the disk surface, instead of the scratching of a needle into a groove or the passing of a tape read head very close to a magnetic surface. This lack of mechanical friction can allow a disk to remain in very good condition even through heavy use.

THE NOTION OF TRANSFER

When so many vital records never take the form of ink on paper, responsible, long-term information management involves not only an understanding of the notions of preservation and storage for archival purposes, but also of transfer, due to the vulnerability of the media on which data are recorded. Records and tape managers must assign both retention and transfer schedules to data sets. In the case of vital records stored permanently on magnetic tape, the tape should be rewound and read at least annually to ensure its viability. Transfer to fresh tape should occur at some time around ten years from the date of the tape's recording, regardless of the amount of read time the tape has had.[17]

As is mentioned earlier, it is harder to predict how optical media will fare in longevity testing. Users of CDROMs, however, report excellent built-in error correction that indicates a disk's wear. By keeping an eye on the amount of error correction per reading, the user can judge when to transfer the data to another, fresher disk. For any optical disk medium, plans should be made and budgets set for periodic transfer of vital data to fresh disks in order to ensure that the data are retrievable and clearly legible through the years.

At the CODMAC meeting, in a discussion of data retention with one of the committee members, that member stated that probably 85 percent of the data sets being preserved by government-sponsored scientific organizations were useless because of the issues of hardware and software dependence mentioned above. Sponsoring organizations continue to allocate money and staff time as a nod to data preservation, even though those data are on the road to obsolescence and everyone closely involved knows it.

In this regard, the elementary notion of transfer must be further extended to its more important and more fundamental tenet: from the outset of the production of data sets to be retained over the long term, budgetary and data processing groundwork must be laid for the eventual transfer of data to successive hardware and software formats. This procedure will prove costly and difficult at the outset, but may in itself usher in, through acknowledgment of the necessity of retaining vital data, an age of standardization, and more important-ly, of accountability in data management.

CASE STUDIES

As mentioned in the introduction, three case studies will be offered to illustrate means of retention of machine-readable data over the long-term. These are practical examples, each with pros and cons--usually cost-related. These are not presented as ideals, but as common solutions to pervasive problems.

The first example, OCLC, illustrates one type of preservation of data on magnetic tape. The second, NASA's Planetary Data System, illustrates both preservation through the use of CDROMs, as well as

the philosophy of distribution of data sets to facilitate local research
and to ease the query burden of a central archive. The third, RLIN,
illustrates means of keeping a large database intact despite the upgrading of system hardware.

OCLC

OCLC and RLIN both serve as electronic catalogues to thousands
of users worldwide. Their databases comprise millions of bibliographic
records, stored online for consultation by contributing libraries and
other institutions. Most of these institutions have individual accounts
with such utilities, accounts which allow the user to consult and update their own holdings online, as well as to consult the holdings of
other member institutions.

All bibliographic utilities offer printed products such as accessions lists, shelf list cards, and catalogue cards, culled from a
client's subset of the main database. As time passes and as a growing
number of libraries close their card catalogues in favor of online
systems, the bibliographic utilities serve to preserve and publish their
holdings electronically.

The electronic publications with which we are concerned include
both the information available daily through telecommunications, as
well as through distributed services. These latter services allow for
a library with an in-house online catalogue to subscribe to tapes of
their own transactions (adds, changes, and deletes) performed on the
utility database. Such tapes are then loaded onto the local system
to allow for public access, circulation, and other in-house functions.
Because of the importance of their role as centralized custodians of
many different, smaller databases, it is of supreme importance to these
utilities that provision be made for the preservation of these data
over the long term.

OCLC (Dublin, Ohio), currently assigns a permanent retention
period to all of the data it stores. This utility generates two types
of back-ups to prevent data loss in case of a sudden, system-related
failure. First, OCLC generates system-wide transaction tapes daily,
sorts them in alphabetic groupings representing the first letter in the
client code (A-C, D-F, etc.), and files them. Second, it generates
periodic "upsaves" which capture the entire database at one time.
These upsaves also are sorted according to client. One copy of the
most recent upsave always remains on-site, in order that technicians
might start work on reconstruction immediately if the nature of a
problem allowed for it. Another copy resides in off-site storage.

Part of the reason that OCLC goes to the trouble of maintaining such a massive tape archive is its emphasis on customer service.
In the case of a client's losing an entire local database in one stroke,
for example, transaction tape retention provides OCLC with the ability

to reconstruct the file by sorting through the tapes compiled since
the beginning of a client's online activity. Another reason involves
the concern with reconstructing the main database in case of a massive system crash.

The keeping of such exhaustive archives necessitates a costly
tape management system, as provisions must be made for new tape,
for periodic readings, and for climate-controlled storage space. With
so many tapes in storage, it becomes difficult to tend to them in as
meticulous a manner as possible. OCLC tape managers wait five years
with no rewinding or cleaning before reading a tape for errors.[18]
No transfer is ever effected, but the older tapes are read periodically
to check for errors, in which case the data can be reconstructed from
other sources.

NASA

In order to ensure successful long-term retention and retrieval
of space science data, the National Aeronautics and Space Administration created the Planetary Data System (PDS), to be centered at the
Jet Propulsion Laboratory (JPL) in Pasadena, California. PDS managers have committed raw data from space missions to CDROMs, and
distributed the disks to researchers in the planetary research community. The project initiated its storage and distribution cycle with
the data transmitted from Voyager 2 during its encounter with the
planet Uranus in the early months of 1986.

Reasons for implementation of such a system reside in the history
of data management at NASA. In most cases of scientific experimentation in space, individuals or institutions are invited by NASA to submit proposals for experiments, and for the instruments which would
perform them, years before the launch of a spacecraft. After a set
of accepted experiments are incorporated into the mission, any data
transmitted from the spacecraft by the scientific instruments on board
are forwarded immediately on magnetic tape to the Principal Investi-
gator (PI) who submitted the proposal, whereupon those data are
processed.

In general, PIs are encouraged to return to JPL the raw data
tapes for permanent archiving, but the tapes do not always find their
way back to the Laboratory. Because of this, tapes of raw data
from space missions become scattered and are therefore inaccessible
for eventual queries from other members of the planetary research
community. In cases when the tapes return to JPL, some have fallen
prey to the problems of hardware and software dependence mentioned
earlier. Like the reels of Mariner data, they may have been properly
tended, but they can no longer be read.

The Planetary Data System proposes to use CDROMs instead of
magnetic tape for reasons of efficiency, of cost, and of expected

longevity. In the first place, making several hundred copies of
planetary data from one master proves far more cost-efficient than
duplicating reels of magnetic tape. Distributing those CDROMs allows
other scientists to review the data after the PIs have finished with
them, and spares them the trouble and cost of tracking down those
data on their own. Further, committing the data to CDROMs saves
NASA the cost of storing and caring for thousands of reels of relatively vulnerable and constantly deteriorating magnetic tape.

PDS directors are aware of the uncertain longevity of the disk
medium, but they are encouraged by the error-correction readings
which can be used as a monitor of deterioration. Data transfer to
newer disks remains a viable option. They are encouraged as well
by the other benefits presented by CDROMs. Of all optical media,
the CDROM is the only one in which disks and readers are being
produced according to an industry standard, set by co-developers
NV Philips and Sony.[19] Standardization provides the assurance
that the highest number of people will be able to view the NASA data
with the least amount of cost and inconvenience.

In addition, storage proves far cheaper, since one CDROM, a
disk 4.72 inches in diameter and less than one-tenth of an inch thick,
stores nearly 540 megabytes of data. For NASA's purposes, this
approximates the amount of data contained on five standard reels of
6250-bpi magnetic tape. A third consideration involves the fact that
CDROMs are not susceptible to heat, sunlight, magnetism, dust, or
to anything short of having the plastic coating peeled off. Hence,
the need for climate and humidity control in a storage environment
is reduced.

RLIN

A change of hardware need not be as traumatic as it proved for
Casalini Libri in the case cited earlier in this article. As stated by
Don Brown at RLIN, in a hardware changeover, data are seldom
actually lost. Any data can be reformatted, but usually at considerable cost. For a small business, this expense can be too heavy to
incur. For a larger concern, such as the Research Libraries Information Network, incurring expense to retain data is not only worthwhile,
it is imperative.

The case of RLIN, a bibliographic utility located in Stanford,
California, is one which illustrates the importance of standards. When
the directors of the institution decided in 1985 to change mainframes,
the massive database was transferred, in Brown's words, "by unplug-
ging one machine and plugging in another."[20] RLIN directors had
chosen to restrict their upgrade choices to systems which were compatible to the existing IBM operating system, and hence the switch over
did not necessitate any change in format of data, nor any adjustments
in protocol.

RLIN currently supports thirty-one member institutions and
some one hundred search-only users.[21] Brown estimates that one
thousand users logon to the RLIN system daily, accessing the single
file which encompasses thirty billion bytes of data. These data
reside currently in ninety-five logical disks, and are shepherded by
an Amdahl 5880.

In order to ensure the integrity of the database in case of a
disk crash or other disaster, twelve copies are kept on magnetic tape
as back-ups, each representing one week's transactions. In the case
of a serious disaster, the database could be rebuilt from the "snapshots" recorded over a twelve week time period previous to the cut-
off. One of these copies lies in remote storage. The other eleven
are stored at RLIN. After the twelve week retention period has
elapsed, the back-up tapes are purged and recycled.

While on the microcomputer level the struggle for standards
continues to wage between IBM and Apple, on the level of higher
computing capability, IBM has decidedly won the day. According to
Brown, the IBM operating system dominates machines of levels of computation up to but short of the supercomputers used in space and
earth science computation. IBM also takes care to ensure that operating systems are upwardly compatible. This fact accounts for RLIN's
having to perform no adaptation of data format or protocol upon the
purchase of the higher-capacity, faster Amdahl system.

Institutions with databases which must be preserved need not
be restricted to a certain type of hardware, as long as they are
willing to pay to provide equipment which can translate between systems. In RLIN's case, all of the telecommunications gear connecting
users across the continent to the Stanford facility is DEC equipment.
Despite the fact that this hardware was designed by and runs on entirely different specifications than those of the IBM or Amdahl, it
nevertheless communicates with those mainframes because of intermediary equipment which RLIN has installed.

RLIN maintains a dynamic database which stores the bibliographic
records for and provides updating services to library users each
working day of the year. Unlike NASA's data which are separated
into discrete and historically distinct sets, theirs is an ever growing
and changing single set. To RLIN, long-term preservation of the
database represents the stock-in-trade for the institution, hence the
attention to efficient and quick transfer of data through the choice
of compatible hardware systems.

CONCLUSION

These case studies represent three separate situations and
three different methods of coping with challenges of long-term retention of data. The element that they share, apart from the preservation

of data in one form or another, is a concern about balancing the worth
of the data being preserved against the cost of preservation.

In OCLC's case, we have a not-for-profit organization intent
on providing for any data-loss eventuality. In light of the archiving
burden OCLC has taken on and the costs it must incur, questions must
be posed about the provisions made to preserve the tape itself. Is
the current refreshment and conservation policy sufficient to preserve
all the data, or might OCLC be paying a heavy toll to carry dead
weight?

RLIN chooses to retain much less data. Twelve days of snapshots will have to suffice to rebuild the main database in case of a
major system crash. Their trade-off involves the risk of data loss
and practically precludes the promise of local database reconstruction,
but it does prove easier for them from both viewpoints of space management and of cost efficiency.

As Don Brown at RLIN affirmed, data are seldom literally lost
through hardware or software changeovers, but they are lost in effect when the cost of recovery becomes prohibitive. By the same
token, systems may be incompatible, but seldom are the cases in which
no hardware can be built or program written to effect data transfer
from one system to another. It just has to be financed.

By choosing an IBM-compatible system for their new mainframe,
the directors at RLIN circumvented the cost and extra effort it would
have taken to bring an earlier operating system into conformance with
a newer configuration. On the other hand the decision to choose
DEC equipment for remote terminals exhibits a case in which RLIN
was willing to provide for the translation from one system to another,
costs notwithstanding. RLIN has chosen not to retain data on storage
media over the long term, but does provide for the long-term retention
of data through its attention to system maintenance.

NASA's PDS combines the sense of scientific purpose with a
sensitivity to costs in its program to store and disseminate planetary
data. Downplaying the risk involved in committing a major retention
program to a relatively new medium, PDS directors focus on the medium's promise of longevity and on the immediate savings which lie
in reduced storage and reproduction costs.

In addition, it cannot be denied that one form of long-term
retention of data is the dissemination of those data. On a very elementary level, this is one of the reasons why off-site storage is
recommended--to provide for back-up in case of on-site disaster. On
a more profound level, though, it can be reasoned that the dissemination of information allows for its absorption by a number of different
people, thereby prolonging the information's life and its usefulness.

Producers of information in machine-readable form should

understand that data may well be destined to outlive the systems on which they are produced, but that often they cannot survive because of neglect. Should data be slated for long-term retention, therefore, from the onset of their production provisions must be made for maintenance through the application of standards and the employment of system-to-system transfer techniques. Further, data managers should understand the vulnerability of any storage medium they choose to employ. Standard operating procedure should include regular testing for error deterioration, particularly in the case of magnetic tape, which is subject to so many environmental adversities. Finally, the most crucial precautions remain the maintenance of archives with proper environmental control, and the transfer of data to fresher or more durable storage media as time passes.

ACKNOWLEDGMENT

The author would like to thank the faculty and staff of the Graduate School of Library and Information Science at Simmons College, Boston, Massachusetts for administrative approval of this article. Special thanks are extended to Dr. Candy S. Schwartz, a member of the faculty, for her boundless support and inspiration.

References

1. Gordon B. Neavill, "Electronic Publishing, Libraries, and the Survival of Information," Library Resources & Technical Services 28, no. 1 (January/March 1984) pp. 86-7.
2. Marc Drogin. Anathema! Medieval Scribes and the History of Book Curses (Totowa, New Jersey: Allanheld, Osmun & Co., 1983), p. 86.
3. Neavill, p. 77.
4. Committee on the Records of Government, Report (Washington D.C., March 1985), p. 9.
5. Ibid.
6. [omitted]
7. Ibid., p. 86.
8. Peter G. W. Keen and Lynda A. Woodman, "What to Do with All Those Micros," Harvard Business Review 62 (Septemer/October 1984), p. 144.
9. Ibid., pp. 142-143.
10. Ibid., p. 143.
11. Committee on the Records of Government, p. 87.
12. Committee on Data Management and Computation. Data Management and Computation (Washington, D.C.: National Academy Press, 1982), p. 10.
13. Planetary Data Workshop, Washington, D.C.: National Aeronautics and Space Administration, Scientific and Technical Information Branch, 1984, p. 137.
14. Committee on Records in Government, p. 29.

15. Meeting of the Committee on Data Management and Computation,
    held at the Jet Propulsion Laboratory, January 8-10, 1986.
16. Ibid.
17. Committee on Records in Government, p. 29.
18. Telephone interview, January 16, 1986.
19. Nancy K. Herther, "CD ROM Technology: A New Era for Infor-
    mation Storage and Retrieval?" ONLINE 9, no. 6 (November
    1985), p. 20.
20. Telephone interview. January 15, 1986.
21. Ibid.

Bibliography

Aveney, Brian. "Electronic Publishing and Library Technical Ser-
    vices." Library Resources & Technical Services. 28 (January/
    March 1984), pp. 68-75.
Brownrigg, Edwin B. and Clifford A. Lynch. "Electrons, Electronic
    Publishing, and Electronic Display." Information Technology and
    Libraries. 4, no. 3 (September 1985), pp. 201-207.
Committee on Data Management and Computation, Space Science Board.
    Assembly of Mathematical and Physical Sciences. National Research
    Council. Data Management and Computation. Washington, D.C.:
    National Academy Press, 1982.
Committee on Records in Government. Report. Washington, D.C.:
    The Committee, 1985.
Craig, Gary. "The Decision to Publish Electronically." Special
    Libraries. 78, no. 4 (October 1983) pp. 332-337.
Herther, Nancy K. "CD ROM Technology: A New Era for Information
    Storage and Retrieval?" ONLINE. 9, no. 6 (November 1985), pp.
    17-28.
Keen, Peter G. W., and Lynda A. Woodman. "What to Do with All
    Those Micros." Harvard Business Review. 62 (September/October
    1984), pp. 142-150.
Kesner, Richard M. Automation for Archivists and Records Managers:
    Planning and Implementation Strategies. Chicago: American Library
    Association, 1984.
Ledieu, Jean. "Commercial Introduction of Digital Optical Disk Tech-
    nology." Journal of Information Science. 9 (1984) pp. 209-215.
Murphy, Brower. "CD-ROM and Libraries." Library Hi Tech. 3,
    no. 2 (1985) pp. 21-26.
NASA Office of Space Science Applications. Information Systems
    Newsletter. Issues 1-4 (April 1985-December 1985).
Neavill, Gordon B. "Electronic Publishing, Libraries, and the Survival
    of Information." Library Resources & Technical Services 28
    (January/March 1984) pp. 76-89.
Planetary Data Workshop. (NASA Conference Publication 2343) Wash-
    ington, D.C.: National Aeronautics and Space Administration,
    Scientific and Technical Information Branch, 1984.
Schenk, Thomas. "Magnetic Tape Care, Storage, and Error Recov-
    ery." Library Hi Tech. 2, no. 4 (1984) pp. 51-54.

Trends in Planetary Data Analysis: Executive Summary of the Plane-
    tary Data Workshop. Summarized by Nancy Evans, Jet Propulsion
    Laboratory, Pasadena, California. (NASA Conference Publication
    2333) [Washington, D.C.]: National Aeronautics and Space Ad-
    ministration, Scientific and Technical Information Branch, 1984.

    Communications to the author should be addressed to Margaret
A. Cribbs, 267 N. Encinitas Avenue, Monrovia, CA   91016; 818/359-
0555.

LIBRARIANSHIP AND INFORMATION RESOURCES MANAGEMENT: SOME QUESTIONS AND CONTRADICTIONS*

Leigh S. Estabrook

The emerging alliance between library education and education for information resources management has seemed a natural one. The study of acquisition, organization, and dissemination of information that is the core of librarianship has been easily applied to organizations outside of libraries. Many in library education have come to share Robert Taylor's vision that "in a metaphorical sense we are moving from a Ptolemaic world with the library at the center to a Copernican world with information at the center and the library as one of its planets."[1] Whether one talks about librarians without libraries or information practice instead of librarianship, there has been an important shift in thinking regarding what librarianship is about--from thinking library education is "about" training librarians and studying libraries to thinking it is "about" information transfer in a variety of settings, including libraries.

This shifting perspective on librarianship and information practice may be understandable, but it raises difficult questions. If the way of thinking about librarianship is changed, what effect will that have on the normative values of librarianship? Is information practice simply a generic form of librarianship as carried out in different settings? Or is librarianship "about" something unique?

This paper seeks to address these questions by looking at one manifestation of library education's broadened perspective: the inclusion of programs in IRM (information resources management) within schools of library and information science. More specifically, it examines the professional bases of IRM and librarianship. Second, it explores the educational and institutional problems that may be raised in trying to reach a common understanding of this issue. Finally, it considers the implications to the profession of librarianship of a shifting perspective on information practice.

*Reprinted by permission of the author and publisher of Journal of Education for Library and Information Science 27:1 (1986) 3-11; copyright © 1986 Association for Library and Information Science Education.

The Professional Base

The rationale for the inclusion of IRM programs within library education derives from the largely tacit assumption that IRM and librarianship share a common theoretical and practical base. Both are concerned primarily with problems of information transfer, and each addresses information use and information users. The emphases of the two have differed, but each is learning from the other. Costing models from IRM can be applied effectively in libraries. Librarians' understanding of the relationship between information resources and information users has enhanced the more technical model of IRM. Although the two fields have been distinguished conceptually, the practical understanding of their difference is based on the fact that their practitioners tend to work in different areas--librarians in libraries; information resource managers in the managerial hierarchy, technical information centers, or other locations not viewed as libraries. Librarians more commonly work with bibliographic records and information retrieval, information resource managers with records and database management. These differences can be attributed more to the evolution of each field than to differences between them in technique. The focus and context of practice are different, not the content. It seems possible that as IRM matures within organizations and as librarianship expands its domain, the two areas will increasingly look alike. At Columbia University, for example, a task force has recommended a transition to an electronic university that will link computer, communications, and information processing systems (including those functions traditionally regarded as in the domain of the library).[2]

There is, however, another important difference--one also related to the nature of each occupational group. Libraries may be only one sort of organization among many in which information transfer occurs, but librarianship as a profession represents certain approaches toward information and its users that are not necessarily taken by all who work with information resources.

Throughout their history, librarians as a professional group and as portrayed to the public[3] have held to the position that information is a public good to which free access is essential. Current evidence of that commitment can be seen in the American Library Association's ongoing work Less Access to Less Information by and about Government.[4] Less Access--a chronicle of U.S. government policies toward information--is just one manifestation of ALA's long-standing position that there should be equal access to any information collected and published by the U.S. government.

This ongoing series of ALA reports is particularly important for understanding the difference between librarianship and IRM, for it is severely critical of policies growing out of the Federal Paperwork Reduction Act, an act designed "to reduce paperwork and enhance the economy and efficiency of the Government and the private sector by improving Federal information policymaking, and for other purposes" (PL 96-511).

This act directed the Office of Management and Budget to establish the Office of Information and Regulatory Affairs (OIRA) and required each federal agency to appoint an administrator responsible for, among other things, "developing and implementing uniform and consistent information resources management policies and overseeing the development of information management principles, standards and guidelines promoting their use" (44 USC 3504).

Information resources management did not originate with this act, but it was clearly christened by it, and the federal mandate for IRM has had a wide impact. The graduate school within the Department of Agriculture trains employees in information resources management as part of a commitment to implementing the principles of IRM throughout the department. The position of systems manager at U.S. embassies abroad, previously defined as having primary responsibility for "keeping the machines running," is evolving into a managerial role with responsibility for all types of data resources, not just computer hardware operation.[5] Within the private sector, Exxon has been perhaps the most visible in its appointment of an information resources manager.[6] Banks, public utilities, and other organizations with heavy capital and labor investment in information-handling activities are becoming committed to IRM.

The primary purpose of information resources management within the government and as it has evolved in other organizations is to treat information in a cost-effective manner. Citing the immense costs of information handling in organizations--costs that are usually absorbed into overhead--proponents of IRM insist that information must be recognized as an organizational resource parallel to natural, human, and capital resources. As such, it should be subject to similar formal controls such as budgeting and accounting. It is precisely these activities that concern librarians and others committed to access to information. Management of information resources within the federal government, in particular, has led to a reduction of information produced for and available to the public. A Washington Post article reported, for example, that "over 900 government publications have been or will be eliminated" with an expected savings of millions of dollars.[7] Librarians are among the more outspoken groups who express fear that information resources management will be equated with management of information, i.e., control over what information will be made available. Information policy will be decided by those responsible for managing the resources.

Forest W. Horton, the director of the Information Management Study for the Commission on Federal Paperwork, shaped the Paperwork Reduction Act and the concept of IRM. Horton is responsible for major writings in IRM,[8] and his energy and vision have directed the development of the field. Horton insists on the distinction between information resources management and management of information, and he notes: "...I believe I share the very real concern that 'managing information' may be viewed by some under certain conditions

as a threat to personal freedoms, a constraint to creative work, or
a barrier to the free flow of ideas in our democratic society. Information is indeed power, and the line between 'managing information'
and 'manipulating information' easily becomes blurred."[9]

This statement is important. It would be a mistake to set up a
straw man and argue that information resource managers are in favor
of limiting access to information--in an ideal sense proponents of IRM
are not. Nor would it be correct to say that librarians oppose cost-
effective delivery of library services. The difference between librarianship and IRM is not that one favors access while the other supports
cost effectiveness; rather, the difference lies in the priorities of each
occupational group. Librarianship's principal professional concern is
access to information; IRM's is cost efficiency in managing information
resources.

There are other important differences between the two as formal
occupational groups. The argument about whether librarianship is
a profession does not have to be settled to recognize that the occupation of librarianship is well organized. Examples of this may be
found in librarian's insistence on the M.L.S. as the accepted credential
for holders of a professional library job, in the efforts of ALA's Washington Office to effect legislation favorable to libraries and the values
held by the library profession, and in the association's accreditation
of M.L.S. programs. The battle to achieve recognition and appropriate status for librarians as information professionals has been difficult and often frustrating. It does, however, have a shape and
history. Institutions such as ALA and ALISE are in place. However
rapidly the library field is changing, those who are members of it
can draw on a long history and a social cohesion that allows them to
identify with one another. Although librarians are identified with
the institutions by which they are employed, their affiliation with one
another is a source of independence from the specific workplace.

Information resources managers have little such independence.
The professional associations[10] to which these individuals belong have
relatively small memberships. If IRM is a separate occupational group,
then it is a profession in utero. Professional norms and values are
more dependent on the specific goals of the organization in which the
manager works than on some external vision of what IRM should be.
There is no accrediting body, no commonly accepted credential, and
no clear boundary around the occupation. Students who enter these
programs often have only a vague notion about what they are committing themselves to. Even if some library school students come with
little more reason than the standard, "I love books and people,"
most have at least a mental representation of a library. Even those
who teach IRM may have problems in visualizing its practice except
in an ideal sense. At present, IRM practices differ widely from organization to organization, and there is no straightforward career
path. These differences in the professional development of librarianship and IRM can be expected to raise important educational and institutional issues within schools of library and information science.

Educational and Institutional Issues

A recent sociological analysis of professionalization, Magali Sar-fatti Larson's Rise of Professionalism, demonstrates that occupational groups work to achieve two ends: "monopoly of expertise in the market [and] monopoly of status in a system of stratification."[11] An examination of the process of professionalization to achieve these ends reveals some of the contradictions that may be encountered in including IRM within graduate schools of library and information science.

Professional education is one dimension of a profession's working to enhance and maintain its monopoly of expertise and status. Without devaluing the important intellectual convergence between librarianship and IRM, the expansion of librarianship can be viewed as part of the process to attain a greater role in information practice. Librarians' expertise in acquisition, organization, and dissemination of information and their knowledge of information retrieval and database management are enhanced when linked to work in systems analysis, records management, database design, and a host of other functions that have become the domain of IRM. Librarians are able both to demonstrate the usefulness of "traditional" library expertise and to expand their market position through this affiliation. Not insignificantly, the addition of a program in IRM may also be seen as a way to enhance the status of librarianship. As a federally mandated function--one that is also highly valued in the private sector--information resources management has a certain cachet. And in this instance, the lack of history may also be advantageous. No stereotyped model of the information resources manager has yet been set.

The fact cannot be ignored that the move to education for IRM by library and information science educators has pragmatic benefits. It came at a time in the late 1970s when library school enrollments were declining, when funds for library services were becoming more restricted, and when the survival of library education was threatened in many institutions. Educating students for IRM is a better strategic way to reposition library schools in the market than to attempt to change the way in which librarians are perceived in society. It is better because IRM does have the sanction from federal policy--it is quicker because there is a substantive relationship between librarianship and IRM. There may be hidden costs in the association.

Professional education is more than the transmission of skills. It also involves acculturating students into professional norms and values through examination of the profession's history, social function, and ideals. Any good academic discussion is bound to involve some argument about exactly what those values are. That argument is appropriate in academia and is part of the challenge and fun of education. There are risks in such a debate, however, when the profession about which one is arguing is in formation. A recent class discussion exemplifies the problem.[12]

During a lecture on costing information services, the instructor
made the point that information centers are frequently expected to
become "profit centers" by their organizations. This led to an analysis of the ways those information centers could price their services
to achieve the expected profit margin. Toward the end of the lecture,
the instructor exclaimed, "But this goes against everything I believe
about the importance of public access to information!" At the end
of class, one of the brighter students said privately, "Does your
statement mean that I shouldn't go into IRM?" The student seemed
unable to question certain aspects of IRM without questioning the
entire profession of information resources management.

The embryonic nature of IRM makes it difficult for students to
face unresolved philosophical questions. It is frightening to students
to enter a professional school and be confronted with fundamental
questions about that profession when they themselves are filled with
uncertainties. The deep historical tradition of librarianship is an
essential condition for passionate arguments about philosophical issues
such as user fees, censorship, or even professionalization. Students
and faculty alike share uncertainties about the directions in which
information resources management will develop. The boundaries are
not drawn. To question fundamental issues such as whether information centers should be profit centers is psychologically difficult because the principles for IRM practice that might provide a framework
for analysis have not been developed. By definition IRM cannot be
faulted for placing cost-effectiveness as its highest priority. Even
a reasoned conclusion that priorities should be changed is unlikely
to affect its actual practice. Faculty may, in some cases, find it
necessary to defer to the norms of the profession for which they are
educating students and as a result may encounter significant role
conflict in trying to exercise their responsibility for creating a new
profession.

Students at library schools have been recruited to a program--
a program that in some respects the faculty and dean must "sell."
As a developing profession, IRM is not only created from the outside
by those who recognize its importance (e.g., Horton) but is also
shaped by members of professional schools who develop curricula,
foster relationships with potential employers, and shape student expectations of the types of jobs they should seek. If library educators
are uncertain about IRM at this formative point in its development
they may undermine its growth either by deterring good students
from entering a program or by making employers question its value.
Alternatively, uncertainty about the relationship between information
resources management and librarianship may threaten the claim of
schools of library and information science to the appropriateness of
including education for information resources management with their
domain. The personal and professional tensions that result from these
dynamics are difficult to confront openly, but may well have an effect
on the evolution of the profession of librarianship.

The Profession(s)

The common way of identifying a profession is by looking at an occupation's claim to expertise, its theoretical body of knowledge, advanced training, code of ethics, etc. It has been argued that the distinction between librarians and information resource managers lies principally in their differing priorities for information practice. The question then arises: are we working with one profession or two? Either librarians and information resource managers must be viewed as members of two different occupational groups, or, if one, the differing value systems of the two must be worked through.

Larson argues that

> Alternative standards and alternative definitions of professional
> morality and worth do, in fact, loosen the grip that the tacit
> and explicit norms of a discipline or profession have on the
> self. This is the significance of dissenting groups or move-
> ments within a profession: while the entrenched elites always
> tend to rule them out as "unprofessional," these groups gen-
> erate their own norms and solidarity. They may arise out of
> an effort to gain recognition for a new specialty, or out of
> full-fledged "paradigmatic battles," or out of the challenge to
> a profession's notion of its social function. [13]

If it is correct to talk about the information profession, then the philosophical differences about access and cost-effectiveness may be seen as representative of a dissenting movement within librarian-ship. Arguments about what is meant by a commitment to access pre-exist the development of the profession of information resources man-agement. These arguments have focused on such questions as chil-dren's rights to adult materials and librarians' handling of proprietary materials. It may even be argued that rhetoric about librarians' commitment to access may often be just that: rhetoric. It may in many cases be boilerplate or commencement oratory. Special librarians who work for the private sector, in particular, have been led to ex-clude proprietary information or information that is seen as a market-able product from the category of material that should be freely avail-able. The philosophical split within the profession seems to have been dealt with primarily by treating librarians who work in the for-profit sector as a group whose norms are mandated by organizations of which they are a part.

If this split is, in fact, representative of a deeper internal battle within one occupational group, evidence suggests that those who hold to the philosophical position that cost-effectiveness must be the highest priority will become increasingly powerful. As noted, information resource managers do not at present have much profession-al independence from the organizations in which they work, and those responsible for IRM's development are concerned about enhancing its status and market position. It is unlikely that members of this group will be able to compromise their philosophical priorities without losing their claim to being information resource managers.

Alternatively, if the different normative positions are understood to be the distinguishing characteristics of two separate professions, the definition of profession is challenged. IRM, special librarianship, and all forms of information practice as it is evolving share many of the attributes of a profession.

It may be difficult and sometimes inappropriate for those who teach IRM within schools of library and information science to address this problem with their students. It may be difficult, but it is not inappropriate to address it with professional colleagues. On the basis of some general understanding of what a profession is and what librarianship is fundamentally "about," it is necessary to answer the question of whether we are one profession or two.

References

1. Estabrook, L. S., ed.: Libraries in Post-Industrial Society (Phoenix, Ariz.: Oryx Pr., 1977). p. xix.
2. Columbia University Task Force on Information Processing: "Final Report," Apr. 20, 1984, mimeo.
3. See for example, "Librarians Rally the Troops to Battle U.S. on Information," New York Times, Apr. 8, 1985.
4. American Library Association: Less Access to Less Information by and about the U.S. Government: V. (Washington D.C.: American Library Assn., Dec. 1984).
5. Estabrook, L. S.: Systems Management in the Foreign Service. 1983. Mimeo available from the author or the Foreign Service Institute, Arlington, Virginia.
6. For background on this development see Robert M. Dickinson, "Can Centralized Planning for Office Automation Ever Work in a Large Corporation?" in Landau, Bair, and Seigman, ed.: Emerging Office Systems (Norwood, N.J.: Ablex, 1982), p. 21-38.
7. Washington Post (Nov. 9, 1981) as cited in ref. 4, p. 3.
8. In addition to his articles and the IRM Newsletter, these include Information Management in Public Administration, ed. with Donald A. Marchand (Arlington, Va.: Information Resources Pr., 1982); Information Resources Management: Concept and Cases, (Cleveland, Ohio: Assn. for Systems Management, 1979); and Information Resources Management Workbook (privately published).
9. Horton, F. W.: Information Resources Management: Concept and Cases. (Cleveland, Ohio: Assn. for Systems Management, 1979), p. 49.
10. For example, the Association of Information Managers, the Information Industry Association, the Association for Federal Information Resources Management, and the Society for Management

Information Systems.
11. Larson, M. S.: <u>The Rise of Professionalism</u>. (Berkeley, Calif.: Univ. of Calif. Pr., 1977), p. xvii.
12. The episode occurred in a class entitled "Concepts of Information Resources Management" at Syracuse University, Fall 1984.
13. Larson, ref. 11, p. 228.

LIBRARY NETWORKS:
A MEANS, NOT AN END*

Patricia Glass Schuman

"There are only two political parties and only two kinds of libraries
in the United States," a colleague of mine recently quipped. "Democratic libraries say: 'We have the book--but we can't find it.' Re-
publican libraries say: 'We have the book--but you can't use it.'"
That characterization hits very close to home.

Networks and the Users

A cousin of mine who lives in a suburban Bay Area community,
an alumni of the University of California, Berkeley, just paid several
hundred dollars to obtain the privilege to use the university-library
for his 16-year-old son. "I don't understand it," he said. "Our
local public library is small--it has very few research materials. When
I was a kid I could find almost anything at the public library." When
he was kid, his local library was the Carnegie Library of Pittsburgh.
Startled, I began to explain the differences between libraries, but
then I quickly stopped. Can we really expect library users to dif-
ferentiate? Can we blame their ignorance when they don't? Or is
the problem endemic to the way libraries operate?

How far has networking between libraries really taken us? The
answer is not simple. Over 80 percent of our librarians work in
school libraries, few of which currently participate in networks. Only
about 7000 U.S. libraries do participate in networks, mainly medium
to large academic and public libraries. I use "networks" in the plural
because, as you know, there is no single network funded by the
national government in the United States as there is in other countries,
nor do we have a national library.

While the Library of Congress does engage in important national

*Reprinted by permission of the author and publisher of Library
Journal 112:2 (February 1, 1987) 33-37; copyright © 1987 by Reed
Publishing, USA. Div. of Reed Holdings, Inc. This article is adapted
from addresses to the New Zealand and California Library Associations.

library programs, its major mandate is to be the library for the
Congress of the United States.

OCLC (The Online Computer Library Center, Inc.) is our largest
network and both the Western Library Network (WLN) and the Research Libraries Information Network (RLIN) have an important influence on our networking environment. OCLC and RLIN are private,
nonprofit corporations.

In addition to these three major bibliographic utilities, there are
close to 500 local, state, and regional networks, systems, cooperatives,
and consortia in the United States.

The Myths of Networks

Of a number of myths about networks that we librarians hold
very dear, three favorites follow:

Myth No. 1: Networks save money. Their shared services will
allow libraries to operate with fewer and less expensive personnel.

Myth No. 2: Networks will blur the lines between technical and
public services, eventually breaking down the bureaucratic structure
of libraries.

Myth No. 3: Networks will break down barriers between libraries,
moving the profession from a philosophy of ownership to a philosophy
of access.

These mythologies held strong sway in the late Seventies--a
time we now refer to as "the golden age" of networking. In the mid-
Eighties, we're beginning to question networks and our mythology
about them. While some of the mythology of networks has some
basis in reality, networking hasn't had quite the effects we expected.

Why No Savings?

Take Myth No. 1--saving money. There is no evidence of overall cost savings because of networks. Nor is there any marked drop
in what we euphemistically call "the rate of rising costs." It is true
that the reconversion of records, staff training, network fees and
dues, rising telecommunications charges, and the costs of library automation projects and new online services may be masking some of
the expected savings. Basically, however, most libraries joined networks with some very naive assumptions about cost accounting, personnel, and technology.

For example, over 80 percent of all titles cataloged through networks require only simple copy cataloging, and some libraries report

even higher "hit rates." Most of this copy cataloging in larger libraries is now handled by a paraprofessional staff and is completed
quicker and cheaper; but, original cataloging backlogs are growing
and there are frequent complaints about the "snail's pace" of original
cataloging.

In fact, there is a clear reluctance on the part of librarians to
do original cataloging. Instead, they wait to see if someone else,
somewhere else, will do it first. This is partially because the task
has become more complicated. To share cataloging you have to accept
cataloging done by others; yours must be the same as everyone else's.
Some library administrators blame the fact that libraries don't save
time or money through shared cataloging because of an inordinate
focus by catalogers on standards, checking, and rechecking, in pursuit of the perfect bibliographic record.

Often, catalogers will accept only cataloging by LC. So they
wait. Others maintain what they call "hit lists" of libraries whose
cataloging they will not accept.

An added complexity is that an individual cataloger's work becomes visible throughout the network. Some say that with this
visibility, some catalogers become immobilized. They suffer from performance anxiety. Richard De Gennaro, director of New York Public
Library, calls it "fear of inputting."[1]

A recent study of catalogers in six large academic libraries demonstrates that they feel isolated from library users. The only evaluation
of their work is done by other catalogers in the network.

There are even a few reports from libraries in universities with
traditional football rivalries whose catalogers use network error reports to disparage competing cataloging departments. Researcher
Ruth Hafter calls it a new form of "Superbowl," played out on video
screens.[2]

According to De Gennaro, "far from becoming extinct, original
cataloging and the catalog maintenance functions in large libraries
are now growth industries."[3]

Which Work Is "Professional"?

We really don't have historical statistical data to scientifically
evaluate the impact of networks on library staffing. Despite some
isolated reports about staff cuts through attrition, and redeployment
of staff, there is no evidence of significant change, either in the
number of people working in libraries or in the proportion of professional to paraprofessional staff.

What is clear after a decade is that networks create new and

different workloads. Our failure to plan for these becomes more
costly after the fact. We're just beginning to discuss the need for
job redesign; reevaluation of work standards; schedules; performance;
training; as well as the need for healthy and comfortable workplaces.

Until recently, library administrators have emphasized the managerial and technological sides of networking. Meanwhile their staffs
are talking about "stress" and "burnout."

The recognition that systems depend on people--not just hardware and software--is fairly new. Library workers want to know
what networks will mean to them personally. They want and need
answers to the following questions:

- Will I lose my job?
- Will my job change?
- Will my salary go up or down?
- Will the system help or hinder me?
- Will I still be important?
- Will I be able to keep up?

In some cases, our mythology about people and networks was
accurate. Networking does tend to move tasks formerly considered
professional downward--particularly in the areas of circulation, cataloging, acquisitions, and interlibrary loan.

On the other hand, some libraries that originally downgraded
positions now recognize that networks bring increased systemwide
responsibilities that require professional skill and knowledge.

Several libraries report recent reclassification of circulation and
interlibrary loan positions back up to professional grades. Nevertheless, paraprofessionals have become the day-to-day operators of our
larger libraries, in charge of many functions formerly in the hands
of librarians.

The Neglected Paraprofessional

Although paraprofessionals comprise two-thirds of the work force
in U.S. libraries, there are few formal educational programs for them.
Qualifications and job titles vary extensively from library to library.
In U.S. libraries there are subprofessionals, nonprofessionals, paraprofessionals, library assistants, library-media technologists, clerks,
library aides, library associates, paralibrarians, library technicians,
and support staff. We pay little attention to their training, job design, or career development. Support staff often feel the most immediate impact from networks.

Their schedules can change often and require uncommon work
hours because libraries must maximize the use of computer time,

including nights and weekends. Their working environment can become uncomfortable, and sometimes dangerous to their health because
of ergonomic factors like furniture design, VDT radiation, and air
flow. Their workload increases, but their output depends upon timely
system functions beyond their control.

All of these concerns impact productivity. A frequent complaint
from paraprofessionals these days is: "I'm doing the same thing a
librarian does or used to do, but I don't get paid for it." As paraprofessionals take over more of the day-to-day library operations,
they ask what the librarians are doing. The answer is unclear.

According to Margaret Myers, director of ALA's Office for
Library Personnel Resources, various studies of job vacancy announcements show that anywhere from 20 to 50 percent require some knowledge of automation or online searching skills.[4]

Some administrators say that specific managerial, technical,
and financial knowledge is essential in a network environment.

Others call for the "best and the brightest" generalists, claiming that though the tools may be different, broad backgrounds for
problem solving, planning, teaching, researching, and coordinating
are necessary.

Lately, conference speakers and writers in the literature reflect
a distinct nervousness about the image of librarians and the future
of the profession. Scenarios and projections range from needing no
librarians at all to the exalted scholar/librarians, generalist librarians,
librarians as intermediaries, information counselors, and information
managers. Notice that the last two terms no longer use the designation librarian. Networks, once a hope for making libraries less labor
intensive, have actually focused our attention more specifically on
library personnel.

Once we thought that networks would displace librarians. Now
we're concerned because we are having difficulty recruiting students
into our library schools. A few graduate programs have closed entirely and many others face uncertain futures.

People, Not Computers, Solve Problems

There are frequent complaints about difficulty in finding applicants to fill jobs--particularly in technical and children's services.
Our experience shows that far from being people savers, networks
are often people eaters. Effective networks depend on effective people.

Until now, we've largely practiced an "it's over there" school
of librarianship, relying on users to find what they need themselves.

But now, the question of "where" is changing all that. The compli-
cations of networks and online services are transferring more of the
labor back to the librarian in terms of teaching the user about new
tools, how to perform online searches and retrieve documents.

For library workers, networks and automation mean change--
some good, some bad. During transition and learning periods, workloads usually increase and become more complex. It's become a
cliché to say that people, not computers, make mistakes. It is true,
however, that human library workers have far less "down time" than
the bibliographic networks they tap.

People solve problems, not computers. Sara Fine, a psychologist and professor at the University of Pittsburgh School of Library
and Information Science, completed the only specific research we have
on "resistance to technological innovation in libraries."[5] Her study
focused on public librarians, but her findings are significant for all
types of librarians.

Fine found no specific evidence of a resistant librarian personality nor of rampant librarian resistance. Her study suggests, however, that the resistance that does exist is important. "If a library
has a staff of 100 professionals, 20 of them will actively or passively
defeat the impact of innovation on an organization," Fine reports.[6]

While the library profession seems to accept, even welcome, new
systems and technology, Fine cautions that this may be seen as a
socially acceptable response rather than a real conviction. Such a
response may really indicate a new kind of traditionalism, not true
adaptability to innovation. Whatever its root reality, the current
stance is no guarantee that future innovations —technological or other-
wise--will gain easy acceptance.

While the librarians Fine surveyed described libraries as open
organizations, a majority also felt that decision making takes place
"without consulting the people who are going to do the work."[7]
The picture painted by those librarians was one of a benevolent but
authoritarian organizational climate in which subordinates agreeably
comply.

A related finding is that library administrators are uncomfortable
with research that focuses on the feelings and reactions of staff.

Stormy Weather?

Fine suggests that the organizational climate and style, and not
the librarian, may be an appropriate target for change.

The conclusions of Fine and other psychologists who have studied resistance are clear. It's not that people dislike change in general,
but they don't want to be coerced to change by an external force.

Successful implementation of networks requires listening to
staff; planning for and with staff; training and developing staff;
and informing and communicating with staff. Attitude can play as
large a part in determining success as the system itself. If library
workers do not accept the system, library users certainly won't.

Psychologist Shoshanah Zuboff of the Department of Organizational Behavior at the Harvard Business School, studied 500 workers
in industry. She suggests that:

> Though information systems can be designed to either serve
> or replace judgment, these choices have frequently not been
> confronted explicitly.... The more managers find ways to
> increase control over work the more employees search out
> ways to subvert that control and gain some personal sense
> of mastery.... In many cases, resistance is the only way
> employees can respond to the substance of change.[8]

Librarians in the United States are beginning to realize that
staff planning and implementation task forces or committees, training,
development programs, and clear and constant communication are essential.

Cost-effective, meaningful library services need effective people
who understand the meaning of the network system and their place
in it. Networks don't save money, but they could help libraries and
librarians become more cost effective.

The Ecumenical Librarian?

What about Myth No. 2? Will networks break down hierarchies
within libraries and blur the line between technical and public services? While networks cause some blurring, there's little evidence
that by themselves they cause substantive organizational change.

The fragmentation of departments and functions within U.S.
libraries is a 100-year-old tradition. Library education programs often
perpetuate the problem. We educate librarians the way we breed
hunting dogs: to be setters, pointers, or retrievers. Three distinct
breeds?

A recent survey of members of the Association of Research
Libraries found that while library managers recognize the importance
of increased communication and involvement, there were few actual
reorganizations taking place.[9]

In reality, blurring the lines usually means that technical services staff spend some time at the catalog information desk, and both
public and technical services staff select materials.

Most respondents ranked integrated automated. systems as the major reason for change. Bibliographic utilities and staff development and morale ranked last. The ARL survey does show increased use of committees and task forces to address mutual public/technical services concerns, and some new multiple reporting relationships for collection development, cataloging, reference, and other functions.

Michael Gorman of the University of Illinois at Urbana has written extensively on what he calls "the restoration of wholeness to librarianship."[10] Gorman believes that an automated system dispenses with the front room/back room library mentality. Rather than define librarians by which function they perform--cataloging, acquisitions, reference--he suggests we define librarians by the "area of service in which they exercise their skills across the whole range of professional librariansnip."

Gorman's "ecumenical" librarian selects materials, develops collections, and performs original cataloging, reference work, bibliographic instruction, and bibliographic services. Of course, in smaller libraries, where there is simply not enough staff to go around, this is often the way it is anyway.

The University of Illinois model abolishes the lines between technical and public services on a professional level and instead creates the librarian specialist, who handles materials by discipline. The professionals are decentralized, while clerical staff become more centralized. But Illinois is an exception.

The Catalogers' Revenge

We could, however, be on the brink of massive change as more and more network members implement online catalogs and integrated systems. As technology moves from behind the scenes to up front-- in the form of online catalogs and online reference databases--public and technical services personnel are becoming more interdependent.

For example, reference librarians using online catalogs have to learn and understand the MARC record. Decisions about which elements of the record can be used to create access points are crucial. When files and catalogs are automated, all librarians become partners in improving the database. Some reference librarians call this "catalogers' revenge."

While networks are primarily used for shared processing functions, shared reference services are increasingly popular.

In California, three-quarters of the public libraries use other libraries and/or network staff for database searching.[11] WLN reports that reference use of the system has grown gradually and consistently.[12]

Networks and automation mean new kinds of questions, new kinds of service. When users and staff have access wherever there's a terminal, there's less mystique and more questioning of why things are done a certain way.

Networks have not yet changed the technical core of librarianship, though they are changing some of the ways librarians operate.

Far from wiping out jobs, networks open up new possibilities and often create jobs. They also require more time-consuming reference, user instruction, more attention to standards, technological fluency, and increased communication between departments, and between professionals and support staff.

From Ownership to Access

It hasn't happened yet, but there's a strong and continuing belief in the idea that networks and technology offer new opportunities to restructure librarianship and libraries completely. This brings us to Myth No. 3--that networking will move librarianship from a philosophy of individual ownership to one of universal access.

Theoretically, libraries are no longer dealing with owned materials, but with "available" ones. There's no doubt that networks have broken some barriers, but issues such as prestige, control, fees, and funding are still sources of frustration. Fragmentation between types of libraries--academic, school, public, and private--and types of librarians is still the norm.

To date, we've enhanced our capabilities to inundate users with citations, but users don't care about our housekeeping procedures or our mysterious codes and standards. They need documents, answers, guidance, information, and evaluation.

Users need what they need organized so they can use it, when they need it. They don't care who owns what; they don't expect libraries to identify resources. They expect libraries to have resources.

Networks now provide access to millions of library holdings. That's a great beginning, but interlibrary loan still accounts for less than two percent of all library circulations.

The concept of ownership is changing, but librarians have made little progress in the actual movement of resources to users. What we seem to do best is to convince library users to wait.

Our professional vision has not yet moved from that of a network that generates catalog cards and locates holdings to a real-time network linking users to information.

Codifying Bad Practice

Networks and automation have too often led to a codification of
bad, complicated, and costly practices. We've spent millions--perhaps
billions--on housekeeping: authority control, conversion to AACR2
and LC. Yet recent user studies of online catalogs present overwhelming evidence that most users search by subject rather than
known item.[13] The average LC nonfiction record has 1.9 subject
headings and we don't classify fiction by subject at all. Studies also
show that users expect to find not only books in online catalogs, but
articles and other materials.[14]

While the majority of U.S. libraries still have card catalogs,
this is changing. As we automate more and more libraries, it's crucial that we move away from our sometimes obsessive focus on production methodologies to a philosophy not only of access, but of dissemination.

Technological myopia is a danger. According to library automation expert Joe Matthews, only 100 online catalogs are now fully
operational, but there are over 30 varieties, each with its own search
protocols.[15]

Combine this with over 2000 available databases and the different
network protocols. You get some idea of the growing "tower of Babel"
library users face.

As a profession, we've devoted massive resources to implementing
networks, but paid little attention to planning and policy setting.
Often the tools, and their inventors, are making policy for us.

Too often we only focus inward, on issues of turf, lack of
funds, and governance, rather than focusing outward, on using our
power, together, to bring about effective change.

Deciding where we are going is not easy in the midst of change,
but we must stop and look at what's behind our network mythologies.
Where are we going and why?

Networks are not a panacea. They can simplify. They can
supplement. They are a means, not an end. Networks can be a tool
for assessing and implementing shared staff development programs,
for developing guidelines for comfortable and safe working places,
and for developing equitable and productive work and performance
standards.

They can be a tool for bringing us together to share expertise,
experience, and knowledge.

Networks and Power

     As individual people, as individual libraries, or even as individual library systems, we have little visibility and even less clout in the political area, or as a market force. There is power in numbers. By joining together, by using networks as a way to build and use a power base, we can insure that libraries have enough resources to share, and that they are effectively delivered to our users.

     Networks, after all, are about, and for, people. We should build them from the bottom up, not from the top down. We can use networks to empower ourselves and our users. We can use networks to break down the barriers and not to create them.

     By working together we can become not merely efficient and competent, but technologically and philosophically fluent, and powerful enough to transform our libraries.

     This takes commitment, participation, and a willingness to share. It means focusing less on the bibliographic record, less on how networks can help us do what we did yesterday, and more on what they can help us do tomorrow. Working together we can move beyond the mythologies to change the realities.

     To paraphrase Shoshanah Zuboff, networks can be used to automate or they can be used to "informate."

     When used to automate, the aim is to replace human skills with technology at less cost and with more control, according to the same logic as mass-production technology.

     In an "informating" environment, comprehension is emphasized. "The work is ... a process of inquiry ... the contributions that members can make are increasingly a function of their ability to notice, reflect, explore, hypothesize, test, and communicate.... An informating strategy," says Zuboff, "recognizes the value and functions of the smart machine, but only in the context of its interdependence with smart people."[16]

     It is the people that can turn networks into opportunities for innovation and change. While no one can predict the future impact of networks, we can all help to invent that future.

References

1. De Gennaro, Richard, "Libraries and Networks in Transition: Problems and Prospects," LJ, May 15, 1981, p. 1047.
2. Hafter, Ruth, "Born Again Cataloging in the Online Networks," in Energies in Transition: Proceedings of the Fourth National Conference of the Association of College and Research Libraries, ALA, 1986, p. 30-33.

3.	De Gennaro.
4.	Myers, Margaret, "Personnel Considerations in Library Automation," in Human Aspects of Library Automation: Helping Staff and Patrons Cope. Paper presented at the 22nd Annual Clinic on Library Applications of Data Processing April 15, 1985, Univ. of Illinois Graduate School of Library and Information Science, in press.
5.	Fine, Sara. Resistance to Technological Innovation in Libraries. 3 pts. Final report to the Office of Libraries and Learning Resources, Office of Education, U.S. Department of Health, Education, and Welfare, 1979.
6.	Ibid., Pt. 3, p. 23.
7.	Ibid., Pt. 3, p. 30.
8.	Zuboff, Shoshanah. Psychological and Organizational Implications of Computer-Mediated Work. Center for Information Systems Research, MIT, 1981, p. 11.
9.	Association of Research Libraries, Office of Management Studies, "Automation and Reorganization of Technical and Public Services," Spec. kit 112, ARL, 1985.
10.	Gorman, Michael, "The Ecumenical Librarian," The Reference Librarian, Fall/Winter, 1983, p. 55-64.
11.	Van House, Nancy A., "California Libraries and Networking: Report of a Survey," in California Conference on Networking, California Conference on Networking, California State Library, p. 137.
12.	Woods, Richard, "The Reality and the Dream for WLN Reference Librarians," RQ, Fall 1979, p. 35.
13.	Matthews, Joseph R., Gary S. Lawrence, & Douglas K. Ferguson. Using Online Catalogs: a Nationwide Survey. Neal-Schuman, 1983.
14.	Ibid.
15.	Conversation with author.
16.	Zuboff, Shoshanah, "Automate/Informate: the Two Faces of Intelligent Technology," Organizational Dynamics, Autumn 1985, p. 10-12.

SUPPLY-SIDE SEARCHING: AN ALTERNATIVE
TO FEE-BASED ONLINE SERVICES*

William A. Britten

While the discussion concerning fees for accessing remote databases
is an old one, a recent study found that the debate has produced
little consensus and that there is a scarcity of current data on fees
for online services. [1] The most recent surveys available indicate
that a majority of libraries charge for searches, and there is little
evidence that the situation is changing. [2] At St. Mary's College of
Maryland, however, online services have grown in both popularity
and productivity over the last five years while the library has continued to subsidize all costs. This article analyzes the attitudinal
paradigm which has enabled feeless searching to prosper, offers a
discussion of why in the current online environment this paradigm may
be appropriate for many college and university libraries, and describes
a methodology for "supply-side" searching.

A QUICK REVIEW

It is not within the scope of this paper to provide a comprehensive review of the arguments for and against fees for online services.
The literature has chronicled the rationale, effects, and implications
of charging or not charging fees for database searching, and some
highlights of the discussion are provided here. Those favoring, or
at least resigned to, charging fees have cited the add-on nature of
online services, the patron-specific costs of searches, the need to
control demand for the services, the financial reality of funds not
being available from other sources, and the supposed acceptance of
fees by library patrons. [3] Counter-arguments point out that fees
have a significant effect on information demand, [4] that it is possible
to offer free searches, [5] and that online services will become so integrated into reference departments that fees will be unjustifiable. [6]
More recently, it has been suggested that funds for searching be
reallocated from the materials budgets. [7] Finally, some libraries

*Reprinted by permission of the author and publisher of The Journal
of Academic Librarianship 13:3 (July 1987) 147-150; copyright © 1987
by The Journal of Academic Librarianship.

have adopted a compromise position, charging for online literature searches, but providing online ready-reference at no cost.[8] Despite the apparent stalemate of the debate in the literature, in practical terms the argument has long been over--the great majority of libraries charge for online searches.

SUPPLY AND DEMAND

It has been pointed out that, notwithstanding a long philosophical tradition to the contrary, libraries have never had the option of providing free and unlimited services.[9] That is, the offering of free services has always been predicated on the assumption that demand for those services would be predictable and manageable, and that the amount of service available (the supply) would be fairly distributed to all who needed it. Traditional reference service, for example, has always been supply-side oriented. Reference librarians routinely adjust the amount of time they are willing to spend with a patron to accommodate the demand for reference assistance. Factors affecting this adjustment of assistance supplied include: the number of patrons waiting, the difficulty of the question, the purpose of the information (a two-page paper versus a master's thesis), and the complexity of the resource. By and large, the strategy of assistance adjustment allows reference departments to cope with peak demand periods.

Demand Orientation

From their appearance in the 1970s, online search services have generally been demand-oriented. The primary purpose of user fees, despite varied arguments in their defense, is to control demand for online searching. The justification for using fees to control demand, even among librarians who are philosophically opposed to fees for services, is that budgetary realities facing virtually all libraries initiating online searching dictate that expenditures must be controlled. However, as Rochell notes, the library profession has focused much attention on the structure and level of fees while failing to seek alternatives.[10]

Supply-Side Alternative

The alternative proposed in this article is to accept budgetary limitations, whatever they may be within each institution, and to control expenditures by limiting the supply of the service in much the same way as in traditional reference service. This is more than a semantic distinction between controlling demand or controlling supply. Although these are two paths which lead to the same destination (the limitation of online services), one uses market forces to exclude students while the other requires librarians to make choices about who will benefit most from an online search. When attitudes shift from seeking to restrain demand through the use of fees to developing strategies for controlling the supply of online searches, a pathway is cleared for a methodology of online services provision that is at once more equitable for the student and philosophically palatable to the librarian. The specifics of this methodology will be discussed later, but first it is important to describe why the context of online searching in the mid-1980s is ripe for supplyside searching.

ONLINE SEARCHING TODAY

An Assumed Service

Several factors characterizing either the online industry or the academic community support a reassessment of priorities, policies, and procedures concerning the way online services are currently offered in academic libraries. First, online searching is now pervasive, normal, and expected. Many entering freshmen who lack an understanding of the scope of printed reference sources in an academic library are well informed on the concept of accessing remote databases. Not offering database searching today would invite a serious loss of credibility for a library. The old argument that online searches are of an add-on or auxiliary nature is no longer defendable.

Access vs. Acquisition

Related to the integration of online services into the mainstream of reference service is the growing priority shift from acquired to accessed information. The Newman report of the Carnegie Foundation for the Advancement of Teaching concludes that when fees are levied for online searches "the result is to discriminate in favor of acquired as opposed to accessed material, and to discriminate in favor of the haves as opposed to the have-nots."[11] Newman goes on to strongly urge research libraries, whose budgets have traditionally favored the acquisition, cataloging, and storage of information, to recast their budgets in light of the increased importance of access to electronically stored information.

Budgetary Support

Despite the wholehearted and long-term acceptance of online services by the academic community, budgetary support has remained disproportionately low. In 1979 Knapp and Schmidt referred to a $20,000 budget to provide online services to 1,600 students as a "bargain,"[12] and more recently Dodd and Anders speculated on a $90,000 commitment (3 percent of the materials budget) to online access of databases in a large university.[13] With a budget reflecting the stature of online searching as part of the standard reference service repertoire, the imperative for fees would be removed and libraries could concentrate on the development of methods to ensure the maximum effect and most equitable distribution of online services.

Technology and End Users

There are two other components of today's online environment, both tending to mitigate the demand for searches. First, the technology attendant to database searching has matured. Microcomputers, highspeed modems, gateway software, and other advances have all contributed to lower the average connect time per search, making searches less time consuming and less costly. Second, end-user searching, whether via dial-up systems or on in-house CD-ROM databases, promises to have a substantial impact on the demand for inter-mediated online searches.

It is interesting to note that while even a bare-bones catalog of CD-ROM databases involves a substantial investment for any library, the emerging literature on the topic has produced no suggestions that user fees would be an appropriate source of funds to pay for data-base subscriptions. Fenichel has raised the issue of access policies and the possible need for restrictive scheduling to ensure that the demand for searching CD-ROM databases is equitably met.[14] It is this author's opinion that while Fenichel's concerns represent the proper attitude toward the installation of optical disk-based reference service, these same concerns are appropriate for the management of traditional online services.

SUPPLY-SIDE METHODS

The literature is far from silent on the subject of methods for cost-effective management of limited online services.[15] These various tips and suggestions, however, have never been articulated as

---

Table 1
Online Service Statistics 1983-1986

	Searches*	Connect Hours	Hours per Search	Cost	Cost per Search
FY 83	152	38.83	.255	$4173.33	$27.45
FY 84	262	50.28	.192	3511.00	13.40
FY 85	296	40.78	.138	3101.00	10.48
FY 86	385	47.71	.124	3540.03	9.19

*A search is defined as one research question answered, regardless of the number of files searched or number of citations retrieved.

---

the basis for a methodology for providing online services. From the start of its database searching service, St. Mary's College of Maryland has used a systematic method for maintaining budgetary control by using a combination of discretionary policies, procedures which encourage frugality, and technological advantages. The library staff, who serve approximately 1,400 students and faculty, currently perform close to 400 searches per year (a search is defined as a research question answered, regardless of the number of databases accessed). During the past four years the number of searches performed has increased 153 percent while the online budget has held steady (see Table 1). This steady decline in per-search costs has occurred despite inflation of vendor charges and is the direct result of a continuous refinement of the components of the supply-side methodology-- that is, the policies, procedures, and hardware.

Policies

First, policy indicates that since the library is absorbing the costs of the service, the searching librarians will make decisions regarding the feasibility and extent of searches. Librarians decide at what threshold research needs require a search and when they can be met by using print indexes. This threshold can be adjusted to ensure that funds allocated for searching are not depleted too rapidly. In addition, the online services policy statement outlines the philosophy that the student carries a major portion of the responsibility for a successful search. Students are required to:

- do preliminary work in printed reference sources to establish the focus of their topic,

- provide keywords (from the thesaurus of descriptors if one is available), and

- be present and willing to interact as the search progresses.

The policies are meant to serve as guidelines, and in practice the librarians are quite flexible and open to negotiation. Students with poorly articulated research needs, with needs inappropriate to online databases, or who are seeking a quick fix to poor planning, however, are quickly referred back to the printed sources. As Champlin has asserted, many of these students are better served in the print indexes and can meet their information needs without an online search.[16]

Cost Effective Procedures

The second component of methodology for maintaining control over the supply of database searches is an ongoing search for procedures which encourage more cost-effective searching.

Search limits. For example, since same-subject databases offered by different producers or vendors contain a significant amount
of overlap, multi-database searching is kept to a minimum. In many
cases searching one or two databases will extract most of the information on a topic, and for the majority of students this will suffice.

BI sessions. Also, by combining bibliographic instruction with
online searching (in a classroom setting or as a postsearch "debrief-
ing"), students become aware of techniques that they can use to
glean the remaining needed citations from a literature search primarily
completed in the databases. In this way the library avoids spending
a lot of money looking for a small percent of citations in an exhaustive
search. The bibliographic instruction/online search connection also
helps to prevent "computer printout syndrome" which causes many
students to assume that since their topic has been searched by computer, the printout must represent everything on the topic. Bibliographic instruction sessions stress the concept of online searching
as just one aspect of an overall research methodology, rather than a
one-stop information supermarket.

Printout savings. Cost-effective procedures can also save on
online printout charges, which have risen sharply in the past few
years. For those databases which are represented by a printed counterpart in the library, citations are printed in the title-and-accession-
number format, which is usually free, rather than the full bibliographic citation format or citation-plus-abstract format, which almost
always incurs a charge. Students can then use the library's
print index to locate the full citation and abstract for promising titles
listed on the printout. This is obviously not the optimal situation for
students, but it is a way of getting better mileage from the online
dollar, and it has the added benefit of continually reacquainting
students with the printed indexes, where browsing and serendipity
are still possible. Again, at St. Mary's College flexibility is the rule,
and students often provide valid reasons for negotiating a full-citation
printout.

Connect-time savings. Additional savings in connect time can
be attained by avoiding the peak hours when database response time
is slow, by making optimal use of descriptors--which are searched more
rapidly than free-text phrases--and by avoiding search strategies
that are bogged down with too many synonyms.

Librarian expertise. Finally, cost-effective searching is, to a
great extent, a function of the expertise of the searcher. The
searching librarians at St. Mary's College have attended many seminars
offered by database vendors, for which the cost and time invested
in attending these seminars has been repaid many times over.

Hardware

The third part of the supply-side methodology is the hardware

and software used for searching. Improvements in technology since
the days of the ubiquitous dumb terminal have been truly revolution-
ary. The literature has thoroughly documented the advantages in
productivity offered by microcomputer-enhanced searching. These
include:

- automatic log-on,

- offline entry of search strategies,

- selective downloading to a buffer or disk,

- effortless accounting,

and in the case of more advanced telecommunications software:

- online help screens, and

- a common command language between databanks.

Modems with a 1200-baud speed are now considered a minimum.
The differential in cost between 300-baud searching on a terminal
versus 1200- and 2400-baud searching on a microcomputer has been
dramatically demonstrated by Kim.[17] Finally, it should be noted
that a high-speed modem connected to either a microcomputer or terminal will feed information from the host database only as fast as the
printer will accept it. In other words, a 1200-baud modem plus a
300-baud printer is not necessarily 1200-baud searching. For this
reason it is essential that the telecommunications software be capable
of temporarily storing data in a buffer or disk file for printing after
logging off the databank.

BENEFITS

What are the benefits of the supplyside approach? Two benefits
are the retention of control over the service and a more equitable
distribution of searches to students. Since searches are distributed
solely on the basis of need without consideration of ability to pay,
librarians can exercise utmost professional judgment in the use of the
service. Also, the student participation and willingness to compromise required by our policies and procedures encourages a more
thorough integration with traditional reference services. Students
asked to look up full citations in the print indexes or use abstracts
as reviewing tools to glean the most relevant citations from an abbre-
viated printout have indicated that they prefer this over a fee-based
service. The library reaps the benefit of reduced online costs while
the students are encouraged to use printed sources in conjunction
with online sources. In fact, it is heartening to note that many students are first introduced to indexes and abstracts in print format
after being drawn to the library by the prospect of an online search.

The synergy between traditional and online reference services has increased the scope of bibliographic instruction while reducing the purely intermediary aspects of performing searches. After several years of exposure to our bibliographic instruction program and online service, students become very adept at making contributions to the search process. For example, many will bring key articles to be used for citation searches or to obtain descriptors which can then be used to locate related articles. A few students have begun asking for search guides to obtain database-specific codes for searching terms or concepts. As students come to realize that online searching is just one component in an overall research strategy of many interrelated components, the perception of computerized research as a quick-fix shortcut diminishes. For a librarian, witnessing this realization is nothing less than a validation of the reference process.

CONCLUSION

The supply-side approach is flexible enough to be applicable in any size college or university library. In large libraries, where demand for traditional intermediated searching may be shared with the demand for in-house CD-ROM databases and end-user searching of remote databases, a feeless-but-negotiated approach to highly specialized research needs might be much more productive than a strictly fee-based approach. And, in small libraries relying solely on librarian-accessed databanks to meet all online needs, it is even more essential to distribute available search time on the basis of need rather than ability to pay. The experience at St. Mary's College of Maryland shows that the demand for searches can be met without fees, and that there are many benefits associated with the management of a feeless online search service.

References

1. National Commission on Libraries and Information Science, The Role of Fees in Supporting Library and Information Services in Public and Academic Libraries (Washington, D.C.: The Commission, 1985).
2. Abbie Landry, "Survey of Computer Database Searching in Louisiana Academic Libraries," RQ 24 (Spring 1985): 341-347; Mary Jo Lynch, "Libraries Embrace Online Search Fees," American Libraries 14 (March 1982): 174; and Connie Lamb, "Searching in Academia: Nearly 50 Libraries Tell What They're Doing," Online 5 (April 1981): 78-81.
3. Sara D. Knapp, "Turf--to be Relinquished Cheerfully," Journal of Academic Librarianship 11 (November 1985): 272-273; Sara D. Knapp, "Beyond Fee or Free," RQ 19 (Winter 1980): 117-119; James A. Cogswell, "On-line Search Services: Implications for Libraries and Library Users," College & Research Libraries 39 (July 1978): 275-280; John Linford, "To Charge or Not to

Charge: A Rationale, Library Journal 102 (October 1, 1977): 2009-2010; and Pat Ensor, "The Expanding Use of Computers in Reference Service," RQ 21 (Summer 1982): 365-372.

4. Mary M. Huston, "Fee or Free: the Effect of Charging on Information Demand," Library Journal 104 (September 15, 1979): 1811-1814.

5. Paula J. Crawford and Judith A. Thompson, "Free Online Searches Are Feasible," Library Journal 104 (April 1, 1979): 793-795.

6. James Rice, Jr., "Fees for Online Searches: A Review of the Issues," Journal of Library Administration 3 (Spring 1982): 25-34.

7. Wendy P. Lougee, "Turf vs. Role? Broadening the Library's Involvement," Journal of Academic Librarianship 11 (November 1985): 270-271; and Jay Martin Poole and Gloriana St. Clair, "Funding Online Services from the Materials Budget," College & Research Libraries 47 (May 1986): 225-229.

8. Carolyn G. Weaver, "Free Online Reference and Fee-based Online Search Services: Allies, Not Antagonists," The Reference Librarian 5-6 (Fall-Winter 1982): 111-118; and Sara Brownmiller et al., "Online Ready-reference Searching in an Academic Library," RQ 24 (Spring 1985): 320-326.

9. Brett Butler, "Why Libraries Can't Stand Success," ASIS Bulletin 12 (October/November 1985): 8-9.

10. Carlton Rochell, "The Knowledge Business: Economic Issues of Access to Information," College & Research Libraries 46 (January 1985): 5-12.

11. Frank Newman, Higher Education and the American Resurgence (Princeton, NJ: Princeton University Press, 1985), p. 152.

12. Sara D. Knapp and C. James Schmidt, "Budgeting to Provide Computer-Based Reference Services: A Case Study," Journal of Academic Librarianship 5 (March 1979): 13.

13. Jane Dodd and Vicki Anders, "Free Online Searches for Undergraduates: A Research Project on Use, Costs, and Projections," Library Hi Tech 2 (Spring 1984): 43-50.

14. Carol Hansen Fenichel, "For Optical Disks and Information Retrieval the Time is Now: A Librarian's View From the NFAIS Meeting," Database 9 (June 1986) 6-8.

15. Crawford and Thompson, "Free Online Searches," pp. 794-795; Joann H. Lee and Arthur H. Miller, "Introducing Online Database Searching in the Small Academic Library: A Model for Service Without Charge to Undergraduates," Journal of Academic Librarianship 7 (March 1981): 14-22; John Budd, "The Terminal and the Terminus: The Prospect of Free Online Bibliographic Searching," RQ 21 (Summer 1982): 373-378; Dick Matzek and Scott Smith, "Online Searching in the Small College Library-- the Economics and the Results," Online 6 (March 1982): 21-29; and Stephen P. Harter and Anne Rogers Peters, "Heuristics for Online Information Retrieval: A Typology and Preliminary Listing," Online Review 9 (October 1985): 421.

16. Peggy Champlin, "The Online Search: Some Perils and Pitfalls," RQ 25 (Winter 1985): 213-217.

17. David U. Kim, "Online Searching with a Microcomputer, a
     High-speed Modem, and a Local Printer," <u>Library Journal</u> 111
     (May 1, 1986): LC16-LC18.

CD-ROM: PERSPECTIVES ON AN EMERGING TECHNOLOGY*

Kay E. Vandergrift, Marlyn Kemper,
Sandra Champion, and Jane Anne Hannigan

PART 1

Finally, we have an answer to information overload. Optical technology will ease it down to fit on a silver platter measuring 4.72 inches
in diameter and weighing a mere .07 ounces. Imagine! We can now
hold in one hand that shiny, indestructible CD-ROM (Compact Disc-
Read Only Memory) equalling 1500 floppy discs or one person typing
90 words per minute for eight hours a day for eight years. Indeed,
CD-ROM products provide volumes of data never before available,
and at a low cost. Furthermore, the same data can be accessed repeatedly without additional cost, and, in many instances, without the
intervention of a librarian.

The most common library applications of CD-ROM are for public
access catalogs and for optical publishing. In July of 1985, Brodart
(Brodart Library Automation Division, 500 Arch St., Williamsport, PA
17705) introduced LePac, its CD-ROM public access catalog, as an
alternative to online public access and COM catalogs. The system
can store one million MARC formatted bibliographic records. With
options, it can hold four million records, print bibliographies and
catalog entries, and can interface with most circulation systems.
Perhaps the best-known publishing venture is the CD-ROM version of
Grolier's The Electronic Encyclopedia. (Grolier Electronic Publishing
Inc., Sherman Turnpike, Danbury, Conn. 06816.) RTI (Reference
Technology, Inc.), one of several sources for this encyclopedia, pro-
duces a version that allows for rapid searching on any phrase or word
in the text of the 20-volume print edition.

*Reprinted by permission of the authors and publisher of School
Library Journal 33:10 and 33:11 (June/July 1987 and August 1987)
27-31 and 22-25; copyright © 1987 by Reed Publishing, USA, Div.
of Reed Holdings, Inc.
Note: the second article was entitled "CD-ROM: An Emerging Technology. Part 2: Planning & Management Strategies."

Bowker's BIP Plus

In researching this topic, the writers conducted a telephone
survey of Bowker's Books in Print Plus (BIP Plus, R. R. Bowker Co.
Electronic Publishing, 245 W. 17th St., N.Y., N.Y. 10011) to obtain
data. Our sample was small, but national in scope. All of the
respondents were exceptionally cooperative in sharing information.
The survey findings, listed below, may serve as indicators of future
trends in library service:

• First, when asked if they perceived a BIP Plus as a tool
for both technical and public services, the respondents indicated
greater use in the public service area than had been anticipated by
the research team. Use of BIP Plus is the heaviest in interlibrary
loan (ILL), primarily for verification of titles. The other use is in
relation to bibliographies which are correlated to the curriculum.
Several respondents indicated that BIP Plus made curriculum work
easier; in one case the development of a new reading program was
enhanced through use of the program.

• Second, no respondent reported direct use by the student
or child; often one machine was in place and frequently it was in a
district center.

• Third, use of BIP Plus for acquisitions was a mixed bag;
several respondents indicated that electronic transmission needed to
be improved. Some respondents said that errors made in ordering
materials as well as those due to someone's dreadful handwriting were
no longer problems since only a few key words yielded the desired
titles.

• Fourth, in almost all cases, additional CD-ROM was in place,
most often ERIC or cataloging programs. CD-ROM is still considered
to be an expensive tool and when many schools exist in a system,
it's not easy to justify a CD-ROM for each site. One respondent expressed concern about its cost-effectiveness and the use of budget
monies.

• Fifth, among the benefits identified from Bowker's BIP
Plus were: speed; accuracy of entry; key word searching; time
saved; and the location of materials in special categories.

Objections to BIP Plus were few. Some respondents indicated
that they are maintaining a "wait-and-see" posture. Updating the
system was raised as one concern, but it has not been in operation
long enough for this to be a real issue. Many said they were eagerly
awaiting the emergence of book reviews on BIP Plus; they feel this
will be a tremendous timesaver and will prove to be the most-efficient
and cost-effective means of evaluating and ordering books.

There is good news here. Recently, Bowker announced that

it will be publishing reviews from School Library Journal, Library Journal, Publishers Weekly and from ALA's journals Choice and Booklist in a forthcoming CD-ROM product called Reviews Plus. Reviews from all sources will be added on a quarterly cumulative basis.

Databases

Probably the two most common public services applications of CD-ROM available to young people are Grolier's The Electronic Encyclopedia and databases such as InfoTrac II and GEOVISION.

The Electronic Encyclopedia uses only 20 percent of the space available on one CD for the equivalent of Grolier's 20-volume, 60-pound Academic American Encyclopedia. In fact, over half of the memory is used for an extensive index that allows users to locate, in just a few seconds, a listing of every entry containing a reference to a particular subject. A further refinement allows a user to narrow any topic by employing two search terms to get a display of entries mentioning, for example, both religion and China. Obviously this capability saves a great deal of search time and may even help students think about and understand the structure and organization of knowledge as well as locate specific information more efficiently.

Several schools use the disc containing the electronic encyclopedia with special education classes; students retrieve a specific article or even two articles for comparative purposes. The success of special ed students in working with the CD-ROM technology has been exciting.

InfroTrac II (Information Access Co., 11 Davis Dr., Belmont, Calif. 94002) appears to have a magic of its own in attracting users. How else can one explain student responses such as, "Wow, look at this! It gives you all this stuff, anything you want!" "Look how fast it goes!" "You have everything you need." "It saves so much time." These responses were made by students at Hialeah High School in Hialeah, Florida using InfoTrac II for the first time. The session was videotaped.

InfoTrac II is a relatively new (Nov. 17, 1986) optical disc reference product that combines magazine index coverage for the current year plus three back years, with several months of current indexing for The New York Times. This database is updated, cumulated, and delivered monthly. The InfoTrac II system, currently on loan in the Hialeah High School's media center, is available to over 2500 senior high students who, without formal training or instruction, search more than 400 general interest magazines and recent issues of The New York Times. Although students had wandered through the labyrinth of alternative strategies for learning to use The Readers' Guide, few remember the skill from year to year. Yet, over and over again, the students who used InfoTrac II marveled that this "new" method of periodical research "even includes the page numbers of the article cited." And that's not all that delighted them about InfoTrac II! They were impressed with the high-speed searching that allows retrieval of print references in seconds and with the fast, quiet printer, that, at the touch of the right color-coded and letter key, delivered a full screen or single citation printout.

The ease with which students adapted to the capabilities of InfoTrac II is a librarian's dream come true. It really is simple to use and it is powerful. Patrons merely type the subject of their search, press the search key and, within a minute or less, they can view a display of articles on their topic. Now comes the only tricky part which, historically, has been discouraging for librarians and users or Readers' Guide. As patrons scan the list of sources, they must make sure their library has them. Keeping an up-to-date, easy-to-read list of periodical holdings posted in the workstation can help ease this problem, or a library can subscribe to all of the magazines indexed.

Taking a closer look at the students and teachers using InfoTrac II, the following was observed:

• First, neither adolescent nor adult patrons wanted background information about the technology as long as it met their immediate needs. Although they were impressed with a quick explanation of the amazing shiny disc, most preferred to go on with their specific searches.

• Second, although InfoTrac II is a high-speed, quick-print device, patrons tended to linger at the workstation longer than expected. The ease with which users can browse a thesaurus and view displays of related subject headings and sub-headings encourages them to examine expanded views of the topic. If another aspect of the topic is of interest, a keystroke brings the citations indexed under that subject heading onto the screen. Many searches take the user on a long journey into the database and heighten his or her awareness of the subject.

Students were fascinated by the expansive coverage of topics on the database. One fellow, stumped by his search in Readers' Guide for articles on drugs in professional athletics, switched his search to InfoTrac II and, in less than one minute, had over 50 citations dealing with drug abuse cases involving professional athletes. Prior to his search, he knew the name of only one ball player in a drug case; by merely browsing through the data display, he picked up names of more than a dozen athletes who have been involved in drug abuse. The search motivated him to request more reading material than he had planned to use.

It is important to note also that, not only did many students seem to grasp a sense of the organization of information using InfoTrac

II, but the ease of the search enabled students of all ability levels
to locate magazine articles for their assignments.

• Third, although students could not access many of the articles desired because the school doesn't subscribe to every magazine
indexed, there were usually so many alternatives that they could find
something to satisfy them on most topics. This surprised the research
team which had predicted that patrons would be upset when they could
not get certain articles.

• Fourth, paper for the printer figured to be a high-cost
factor. Even when a patron needed only one citation, the printer
advanced a blank sheet of paper in addition to the single piece of
paper used for that citation. The ink cartridge, which is simple to
insert, had to be replaced after nine days of use, during which approximately one-third of a package of paper had been consumed.

• Fifth, very few patrons complained that only one InfoTrac
II workstation was available. Sharing came naturally, and students
were willing to wait their turn in order to save themselves time in
the long run.

• A sixth, totally unexpected, finding, was that the clerical
staff discouraged use of InfoTrac II because the frequency of requests
for magazines meant an increased work load for already overburdened
para-professionals.

It is too soon to know whether this product will increase student's ability to integrate and synthesize information from a large
database. We do know that it increases their ability to access information from a large number of sources. It may expand their horizons
and vastly multiply the amount of information they can easily access,
but three questions remain: Has the technology changed the user?
Do we have more knowledge or does increased information give us the
illusion of knowing? And, finally, will this illusion of knowing keep
us from wondering and thinking? For now, InfoTrac II serves as a
convenient, timesaving, inexpensive, and impressive tool for both
patrons and media specialists. Research into some more manageable
questions than those above is being done by Nellie Kreis and James
L. Buchholz. Kreis, media specialist with the Dade County (Fla.)
Public Schools, is developing a study to compare manual searches
with CD-ROM searches. That study will include a cost-analysis. The
implementation and evaluation of Bibliophile, a bibliographic retrieval
system, is now being examined in the 103 schools of the Palm Beach
County School System, by Buchholz, its head of technical services.

GEOVISION: A very different educational product available
on CD-ROM is GEOVISION's On the World, a software package containing GEOdisc maps from such sources as the United States Geological
Survey DLG, the National Oceanic and Atmospheric Administrations,
the Census Bureau, and the Earth Observation Satellite Company.

(Available from GEOVISION Inc., 303 Technology Park, Suite 135, Norcross, Ga. 30092.) This application program runs on a personal computer in the Microsoft Windows environment allowing the user to manipulate, access, and display the information on a GEOdisc. The user also has the flexibility to create either graphics, symbol overlays, or text to accompany the GEOdisc data. GEOVISION operates on the premise that a PC approach to geographic information systems' problems is a cost-effective solution in the fields of education, government, and business.

Palenque--a prototype: Clearly the most exciting use of this technology is represented by Palenque, a CD interactive, audio/video research prototype developed at the Center for Children and Technology at New York's Bank Street College of Education under the direction of Kathleen Wilson. The Palenque Project is a further development of the Maya explorations of the Second Voyage of the Mimi, a multimedia educational package which includes the televised program, computer software, and print materials, also produced by Bank Street.

Using a joy stick control, the user is able to wonder through an actual Mayan dig and to investigate, following up, down, and around the screen as interest compels them. For example, at one point the user could examine a multitude of artifacts in a museum and then ask questions of an archeologist to gain information, while at another point the user could go through a rain forest to find birds and animals and even hear the sounds of their cries. This prototype, which is not easily described, is one of the most exciting educational endeavors being developed for CD-ROM. Its potential for learning processes is high since it allows for a variety of alternatives without forcing conformity to a predictable pattern.

CD-ROM: A Selected Book List

Alberico, R. "Justifying CD-ROM." Small Computers in Libraries 7 (Feb. 1987): 18-20.
    Costs and benefits of CD-ROM products are compared to those of online and print products. The author notes that as the number of individuals utilizing CD-ROM databases increase, the cost per search will decrease since the cost is a fixed expense.

Allen, R. J. "The CD-ROM Services of SilverPlatter Information, Inc." Library Hi Tech Issue 12 (1985): 49-60.
    SilverPlatter Information supplies an array of databases on CD-ROM as well as the software and hardware that permit these databases to be used. A complete stand-alone system, this includes an IBM or IBM-compatible personal computer, one or more SilverPlatter compact digital discs containing fully indexed databases such as ERIC or PsychLIT, a compact disc drive, and the SilverPlatter retrieval and search software.

Bairstow, J. "CD-ROM: Mass Storage for the Mass Market." Hi
Technology (Oct. 1986): 44-49.
  Excellent information on CD-I and a list of CD-ROM discs featuring
  the High Sierra Group and Standards.

Bardes, D'Ellen. "Implications of CD-Interactive Direction, Specifications, and Standards." Optical Information Systems 6 (July-August
1986): 324-328.
  CD-I and its impact on market and product development, optical
  publishing, and CD-ROM are discussed.

Brewer, B. "Multimedia Media Mastery." CD-ROM Review: The
Magazine of Compact-Disc Data Storage 2 (March/April 1987) 14-18.
  According to Brewer, while current CD-ROM applications mainly
  focus on software or textual data, a widespread future use of multimedia CD-ROM will occur in the field of training. Existing software tutorials will be enhanced with visuals and audio. Inasmuch
  as narration and vocal instructions can supply additional material
  without interrupting the screen display, audio can play an especially significant role in teaching the learner how to utilize a
  software product. The same technology employed to train business
  users can likewise be employed in children's educational software.

_____. "Ready When You Are, CD-I." PC World 5 (April 1987):
252-255.
  CD-I merges pictures, sounds, and text on a 552MB optical disc
  that promises to trigger new techniques for displaying and communicating information. Designed to plug directly into stereos and
  television sets, CD-I is geared for the educational and home markets. Sony and Philips International envision a wide array of CD-I
  products including graphics accompaniment to music, interactive
  home reference materials, multimedia educational programs, interactive games, automobile navigation aids, and talking books.

Byers, T. J. "Built by Association." PC World 5 (April 1987):
245-251.
  CD-ROM, with its capacity to make gigabytes of data available on
  a personal computer, holds both challenge and promise. The vast
  storage capacity that makes CD-ROM so attractive is also its largest
  drawback. A visionary concept based on an interconstellation of
  knowledge known as hypertext may be the most practical approach
  for tagging and retrieving.

Chen, Ching-chih. "Libraries in the Information Age: Where are the
Microcomputer and Laser Optical Disc Technologies Taking Us?"
Microcomputers for Information Management 3 (Dec. 1986): 253-265.
  Special emphasis is placed on the effect of microcomputer and laser
  optical disc technologies on library services and information re-
  source management. Trends discussed cover developments in CD-
  Audio products, CD-ROM and WORM technology, and the potential
  of interaction between video/optical discs and microcomputers.

Cummings, S. "Mastering Corporate Data." PC World 5 (Apr. 1987): 232-235.
    A vast array of prototype CD-ROM applications ranging from disc-based encyclopedias to repositories of stock quotations and medical data has been developed in the last year. Businesses are similarly starting to exploit CD-ROMS for records management. In-house CD-ROM applications under development are designed to facilitate effective information retrieval and simplify archival management.

Desmarais, N. "Laserbases for Library Technical Services." Optical Information Systems 7 (Jan.-Feb. 1987): 57-61.
    Covers CD-ROM products for cataloging applications, based on the public domain records in the Library of Congress MARC (MAchine-Readable Cataloging) database, and CD-ROM products for public access catalogs, acquisitions, and serials. As CD-ROM technology matures, technical services librarians will find available an array of CD-ROM and videodisc products to streamline their work.

Gail, J. C. "Text Retrieval." CD-ROM Review. The Magazine of Compact-Disc Data Storage 2 (March/April 1987): 20-23.
    Since CD-ROM has a slower access time than magnetic media, retrieval software must be created with this constraint in mind. To optimize response time without sacrificing search flexibility or ease of access, Gail notes that perhaps the most effective approach is to have two types of interfaces. One interface would feature a menu-driven system designed to provide an easy access to the data for the novice while command driven systems would satisfy sophisticated search capabilities demanded by trained searchers.

Helgerson, L. W. "CD-ROM: A Revolution in the Making." Library Hi Tech Issue 13 (Spring 1986): 23-27.
    Manufacturing processes for drives and discs and the appearance of useful software contributed to the popularity of CD-ROM as a storage and distribution mechanism. Types of information that can be stored on a CD-ROM platter include image, data, voice, text, and graphics. Possibilities for the utilization of CD-ROM for information management are virtually unlimited.

_____, and Ennis, M. The CD-ROM Sourcebook. Falls Church, Va.: Diversified Data Resources, Inc., 1986.
    Topics range from software and data preparation to mastering and replication, to software, publications, and CD-ROM titles.

Hendley, T. CD-ROM and Optical Publishing Systems. Westport, Conn.: Meckler, 1987.
    This report highlights the potential applications of CD-ROM in the commercial and technical publishing fields, as well as applications in education, from primary school through to the university level.

Herther, N. K. "CD-ROM Technology: A New Era for Information

Storage and Retrieval?" Online 9 (Nov. 1985): 17-28.
The history, background and developments of CD-ROM technology
along with current applications and the market for CD-ROM products are addressed. A diagram features the steps involved in
the production of CD-ROM by 3M. Factors important in the selection of CD-ROM technology for original applications are highlighted.

Hiscox, M. & S. "A Level-Headed Look: The Potential of CD-ROM
in Education." Tech Trends (Apr. 1986): 14-20.
The authors write about realistic educational applications.

Jones, M. K. "Interactive Videodisc and the Self-Directed Learner."
Optical Information Systems 7 (Jan.-Feb. 1987): 62-65.
Applications focusing on interactive videodiscs for adult cognitive
learning are highlighted. Self-directed learning situations are
well suited for utilization of interactive videodiscs because they are
characterized by participants heterogeneous in aptitude and background, but mature and highly motivated.

Lambert, S. and Ropiequet, S., eds. CD-ROM: The New Papyrus.
Redmund, Wash.: Microsoft Press, 1986.
CD-ROM: The New Papyrus is comprehensive in scope, covering
articles ranging from an overview of the CD system and CD-ROM
production techniques to CD-ROM publishing, market considerations,
and medical, legal, geographic, archival, and library applications.

Levine, R. "Optical Storage." DEC Professional 6 (Feb. 1987):
30-38.
Levine highlights the advantages of optical disc technology. While
other storage media can store only text, CD-ROM has the capability of recording a mix of images, audio, and text. This capability
makes CD-ROM an ideal candidate for educational materials.

McManus, R. "The Reference ROM." PC World 5 (April 1987): 236-
239.
Microsoft Bookshelf, a set of ten databases featuring a single CD-
ROM platter, is profiled. The World Almanac; Houghton Mifflin's
Roget's II Thesaurus, Usage Alert and Spelling Verifier and Cor-
recter; The Chicago Manual of Style; Bartlett's Familiar Quotations;
and the American Heritage Dictionary. Additionally, the University
of California's Press Business Information Sources; the U.S. Postal
Service's Zip Code Directory; and Microsoft's Common Business
Letters are included. The reference data featured on this CD-ROM
disc can be inserted directly into a word processing document,
making it instantly usable.

McQueen, J. and Boss, R. W. Videodisc and Optical Digital Disk
Technologies and Their Applications in Libraries, 1986 Update. ALA,
1986.
This report focuses on the potential impact of optical media in
library applications. Compact audio, video, and CD-ROM disc

projects and products designed for library technical services use,
and those with a research and reference orientation, are examined.

Moes, R. J. "The CD-ROM Puzzle: Where Do the Pieces Fit?" Optical Information Systems 6 (Nov.-Dec. 1986): 509-511.
  The evolution of the three compact disc standards, namely, those
  for compact disc audio, CD-ROM and CD-I are highlighted; an
  analysis of their positions in the marketplace is also presented.
  The CD-ROM standard functions as the foundation for CD-I, and
  CD-ROM products presently available will also operate in a CD-I
  system. Through its ease of use and degree of standardization,
  CD-I enhances the market potential of compact disc products designed for mass market consumers.

O'Connor, M. A. "Education and CD-ROM." Optical Information
Systems 6 (July-August 1986): 329-331.
  O'Connor profiles CD-ROM applications in the educational environment. One area where CD-ROM can supply real value to the instructional process is facilitating access to hundreds of online
  databases. Other products include creation of a school administration reference base featuring administrative policies, procedures
  and reports, and a compendium of lesson plans and worksheets
  with materials from instructors nationwide indexed by learning objectives, subject, level, and type.

Ropiequet, S., ed. CD-ROM Volume 2. Optical Publishing. Red-
mond, Wash.: Microsoft Pr., 1987.
  Profiling developments highlighting the state of the CD-ROM industry, this book covers such topics as text preparation and retrieval, the CD-ROM environment, sound and image preparation,
  data protection and updating, and disc production. Case studies
  concerning a medical database and a card catalog on CD-ROM, a
  resources guide, and a glossary enhance the text.

Roth, J. P., ed. Essential Guide to CD-ROM, Meckler, 1986.
  Roth introduces the basics of CD-ROM. Topics range from an introduction to CD-ROM technology to software and applications.
  Appendices on standards, CD-ROM technical terms and acronyms,
  firms and organizations working with CD-ROM technology, and
  recommended readings enhance the material presented. Reference
  Technology's Software Library CD-ROM Disc comes with the text.
  This disc features 8,800 files of programs that are either in the
  public domain or user-supported.

Strukhoff, R. "Finding a Common Ground." CD-ROM Review. The
Magazine of Compact-Disc Data Storage 2 (March/April 1987): 24-31.
  Strukhoff discusses the role and evolvement of standards in the
  marketplace along with specifications in the CD-ROM industry.

PART 2

Libraries are becoming increasingly dependent on sophisticated technological systems for information collection, storage, and dissemination.
CD-ROM (Compact Disc-Read Only Memory) competes for scarce library dollars with innovative services that provide data distribution,
including facsimile, online databases, local area networks (LANs),
integrated services digital networks (ISDNs), packet radio networks
(PRNs), electronic mail (E-mail), and bulletin board systems (BBSs).

CD-ROM, one of a variety of optical storage media that include
write-once discs, erasable optical discs, and digital videodiscs, is
transforming the information environment, presenting new challenges
and supplying expanded opportunities. Effective application of CD-
ROM technology in the library setting calls for the development of
a conceptual framework which guides the decision-making process.
Planning for CD-ROM involves the organization of activities to achieve
specific results which are consistent with the library's mission, its
short-range goals and long-term objectives.

Although libraries serving children and young adults may not
yet have any of the technological systems mentioned, it is critical
that they be included in the planning process for this new technology.
Children's librarians still fighting to get that first microcomputer into
their libraries need to be thinking years ahead so they can make the
best decisions now. For instance, those school librarians who have
been working to make online database searching available to students
might consider whether they should skip online systems and move
directly to CD-ROM.

The stages in the decision-making process outlined here were
constructed within the context of a large library system, but even
practitioners working in a small, one-building library would do well
to follow these basic suggestions.

Establish the Project

Generally, a project manager or a task force is responsible for
estimating the potential costs and evaluating the benefits of a CD-ROM
project. For youth services librarians, this is likely to be done at
the district or county level. The size of the library system and the
staff's experience with electronic information technologies as well as
internal constraints, conflicting subgoals, and local politics can determine not only Who makes the decisions, but what decisions will ultimately be made.

The CD-ROM task force may be comprised of: top administrators
who will be users; information professionals, including children's librarians; and representatives from management (perhaps a children's
or a YA coordinator).

Conduct a Feasibility Study

Many questions must be answered in determining the feasibility of CD-ROM. Are the discs readily searched? Are searches on CD-ROM cheaper than searching online databases? How current are the CD-ROM discs? Are players compatible? What are restrictions on usage? Should the library buy what is currently available in the marketplace or wait until the technology is further advanced?

To determine if the technology is feasible within a specific library setting and how that technology will supplement and/or enhance library services, a review should examine:

- print and nonprint tools, including microfiche and microfilm;

- access to online databases;

- subject boundaries of the collection;

- programs or user needs that must be supported;

- clients served;

- staffing: i.e., coverage, staffing levels, and degree of reference services;

- equipment inventory: including types of microcomputers in-house; personal computers accessible for public access; printers accessible to patrons.

- budget considerations: in libraries under financial constraints, pricing may play a pivotal role in determining which system is selected.

- users' information needs, both currently unfilled and projected.

- the competitive environment, which requires an assessment of technological trends; evaluation of legal and regulatory restraints.

Create a Planning Document

The primary responsibility of the project manager or the CD-ROM task force is the creation of a planning document, which should contain statements or descriptions of the following:

- Library objectives. Outline ways in which CD-ROM can fulfill these objectives.

- Personnel requirements. Staff must have time to train
  clients, deal with queuing problems, maintain equipment
  (making sure that printers are supplied with ink and paper),
  and insure security.

- Equipment. The number of individuals that can use the CD-
  ROM system is determined by the number of available workstations.

- Facilities. A station for CD-ROM generally includes a 40
  square-foot carrel, a microcomputer, a printer, and an optical disc drive.

- Expenditures. The purchase price for the CD-ROM depends
  upon what configuration is selected. Declining prices of information technology equipment coupled with their increasing
  memory storage capability have altered the economics of CD-
  ROM implementation.

Evaluate Hardware/Software

The hardware for a single workstation (an optical disc drive,
a microcomputer, and a printer) is a onetime expenditure, ranging
between $2,000 and $3,000. With the CD-ROM drive or player, data
can be retrieved from the CD-ROM disc. CD-ROM drives are similar
to the players developed for compact audio discs, however, they have
the capacity for greater error detection and are more durable. They
also have different circuitry. The trend in CD-ROM drive design and
development is towards a plug-and-play operational format with personal computers. Retrofitting CD-ROM drives with audio adaptors
permits CD-ROM drives to utilize CD-ROM discs and digital audio
compact discs. The capability for interface between CD-ROM drives
and computers has a major impact on the adoption of CD-ROM technology. While CD-ROM can be used with all computer systems, CD-
ROM will generally be employed with microcomputers. In theory, any
CD-ROM disc can be played on any CD-ROM drive and that CD-ROM
drive can be interfaced to any personal computer. In actuality,
different CD-ROM publishers have created interfaces that are operational for only a limited range of player-computer configurations.
Corporations that manufacture CD-ROM drives include: Denon America; Hitachi; Philips; Reference Technology Inc; and Sony.

Despite the wide array of applications being developed for CD-
ROM, industry-wide standards have yet to be implemented for hardware systems. Until the industry matures, the burden is on the
library professional to become well informed about which of the many
available systems will satisfy specified needs.

- Evaluation & Selection. Selection of CD-ROM titles involves
  establishing specific criteria ranging from frequency of

updates and formats covered (i.e., conference proceedings, journal articles, maps, monographs) to the provision of options to the user for accessing the data. Sources available include serials, trade publications, and textbooks as well as workshops and training sessions.

- Service options. Increased competition among CD-ROM vendors has triggered offers of service bundling and flexible packaging customized for individual end users.

- Hardware. Consideration of equipment required.

- Software. Data can be printed and searched locally or downloaded for flexible manipulation using appropriate software.

- Analysis of costs. Consider the cost of such items as applications software, players and their interfaces to microcomputers, operating system software, and the CD-ROM discs.

- Development of an RFP (Request for Proposal) with criteria for reviewing each vendor's response.

- Timetable for implementation. A PERT (Program Evaluation and Review Technique) Chart delineating the relationship between the estimated total elapsed time and various tasks for finishing the project should be developed so that the selection process can be completed within a reasonable time frame.

Devise Procedures & Policies

CD-ROM, a new technology, must be integrated into the existing library environment in order to exploit its information retrieval capabilities. To facilitate acceptance and overcome resistance, paraprofessional and professional staff should receive hands-on training. Library-sponsored workshops and seminars facilitate dialogue among information professionals, thereby helping them to keep up with advances in the field. Special training sessions, self-guided study and interactive presentations, for example, should also be scheduled for the library's clientele.

- Policies. Guidelines for staff and patron use should be delineated prior to CD-ROM deployment. To avoid long queues at public access CD-ROM workstations, a sign-up sheet can be posted at each station and a log maintained at the reference desk.

- Documentation. A one-page sheet of instructions should be posted at each CD-ROM workstation. Policies, objectives, and constraints should be spelled out. In-house written manuals and vendor supplied documentation should also be made accessible to users.

- Maintenance. A staff member should be assigned the responsibility of monitoring CD-ROM implementation since users may be unfamiliar with it and may not know about all the available options for the system.

- Vendor support. Factors to be considered in the selection of a vendor for the CD-ROM system can include the provision of specialized services, such as:

Does the vendor offer discounts for multiple purchases of a CD-ROM title?

Does the subscription to the system include the microcomputer with built-in CD-ROM player, keyboard, monitor, printer, software, and discs?

Does the subscription include customer assistance and all maintenance?

Is a 24-hour telephone hotline available?

Can recommendations from satisfied library consumers be supplied?

Is immediate shipment possible?

Does the equipment come with a factory warranty?

Analyze Contracts

At present, most CD-ROM use occurs in conjunction with subscriptions to databases, and users lease discs rather than own them. Usually the company providing the data also supplies at least some of the equipment required to access that data. Librarians entering into contractual agreements with these corporations will find it essential to study the subscription or licensing agreement, keeping in mind some of the following areas.

Questions regarding price and payment include:

- Is the cost guaranteed for the life of the contract or does the company retain the right to pass price increases on to the subscribers?

- Are payments made annually, along with other subscriptions, or monthly? Is this optional? Is there any discount for annual payment? Do payment dates correspond with existing budgeting and payment schedules?

- What the term of the contract? Are costs likely to increase
  with each new contract? Is it possible--or wise--to arrange
  for a longer term contract to avoid such increases?

Questions regarding delivery and installation are:

- Is there a guaranteed date of delivery for everything required to make the system operational? If the optical disc
  drive is included in the licensing agreement, is all the related equipment also included?

- Who is responsible for the installation of equipment? Is
  there a separate installation cost? Is your current microcomputer compatible with the CD-ROM equipment? What is
  the schedule for delivery of updated copies of the database?

Questions about documentation and training:

- Is the documentation adequate to your needs?

- Is there an initial training session in the use of the system?
  Is training included in the licensing agreement? Or is this
  an option at additional cost? Will the trainer come to your
  library? If so, is the library responsible for travel and expenses? How many people can be included in the training
  sessions(s)? How much time is required for training?

Questions regarding service and support are:

- Does the licensing agreement include a maintenance contract?
  Is both hardware and software included in that contract?
  What is the time frame for the replacement of defective equipment or software? Is there a local agent who can provide
  service? Is there an 800 number to call for assistance?
  Is there a cost adjustment for time the system is not in service?

What you should know about limitations and use restrictions.

- Can the system be used with more than one microcomputer?
  Can the database be networked to several schools or public
  libraries in a single district? Is downloading permissible?
  Can the system be used for group presentations?

The following explanation, excerpted from an actual contract,
relates some of the restrictions regarding use:

> The Data, Equipment and Software may be used only in the
> internal operation of the Subscriber's business, and may not
> be made available for any other use by loan, rental, service
> bureau, external timesharing or similar arrangement or

otherwise. The Data, Equipment and Software may be used
only in conjunction with a single microcomputer permitting
access by one individual user at one time, and may not be
made available to multiple users at one time through any networking, terminal access, downloading, internal timesharing
or similar arrangement or otherwise. Upon receipt of an updated copy of any Database, the Subscriber shall promptly
cease all use of any prior copies of that Database.

Ask about the termination of a contract.

• Under what conditions can the contract be terminated?

• Can either party terminate?

• What procedures and time frame are required for termination?

• What financial adjustments are made in the event of termination?

Those who need complete, detailed information about automated
library systems and contracts may want to consult Proposals and
Contracts for Library Automation: Guidelines for Preparing Successful RFP's by Edwin M. Cortez, co-published by the American Library
Association and Pacific Information, Inc., 11684 Ventura Blvd., Suite
295, Studio City, Calif. 91604. The 225-page paperback (ISBN
0-8389-2043-8) is $29, and will be released by ALA's Publishing
Services, 50 East Huron St., Chicago, Ill. 60611, in November.

A Final Note

The effective application of CD-ROM technology along with careful planning, advance preparation, and adequate staff training, combined with a visionary approach to offering patrons new ways of accessing information, will make CD-ROM systems both a feasible and
plausible means of providing improved information services in school
and public libraries.

Serials: A Selected List

Advanced Technology/Libraries. (monthly). G. K. Hall & Co.,
70 Lincoln St., Boston, Mass. 02111.
   Highlights news in the CD-ROM field including new products,
   software, and applications.

Byte Magazine. (monthly). McGraw-Hill, 1221 Avenue of the Americas,
New York, N.Y. 10020.
   Features new CD-ROM products and developments.

CD-ROM Review: The Magazine of Compact Disc Data Storage. (bimonthly). CW Communications/Peterborough, Inc., P.O. Box 921,
Farmingdale, N.Y. 11737-9621.
  Covers all facets of CD-ROM technology including data preparation,
  standards, hardware, and software plus reviews of products and
  updates of CD-ROM companies.

Database: The Magazine of Database Reference and Review. (bimonthly). Online, Inc. 11 Tannery Lane, Weston, Conn. 06883.
  Includes columns, special features, and news about all facets of
  optical media.

Library Hi Tech. (quarterly). Pierian Press, P. O. Box 1808, Ann
Arbor, Mich. 48106.
  Supplies in-depth coverage of new technologies such as CD-ROM,
  including evaluations and descriptions.

Library Hi Tech News. (monthly). Pierian Press.
  Contains news of CD-ROM products and technological developments
  related to library operations.

Online: The Magazine of Online Information Systems. (bimonthly).
Online, Inc.
  Features news of CD-ROM technology as well as articles on appli-
  cations in libraries and information centers.

Optical Data Systems. (monthly). Microinfo, Ltd., P. O. Box 3,
Newman Lane, Alton Hants, ENG. GU34 2PG.
  Covers international developments in the field of optical data storage systems, including CD-ROM, videotex, optical data discs and
  videodisc applications.

Optical Information Systems. (bimonthly). Meckler Publishing, 11
Ferry Lane West, Westport, Conn. 06880.
  Provides news and notes on videodisc, CD-ROM and compact disc,
  optical disk and LaserCard, and related technologies along with a
  videodisc projects directory, publications announcements, and
  articles covering a wide range of topics related to CD-ROM technology. (Continues Videodisc and Optical Disc.)

Optical Information Systems Update. (biweekly). Meckler Publishing.
  Highlights events which have an impact on the field of optical publishing and storage.

Optical Information Systems Update/Library and Information Center
Applications. (bimonthly). Meckler Publishing.
  Contains news of developments in optical media and its utilization
  in libraries and information centers and case studies, reviews,
  tutorials, and interviews.

PC World: The Comprehensive Guide to IBM Personal Computers

and Compatibles. (monthly). PCW Communications, Inc., 501 Second
St., San Francisco, Calif.   94107.
   Features product reviews, interviews of people in the industry,
   and articles about CD-ROM.

T.H.E. Journal: Technological Horizons in Education.   (monthly,
except July and Dec.).   Information Synergy, Inc.   2626 South Pull-
man, Santa Ana, Calif.   92705.
   Covers CD-ROM and CD-I applications in schools and contains
   descriptions of new products.

NOTES ON CONTRIBUTORS

JOAN ATKINSON is on the faculty of the Graduate School of Library Service, University of Alabama, Tuscaloosa, AL.

JOAN M. BECHTEL is a librarian at Dickinson College, Carlisle, PA.

JAMES GREGORY BRADSHER is Archivist, Planning and Policy Evaluation Branch, National Archives and Records Administration, Washington, DC.

ROBERT S. BRAVARD is Director of Library Services, Stevenson Library, Lock Haven University, Lock Haven, PA.

WILLIAM A. BRITTEN is Assistant Professor and Systems Librarian, Main Library, University of Tennessee, Knoxville, TN.

SANDRA CHAMPION is Head Media Specialist, Hialeah High School, Hialeah, FL.

MARGARET A CRIBBS is currently Operations Engineer at Magellan Data Management and Archive Team, Jet Propulsion Laboratory, Pasadena, CA.

BRUCE W. DEARSTYNE is Principal Archivist for External Programs and Services at the New York State Archives and Records Administration, State Education Department, Albany, NY.

LEIGH S. ESTABROOK is Dean of the Graduate School of Library and Information Science, University of Illinois, Urbana, IL.

CAROLYN M. GRAY is Associate Director, Brandeis University Libraries, Waltham, MA.

AGNES M. GRIFFEN is Director of Montgomery County Department of Public Libraries, Rockville, MD.

JANE ANNE HANNIGAN is Professor Emerita at the School of Library Service, Columbia University, New York, NY.

ROBERT HAUPTMAN is on the faculty of St. Cloud State University, St. Cloud, MN.

THOMAS J. HENNEN, JR. is Administrator of Lakeshores Library System, Racine, WI.

CAROL HOLE is Community Services Manager, Alachua County Library, Gainesville, FL.

VIRGINIA G. HOLTZ is Director of the Center for Health Sciences Libraries, University of Wisconsin, Madison, WI.

STEPHEN E. JAMES is Assistant Director of the Public Libraries of Saginaw, Saginaw, MI.

HELEN JOSEPHINE is Information Manager, F.I.R.S.T. (Fee-based Information and Research Service Team), University Libraries, Arizona State University, Tempe, AZ.

MARLYN KEMPER is Assistant Professor and Director of Information Sciences, Center for Computer-Based Learning, Nova University, Fort Lauderdale, FL.

LEONARD KNIFFEL is a librarian at the Detroit Public Library, Detroit, MI.

CONSTANCE A. MELLON is on the faculty of the Department of Library and Information Studies, East Carolina University, Greenville, NC.

SAMUEL PICKERING, JR. is Professor of English, University of Connecticut, Storrs, CT.

GAIL POOL is Book Review Editor of Wilson Library Bulletin and the Radcliffe Quarterly, and a book reviewer for The Christian Science Monitor.

CATHERINE SHELDRICK ROSS is on the faculty of the School of Library and Information Science, University of Western Ontario, London, Ontario, Canada.

PATRICIA GLASS SCHUMAN is President, Neal-Schuman Publishers, Inc., New York, NY.

CHRISTOPHER E. SMITH is Assistant Professor of Political Science, University of Akron, Akron, OH.

TED SOLOTAROFF is Senior Editor of Harper & Row, New York, NY.

NORMAN D. STEVENS is Director of University Libraries, University of Connecticut, Storrs, CT.

MARGARET F. STIEG is on the faculty of the Graduate School of Library Service, University of Alabama, Tuscaloosa, AL.

KAY E. VANDERGRIFT is on the faculty of the School of Communication, Information and Library Studies, Rutgers University, New Brunswick, NJ.

DAVID C. WEBER is Ida M. Green Director, Stanford University Libraries, Stanford, CA.

RONALD J. ZBORAY is Microfilm Editor of the Emma Goldman Papers at the Institute for the Study of Social Change, University of California at Berkeley, Berkeley, CA.